MW00637103

Sending Flowers To America

Sending Flowers To America

Stories of the Los Angeles Flower Market and
the People Who Built an American Floral Industry

By Peggi Ridgway
and Jan Works

American Florists' Exchange, Ltd. / Los Angeles Flower Market

ISBN 0-9798285-0-3
ISBN 978-0-9798285-0-8

Library of Congress Control Number: 2007905661

Researched and written by the team at Wordpix Solutions:
Peggi Ridgway, chronological history, special features/sidebars and project management
Jan Works, Profiles in Progress stories and general consulting

Dust jacket design by Michael Wheary, Foresight Design
Interior design by Theresa Padilla Fajardo, Mind2Eye Studios
Current photography of the Los Angeles Flower Market and environs by Julie Diebolt-Price, JDP Photography
Project liaison Jon Prechtl

Printed in China by Everbest Printing Co., Ltd.
Pre-press production by Everbest Printing Co., Ltd.

Photos/front cover/dust jacket – clockwise from left: The Mellano brothers Johnny and Michael with their father and workers; Gebhard Prechtl; five little girls from back left – Dorothy (Willard) Trowbridge, Anna Lee (Gorini) Gallizio, Lena Gorini and, in front, Inez Ghigo; Paul Ecke Sr.
Photos/back cover/dust jacket – clockwise from top: from left, Jack Hauquitz, Eddie Battistessa and Bert Johnson; C.J. Groen; unknown gentlemen in front of American Florists' Exchange; Victor Hasson.
Florals by JDP Photography and Wordpix.

Orders and Information:
Publisher
American Florists' Exchange, Ltd.
Los Angeles Flower Market
754 Wall Street, Los Angeles, CA 90014
(213) 622-1966
www.flowermarkethistory.com

Wordpix Solutions
P.O. Box 218
Buena Park, CA 90621-0218
(714) 228-1101
www.wordpix.com

Contents

Index to Sidebars

Profiles

Profiles in Progress

Florists & Designers

Acknowledgments

The authors express our deepest gratitude to the people and organizations that helped to make this book a reality. Many called or wrote us to volunteer information; others responded enthusiastically to our requests. We sincerely thank all the individuals and families for their part in creating this story of progress, and:

Sylvia Foltz, who had the foresight in 1981 to record interviews with Paul Ecke Sr. and Frank Kuwahara, transcripts of which were a very helpful resource; Norman Amling and Stella Berry, who provided names and telephone numbers for many people who otherwise might not have been interviewed or included; Carolyn Cole, photo archivist with Los Angeles Public Library; Alex Moreno Areyan for introducing us to the flower growers and festivals of the South Bay and leading us to Tike Karavas, who became an invaluable source; Mike Branch, president, Branch-Smith Printing, for access to early *Southern California Florist & Nurseryman* articles about how the Los Angeles Flower Market operated in 1950; Marie Barnidge-McIntyre, horticulturist with Rancho Los Cerritos in Long Beach, California, for introducing us to Victoria Padilla's book, *Southern California Gardens*, and for her welcome comments and contributions to the text of this book; Rod Crittenden, executive vice president of the Michigan Floral Association, for connecting us with floral wholesalers and retailers who have historically done business with California growers; Judith Carter, archivist with San Marino Historical Society, for her information about florist Erna Thurnher; Dr. Michael Reid in the Plant Sciences Department at the University of California, Davis, and Ann Quinn, executive director of the California State Floral Association for their observations and insight; Jim Sherman, Emma Roberts and other helpful librarians at the Los Angeles Public Library; Michael Wheary for retrieval of old *Bloomin' News* photographs; Morgan Yates, corporate archivist for Auto Club of Southern California for access to early articles about the Los Angeles Flower Market; Galen Beery, president of the Historical Society of La Verne for his background about Cecil Houdyshel; the volunteer ladies at the Alhambra Historical Society for their dedication to uncovering priceless gems about the life of Captain Gray; Naomi Hirahara for sharing her experience in the writing of *A Scent of Flowers;* Theresa Padilla Fajardo, Earl Russell and Jared Stevens, who worked out the technical challenges of the electronic version of the layout; Nick Gandolfo, whose review of the completed galleys addressed questions of an editorial nature; the Tournament of Roses public information office; and all the researchers and writers who blazed the trail of recorded local history and floral industry history.

JDP Photography

Project Partners

We are especially grateful for the generous and heartfelt sharing of a handful of companies and people who felt so inspired by this history project that they were led to contribute financially to its success.

We extend our deepest gratitude to:

Our Rose Partners
Barbara Winter
California Association of Flower Growers & Shippers
Groen Rose Company/Sylvia Foltz
Lizbeth Ecke
Mellano & Company

Our Lily Partners
California State Floral Association
Albin Hagstrom & Son, Inc.
The Bert N. Johnson Family
Mario & Doris Ann Del Fante
Ecke Ranch
Ray Winter
Duane Rodriguez-Winter
Ghigo Greens/Inez Ayala
John Noonan Wholesale Florist
Hollandia Produce

Flower Market Q&A

Q. **What is the correct name of the Los Angeles Flower Market?**

A. Commonly referred to as the Los Angeles Flower Market, the legal name is: The American Florists' Exchange, Ltd. doing business as the Los Angeles Flower Market.

Q. **Is that the same as the Japanese American Flower Market?**

A. No. The Southern California Flower Market, started by Japanese Americans in the early 1900s, is a separate entity. It is located directly across the street from the American Florists' Exchange.

Q. **How large is the American Florists' Exchange (Los Angeles Flower Market)?**

A. Today's Los Angeles Flower Market, including merchants who lease space in adjacent and nearby buildings, occupies five acres. The main sales floor of the Market occupies around 50,000 square feet.

Q. **What is the Flower District?**

A. The Los Angeles Flower District is a badge membership program that offers wholesale pricing to its members. Its 2008 membership is more than 4,500 individuals, representing approximately 2,000 retail florists, 300 event planners, 600 interior decorators, and others. Visit LAFlowerDistrict.com for more details.

Q. **How does the Flower District fit into the Fashion District?**

A. The Los Angeles Fashion District encompasses a 90-block area of what has traditionally been called the wholesale district. The Flower District is a resident of that area along with the textile, fashion, jewelry and produce wholesale markets.

JDP Photography

Q. **How many people visit the Los Angeles Flower Market and the District?**

A. Every year, more than 250,000 members of the general public visit the Flower District. In addition, some 45,000 or more visits are made by District badge members.

Q. **What are the busiest days at the Market?**

A. Wednesdays and Fridays, when retail florists and event planners stock up for their weekend orders and events, are the busiest days.

Q. **What's the parking situation in the area?**

A. Street parking is available, and there is usually plenty of parking space on the two garage parking levels accessible from the entrance on San Julian Street. The Southern California Flower Market offers garage parking also.

Q. **Can I bring my group to visit the Flower Market?**

A. Yes, the Flower Market welcomes groups. Please contact the Los Angeles Flower District operations office to make special arrangements (213 627-3696).

Q. **Does either the District or the Flower Market publish a newsletter?**

A. The American Florists' Exchange/Los Angeles Flower Market publishes a bi-monthly, full-color newsletter called *The Bloomin' News*, which shares local, national and world news of interest to Southern Californians connected to the flower industry. For subscription information, please visit BloominNews.com.

JDP Photography

From the American Florists' Exchange

The Board of Directors of the Los Angeles Flower Market of the American Florists' Exchange, LTD, welcomes you to the history of our Flower Market. It all began back in 1921 when a group of European immigrants came together to form an alliance to market their floral products and began sending flowers to America.

It is not often that a historical story such as this has the opportunity to be told. For that, we commissioned two very capable writers to compose the story of the Los Angeles Flower Market. We are so thankful to Peggi Ridgway and Jan Works for their tireless efforts to meet with and interview many of the families who have been an integral part of the history of our flower market.

We hope you will thoroughly enjoy the history, pictures and memories of the Los Angeles Flower Market and pass along the message of the book to other members of our flower family.

Board of Directors of the Los Angeles Flower Market of the American Florists' Exchange, Ltd.

From left, standing, John Williams and Johnny Mellano; seated are Lizbeth Ecke, Bert Johnson and Jon Prechtl. *The Bloomin' News,* January 2007.

Prologue

There are a hundred places to start a book about flowers. We chose to start this one where the flower growers began, that is, in the hearts of people who longed to bring color and beauty to the half desert, frontier land that had become their new home. It was in those hearts and in that place with its unique confluence of geography and climate, that the longing morphed into Southern California's spectacular flower fields and the commerce associated with them.

Sending Flowers to America speaks to the dreams people hold close and dreams they and their descendants proudly shared during the writing of this book. These were the hopes of immigrants who sailed away from war and impoverishment to the promise of America and who made their way across our land to California. We are pleased to present their stories, intertwined with the Los Angeles Flower Market history, here.

As we dove into the dozens of newspaper and magazine articles written about the Los Angeles Flower Market over the last century, we encountered misconceptions worthy of note here.

Locally, journalists loved to write about the special seasons of the year when the Market buzzed with activity and thousands of flowers filled it with spectacular color.

Nationally, the Market earned deep respect from the floral industry for its sheer volume of sales and collective, positive impact.

The problem was that most journalists and the public believed there to be but one flower market. Few who wrote about the Market (or "Mart") realized that there were two separately organized markets operating across the street from each other: The American Florists' Exchange (Los Angeles Flower Market) and the Southern California Flower Market (affectionately called the "Japanese market" and the older of the two). We hope that *Sending Flowers to America* will finally give the American Florists' Exchange its due.

As we worked, we realized that this book represents the period of the greatest advancements in human history. It begins in the earliest years of photography and before the advent of the automobile, airplane and computer and it progresses in floral history with the advancing of those technologies. (Many of the more than 500 photographs lent to the project were black-and-white taken before color photography was perfected, with lovingly tattered corners.) By the time our book ends, our story is illustrated with full color images received electronically. What's more, this history takes us from horse-and-buggy to supersonic speed, from handwritten notes to computer-generated reports.

We noticed also that the flower business depends upon personal connections of people, from farm to florist to consumer. It's personal and it's special. That's why *Sending Flowers to America* shares the personal lives, personalities and dreams of the people who formed the foundation of the Southern California flower industry and the American Florists' Exchange. These are the people who helped to build the flower industry.

Peggi Ridgway
Jan Works
May 2008

CHAPTER 1

JDP Photography

Timeline: 1800s

1850	California celebrates statehood on September 9.
1861	The Civil War begins.
1865	America's Civil War ends.
1873	California's first two citrus trees arrive, gifts from one housewife mailed to another. (Joseph S. O'Flaherty, *Those Powerful Years*, 1978) Mrs. Elsa Tibbetts receives two orange trees from the Department of Agriculture. When they bear fruit, the navel orange revolutionaizes California's orange industry.
1874 – 1890	First commercial cut flower growers in Los Angeles area were housewives seeking to supplement the family income. First prominent commercial cut flower grower in the Los Angeles area, Captain F. Edward Grey of Alhambra, grows and sells flowers in Alhambra. Captain Grey advertises his flowers in the *Land of Sunshine* magazine.
1875	The Southern Pacific Railroad reaches Anaheim.
1876	The American Association of Nurserymen, Florists and Seedsmen is formed. Southern California Horticultural Society holds its first annual exhibit. Los Angeles and San Francisco are finally linked by railroad. "Mr. Watson, come here, I want to see you." Alexander Graham Bell speaks these words into his new invention of the telephone.
1880	The population of Los Angeles is about 64,000. Five-year-old Nan Bixby presents a bouquet of California flowers, a gift from a local florist, to the first president to visit California, Rutherford B. Hayes, and his wife.
1882	On New Year's Eve, thousands flock to hilltops to view a city emerging from traditional darkness with arc lighting created by two 50-horsepower steam engines for two Brush Electric Company machines.
1884	After growing and selling informally and analyzing the marketplace, Theodosia Shepherd, a Ventura housewife, goes into business as a professional seed and bulb grower. Her business would become nationally known and recognized as the start of the seed industry. Society of American Florists is founded. The Statue of Liberty arrives in New York Harbor from France. The first Flower Festival of consequence is held in Los Angeles. Los Angeles becomes the first U.S. city to be exclusively lighted by electricity. (Boyle Workman, *The City That Grew*)
1885	Hiroshi (Kan) Yoshiike returns to San Francisco from Japan with chrysanthemum seedlings, to pioneer growing techniques for mums with large blooms. The railroad arrives in Los Angeles on September 16. Nurserywoman, writer and lecturer Kate Sessions opens a nursery in Coronado and a flower shop in San Diego.
1889	Orange County is formed from Los Angeles County, with Santa Ana as county seat.
1890	The first Tournament of Roses parade is held in Pasadena on January 1, 1890. The population of Los Angeles is around 201,000. The Southern California Floral Society holds a flower show.
1890s	Sotaro Endo, the first Japanese-American commercial flower grower, leases two lots at South Main and West Jefferson to grow carnations Refrigerated rail cars appear, catapulting Southern California into the business of supplying the nation's citrus and avocado produce and assuring the quality of fresh flowers.
1892	Edward L. Doheny discovers oil at Second Street and Glendale Boulevard in downtown Los Angeles.
1893	Japanese immigrants growing carnations near South Main and Jefferson. Los Angeles business owners form the Merchants Association.
1897	Japanese grower Kametaro Endo growing chrysanthemums and sweet peas near the intersection of South Main and Jefferson
1898	W. J. Cowee introduces machine-made flower stems, replacing florists' need to support flower stems with toothpicks and stakes. The Spanish American War begins, ending eight months later with a signed treaty between the United States and Spain.
1899	Edwin James Vawter begins commercial development of carnations and other flowers in Santa Monica.

JDP Photography

Discovering Southern California (1800-1899)

"Tuesday, February 5, we came on to Los Angeles and camped again on the site of our first camp. We passed over the lovely plains of San Gabriel, El Monte and Los Angeles, with their thousands of cattle, horses, and sheep feedings; tens of thousands were seen... The plains and hills were green, men were putting their vineyards in order, and fruit trees were coming in bloom here..."

— William Brewer, *Up and Down California in 1860-1864* [1]

The words of William Brewer [2] echo those of countless writers who have described the early, pastoral scenes of the Los Angeles area before the world rushed in. When Brewer first visited in 1860, the population was just over 4,000 – so small that it was not included in the 100 largest cities of the United States. The inner city was a small, bustling village with dozens of ranches dotting the surrounding hillsides. It was an agricultural town, started by a group of residents from the Spanish mission at San Gabriel. With no hint of its eventual development, El Pueblo de la Reyna de Los Angeles was poised for growth in a vast ocean of promise.

In 1850, thousands of acres within a day's travel of the Pacific Ocean, in fact, the entire Southern California region from the Tehachapi Mountains northeast of Santa Barbara to the Mexican border, lay mostly undeveloped and largely unexplored. Spanish soldiers and padres, Mexican-American residents and thousands of Native American Indians had traversed its hills and valleys, creating a network of foot trails, modest dirt roads and small villages associated with nearby missions established in the late 1700s by Father Junipero Serra. With this activity, the population of all of the area we know today as thriving, bustling Southern California, was still under 25,000.

Along the western coast lay a land of potentially great agricultural wealth and extraordinary riches for the visionaries of the time. Of contradictory influences, its coastal strip of semi-desert but fertile land resided in a warm climate enjoying the benefits of cool, moist ocean breezes daily. No farmer or orchard owner could ask for a more perfect arrangement for agricultural enterprise. Not truly tropical nor Mediterranean, it offered the ideal conditions of both.

In the eighteenth century, Southern California was a much wetter region than it is today. Rivers, such as the San Gabriel and Los Angeles rivers, flowed unchecked in the days before their confinement to rigid concrete channels. During heavy rains, they raged out of control across the land, resulting in floods and often creating watery marshes and rivulets on their own. Such history conflicts with the misconception that the Los Angeles Basin resides in a "desert" climate. In those days, the challenges were the unpredictability of water's availability and the difficulty of getting it where and when one needed it.

Connections North and East

Southern California's history has always been linked with that of Northern California, in spite of attempts to separate the two into individual states and regardless of the mountain ranges and deserts that divide them. The Gold Rush of 1849 brought thousands of immigrants from Eastern cities of the United States to Northern California. Many of those gold seekers found their way to Los Angeles and brought with them their ideas and dreams, culture, industry, technology and tried and proven farming techniques. Along with thousands of foreign immigrants, and the resident population of Native American Indians and Mexican immigrants, they helped create a framework for growth.

While by 1860, cities of the Eastern United States enjoyed the luxuries of roads, passenger trains and established business districts and populations of upwards of 5,000 (New York City's surpassed 300,000), Los Angeles had barely gotten started. Although it would take only 30 years to become a major metropolitan area (a phenomenon for its rapidity), during the years of America's Civil War (1860-1864), California was still a mostly unknown frontier and Los Angeles a dusty little village.

Who could have imagined that, less than 100 years later, a mostly-uninhabited desert beside an ocean would produce a major metropolis and glorious chrysanthemums, dahlias, roses and gladiolus enjoyed by millions of Americans? In 1860, in a land where many men went about their business armed with revolvers, where tensions between Anglos and Native American Indians were intense if not sometimes violent, and where agriculture and farming were difficult because water supply was unpredictable, who would even have cared about flowers as a business enterprise?

Taming the Land

California was young, brash, wild and a frontier known to Easterners only through letters and reports sent by travelers across the mountains and prairies. The expansive, exciting West beckoned the adventurous to leave their cushy parlors and discover new freedoms. Where once the challenge was to reach the frontier at its westernmost point of Pittsburgh, Pennsylvania, it was now 2,000 miles beyond. The frontier had moved to the Pacific Ocean; and it was a land of milk and honey.

In 1827 and 1828, Jedediah Smith, at age 27, had led the first expeditions from the Midwestern and Eastern United States ("the states," as everything east of California came to be called). As the Spaniards had

Downtown Los Angeles around 1895. Pictured here is Second Street looking west from Spring Street. The building at close left is the Wilcox Building and at far left the Hollenbeck Block. At the far right is the Bryson-Bonebrake Block. Notice the telegraph office at left and the horse-drawn vehicles and streetcars. ***Security Pacific Collection/ Los Angeles Public Library.***

once linked California to their oceanic route, Smith established the land link. Trail guides and opportunity seekers set out to make their own trails and to discover their own new land and adventures in the West.

Over the next few decades, Southern California saw the arrival of courageous families who had endured nearly insurmountable obstacles during their wagon-train trek to the West, including Indian ambushes and cruel weather, across the prairies, deserts and mountains. Also finding their way along the dirt trails leading to Los Angeles, Santa Ana and San Diego were miners whose luck had run out in the gold mines of the American River and its tributaries in Northern California; transplants from the San Francisco area; thousands of Chinese immigrants employed to help build the railroads; farmers with families, Civil War veterans, people who had nowhere else to try their luck or get a fresh start and others who had heard the word of balmy breezes and plentiful land at little cost. Others purchased passage on ships and sailed around the tip of South America, then north to San Francisco. Every route was long and difficult and came without guarantee of safety. The new citizens helped to populate a brand new state (statehood was celebrated in 1850) and built new lives.

These new California residents tamed the virgin land with vigor, vision and an ingenuity that foreshadowed the great achievements of the twentieth century. They brought their skills and knowledge, trades and professions; and they brought their tools and machinery. Once they got here, they adapted the land to fit their needs, inventing processes and machines to solve problems and increase production. California has always been a land of immigrants and its early years depended upon the importing of the knowledge the first immigrants brought with them. They laid a foundation for industry.

An Appreciation for Beauty

As families built and settled into their Southern California homes in the 1850s and 1860s, housewives planted the flower and vegetable seeds sent to them by relatives in "the states" (everywhere east of California). Backyard gardens and landscaped yards appeared and, to supply them, nurseries. Housewives shared with each other the choice bulbs and seeds that gave them good results. The nursery industry grew as horticulturists discovered new plants, seeds, bulbs and rootstock from around the world. California was like a blank canvas, just waiting for its citizens to splash it with colorful flowers, to paint it with their dreams.

Los Angeles Chuckles

A *Los Angeles Times* brief on March 4, 1887 tells of the difficulty of getting fresh flowers to present to performers at a Fariai concert in San Diego. It seems the patrons from Los Angeles scoured the town for flowers but were able to produce nothing suitable.

Finally, after a "long and bootless search," they made the acquaintance of a San Diego florist who offered them hope. Could he prepare three floral bouquets, they asked. "Well, no," he responded, he couldn't make them right now, but if the flowers he ordered arrived from Los Angeles by Express in time, he would certainly make the bouquets!

The article notes that the only bouquet presented that night at the San Diego opera hall was one sent to a lady in the Fariai performing company – by a gentleman in Los Angeles.

It helped that by 1875, the Impressionist style of painting had become the rage for collectors of art and those who cultivated an appreciation for beauty, and that many Impressionist painters chose flowers as their subjects. Refreshingly, painting styles had evolved from dark, somber and depressing depictions of dramatic events to happy scenes with color and loose, almost casual brushstrokes. Paintings depicting roses, which dominated the art scene from 1840 to 1900, were bold and full of life and glorious color, inspiring those who saw them to grow or buy flowers so they could duplicate the scene for themselves.

Homemakers were becoming increasingly interested in creating pleasant surroundings for their families both inside the home and in the garden. Popular women's magazines featured articles about flower care and display. Flowers and flowering plants, with all their color and magic, were decorating dining tables and living rooms everywhere.

In Los Angeles, Ozro W. Childs started a nursery on a tract of land just east of Main Street. In 1857, he and W. Huber became partners in the Los Angeles Nursery and Fruit Garden, a highly profitable enterprise. Childs introduced new fruits, nuts, vines and flowering shrubs and cut flowers (gladioli, tuberoses, roses, fuchsias and others), importing seeds and plants from Europe and South America and laying the foundation for the nursery business in the area. In 1884, with urbanization already in play, Childs subdivided his large property, which had become a tourist attraction, retaining only a ten-acre tract around his home. Of the wealth Childs accumulated from his success, he gave back generously. In exchange for his gift of a sixteen-hundred-feet-long water ditch (a zanja), the city gave him a parcel of land approximately the size of the central business district of today's Los Angeles. [3]

In March 1855, William B. Osborne, another early commercial nurseryman in Los Angeles, advertised that he had received a shipment of roses and shrubs, including lilacs, from the East. Residents turned to Osborne for flowering plants and shrubs. Like many local residents who took advantage of local nursery supplies and seeds available through postal mail, Dr. T. J. White bordered and decorated his expansive lawns with a variety of trees and flowering shrubs. Gardening was a fascinating side interest for many, and a lot of the do-it-yourself gardeners were men.

The beauty of residential gardens was marred only by the frustration of watering them. An expensive commodity, water could be obtained by irrigation or by paying someone to carry buckets of water from the nearest water source. If the home sat near a water canal, the homeowner simply helped himself. Regardless of the source and the fact that carrying buckets of water to the garden was laborious and time-consuming, beautiful gardens became the talk of the town and some lasted into the twenty-first century.

Disruptions to the Dream

At the beginning of the 1860s, beyond the parameters of the lovely estates and private gardens in urban areas, Southern California was a place of broad expansive vistas, of large ranchos with thousands of cattle that grazed their pastures. And then the rains came, pouring torrents of water and washing away many beautiful gardens. When the rains finally stopped, a long dry spell set in. The land turned barren and brown and the carcasses of cattle littered the countryside.

Continued to page 7...

Captain Gray's Colorful Path to Alhambra

The man credited with being the first in Southern California to grow flowers commercially under glass brought a fascinating personal history to his position in the annals of horticultural fame.

Francis Edward Gray was eighteen years old when he enlisted in July 1862 in the Massachusetts Infantry 37th Regiment to fight for the Union Army, giving his occupation as farmer. His hometown of Springfield presented him with a beautiful sword carrying an engraving of his name, which he carried into war but lost in battle. Almost immediately after enlisting, he was thrust with other recruits into the fray of war.

On September 19, 1864, First Lieutenant Gray was wounded in the Third Battle of Winchester (Opequon Creek) in Virginia, during General Philip Sheridan's Shenandoah Valley Campaign. Two months later he attained the rank of Captain. He mustered out soon after the war ended on June 21, 1865, as Captain of Company I.

Like many military men who heard tales of the Golden West from fellow soldiers, Gray later moved to California to live. In 1876 he settled in Alhambra, where he built a beautiful estate and park and became a prominent citizen. He served as Los Angeles Tax Assessor, 1891-1893.

A small, pleasant man who stood erect, Gray's claim to fame was in his horticultural expertise. He was the landscape architect for San Diego's Balboa Park, living in San Diego as he completed that project, and the Superintendent of Gardens for the Panama Pacific International Exposition held in San Francisco in 1915. *

He operated a nursery at El Molina and Wilson Avenue north of Huntington Drive in San Marino, the 30-acre Ingleside Floral Company nursery midway between Pasadena and Alhambra, and is believed to be the first Californian to grow roses under glass for the purpose of selling them.

As a horticulturist, he was well known for breeding the Kate Gray canna lily, named after his wife, and developing many interesting flowers in his greenhouses, including carnations, his specialty. Enthusiastic about his flowers, he operated several large greenhouses with one devoted to maidenhair fern and another to roses.

The Captain also hybridized and produced some of the largest and most prolific gladioli, cannas and amaryllis. Buyers from around the world sought his spectacular amaryllis, which measured twelve inches across. The weekly production of the Ingleside operation was well into the thousands, with sales of a half-million dollars to the City of Los Angeles alone in 1895.

Captain Gray was the first Los Angeles horticulturist to advertise his flowers, promoting them in the periodical, *Land of Sunshine*, a magazine founded in 1894 to promote California. The "Captain Gray" name caught the eye of one special reader. Learning of the Captain's whereabouts led that reader to return the long-lost engraved sword which had long ago been presented to the captain as a teenage soldier by his hometown.

Captain Gray died in September 1929.

The sources for this article include a June 5, 1968 letter from Mrs. H. W. Purnell, Captain Gray's granddaughter (representing the Alhambra Historical Society), a 2002 essay by William H. Gerdts called "The Land of Sunshine" (Irvine Museum online archive), documents residing in the collection of the Alhambra Historical Society, *Southern California Gardens* by Victoria Padilla, an early history of Alhambra published in *The Life and Times of Norma Yocum* by Norma Yocum, Civil War Soldiers & Sailors (System Search Detail) found at the website www.itd.nps.gov and Civil War military history published online at www.pueblo.gsa.gov.

*The Panama Pacific International Exposition was the 1915 "world's fair" held in San Francisco, California. The fair boosted the economy of the city, which had been almost destroyed by the great earthquake and fire of 1906. The exposition celebrated completion of the Panama Canal and commemorated the 400th anniversary of the discovering of the Pacific Ocean by Balboa.

Hurt beyond repair from the 1860s' floods and drought, large rancho owners in the San Gabriel and Santa Ana valleys quit farming and subdivided and sold what they could of their lands. It wasn't long until the great ranchos of early California were a thing of the past and the Southland was on its way to urbanization. The latter part of the decade witnessed the growth of the citrus industry and the further development of irrigation and cultivation.

Meanwhile, the "city" of Los Angeles was undergoing a transformation of its own. In the early 1880s, a man named Remi Nadeau built a four-story hotel in the center part of the Los Angeles of that day, speculating that the as yet undeveloped area would take a hint from him and that development would follow. It did. Commercial enterprises sprang up along the streets. By the late 1880s, land in the Sixth and Main streets area had increased 40 times in value. In 1893, the Bradbury Hotel, with its central atrium an explosion of light and its steel trusses ahead of their time, was constructed at 304 South Broadway. In 2008, it remains a beautiful architectural specimen and the oldest commercial structure in downtown Los Angeles.

In the 1880s and 1890s, South San Pedro Street and other streets around today's Los Angeles Flower Market were agricultural land and home to early nurseries. Thomas A. Garey operated a 72-acre nursery on South San Pedro Street and Mrs. H. Shaw's 35-acres of fields and nursery facilities were situated on San Pedro Street. Some of the nurserymen who made a substantial contribution to ornamental horticulture in the Los Angeles area included Jacob Dieterich, Louis Stengel and Eugene Germain, all of whom continued their operations into the twentieth century. [4]

A Climate for Business and Flowers

By the 1880s, the effects of big business were noticeable. As word of opportunities of the West reached entrepreneurs of the East, the railroads wasted no time expanding their market. Snaking across the prairies and over the mountains, by 1876 a railroad tunneled through the Tehachapi Mountains, effectively connecting the East and West coasts. When the Atchison, Topeka & Santa Fe railroad reached San Bernardino in 1885, Los Angeles two years later and San Diego a year after that, all areas of California became connected. An economic boom followed that author Kevin Starr, in *California, A History* [5], describes as finalizing the Americanization of Southern

This tourist advertisement, "Meet Them with Flowers," displayed prominently at the back end of the Los Angeles Limited. The poster shows a young couple welcoming their tourist friends to Los Angeles with flowers. ***Security Pacific Collection/Los Angeles Public Library.***

California. Formerly isolated by mountains and desert, the land south of the Tehachapi range was finally part of the land north of the range. The icing on the railroad cake was that thousands of people began to travel by train to California and to forever alter its lifestyle.

Southern California was an exciting place to live and work in the 1880s. Rows of grapes, sugar beets and orchards blanketed the picturesque ranchos, modern machines accelerated industrial efforts, small towns sprang up and new residents arrived frequently, eager to create new enterprises and explore opportunities.

The region was aggressively advertised to Eastern and Midwestern residents by land developers and railroad companies, who put a premium on Southern California's weather. The story goes that one potential customer remarked to land speculator Lucky Baldwin that his asking price of $200 per acre for bare land without a sure source of water was ridiculously high. "Hell! We're giving away the land," replied Baldwin. "We're selling the climate." [6]

The influx of tourists and immigrants from the States continued. The population of Los Angeles grew from 5,728 in 1870 to 50,350 in 1890, proof that, except for a brief economic downturn in 1873, a boom of unprecedented growth had indeed occurred. Southern California had been discovered by the American people and the floral industry was beginning to form its foothold.

Near Santa Clara, sweet pea flowers were being cultivated for their seeds. In a few short years, the expansive flower seed production fields around the town of Lompoc would earn the area the name of The Valley of Flowers.

In Ventura in the 1880s, a quiet housewife and mother of four named Theodosia Shepherd, who came to California for her health (she suffered from tuberculosis), turned her backyard into a flower seed production field. Converting an old piano crate to a greenhouse, Mrs. Shepherd is credited with starting today's California flower seed industry. Encouraged by letters from Peter Henderson, considered the father of modern American floriculture, she became one of the first to ship seed to customers outside California. In 1892, she was cultivating eight acres and selling the seeds of begonias, smilax, calla lilies, cobaea scandans, Mexican orchids and cacti to seedsmen across the United States.

In Los Angeles, the florist Mr. Weinhold, on First Street between Spring and Main, advertised a special sale in March 1883; [7] and John Lunkenheimer, a florist and landscaper who also sold fruits and vegetables, took orders through the S.M. Perry store on South Main. [8]

In 1885, a beautiful young teacher named Kate Sessions, who had relocated from her native home in San Francisco, opened a retail flower shop in San Diego and a small nursery in Coronado. She would go on to inspire countless gardens and the planting of flowers throughout the city, hastening the development of the area and instilling a keen awareness of flowers among the general public.

In Santa Barbara in the late 1800s and early part of the twentieth century, where nurseryman Joseph Sexton had already made his place in floriculture history by introducing exciting new plants from South Africa and around the world, three men set the pace for floral appreciation: Dr. Francesco Franceschi, an Italian im-

Celebrating the arrival of the first train. Many people attended the opening day of the Los Angeles and San Gabriel Railroad between Los Angeles and Pasadena, to greet the arrival of the first Santa Fe train on September 16, 1885. This picture shows the large pavilion erected for the event on the Central School Park. The pavilion was built of rough lumber open on all sides and covered with freshly cut cypress boughs. The tables were set up under the pavilion for a dinner celebration. ***Security Pacific Collection/ Los Angeles Public Library***

migrant who introduced more plants to the United States than anyone else and published guides to existing area flora; Edward Orpet, from England, a horticulturist with experience in several Eastern states, who, after arriving in Santa Barbara, hybridized Cattleya orchids for the first time and inspired the landscaping and beautification of the city; and Peter Reidel, of Holland, whose work with cataloging flowers and plants, in landscaping around the city and in teaching classes made him a popular expert of the area. [9]

Distribution and Transportation

In the last quarter of the nineteenth century, several major achievements paved the way for expansion of floral shipping and distribution, indeed all commerce conducted in California. In 1876, with the completion of the railroad over the Tehachapi mountain range north of Los Angeles, Southern California and Northern California became connected for the first time. This feat alone catapulted commerce within the state to unimaginable levels. Following on its heels was the completion eleven years later of the Transcontinental Railroad, thanks to the ingenuity (and perhaps more than a little greed) of railroad companies and the hard work of thousands of Chinese immigrants brought here for the sole purpose of building the line. The Transcontinental connected the rest of the country with Los Angeles and, in 1888, with San Diego.

With the arrival of railroads, there was nothing to stop progress. Now, thousands of tourists arrived weekly to see the land of sunshine and opportunity they had only read about in romance and Western novels and in advertisements financed by the railroads.

By 1890, the availability of refrigerated rail cars made it possible to ship fresh produce to the East Coast in one week. It would not be long before fresh flowers would join the oranges, lemons and avocados destined for New York and Chicago markets. Not truly "refrigerated," the early trains were stocked with ice and forced to make stops along their routes for the purpose of re-icing their perishable cargo. The quality of the goods upon delivery could not be guaranteed, but aggressive efforts were made by growers and sellers in the name of national sales and distribution.

Due to a price war between the Southern Pacific and Santa Fe railroads, the year 1887 saw increased numbers of tourists and new residents traveling to Los Angeles. The Southern Pacific alone delivered 120,000 people that year, with the Santa Fe Railroad not far behind.

The railroads and their promoters laid out townsites, planning the first hotel and the railroad depot and then promoting the development to Easterners. Many promotions focused on the agricultural possibilities of the area, to attract farmers from "the states." More than 60 new towns, most of them carefully mapped and planned in advance by developers and railroad interests, appeared in Southern California between January 1887 and July 1889. The land along the San Gabriel and Los Angeles rivers, which had been broken up into small ranchos during the years following statehood, were being subdivided into townsites by the new American arrivals.

All this growth was achieved without the benefits most growing, established cities enjoy. There was no reliable supply of water and little fuel. The area featured few mineral resources or forests. Aside from San Diego, there was no natural harbor in Southern California. Boosters were forced to promote the area or leave it.

Although the boom years slowed to an economic depression by 1890, and many of the fancy new towns disappeared, core businesses continued and Southern California growth went on. The boom had deposited substantial wealth and population, with losses mainly seen in the absence of anticipated profits.

Water: Now You See It, Now You Don't

Water was as precious in the 1890s as it is today in Southern California. Early Californians found ways to re-route water as they needed it. William Brewer speaks of coming upon the mission at Santa Barbara, in ruins at the time of his visit in 1861, but with its manmade water

Eighth and San Pedro in 1896. The east side of San Pedro Street at the corner of Eighth Street, showing the City Gardens, established in 1874, with a windmill. ***Security Pacific Collection/ Los Angeles Public Library.***

system intact. A strong cement dam had been built by Native American Indians working for the mission, so water could flow via an aqueduct made of stone and cement, to then flow into two large, cement reservoirs.

William Brewer speaks of the San Fernando Valley, where the runoff from mountain streams was absorbed by porous rock or granite. Of camping in the San Gabriel Mountains, he describes getting water through irrigating from a stream in a long ditch, "over twenty miles distant."

Long dry seasons followed by torrential rains meant vegetation grew rapidly when it grew at all. There were many rivers, but little water when the farmer needed it. Irrigation ditches were common. Later, the discovery of natural artesian wells in the Los Angeles farmland eased the water burden, until they dried up. Beginning in 1903, formal steps were taken by officials to dig wells and tunnels and, later, a large aqueduct.

Growing Cut Flowers in Southern California

With commercialization occurring in all sectors of the industrial world, the growing of cut flowers in Southern California began to take on more serious possibilities for those who recognized the area's unique climate and growing conditions. Although less than 100 acres were being used to grow cut flowers in the preceding decade, Southern California residents had begun to sell the flowers from their yards and small flower farms had been started by Japanese-American farmers.

In his book, *Southern California: An Island on the Land*, Carey McWilliams [10] notes that "It was not only the size but the rapidity with which things grew in Southern California" that amazed newcomers. The joke was that you had to get yourself up on a horse's back in order to pick a melon in this part of the state. There was no questioning the fact that although some areas of the broad Southern California countryside might offer loamy soil and others rich bottomland, with natural conditions and the addition of water, anything planted would thrive and grow quickly.

By 1890, the housewives of Southern California had firmly established themselves as the growers and sellers of cut flowers. By hand-watering, often with water recycled from household use, these industrious women transformed their backyards into flower factories, harvesting calla lilies and other blooms for local florists and their own homes. It was common to see vases of fresh flowers, placed on hand-crocheted doilies, on the dining tables and buffets of area homes. Californians were increasing in number and so were the flowers.

To meet the demand of a growing population, enterprising individuals gathered together to sell their vegetables, fruit and flowers in the center city. There was an open air market in the vicinity of the original Plaza, near today's touristy Olvera Street. Another market evolved at Ninth and San Pedro streets; still another at Seventh and Alameda. Don

Southern California's "Flower Basket" Climate

Mother Nature has generously endowed Southern California with a growing season of twelve months a year.

In Southern California, a grower could raise a certain crop along the coast in winter and when it became too cold there, a grower farther inland, where it is always warm, would produce that same type of crop. In this fashion, during Southern California's flower-growing heyday, it was possible to produce just about any crop year-'round and satisfy a demand that knew no seasons.

Morning fog along the coast in May, June and July provides ideal conditions for young flowers, like Giant and King Asters. These flowers can withstand the intense heat that breaks through as the clouds dissipate, because, thanks to the fog, the heat is only for a few afternoon hours and it is accompanied by a moist ocean breeze.

Pompon mums love sunshine and moisture. Because they don't do well in Southern California's intense summer heat, an early crop could be harvested in the Fall in the San Fernando Valley, overlapping the main crop.

Stocks do well in Southern California's winter weather, loving sunshine but not excessive heat. They are harvested in January and February in the inland valleys; and from March to May in the coastal fields.

Temple is said to have built the first produce market in 1859. Temple City Market, the first two-story building in the business district, offered a market on the first floor, theater, courthouse and city hall upstairs and a clock tower above all. The market stalls were 10x15' and rented for $20-$40 per month. Temple didn't grow flowers for the trade but his two-acre garden at Rancho Los Cerritos in Long Beach was famous for its flowers and fruit.

Shipping flowers out of California was impossible, as refrigeration had not yet been introduced. Early flower markets served local demand only. As area florists could purchase their flowers locally during warm weather, the informal Los Angeles flower markets operated only during the winter months when farmers brought their flowers in from the warmer valleys.

Throughout California, flower and gardening societies enjoyed growing memberships, shared growing tips and sponsored flower shows and festivals. Retail florists, floral designers and decorators were enjoying great interest in their professions. Flower festivals and parades were com-

The Legacy of Theodosia Shepherd (1845-1906) Founder of California's Flower Seed Industry

In 1881, with her husband of six years, Theodosia Burr Shepherd left her home in Keosauqua, Iowa for the warm climate of Ventura, California. She was a petite woman who suffered from tuberculosis and she hoped the balmy weather of the Coast would bring improvement to her health.

Mr. Shepherd, an attorney, found it hard to build a new law practice and Mrs. Shepherd determined to supplement the family's income so they could enjoy the finer things of life. It didn't take long for her to discover the flowers and fern on the hillsides and the shells on the ocean sand, which she then tamed and used in decorative arrangements. She quickly became known for her floral pieces.

Mrs. Shepherd found further joy in cultivating flowers in her 80x100-foot backyard garden and created a business from that activity. She began by exchanging calla tubers for gardening tools and flower arrangements for seeds from Europe. She also sent some of her work to Peter Henderson, a respected Eastern horticulturist who encouraged her to pursue the flower seed business.

Image by Theresa Padilla Fajardo

After two years, she was running a full-time business raising seeds and cuttings. She expanded by purchasing two adjoining acres on which her husband then built a greenhouse. In 1889, she published her first seed catalog and in 1902, she incorporated as the Theodosia B. Shepherd Company.

Mrs. Shepherd wrote articles considered to be among the finest descriptions in the United States, and gave talks about her hybridization and cultivation work with begonias, Smilax, Calla lilies, Cobaea scandans, Mexican orchids, cacti, geraniums, chrysanthemums and other varieties to which she introduced brilliant color and size. She sent seeds to growers and wholesalers throughout the world.

Theodosia's own garden was regionally famous. It was, as Victoria Padilla says in *Southern California Gardens,* "like one huge old-fashioned bouquet, a riot of color and beauty without any particular form."

Sources: Southern California Gardens by Victoria Padilla; (B) "Finding Aid for the Theodosia Burr Shepherd Papers, ca. 1900-1040," in the Online Archive of California 2006, http://content.cdlib.org/ark:/13030/tf8h4nb5hq/>

mon. Residents, usually women, organized floral carnivals at wooden pavilions. Finally, organizers with bigger ideas came along.

1876 Southern California Horticultural Society Exhibit
This first annual exhibit was held for five days in a Temple Street pavilion erected just for the occasion. Although the emphasis was on citrus displays, the exhibits also included musical instruments, silk hats, other agricultural products and an entire section of flowering plants.

1884 Flower Festival
Organized by the Los Angeles Women's Union, the show aimed to raise money to build a home for working women and newcomers to the city. Rain may have caused some folks to stay at home, but the event succeeded in raising more than $2,300 for its cause. Subsequent events in 1885 and 1886 were even more successful.

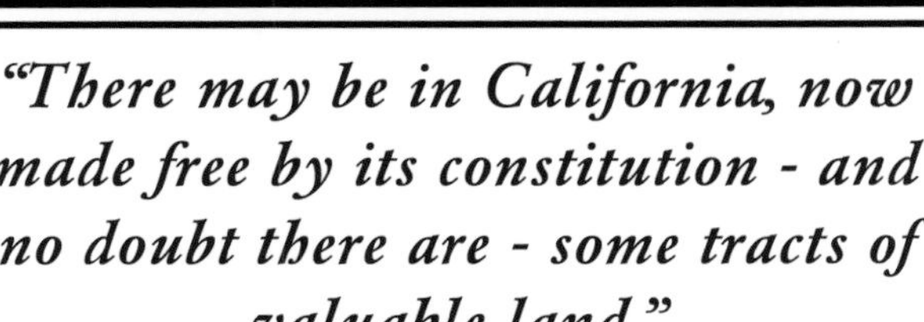

"There may be in California, now made free by its constitution - and no doubt there are - some tracts of valuable land."

— Daniel Webster as expressed in the U.S. Senate in 1850

1888 Los Angeles Flower Festival
A notice of the Flower Festival to be Held at Hazard's Pavilion, April 17, 1888, which appeared in the *Los Angeles Times* on March 23, 1888, invited "every town" in Los Angeles County to make an exhibit at no cost. It called upon area "Florists and other large growers who desire to enter exhibits" and it sponsored a floral design competition for florists. The exhibit hall was the largest auditorium in Los Angeles.

Two prizes of $200 and $150 were offered for the best and second best exhibits of flowers; and two prizes of $100 and $75 were offered for the handsomest original floral designs. The Southern Pacific and Atchison, Topeka and Santa Fe railroads offered free freight for flowers, food and fruit donated to the festival. The event benefited the "little ones" of the Los Angeles Orphans Home.

1890 Flower Festival
The Flower Festival Society's April 24 show was, in the words of a *Los Angeles Times* writer, "a resplendent carnival of flowers." Dozens of city wards, companies, nurseries and florists (including nurseryman and florist Joseph Sexton of Carpinteria and Santa Barbara) presented florals in exhibit booths and there was an art show of paintings by local artists. The Society treated 55 flower-decked orphan boys to cake and ice cream, who came trooping into the hall like a little army. "The fragrance of the thousands of blossoms was not more penetrating than was their shouts of gladness … how they cheered at the information that a second dish of (ice) cream would be served them." [12]

1894 Flower Fiesta
The "Fiesta de Las Flores" was organized by one Max Meyberg, who patterned the event after Rome's famous carnival and the Mardi Gras in New Orleans, both of which he had attended. The Los Angeles event featured an enormous Chinese dragon, composed of heavy red silk with embroidery of solid gold, and trucks were brought in from Kansas City for the presentation of floral floats. A masked ball was held at Hazard's Pavilion, at which hundreds of flowers were displayed.

These floral events came about because people shared their interest in flowers and organized to showcase them. Organizations were formed, including a state floral society in the San Francisco area (1888), the Floral Society of Los Angeles (1890) and the Southern California Floral Society (1890) which sponsored its first exhibition in Hazard's Pavilion that same year; the San Diego Floral Association formed in 1904. [13]

In Pasadena in 1890, to tell the world about Southern California's mid-winter flowers, citrus fruit and the ideal weather of their new-found paradise, members of the

Valley Hunt Club held a New Year's Day parade of floats and cars decorated with locally-grown fresh flowers. The Tournament of Roses would become an annual ray of sunshine during the cold and dreary winter for millions of people the world over.

By the time the nineteenth century began to wind down, as evidenced by the many flower festivals, events and gardens, ornamental horticulture had taken California by storm. Cut flowers were well on their way to doing the same. Up in Oakland in the San Francisco area and in Southern California, Japanese Americans had begun growing chrysanthemums and other fresh flowers commercially, setting the stage for California's cut flower industry.

Sowing the Seeds of the Cut Flower Industry

In Oakland, in 1886, Hiroshi Yoshiike became the first person to grow chrysanthemums commercially, while the Domoto family created the first truly large-scale Japanese nursery in America. [14] Yoshiike is known to have sold his chrysanthemum plants to Sotaro Endo, who in 1890 leased two lots for growing the plants in Los Angeles at South Main and West Jefferson. Endo was joined in his Los Angeles business by Jinnosuke Kobata, a flower grower who author Naomi Hirahara says would become like "a trunk of a tree," supporting "many branches of Japanese men, training them in his field before they broke off to launch their own independent enterprises." [15] Jinnosuke, a chrysanthemum grower, was described in *The Bloomin' News* (July 1966) as being the "first known recorded commercial cut flower grower in Southern California."

In the 1890s the Jotham Bixby Company owned Rancho Los Cerritos and about half of Rancho Palos Verde. Ranch manager Harry Phillips introduced farming, raising cattle, farming barley for hay and grain, and lima beans. When land values made it uneconomical to graze cattle, George Bixby, owner of the ranch, leased the land to Japanese farmers for about ten dollars per acre. Many of these precious acres would soon convert to flower farms.

In Alhambra, a Civil War veteran, Captain Edward Gray, who served Los Angeles County as a tax assessor from 1891-93, tried his hand at growing flowers on the large lot surrounding his beautiful home at 226 South Sixth Street. A Massachusetts farmer before the war, Captain Gray grew many different flowers and hauled them after harvesting to a flower market in Los Angeles. This farmer-turned-soldier-turned-horticulturist was also a florist, owning the Ingleside Floral Company, midway between Alhambra and Pasadena. And he operated a nursery at El Molina and Wilson streets in Alhambra. The Captain held the honor of having designed the gardens of San Diego's Balboa Park.

Captain Gray is said to have cultivated several fine strains of the carnation, and he raised exceptional gladioli. The first California nurseryman to raise flowers commercially under glass, he devoted one greenhouse to roses, one to maidenhair fern and others to asparagus and plumosus fern and smilax.

Also among the pioneers of the flower industry in California was a very determined Englishman named John Bodger. Settling in the Santa Paula area, Bodger started the John Bodger and Sons, Inc. seed company, now in its fifth generation of family management and operation with headquarters in El Monte, California. John Charles Bodger, his son, became president of the firm and a founder of the American Florists' Exchange.

An Alhambra, California blacksmith shop, 1800s. ***Courtesy Alhambra Historical Society.***

The Paths of Progress

Before the new century would begin, in 1898, Americans would experience an eight-month Spanish-American war, the annexation of Hawaii and the extension of the rule of the Philippines by the American government. These events opened the frontier beyond the California coast. They reinforced the need for a global attitude in a state destined to become what some have called a "country state" and one of the world's largest economic entities.

Within the few final years of the twentieth century, progress perched upon the horizon with a strong reflection of the innovations of the last quarter century and a beacon to the enormous strides about to be taken in Southern California.

The visionaries of Los Angeles would experience their first mental images of the great harbor that was possible if they could but tie together the factors of engineering talent, railroad accessibility and control, the clash between Santa Monica and San Pedro for the port's location, and money and politics. Ocean shipping would become important in the transport of cut flowers and greens in coming decades.

The automobile roared into Southern California in a big way after 1900, but several wealthy local leaders "tested" autos for themselves even earlier. Early cars had their gears on the outsides and they had to be cranked to start them. Riding in an automobile over dirt roads, one felt the bumps most severely. Motorized vehicles would soon change the way the flower growers, wholesalers and shippers conducted their businesses and made money.

Think wireless technology only appeared in the late twentieth century? Author Boyle Workman recalls the "wireless" service between California's mainland and the town of Avalon on Catalina Island. In about an hour, you could send a message across the channel, thanks to the ingenuity of homing pigeon owners Otto J. Zahn and Oswald F. Zahn.

Discoveries of oil in the Los Angeles area had begun to create an infrastructure for industry beginning in the 1890s. No one could have imagined the drama that commodity would play out in the new century, in key cities of the region.

Today, the cities and towns of semi-arid Southern California are irrigated with water, the lifeblood of our land. In the 1890s, irrigation districts were still being formed. The future of the flower growers (and everyone else) depended upon a reliable water source and system of water delivery.

Naming Los Angeles

Los Angeles was originally called Nuestra Senora de Los Angeles de la Porciuncula (Our Lady the Queen of the Angels of Porciuncula, with Porciuncula referring to the Los Angeles River and referencing a church in Spain) by Friar Juan Crespi. Fr. Crespi was a member of a group of European missionaries who camped in the area while exploring it in 1769.

In 1781, by order of King Charles III of Spain, a mission was established on the Los Angeles site. Eleven families, recruited from Mexico by Captain Rivera y Moncada, left the original mission at San Gabriel (established by Father Junipero Serra ten years earlier) to establish a mission in present-day Los Angeles. The families included eleven women, eleven men and 22 children. The village was named El Pueblo de la Reyna de Los Angeles (The Pueblo of the Queen of the Angels) and was part of the King's plan to secularize the settlements and expand them into agricultural and commerce centers. As the little pueblo grew, activity became centered around Wine Street, later named Olvera Street and preserved today as a visitor attraction.

As the years went by, the long name was shortened to the Ciudad de Los Angeles (City of Angels) and eventually to Los Angeles.

Sources: Olvera-Street.com; Wikipedia (Pueblo de Los Angeles)

Near the end of the nineteenth century, the prospect of electric lighting shone brightly. The Los Angeles Gas & Electric Company, formed as Los Angeles Electric Company in 1882-84, built a power house of 400 horsepower capacity and seven 150-feet-high towers. The city's shopping area was illuminated before 1900. Los Angeles became the first city in America to be completely illuminated by electricity.

> *There were many objections voiced to electricity. It was said to be a menace to ladies' complexions, to be bad for the eyes, producing color blindness. It was accused of causing optical illusions, of magnifying objects. Chicken owners were warned that the light would keep their chickens awake. And it was condemned as a costly experiment.* [16]

During these development years for Southern California industry, individual flower growers concentrated on selling to the market in the Los Angeles area. They tied their flowers in bunches of 25, packing them carefully into five-gallon oil drums, and hauled them by horse and wagon to the downtown flower and vegetable market and to florists' establishments. For a short time, until management realized how small the growers' volume was, the Pacific Electric Railway offered transportation to Los Angeles. It was offered just long enough to spoil the farmers before they went back to using the horse-and-wagon mode.

The days of horse-and-buggy transport, dimly-lit gas lamps and Artesian wells for water were numbered. Everything was about to undergo revolutionary change.

[1] William H. Brewer was a Yale-educated natural sciences teacher and botanist who assisted in the first geological survey of California from 1860 to 1864. His descriptive letters to his brother back in New York State were published by the University of California Press.

[2] Brewer, William H., *Up and Down California in 1860-1864: The Journal of William H. Brewer*, Fourth Edition, University of California Press (2003)

[3] [4] Padilla, Victoria, *Southern California Gardens, An Illustrated History*, University of California Press (1961)

[5] Starr, Kevin, *California, A History*, The Modern Library (2005)

[6] O'Flaherty, Joseph S., *Those Powerful Years*, Exposition Press (1978)

[7] *Los Angeles Times*, classified ad #12, March 31, 1883

[8] *Los Angeles Times*, classified ad #4, January 23, 1885

[9] Hirahara, Naomi, *A Scent of Flowers*, Midori Books, Southern California Flower Growers, Inc. (2004)

[10] McWilliams, Carey, *Southern California: An Island on the Land*, Gibbs-Smith Publisher, Seventh Printing (1988). Carey McWilliams was an author, editor and lawyer and served for four years as head of California's Division of Immigration and Housing. He was an outspoken advocate for a number of causes and a prolific writer.

[11] Laris, Sue, *Dining Guide,* (Downtown Los Angeles), "Old Photo Gets Explained," April 11, 1978.

[12] *Los Angeles Times*, "Flower Festival – the Pavilion Crowded Day and Evening," April 24, 1890

[13] Hutchison, Claude B., ed., *California Agriculture*, University of California Press (1946)

[14] Kawaguchi, Gary, *Living with Flowers, History of the California Flower Market,* California Flower Market, Inc. (San Francisco) (1993)

[15] Hirahara, Naomi, *A Scent of Flowers*, Midori Books, Southern California Flower Growers, Inc. (2004)

[16] Workman, Boyle, *The City That Grew*, Southland Publishing Company, Los Angeles (1936). Workman (9/20/1868 – 12/25/1942) was the first to represent the Fourth District on the Los Angeles City Council under its new charter. He served from 1925 to 1927.

JDP Photography

Timeline: 1900-1920

1900	Less than 100 acres were used for growing cut flowers in Southern California. Flowers were purely seasonal and only what could be grown and harvested in winter was available in winter. The flower markets were closed during summer months. Eastman introduces the first mass-marketed camera (the "Kodak"). The life expectancy for men is 45.6 years, for women 49.9. The population of Los Angeles is 102,000.
1902	The Paul Ecke family moves to the Los Angeles area. The Domoto brothers purchase land in Oakland which will become America's first large Japanese nursery. The first Rose Bowl game is played in Pasadena's Tournament Park. (Michigan routed Stanford, 49-0.)
1905	The first Los Angeles flower market is in business at 522 South Spring Street, established by Vawter Carnation Fields of Redondo Beach, California. (Los Angeles Chamber of Commerce, April 1947) The Ecke family grows chrysanthemums and poinsettias on its farm in Eagle Rock. In April 1906, a great earthquake in San Francisco ruptures the San Andreas Fault for 296 miles, resulting in a terrible loss of life and severe economic impact.
1906	Many Japanese growers move to Los Angeles from San Francisco after the April 18 earthquake.
1907	Japanese growers enter commercial floriculture. "They went into (the) chrysanthemum culture on a large scale and to less scale poinsettias and other flowers…" The San Diego Floral Association begins in Balboa Park.
1907 or 1910	Shumiti Murata purchases his employer's shop at Sixth and Broadway and converts it to a headquarters for the 30 to 40 Japanese growers in the city.
1909	The Domoto brothers locate their San Francisco wholesale flower market to 31 Lick Place.
1910	Florists Telegraph Delivery Association (FTD) is founded. The Los Angeles Times building is blown up in labor-related strife.
1912	Southern California Flower Growers Association forms in Los Angeles by 27 Japanese growers on April 12. California Flower Market incorporates in San Francisco with 54 Japanese flower growers as shareholders. The John Henry Company is founded to supply waxed and assorted paper products to the retail florist industry.
January 1913	Southern California Flower Market opens at 421 S. Los Angeles Street in a building that was only 20' wide by 60' deep.
1913	California Alien Land Law enacted, prohibits all aliens ineligible for citizenship from owning land. William Mulholland's aqueduct brings water to Los Angeles from 200 miles north.
1914	Southern California Flower Market is incorporated on February 6; moves to 421-423 South Wall Street on July 31. Henry Ford's company sells a quarter million Model T cars, each selling around $490, this year. The United States enters the war in Europe.
1915-16	Additional lots leased and a new building constructed by Southern California Flower Market
1917	American Florists' Exchange organized, opened market at Fourth and Winston streets. The Ecke family joins the group of immigrant and American families who are flower wholesalers in buying the building at Fourth and Winston, next to Armacost and Roysen and other floral industry shippers and suppliers.
1918	A war relief fundraiser is held in the form of a flower market in Central Park (now Pershing Square) in downtown Los Angeles.
1919	Albert Ecke dies.

JDP Photography

Planting the Seeds of California (1900-1920)

"The growers tied the flowers in bunches of twenty-five, packed them in five-gallon oil tins, and shipped them on Pacific Electric Railway cars. This service was abandoned after a short time by the Pacific Electric, as the volume of business was too small to pay for the expenses involved. The growers then had to resort to horses and wagons, and they peddled their blooms from florist to florist in the city of Los Angeles."

— Victoria Padilla, *Southern California Gardens* [1]

The great technological and industrial advancements of the latter part of the 1800s moved Southern California into an excellent position for growth in the new century. Mechanization, electricity, dams and waterways, improved methods of communication and transportation, and a functional infrastructure opened doors of opportunity for industry. Southern California became one of the fastest-growing regions in the United States. The wild and woolly frontier at the edge of the Pacific had, to a large degree, caught up with the long-established cities of the Eastern and Midwestern states.

The floriculture industry in California's Southland was, however, in its infancy. Just over 100,000 people resided in Los Angeles, but only five retail florist shops are known to have existed in 1900. Production of flowers was seasonal, occurring mostly in the winter months to address off-season demand that could not be filled by backyard growers and nurseries. Promoted nationwide for its great agricultural potential, the region had not yet discovered the soon-to-be multi-million-dollar cut flowers and greens industry.

The arrival of a new kind of immigrant in the first decades of the 1900s added texture and variety to the flower industry. Today our reflections of the past make one thing certain: The Southern California flower business was molded by people who sought a better life in their new-found land of equality than the life they left behind.

They followed in the impressive footsteps of those who had immigrated to California in the nineteenth century from other American states. The new refugees left hunger, joblessness, persecution, war, crop failures, floods and disease on the faraway shores, plains and mountains of Italy, Turkey, Greece, Japan, Holland and countless other nations, and they carved out new lives for themselves in the Golden Land.

The Official Welcome

In February 1890, U.S. Treasury Secretary William Windom advised that, beginning in April, the federal government would assume responsibility for immigration, which had until then been managed by the State of New York. After lively discussion, a congressional committee decided to discontinue the use of Castle Garden, an immigration processing station at the southern tip of Manhattan, and to build a new station on Ellis Island near the New Jersey shore. Sharing the three-acre island with the Statue of Liberty, the new station opened on January 1, 1882, to the celebration of steamships already waiting to discharge the very first passengers.

America's first official immigrant to process through Ellis Island was a fifteen-year-old, rosy-cheeked girl from Ireland, where famine had killed thousands of her countrymen in recent years. Ship living conditions were intolerable in previous years and many immigrants, upon arriving at the old Castle Garden station, had been deceived, misled and robbed. Under the new rules of the U.S. government, steamship lines were expected to screen passengers before boarding. Upon arriving at Ellis Island, immigrants were interviewed by doctors and clerical personnel and directed to holding areas, depending upon whether they planned to remain in New York or were traveling by train to another destination. Only one-third of immigrants stayed in New York City, with the rest continuing on to New Jersey and western states.

More than four million people first set foot on American soil at Ellis Island from its opening in 1892 until its closing in 1954. In the peak year of 1907 more than one million people were processed on the little island. [2]

Many families of early immigrants who made their living in the flower business were interviewed for this book. Without question, the pride of ownership and the rewards of achievement remain as bright stars for these proud Americans as they share their long-treasured memories, connections to their homelands and the reasons their ancestors came to America.

Many new arrivals to Southern California received the helping hand of a friend or family member who had made the ocean journey before them. An uncle or older brother were often employed as a field worker or helper in the processing shed of a flower grower's farm in the South Bay area near Los Angeles, near San Francisco or elsewhere in the agricultural area. When harvest time arrived or an employee quit, the new guy, speaking broken English and eager for work, slid easily into the fold. It was not uncommon for him to strike out on his own after getting some experience. He was sometimes helped to take this monumental step by his employer who generously let him farm and care for a small growing area of his own in order to get the required experience first.

City's Growth Paves the Way

In Los Angeles in the early 1900s, agriculture boomed. The city annexed the spacious, agricultural treasure called the San Fernando Valley, which enjoyed a reliable water supply, coastal climate and around twelve precious inches of rain each year.

Throughout Southern California, cattle ranching enterprises once operated by the large ranchos, now subdivided and gone, were gradually being replaced by crop farming. The landscape resembled a patchwork quilt with its orchards of fruit and olives and fields of wheat, vegetables and flowers. Interspersed among the oil derricks that punctuated the open areas in the San Gabriel Valley and around Artesia and Norwalk, the dairy farms appeared.

Fewer open spaces existed in Los Angeles proper, however, as a building spree such as the area had never before experienced began with fervor. The central financial district had evolved near Fourth and Spring not far from where the Los Angeles Flower Market was slowly taking shape. Thirteen-story-high buildings (the height limit) popped into view as the outline of an impressive cityscape developed. City blocks that previously housed nurseries and bungalow homes gave way to hotels, banks and department stores.

As they farmed, the flower and vegetable growers and orchard operators saw the city creeping closer and closer. New towns came into existence, brought about by the tremendous influx of new immigrants from the other states and overseas. Towns became larger and farms became smaller. The trend toward urbanization, evident early in the century, was a symbol of growth and a precursor to the future.

Several important innovations and improvements urbanized and mechanized the whole of Southern California and set the stage for changes in industry and agriculture. They would eventually support the growing flower industry. In 1905, the arrival of the San Pedro, Los Angeles & Salt Lake Railroad brought the Union Pacific Railroad to Southern California, boosting population substantially. The automobile, which had been tolerated by most people as a noisy nuisance in its first few years, became extraordinarily popular when Henry Ford's mass-produced, cheap, reliable and easy-to-repair Model T arrived in 1914. Suddenly, the ordinary person could become mobile easily. Voila! He could reach destinations in one-fourth the time his horse and buggy might have taken.

As innovations and progress occurred, the film industry discovered Southern California. The thought of 350 days a year filled with sunshine proved irresistible for investors, directors and companies in an industry experiencing the same revolutionary strides as others. It wasn't long before the little village of Hollywood was a big star in the minds of would-be actors and thousands who came to California to make their living from the silver screen.

Opposite: C.J. Groen with flowers loaded and ready to drive to the Market in Los Angeles, circa 1912.
Sylvia Foltz collection.

California Seeds the World

"Seeds are the foundation of human and animal life on earth," begins the text on the website of the American Seed Trade Association. Without seeds, food, fiber and many of the products we use from day to day would not exist.

It is especially satisfying to Californians to know that their state supplies a large proportion of the seeds that give life to the earth; and a substantial portion of the seeds used to grow cut flowers around the world.

Seven prominent professional flower seed companies that provide varieties to cut flower and greenhouse growers operate in California. In the northern part of the state (with volume very close to those in the southern counties) are Goldsmith Seeds, Syngenta, Sakata and Takii Seed. In the well known seed-producing areas of Southern California, the long-established Bodger Seeds Ltd. has its production and breeding headquarters in Lompoc and its company offices in El Monte. Floranova operates its breeding facility in Lompoc. Pan American Seed Company's production and breeding headquarters reside in Santa Paula.

These firms also operate extensive production facilities overseas in countries with low labor costs.

Reclamation seed and home gardener flower seed companies, on the other hand, include companies in the Midwestern and Western states, and California. They produce a wide range of products from wildflowers to garden flowers, most of which end up in seed packets.

Cut flower growers and greenhouse growers purchase the seeds harvested in California through seed distribution companies.

Our thanks to Jack Bodger, President, John Bodger & Sons Company, for his assistance with this story.

From Santa Barbara to San Diego, the agricultural areas were boosted by new sources for water and electricity. A municipal waterworks system came to Los Angeles in 1902 and, in 1913, a 233-mile-long aqueduct was built to deliver water from the Eastern Sierra Mountains. An added benefit of the aqueduct was that it increased electric power throughout the city. In 1917, distribution of municipally-generated electricity was introduced in the city of Los Angeles, replacing many of the gas lamps that had dimly lit the streets and business areas. Invention and ingenuity were transforming the way business worked and people lived.

Breaking News: World War I Begins

War arrived in the summer of 1914, the United States entering a fray that eventually involved 137 predominantly European countries. For four years, Southern California appeared as a microcosm of the entire country, so deeply absorbed were its people in the conflict overseas. The heart of the Southern California working force, indeed, a large part of the immigrant community, represented the nations now at war. Thousands of families were connected or, depending upon events of the war, unconnected with their homelands and loved ones.

Camp Kearny in San Diego was designated as a location for one of sixteen Army training centers and a staging area for the 40th Division. Before long, thousands of soldiers had relocated to the camp from other states and many others rode the trains through Los Angeles to reach their wartime destinations.

During the years of the First World War, millions of Europeans became refugees. Following the close of the war, in 1920, the numbers of people relocating to America swelled from 26,731 in 1919 to 225,206 in 1920 and to 560,971 in 1921. Their sheer numbers forced the ill-equipped, over-worked steamship and immigration workers to treat the refugees more like numbers than people, yet they came by the hundreds of thousands. In 1921, Congress imposed a quota which reduced the numbers. It replaced those regulations with even stricter ones in 1924.

Continued to page 23...

Bodger – A Name Synonymous with Flower Seeds

They would become known for developing the American Beauty Aster, Giant Imperial Larkspurs, the Dahlia Flowered Zinnia, the first red (Firechief) Petunia and many other national and global award-winning flowers over their 118-year history.

Bodger Seeds' long history of innovative flower breeding began in earnest in 1904 when John Bodger purchased land in Gardena, southwest of Los Angeles. Within a few short years, that modest parcel of land evolved into 350 acres and in 1916 was said to be the world's largest single field of sweet peas at the time.

John Bodger, an exceptional seedsman from England, came to America at the age of 45 and worked briefly for Theodosia Shepherd, California's famous flower seed lady. Seeing the difficulty Mrs. Shepherd's firm had in filling large orders, John and his son Will left to form John Bodger and Son. They began by growing flowers in the cool ocean breezes of Santa Paula.

The purchase of the Gardena Ranch in 1904 helped the company to service

Above right: John C. Bodger and his brother Chuck in an early day photo. ***Bodger Seeds, Ltd. collection.***
Above: John C. and Bertha Bodger in their aster fields. ***Bodger Seeds, Ltd. collection.***

larger accounts. Soon, they were also growing at Lompoc, 150 miles north of Los Angeles and eventually on leased land in other areas, until in 1919 they found a permanent home in El Monte. The firm constructed its offices in El Monte and the Lompoc ranch became its greatest growing field.

In 1909, the founder transferred ownership to his sons, John C. and Walter, who took the firm to new levels of success. John C. Bodger became a signer of the Articles of Incorporation of the American Florists' Exchange, Ltd. in 1920. Both he and Walter, along with family members who followed, were very active in the American Horticultural Society and other trade and civic associations.

After reorganization in 1930, Bodger Seeds Ltd was formed as a wholly owned subsidiary of John Bodger and Sons Company, ushering in an era of great innovation. Many changes occurred over the years since that new beginning, and four generations of the Bodger family have cemented the company's position as a leader in the world of flower seed hybridization and production.

Today, Bodger farms 350 acres at Lompoc and produces flower seed through contractual farming worldwide, selling its products through distributor seed companies. The company's vegetative cuttings are marketed as Bodger Botanicals, its wildflower seeds as Environmental Seed Producers, and the headquarters for Bodger Seeds, Ltd. and the company's real estate ventures are based in El Monte.

Sources: The House of Bodger *by Louise Bodger Whitman;* Southern California Gardens *by Victoria Padilla; and Bodger Seeds Ltd.*

To stop the practice of inspecting and sending thousands of non-qualified immigrants back to their homelands, the 1924 law moved the inspection process to overseas-based American consulates. Now immigrants were required to obtain visas in their countries of origin before setting forth for the United States. This single change in procedure reduced the numbers of immigrants to a trickle. Control and better-organized procedures were gained, although, as the 1928 commissioner general of immigration said so succinctly, "Ellis Island has lost its proud place in the grand immigration scheme." [2] The numbers of immigrants arriving at Ellis Island and other official U.S. ports of entry experienced many declining years after that.

Although the production of automobiles and other commodities and goods used by Americans was curtailed during the war years, and many retail shop owners saw the departure of employees who entered military service, this was an era during which demand for flowers continued and retail florists implemented many innovations and new technology.

Some shops began to embrace refrigeration, replacing the almost daily deliveries of ice to fill the "ice box" to keep flowers cool. Shops were redesigned to achieve greater efficiency. Themes, such as an Italian Garden or Hawaiian exotic flowers, were employed frequently. Most importantly, wire service by Florists Telegraph Delivery (today's FTD), introduced in 1910, increased in popularity and encouraged the ordering of flowers from state to state. Finally, demand from Eastern florists and wholesale houses for California flowers was cause for Los Angeles growers and shippers to explore new, improved packaging, shipping methods and technology.

On the immigration front, thousands of Ellis Island-processed immigrants joined the Japanese, Chinese and others who entered the United States through the port at San Francisco, making their home in California and their life's work in the flower fields. Working at the Los Angeles Flower Market became the dream of many. One can only imagine the sounds of the Market in those days,

Wordpix

as the thick Greek and Italian accents of flower growers and retail florists mingled with the Danish, German and Japanese tongues. Commerce was conducted with broken English and body language.

The list of Southern California immigrant families who farmed the flowers that filled florists' orders from the Pacific Ocean to the Atlantic Ocean is very long. Here are just a few:

- Dan Stamis, who came from Greece, became a grower of King Asters and then, for the last 30 years of his life a wholesaler at the Market. His business, Dan Stamis Wholesale Flowers, continues today at the Los Angeles Flower Market.
- Cornelius J. Groen's immigration from the Netherlands around 1912 helped establish the rose industry in Southern California. C.J. Groen's greenhouses in Santa Barbara County serve as a research station today.
- Italian immigrant Giovanni Mellano, enticed to make America his home instead of Argentina, established the state's largest foliage business. Mellano is one of the country's largest flower growers and wholesalers.
- John Polder, a Montebello grower originally from Holland, served on the original committee that arranged for the purchase of the American Florists' Exchange building.
- Chris Colombo Brevidoro, from Italy, founded the Colombo Lilac Ranch in Acton, California.
- John C. Bodger, an English gardener and seedsman, founded Bodger Seed Company, which today cultivates and supplies seeds through distributors to cut flower growers and greenhouses, nurseries and garden centers around the world.
- Jack Mayesh, after immigrating from Turkey, left his hot dog concession at Madison Square Garden, moved to Los Angeles and built one of the largest floral wholesale companies in America.
- Joseph Shinoda, born of Japanese American parents in Oakland, led the San Lorenzo Nursery Company to remarkable growth. The prestigious Shinoda floricultural educational scholarship foundation bears his name.
- Germany's Gebhard Prechtl found his niche growing calla lilies, paperwhites, Easter lilies and Scotch heather. It was he who miniaturized the calla.
- From the island of Cephalonia in Greece came Jerry Defterios. The company he founded today supplies fresh flower bouquets to supermarket chains.
- Leon Moskatel, from Turkey, established one of the most successful, high-volume florist supply stores in America as a Los Angeles Flower Market merchant.
- Finally, Albert Ecke, having emigrated from Germany, established the poinsettia forever as the "Christmas flower" in the floral marketplace.

Immigrants took the flower industry to new levels in other parts of the United States as well, as the histories of markets in San Francisco, New York and Boston attest. A number of Japanese American and Italian American growers in the San Francisco Bay Area also sold flowers in the Southern California Flower Market across the street from the American Florists' Exchange.

On the national front, thousands of blooms shipped from California to florists and wholesalers across America as early as the first decade of the century. In 1905, the Los Angeles Terminal Railway station in the settlement of Burnett (now Signal Hill, in Long Beach, California) was reported to have shipped on one day 400 pounds of Easter flowers grown by Japanese farmers nearby. [3]

Were there room in this book, our list of immigrants and their American counterparts who took the fledgling California floral industry to a leadership position in the twentieth century would go on and on. Some of the people named on these pages helped to establish the American Florists' Exchange just after World War I ended. Many of their names hold special places in the annals of floral history. (Their stories comprise our "Profiles in Progress" section.)

G.K. Defterios

Jerry Defterios at Redondo Beach flower field and storefront, early 1900s. ***Delta Floral Distributors Collection.***

Early Los Angeles Flower Markets

Going into the twentieth century, farmers hauled fruits, vegetables and flowers straight from their fields to a large produce market in Los Angeles. Paul Ecke Sr., who took his father's poinsettia growing operation to heights Albert Ecke could hardly have dreamed possible, recalled in later years that he accompanied his father every week to the big vegetable and flower market at San Pedro and Ninth Streets. Between 1902 and 1918, he recalled, they hitched up the horses, loaded the buckboard and left for market at 2 o'clock in the morning.

Traveling from Eagle Rock, and later on from their Hollywood fields, Ecke remembered, "We would get to the vegetable and flower market at 4:00 in the morning. It took us two hours to come down by horse and wagon, and then about an hour-and-a-half to drive home after the market." [4]

Paul Ecke also remembered his fascination with the hustle and bustle of the market, its fruits, vegetables and flowers in colorful array, and the florists who bought Ecke products regularly. [5]

Japanese American flower growers of the area were among the early flower peddlers in downtown Los Angeles. In 1909, growers Heiichiro Higashi and Yukitaka Ohta operated a small wholesale market on Spring Street; and in 1910, more than 30 Japanese growers were selling their flowers along South Broadway, near Sixth Street. [6]

Several flower "markets" were held as one-day or weekend events, usually to benefit a charity organization, during the years leading up to the formation of the American Florists' Exchange. In fact, a *Los Angeles Times* writer suggested in a September 16, 1907 article titled "A Fruit and Flower Market," that the city should build a "large, airy, artistic retail fruit market, devoted entirely to the sale of fruit and flowers." The writer went so far as to suggest the market be constructed "largely of glass," emulating Covent Garden in London.

One of the early flower "market" events, titled simply, "The Flower Market" was described in the "Red Cross Affairs" column of the *Los Angeles Times* on April 19, 1918. The event was to be held on May 4, 1918, in Central Park (today's Pershing Square) to benefit "war relief" and it was organized by the Needlework Guild of America, which was affiliated with the Red Cross.

May 4 is Flag Day and it is planned to have the parade that day march around the park and disband there, after which there will be an invasion of the market by the soldiers and sailors, each of whom will be presented with a boutonniere. – Los Angeles Times, "Flower Sale for War Work," April 28, 1918 [7]

Flowers seemed to be everywhere in the early part of the last century. They were sold on street corners and in little stalls and doorways throughout the city, making it easy for shoppers and residents to enjoy their beauty and fragrance. The Greek farmers were easily recognized as they carried bundles of flowers on their shoulders, hawking their blooms throughout the business district. Today's famous poinsettias produced by the Ecke Ranch in Encinitas got their start in the early 1900s when Paul Ecke Sr. sold them streetside in Hollywood, straight from the field. Setting up stands on Sunset Boulevard and busy intersections, family and friends pitched in to help meet the growing demand for the new Christmas flower. Area residents could purchase poinsettias easily from the Ecke family's local flower stands.

The Tournament of Roses: Every New Year Begins With Flowers

Throughout the world, thanks to the miracle of television (in living color), every new year begins with flowers in a spectacular display from Pasadena, California. Southern California farmers grow many of the flowers for the event, Flower Market wholesalers supply dozens of semi-truck-loads of flowers, retail florists assemble the floral arrangements for the floats and hundreds of volunteers help the event succeed. The entire Southern California community is involved.

- The one season of the year that is unusually quiet for retail florists and wholesalers around the world is crazily busy in Southern California.
- Float-building companies place their orders weeks in advance through local wholesale companies. Some orders are placed direct with growers.
- Deliveries to the float construction area in Pasadena take place from the day after Christmas right up until a few hours before the parade kicks off on New Year's Day. Deliveries of leaves, seeds and bark, used for color and texture, may occur weeks before the event.
- Delicate flowers, like orchids and roses, are the last flowers to be added to the float assembly, so their growing is carefully planned, their harvesting precisely timed and their deliveries made within mere hours of float completion. A truck-load of roses picked a day too soon (or too late) could be disastrous.
- As weather and other unpredicted factors affect harvest and delivery, wholesalers at the Los Angeles Flower Market must often make last minute purchases and order changes with their grower-suppliers, making the final week before the parade quite hectic. It is not unusual for buyers and wholesalers to work around the clock during that week, missing many holiday activities with their families. Experienced wholesalers know precisely what similar

Top left: Onlookers line the street awaiting the 1901 Rose Parade.
Above (color): In 1952, this Southern California Floral Association float won the Sweepstakes Award in the Tournament of Roses parade.
Bottom right: The City of Long Beach float, 1934.
Photos from the *Tournament of Roses collection.*

flowers to substitute and where in the world they can be purchased.

- Just before the flowers are delivered to Pasadena, it looks like a field of flowers in the cool storage areas of the large wholesalers at the Los Angeles Flower Market. Mellano's 3,500 square feet, 25 feet high cooler is stacked two levels high with flowers that won't be touched until they are loaded into semi-trailers and delivered for the parade.

- The average Tournament of Roses float uses more flowers than most retail florists use in five years.

- Before the planning system was refined, Tournament of Roses float purchases created flower shortages in the area's retail flower supply. Now, growers supply the event with advance planning and planting.

- In years past, floral wholesalers at companies like Mellano & Company and Mayesh Wholesale Florist acted as consultants to the float construction companies, helping them select the best flowers and fillers and calculate the numbers. Today, the float companies employ professional staff and consultants who fill that role.

Top: 2008 "Magic of Mardi Gras" float entry by Florists' Transworld Delivery, Inc. (FTD) won the Tournament Special Trophy award. Float riders were survivors of Hurricane Katrina and residents of the newly-constructed New Orleans Habitat Musicians' Village.

Above: The Raymond Hotel float in 1917.

Left: The Los Angeles Chamber of Commerce's float celebrates the peace and victory, World War I having just ended, 1919. Note the photographer at left. Photos from the *Tournament of Roses collection.*

Early Bloomers in the Field of Flowers

All over Southern California in the first decades of the 1900s, flowers adorned ladies' hats and dresses and decorated the tables and vestibules of public and private events. Home gardens, many of them covering large areas and surrounding their homes and walkways, were enormously popular, especially within affluent communities. Garden clubs – including the San Diego Floral Association formed in 1907 — were numerous.

Although not directly concerned with cut flowers, serious nurserymen from Santa Barbara to San Diego created an appreciation and awareness of the beauty of flowers among the people of Southern California.

A Massachusetts farmer named **Captain Francis Edward Gray**, who moved to California after the Civil War, is believed to have been the first Southern Californian to grow flowers commercially under glass. Captain Gray operated greenhouses and a nursery in Alhambra and the Ingleside Floral Company retail shop where he was the florist.

Englishman **Theodore Payne**, an early employee of the Germain Fruit Company in Los Angeles, purchased a nursery from Hugh Evans at 440 South Broadway, then made it his life's passion to call attention to the beauty of California's wild flowers.

Dr. Francesco Franceschi, an Italian immigrant, is recognized for making the nursery industry aware of the vast resource of exotic plant material available right here in Southern California.

Peter Riedel, from Holland, perpetuated the work of Dr. Franceschi, his predecessor in the Southern California Acclimatizing Association, and cultivated thousands of plants while testing and assuring their adaptability to Southern California growing conditions. He is known for publishing several important books, the accumulation of his lifetime of knowledge and experimentation.

Mrs. Theodosia Shepherd, who moved to Ventura from Iowa in 1873, is widely recognized as the catalyst for the flower seed industry in California. Mrs. Shepherd's backyard flower growing venture evolved into big business. Eventually, she cultivated eight acres and sold seed and bulbs to seedsmen nationwide.

Ralph D. Cornell, Dean of Landscape Architecture, renowned plantsman, lecturer and photographer, took time from planning cities and designing landscapes to train judges for flower shows as well as acting as a judge himself.

In Los Angeles, German-born **William Hertrich** turned the orchards and barley fields of Henry Huntington's 650-acre ranch, in San Marino, into a place of indescribable floral beauty known today as the Huntington Gardens.

Down the coast in San Diego County, a lady named **Kate Sessions** made her mark by introducing many valuable plants from Australia and South Africa. Those included a number of bougainvilleas which cover the hillsides of Southern California today.

Because of these passionate flower and plant people and others the Southern California landscape of the 1800s was alive with the color and fragrance of flowers.

Other growers sold on street corners as well. Neeta Marquis' article, "Streets of Glory" (*Los Angeles Times*, January 1, 1915), relates the comments of a Chicago woman whose love for Los Angeles was based on streetside "flower stalls." Marquis compares the many flower stalls of the city with those of "picturesque foreign cities."

Neeta Marquis' 1915 article also describes the "big flower market" on Wall Street, where Japanese, Greek, American and Chinese workers sold carnations (in bunches of 50, from the "great fields of Hermosa Beach, with a few from Hollywood and Santa Monica"), violets (small clusters from Long Beach and Newmark), fern asparagus, exquisitely fragrant sweet peas, Chinese lilies, rosebuds, Cecile Brunner ("raised at Montebello") stock, California poppies ("two months in advance of the general season") and other blooms.

The First Flower Market

The first wholesale flower market in Los Angeles, according to 1947 Los Angeles Chamber of Commerce records, was operated in 1905 by Vawter Carnation Fields at 522 South Spring Street. Its owner was Edward James Vawter, a prominent businessman and a grower known for his production of top quality carnations and other flowers. Vawter was founder of the Santa Monica Commercial Company, organized to conduct real estate, banking, railroading and other matters. He also organized the First National Bank of Ocean Park and served in many civic roles. His small flower market lasted only three years.

Flower sales seemed to be centered on Spring Street around First and Second streets. Paul Ecke Sr. recalled in a 1981 interview with Sylvia Foltz of the Groen Rose Company that his family hauled (riding the streetcar, or "red" car) chrysanthemums to the Borden Floral Company, a retailer located at Fourth and Spring. In another interview conducted by Sylvia Foltz, Frank Kuwahara, long-time manager of the Southern California Flower Market, recalled a wholesale floral center around First and Second streets on Spring Street, to which the European growers took their flowers to sell.

The Alien Land Law drew attention to the Japanese and was the underlying reason for changing the name Japanese Flower Market to Southern California Flower Market, Inc. Although the law could have limited the successes of Japanese farmers, the Japanese Americans were not deterred. Like many of those seeking a new life in the land of opportunity, they simply regrouped and found other avenues to grow their businesses.

The wholesale market started by the Japanese growers moved in 1914 to larger quarters in the 400 block of South Wall Street. In that same year, they started a rail transport company and opened a field office in Chicago to facilitate shipping to eastern and southern states.

The Japanese Americans Organize a Flower Market

Following on the heels of the new wholesale market in San Francisco [8], the Japanese American flower growers of the Los Angeles area formed their own market association. Fifty-four Issei (first-generation Japanese) flower farmers first organized into a wholesale flower group with shareholders, incorporating in January 1912 as the California Flower Market. Several months later, nine Japanese growers met at the Hotel Grand and organized as the Southern California Floral Industry Association. In January 1913, the new organization opened its Southern California Flower Market at 421 Wall Street in Los Angeles. The building was 20 feet wide and 60 feet deep, a far cry from today's two-story, $10 million facility across the street from the American Florists' Exchange. The membership fee was $25. Initially called the Japanese Flower Market, the directors later changed its name to the Southern California Flower Market, Inc.

California politicians of the era took a hard line against Asian immigrants, to the embarrassment of many Southern Californians and United States presidents Theodore Roosevelt and Woodrow Wilson. The atmosphere led to the passing of the Alien Land Act in 1913 which effectively prohibited non-citizens, including Japanese, Koreans and Chinese, from buying or leasing land for longer than three years. It was the first of several acts and extensions.

The American Florists' Exchange Organizes

During the formative years of the Japanese flower growers' market, and while many flower-themed events were sponsored and garden clubs rose in popularity, when spectacular gardens were developed on large estates and backyard lots, and as the numbers of retail florists increased, the European immigrants who had found their way to the flower fields grew in number, coming together in their own wholesale flower market and building bigger dreams. It should come as no surprise that many of them found their way to the produce and flower markets in the central city, or that before 1919 they began to talk about formally organizing as a flower market. The Japanese had blazed the trail and shown that a corporation owned by flower growers could be successful.

Led by Los Angeles florist Tom Wright, who was also a gardenia and orchid grower in Gardena, 30 flower growers organized the American Florists' Exchange in 1919, their first official place of business a garage on Winston Street, which intersects Wall Street, between Fourth and Fifth streets. It was a move no doubt emboldened by the early informal flower markets, the proliferation of flowers in a fast-growing city and the success of the Japanese growers' market. On December 31, 1920, the Articles of Incorporation were signed by the first five directors: T. H. Wright, John C. Bodger, Roy F. Wilcox, Albert Goldenson and H. N. Gage, each of whom received one $50 share of preferred stock.

The founders of the American Florists' Exchange included both the signers of its Articles of Incorporation and a handful of other men devoted to the vision of a grower-owned wholesale floral market. Some of these visionaries included:

- Ernst C. Amling, founder of today's Amling Brothers Company
- Walter Armacost, whose partnership with Fred Royston gave support to the growing flower industry and American Florists' Exchange
- John C. Bodger, president of Bodger Seed Company, a signer of the AFE's Articles of Incorporation
- Paul Ecke Sr, responsible for the poinsettia becoming America's "Christmas flower," who served as the organization's president for many years
- H. N. Gage, a Montebello flower grower and signer of the AFE's Articles of Incorporation
- Wall "Pop" Godfrey and Donald Briggs, commission men
- Albert Goldenson, a florist operating at 132 W. Sixth Street, Los Angeles, a signer of the AFE's Articles of Incorporation
- C.J. Groen, founder of the Groen Rose Company
- Gebhard Prechtl, the AFE's second president, who served as president until his death in 1946
- Herman Seidler, an investor
- Waandert Jacobus (W.J.) Vander Bruggen, Montebello horticulturist and grower
- Constantine ("Connie" or C.P.) Pierre Von Herzen, who served for 50 years as legal counsel for the group
- Roy F. Wilcox, a pioneer in the indoor decorative plant industry and a signer of the AFE's Articles of Incorporation
- Tom Wright, the first president of the American Florists' Exchange, a signer of the AFE's Articles of Incorporation

Shares of stock were sold at $50 each to those who held the dream of success for the American Florists' Exchange.

The Articles of Incorporation, witnessed by J.S. Whyte, secretary, believed to have been a banker in Montebello, were filed with California Secretary of State Frank C. Jordan on January 22, 1921. It would not take long for the corporation name, the American Florists' Exchange of Los Angeles, to become known across the country as The Los Angeles Flower Market.

Endnotes

[1] Padilla, Victoria, *Southern California Gardens, An Illustrated History*, "The Cut Flower Business," University of California Press (1961)

[2] Reeves, Pamela, *Ellis Island: Gateway to the American Dream*, Dorset Press (1991)

[3] *Long Beach Evening Tribune*, "Easter Flowers Grow at Burnett," April 18, 1905

[4] Dutter, Vera E., *Poinsettia King,* Ecke family history, circa 1975

[5] From transcripts of interviews conducted by Sylvia Foltz, daughter of C.J. Groen of Groen Rose Company, with Paul Ecke Sr. and Frank Kuwahara in June 1981.

[6] Hirahara, Naomi, *A Scent of Flowers*, Midori Books, Southern California Flower Growers, Inc. (2004)

[7] Central Park in mid-city Los Angeles was renamed as Pershing Square in November 1918 to honor World War I General John J. Pershing. During that war, the park was often the location of militia receptions and served as a sounding place for public speakers. It is located in the heart of downtown at 532 S. Olive Street.

[8] In 1906, soon after a devastating earthquake, the California Flower Growers Association was established in San Francisco. In 1909, the organization's previously open-air wholesale market found a home at 31 Lick Place. *Living with Flowers,* California Flower Market, Inc., San Francisco, CA, page 24-26.

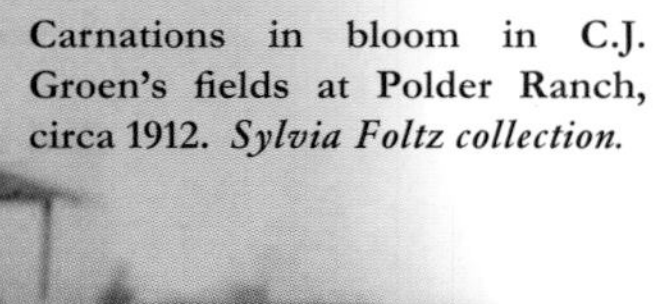

Carnations in bloom in C.J. Groen's fields at Polder Ranch, circa 1912. *Sylvia Foltz collection.*

Wordpix

Timeline: 1920-1939

1920	The Mexican government introduces the Bracero Program, which requires Mexican workers going to the U.S. for jobs to have a contract signed by an immigration official and demands that U.S. ranchers allow workers from Mexico to bring their families with them during the period of the contract. American Florists' Exchange incorporates and moves to 754 Wall Street. Standard Oil Company drills first successful oil well in Huntington Beach; land boom follows. The country is producing 106 million barrels a year, a quarter of a million barrels of it coming from Signal Hill, south of Los Angeles.
1921	The Articles of Incorporation of the American Florists' Exchange (Los Angeles Flower Market) are filed on January 22.
Feb. 17, 1923	Southern California Flower Market moves to 753-755 Wall Street. San Francisco's Italian greens growers incorporate as the San Francisco Growers Association.
1924	Ecke Ranch begins growing flowers in the San Diego area. First crop of poinsettias grown at the Encinitas farm destroyed by an unexpected freeze on December 17. American Florists' Exchange moves to its new building at 754 Wall Street. U.S. Border Patrol is created and the definition "illegal alien" is born. The Los Angeles City Directory lists nearly 100 movie producers, 150 movie theaters and 112 retail florists. In San Francisco, the California Flower Market moves to Fifth and Howard streets. The Society of American Florists & Ornamental Horticulturists holds its annual convention in Los Angeles. Roy F. Wilcox, one of the founders of the American Florists' Exchange, calls the general meeting to order. Rose petals blanket Clover Field in Santa Monica as Donald Douglas's three World Cruisers land to a cheering throng after circumnavigating the globe.
1925	Giovanni Mellano relocates from San Francisco to Los Angeles, becoming a partner with the Rainero brothers' wholesale greens company. Shortly thereafter, he started Mellano & Company.
1926	Wholesale Commission of Florists of America forms (later renamed to the Wholesale Florist & Florist Supplier Association).
1927	Home refrigerators accelerate in popularity.
1928	Southern California Flower Market purchases three additional lots. The St. Francis Dam, part of the Los Angeles Aqueduct system, collapses on March 12, killing hundreds of people.
1929	The stock market crashes on October 29, followed by several additional plunges in the following weeks.
1931	Southern California Flower Market completes plans for new building. Los Angeles International Airport opens.
1933	The Southern California Floral Association is formed. Long Beach earthquake, 6.5 ms, occurs on March 10, 1933, 5:55 p.m. The National Industrial Recovery Act becomes law on June 16. Albert J. Amling and Ernst C. Amling of Orange, the first Californians to apply for a rose patent, are granted the patent for their Red Talisman rose.
1934	Southern California Flower Market moves into new 9,000 square foot building.
1935	The National Industrial Recovery Act of 1933 is overturned by the Supreme Court.
1936	Hoover Dam begins transmitting electricity to Los Angeles.
1936-39	Southern California Flower Market purchases 10 additional lots.
1937	E. Manchester Boddy, *Los Angeles Daily News* publisher, purchases the 160 acres that will become Descanso Gardens.
1938	The Southern California Floral Association's Bowling League is formed. It would grow to more than eighteen teams, playing at Western Bowl for more than 30 years. The first Annual Headdress Ball, a benefit for the Rancho Los Amigos National Rehabilitation Center, is held by the Las Floristas organization.

Wordpix

Growing the American Florists' Exchange (1920-1939)

"There doesn't seem to be the slightest excuse for not having flowers these days – not in California, certainly!"

— *Los Angeles Times*, "The Easter Pageant," Helen W. King, April 5, 1931

In 1924, the American Florists' Exchange moved to the "White garage," a former taxi cab garage at 754 Wall Street. The new facility, a 40-foot lot, was conveniently located across the street from the Southern California Flower Market, which had relocated a year earlier to its own newly-constructed building at 753-755 South Wall Street. Both markets operate in those locations today.

From its earliest days, the flower business in Los Angeles was anchored in the downtown wholesale district. The wholesale flower markets followed the success of early nurseries that lined San Pedro Street a block from the site of today's Flower Market, of early Japanese American flower growers with their first farms in the area, of an increasingly popular city produce market, and retail flower stands throughout the area. More than 112 retail florists were located in the city limits in 1924. [1]

The early 1920s were ripe with opportunity, as the establishment of California floral businesses attests. San Francisco's California Flower Market took space in 1924 in a building on the city's Fifth Street following the 1909 forming of its California Flower Growers Association on Lick Place. The Los Angeles wholesale operation would find many occasions in coming years to sell to and buy from wholesalers in that market.

In downtown Los Angeles, a floral niche was forming. Around 1918, Tom Wright, who later became a signer of the Market's Articles of Incorporation, had purchased the Ocean Park Floral wholesale market from E.J. Vawter, the "carnation king," at Fifth and Spring to begin to create his downtown presence. In 1925, commercial orchid producer Walter Armacost built a new store on Wall Street for his downtown wholesale operation.

The San Lorenzo Nursery Company, a family-run Oakland growing firm, expanded by establishing a wholesale operation near the Flower Market in 1921. Joseph Shinoda, who became a respected floral industry leader, became its president in 1933.

Also in 1925, the Japanese Americans formed the San Pedro Firm, Inc., which took space in its new 28,677-square-foot building on San Pedro Street in Little Tokyo.

It was around 1930 that Leon Moskatel opened a retail flower shop on Wall Street just north of the Los Angeles Flower Market, a shop that would soon become a favorite supply store for florists.

In 1930, the Union Flower Market, comprised of Japanese American and European growers and shippers, formed on Wall Street just north of the Southern California Flower Market.

In 1931, Buford W. Hall started his wholesale business at Eighth and Wall streets.

In 1934, Giovanni Mellano and Colombo Brevidoro launched Mellano & Company in the American Florists' Exchange.

"You know, it seems that the Market just attracted more people as the markets (businesses) came down here," said Frank Kuwahara in 1981. [2] Kuwahara recognized the magnetism and influence of the district. Even flower growers who later moved to farms in San Diego County continued to sell through the Los Angeles market, trucking their fresh product several times a week to Los Angeles, years before the I-5 freeway appeared.

The two major markets became complementary to each other, growing at nearly the same rate and providing convenience to customers by selling from the same block, just across the street from each other. Each purchased adjacent and nearby properties as well, to expand parking facilities and make space available for tenants. The American Florists' Exchange purchased property on San Julian Street (behind its market on the east side) and it bought strips of property extending from Wall Street through the Market to San Julian Street.

"In those days, we paid $40,000 apiece for those lots with the apartment houses and had to rip the houses down," recalled Paul Ecke Sr. [3]

Early entrepreneurs like Gebhard Prechtl visualized the potential of the flourishing flower market area and purchased properties there, sometimes convincing the American Florists' Exchange board to do the same. In 1942, Prechtl bought an apartment house from the elderly Tomiko Minamiki, then arranged for her to live there rent-free. Later, when the AFE wanted to expand, Prechtl moved Ms. Minamiki to a nearby building at Eighth and Wall Streets, which was jointly owned by himself, Paul Ecke Sr and C.P. Von Herzen, attorney for the AFE. Prechtl's young grandson, Jon, received a handmade present from Ms. Minamiki every Christmas until she passed away.

C.J. Groen, who was instrumental in the organization of the AFE in 1919 and, like Gebhard Prechtl, was very dedicated to its success, loaned the AFE money in 1945 so it could purchase five lots from Gladys Greenlee, who owned extensive property in the immediate area.

From 1925 through the 1940s, the board approved purchases of various lots and buildings which are today part of the overall Flower District and AFE holdings. Lots described as residing in the Goldsworthy, Lankershim, Maple Avenue and Widow Botiller tracts and others became the property of the AFE. Many of the surrounding properties contained small, ramble-shack frame buildings. These were torn down to make way for the businesses that soon arrived and were rebuilt or constructed anew on those lots. The main 754 Wall Street property was bought in December 1924 with a loan of $30,000. It contained the brick one-story taxi garage of 79.1 feet frontage and 150 feet depth, that housed the Los Angeles Flower Market at the time. The interest rate on the loan was seven percent.

Innovation and Ingenuity

In the 1920s, the two markets, still in their formative stages, responded quickly to improving modes of transportation. Wholesale floral shipper Armacost & Royston advertised in *The Florists' Review* that it had started weekly rail service to El Paso, Houston, San Antonio

Two Amling Brothers trucks parked in front of the American Florists' Exchange, 1920s. ***Mellano collection.***

and New Orleans. To ship flowers to out-of-state customers, growers delivered their products directly to a Railway Express office for placement on eastbound trains. The rail service attempted refrigeration by packing bunches of flowers in blocks of ice to preserve their quality and fragrance.

Flower shipments had become significant to the point of mention in the "Southern California Acreage" report published in the *Los Angeles Times* on January 3, 1928, by the State Department of Agriculture. Among reports on the production of artichokes, cabbage and other vegetables, it mentioned:

"The growing of flowers for shipment into all parts of the West is a growing activity, especially around Los Angeles and San Francisco. Bulbs are produced chiefly around Santa Cruz and in Los Angeles and San Diego counties ... trade estimates the annual income to California for bulbs alone to be two or three millions of dollars. In Los Angeles there are two wholesale flower exchanges supplying about 189 retail florists."

Increasingly through the 1920s and 1930s, florists and wholesalers from Miami to New York, from New Orleans to Chicago, ordered flowers from Southern California companies. "The demand is constantly becoming greater," said G.G. Greenwait, commercial agent for the shipping firm of American Express Company. [4] Greenwait went on to say that in the Fall, for All Saints Day, New Orleans customers ordered up to 20 (train) carloads of chrysanthemums and many carnations and roses. Millions of blossoms were shipped from the Los Angeles Market during the year for non-holiday occasions as well.

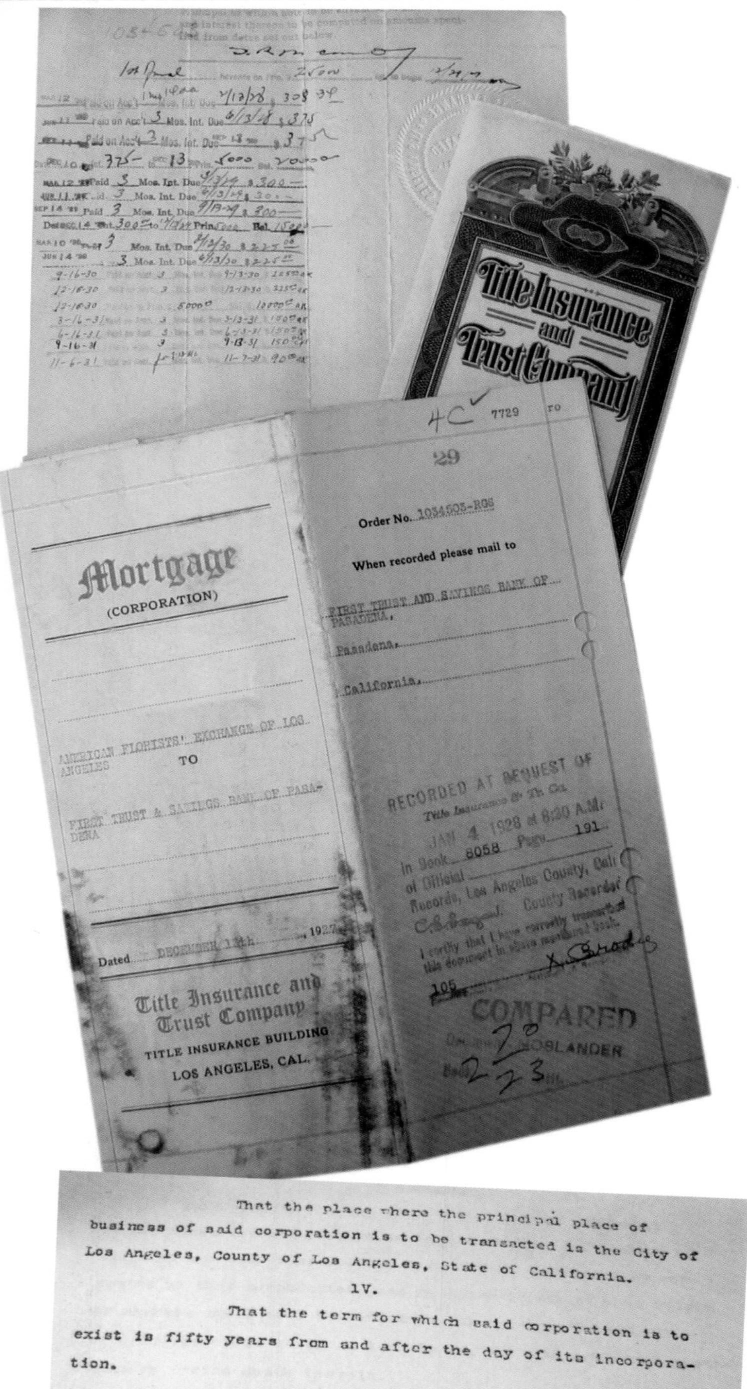

That the place where the principal place of business of said corporation is to be transacted is the City of Los Angeles, County of Los Angeles, State of California.

IV.

That the term for which said corporation is to exist is fifty years from and after the day of its incorporation.

V.

That the number of directors or trustees of said corporation shall be five (5), and that the names and residences of such directors and trustees who are appointed for the first year to serve until the election and qualification of such officers, are as follows:

NAMES.	RESIDENCES.
T. H. Wright.	Los Angeles, California.
John C. Rodgers.	Los Angeles, California.
Roy F. Wilcox.	Los Angeles, California.
Albert Goldenson.	Los Angeles, California.
H. N. Gage.	Montebello, California.

Top: Early legal documents of the American Florists' Exchange.
Bottom: Original signers of the American Florists' Exchange Articles of Incorporation, 1920.

In the middle of the explosion of demand for California flowers, the Japanese growers found themselves unable to expand their farming operations because of discriminatory laws. With the Alien Land Law a sticking point for everyone, local attorneys helped them establish guardianships and purchase land in the names of their children and through other creative means.

The Greek Flower Market

Just to the north of the American Florists' Exchange, at 744 Wall Street, the Greek flower-growing community established a wholesale market for its blooms, having first operated in a parking lot. Well known for their splendid and sizable asters, the Greeks were ambitious, hard-working and determined. Their Growers Market was used by wholesalers who were Greeks, Sephardic Jews, Filipinos and anyone who had not yet been accepted into the fold of tenants and vendors at the two larger markets down the street.

Many families from the Greek island of Cephalonia and the Turkish island of Rhodes had come to the United States, along with immigrants from other countries, in the early 1900s. Although not as large in number as those of the teen years, the 1920s continued to welcome hundreds of thousands of immigrants annually.

One descendent put it this way: "You go where your countrymen are." Once they were established in California, most immigrants then helped their family members to come to the United States. The Stamis family, the descendents of which still operate the Dan Stamis wholesale greens counter at the American Florists' Exchange market, along with the families of Karavas, Stephanatos, Priamos, Defterios, Katsogianes and many others formed the backbone of the Greek Flower Market.

Early AFE Flower Market Operations

Around 50 wholesale companies were based in the American Florists' Exchange in 1928; the Southern California market had around 140 members. Monday, Wednesday and Friday mornings were the especially busy periods, as they are today, with Saturday mornings also very busy.

Flowers grown in fields all over Southern California supplied the markets. From a radius of about 100 miles, as far south as Encinitas in San Diego County, north to Carpinteria in Santa Barbara County, and Redondo Beach along the western coast, growers hauled their just-cut blooms to market in the central city. Roses, lilies, carnations and dozens of other flowers found their way to Wall Street by truck, van and auto, causing one observer to call the increasingly busy, flower-decorated avenue "the Street of a Million Flowers." [5]

The sheer variety of flowers sold at Market, along with the year 'round availability of what Americans back East and in the Northern states called "off" season flowers, astounded visitors and kept the flower industry moving from coast to coast. One could buy lilies and gladiolus in the middle of the cold winter months when they could not be grown outdoors anywhere except in Southern California. Growers in Michigan, for example, obtained their pom pons, asters and gladiolas from Los Angeles area growers during winter. Business didn't stop when there was snow on the ground. Funerals and weddings occurred, depending for their expressions of sympathy and joy upon California-grown chrysanthemums, carnations, callas and gladiolas. Valentine's Day still called upon California to supply roses in the coldest days of Eastern and Northern winters when the greenhouses of Illinois and New York could not keep up with demand.

> "The first experience we had with California flowers was when they shipped them in refrigerated rail cars and it took about three days," said Jon Anthony of Jon Anthony Florist in Lansing, Michigan, in 2007.

Top: These five little girls posed in Guiseppe and Aurelia Gorini's tulip farm in the 1920s. In the back row at left is an unknown friend. To her left are Dorothy Willard (now Trowbridge), Anna Lee Gorini (now Gallizio) and Inez Ghigo. The dark-haired girl in front is Lena Gorini (now Pianta).

Center: In the back row, Mrs. Gebhard Prechtl (grandmother to Jon Prechtl, who worked as manager for Mellano & Company) and Lavina Groen (wife of C.J. Groen, the rose grower) pose in 1927 with Mrs. Groen's baby Sylvia (now Sylvia Foltz) and her big sister, Julia. Mrs. Prechtl's daughter Erika is at left.

Bottom: Anna Lee Gorini-Gallizio (in bonnet) with a worker in the Gorini tulip field, 1930s.

When he was a child, Anthony's parents operated a retail shop in Flint, Michigan, ordering carnations, snapdragons and pom pons direct from California sellers. Today, many florists, as well as wholesalers and distributors in florists' exchanges and markets throughout the United States, still order from California in an effort to stock up their wintertime inventory with the extraordinary color, variety and beauty available in California blooms.

Meanwhile, California flower growers were making names for themselves. Albert J. and Ernst C. Amling of Orange, the first Californians to apply for a rose patent, were awarded a patent for their "Red Talisman" rose in 1933. Many new roses were introduced in the 1930s including, in 1936, one from Germain's, one from Paul J. Howard, six from Howard and Smith, four from Armstrong Nurseries and one from Armacost, all of Southern California. In that year, Americans outpaced Europe for the first time in the number of new roses introduced. [6]

Also in 1936, the Bodger Seed Company won the All America Selections champion gold medal for its cosmos "Early Klondyke Orange Flare," the first of many awards to come. In 1936, Cecil Houdyshel, a bulb expert who grew and judged gladiolus, was honored for his work by the American Amaryllis Society, an organization he helped to establish. Some flowers, like the larger chrysanthemums and daffodils, were still being trucked from the northern part of the state, and many of those shippers and growers would soon open businesses in Los Angeles.

Enter the Southern California Floral Association

The National Industrial Recovery Act, passed into law in June 1933 and part of Franklin D. Roosevelt's New Deal, was probably the single event most responsible for the forming of the Southern California Floral Association. Supported by leading businessmen, the law created an agency that exercised powers delegated to it by Congress. In an attempt to stimulate the U.S. economy, it created jobs for the unemployed, promoted competition, made thousands of business practices illegal and put forth an endless stream of regulations.

In addition, in 1933, State of California legislators passed the California Retail Sales and Tax regulations, putting further pressure on the wholesale markets to standardize their practices.

Leaders of the two Los Angeles wholesale flower markets, who frequently found themselves in positions of mistrust and misunderstanding due to language barriers and contradictory business practices, were forced to collaborate. In 1933, they incorporated a nonprofit trade group called the Southern California Floral Association. The SCFA became a vehicle through which growers, wholesalers, retailers and allied tradesmen could communicate with each other and work together for their common interest. Standardized pricing and business practices evolved and those who wanted to do business through the wholesale markets were invited to become SCFA members. Until 1966, SCFA membership became virtually mandatory for those who wanted to trade at the two markets.

Left: Paul and Magdalena Ecke on the steps of their original ranch house in Encinitas, California, 1925.
Center: Montebello oil derricks hover over agricultural lands in Montebello, 1926. ***Herald Examiner Collection / Los Angeles Public Library.***
Above: The Alhambra Nursery, established in 1893, was located at 315 W. Main Street between Second and Third and across from the Alhambra High School. Nursery owner Glen McKay is pictured here in the early 1920s. ***Alhambra Historical Society Collection.***

Finally, the European American and Japanese American floral industry leaders sat down with each other, putting suspicions and mistrust aside, to set goals for the good of all. Meetings attended by representatives of both the American Florists' Exchange and the Southern California Flower Market were held regularly. A young Nisei (second generation Japanese American) named Frank Kuwahara stepped up to translate for his people, helping to eliminate the language barrier and facilitate dialogue. It was the work of Frank Kuwahara and Gebhard Prechtl that opened the doors and encouraged shoppers to move freely between the two markets.

SAF Brings the Country to California

In August 1924, Los Angeles put on its friendliest face for attendees to the Fortieth Annual convention of the Society of American Florists and Ornamental Horticulturists. *Southern Florist and Nurseryman* writer Aaron Smith said in his report that California had "set a mark for high class and pleasurable entertainment which will be difficult for future host cities to equal."

SAFOH's vice president Roy F. Wilcox, one of the founders of the American Florists' Exchange, called the session to order in the theatre of the Ambassador Hotel. Following the singing of "La Paloma" by Miss Los Angeles, Ruth Helen Miller, the crowd was greeted by Walter Armacost of Armacost and Royston, "in his inimitable and warm-hearted way making everybody feel welcome."

Smith reported that, "At noon, the florists and their ladies enjoyed a luncheon in the Ambassador ballroom."

Noted botanists, horticulturists and business advisors made reports and presentations, including Chancellor K. Grady, secretary of the California Association of Nurserymen, Fred C. McNabb, prominent member of a Los Angeles flower seed house, and H.A. Nater of the Los Angeles branch of the Bank of Italy (now Bank of America).

The only occurrence to mar the event was the collapsing of temporary seats for visitors having their picture taken. Miraculously, none of the 400 people involved were injured.

Southern Florist & Nurseryman, "Los Angeles Puts On Successful Convention," by Aaron Smith, August 22, 1924.

In 1935, the National Industrial Recovery Act was ruled by the federal government to be unconstitutional. The Southern California Floral Association, finding its effectiveness growing among the two market communities, continued. Frank Kuwahara was elected to its board of directors.

While all would seem to have gone smoothly from that point, points of contention continued to exist between the two flower markets. A 1935 lawsuit for $100,000, filed by the American Florists' Exchange against the Southern California Flower Market, was settled out of court, according to *Rafu Shimpo*, January 21 and March 23, 1935. Differences involving policies, attempts to control prices and operations were often difficult to resolve.

The Depression Years

In 1928, the economy of the world began an ugly, downward spiral. The downturn accelerated in the United States when the stock market crashed on New York's Wall Street on October 29, 1929. The effects of the crash were felt in California in ensuing waves and, owing to the state's diverse commercial base, a bit less depressing than in other areas of the country. On a broad scale, the effects in the United States and internationally were devastating to trade, and personal income declined steadily.

For some California flower growers, ironically, sales seemed to enjoy an upswing during the height of the Depression. People may have bought flowers to help themselves feel better or as a gift to pick up the spirit or mood. "Flowers are life. They represent hope. They deliver a message to hang in there and don't give up" is how one descendant of a Depression-era flower grower described the phenomenon recently.

For others in California's flower industry, things were not so bright. Many growers were heavily leveraged and many were dependent upon credit. It was tough to pay the bills, keep the business going and control the rising mountain of debt. Some turned to growing vegetables or other occupations, just to get through the difficult era.

Hardwig Prechtl recalled his father, Gebhard Prechtl, pulling his paperwhite bulbs out of the ground so he could sell them to John Bodger's seed company to raise money to pay the taxes on Prechtl's flower field. In another family, a daughter delayed plans to attend college so she could work at the Market for a dollar a day.

Even while bad economic times took their toll, Southern California's infrastructure was built. After the collapse of the St Francis Dam near Saugus in 1928, which killed 400 people, the formidable Boulder Dam was constructed by 1935 on the Colorado River at the Arizona and Nevada borders. Together with hydroelectric power generated by the dam's turbines, water from Lake Mead, created by the dam, was soon delivered to Southern California flower farmers.

The Metropolitan Water District had engineered and built an effective delivery system by the end of the decade, creating a base for agricultural irrigation and the aerospace manufacturing soon to come. To the north, the construction of the federal government's Central Valley Project was begun in 1935. It would integrate the reservoirs and dams, pumping stations and power plants in California's great agricultural region.

In 1938, construction was begun on a freeway intended to link Pasadena and downtown Los Angeles. The Arroyo Seco Parkway was dedicated on December 30, 1940, two days before the Tournament of Roses parade. Now, farmers in the Pasadena area and in the towns along the 710 Freeway route could get their flowers to Market much more quickly.

Oil wells continued to be drilled, and oil companies grew into large corporations. Co-existing beside colorful fields of flowers,

Top right: Partial view of the Buford W. Hall Wholesale Florists packing room in 1939.
Right: Los Angeles Evergreen employees on Wall Street during the 1934 Christmas season, making garlands for the department stores. The inscription on back identifies the people as: Background – the two girls are Doris and Julia Gandolfo. From right to left, the workers are: Caesar Rainero, John Rainero (partner), John (Giovanni) Mellano (partner), Nick Gandolfo (Senior, a partner), an unknown man, Emilio Lombardo and Albert Mongi.

sugar beets and countless citrus groves, derricks loomed throughout the Los Angeles Basin. They appeared "planted," in large and small groups and in some places in row after row, like tall, dark sentinels. Landmarks of an era, like the fields around them, they would soon fade into the mist of urbanization.

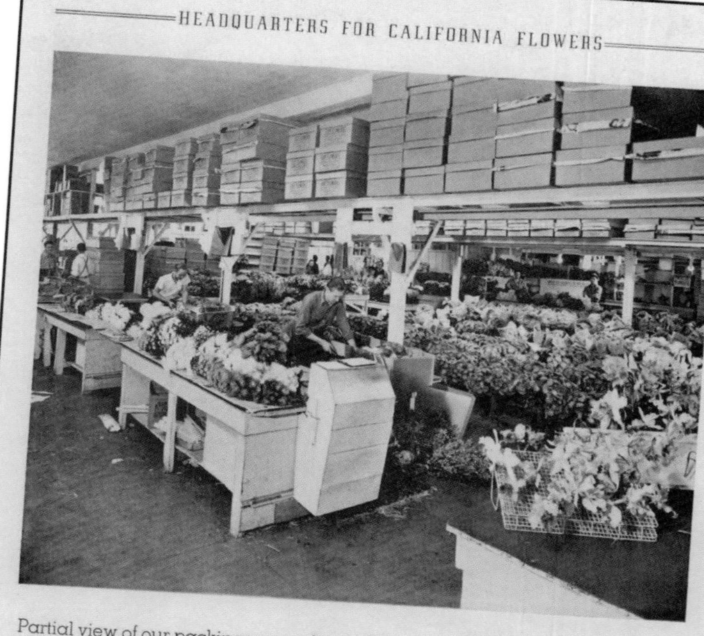

The Promise of Labor

The difficult 1930s saw an influx of yet another kind of immigrant. These were the thousands of out-of-work laborers who relocated to California, the land of promise, from Midwestern states. They took their places in the flower disbudding and picking fields and processing sheds all over California, learning from Greek and Italian workers who were now joined by itinerant laborers from Mexico.

Labor became a sensitive, often volatile topic in the 1930s. More than 300,000 agricultural workers worked in California, many from the drought-stricken Southern,

HEADQUARTERS FOR CALIFORNIA FLOWERS

Partial view of our packing room where fresh cut flowers are shipped out the day they are purchased. Buying begins at 3 a.m. to insure an adequate supply of the choicest flowers available for the day's requirements. Our service is a "year round service" from the year round market — *Los Angeles!*

Very truly yours,

Employees of

Buford W. Hall Wholesale Florists

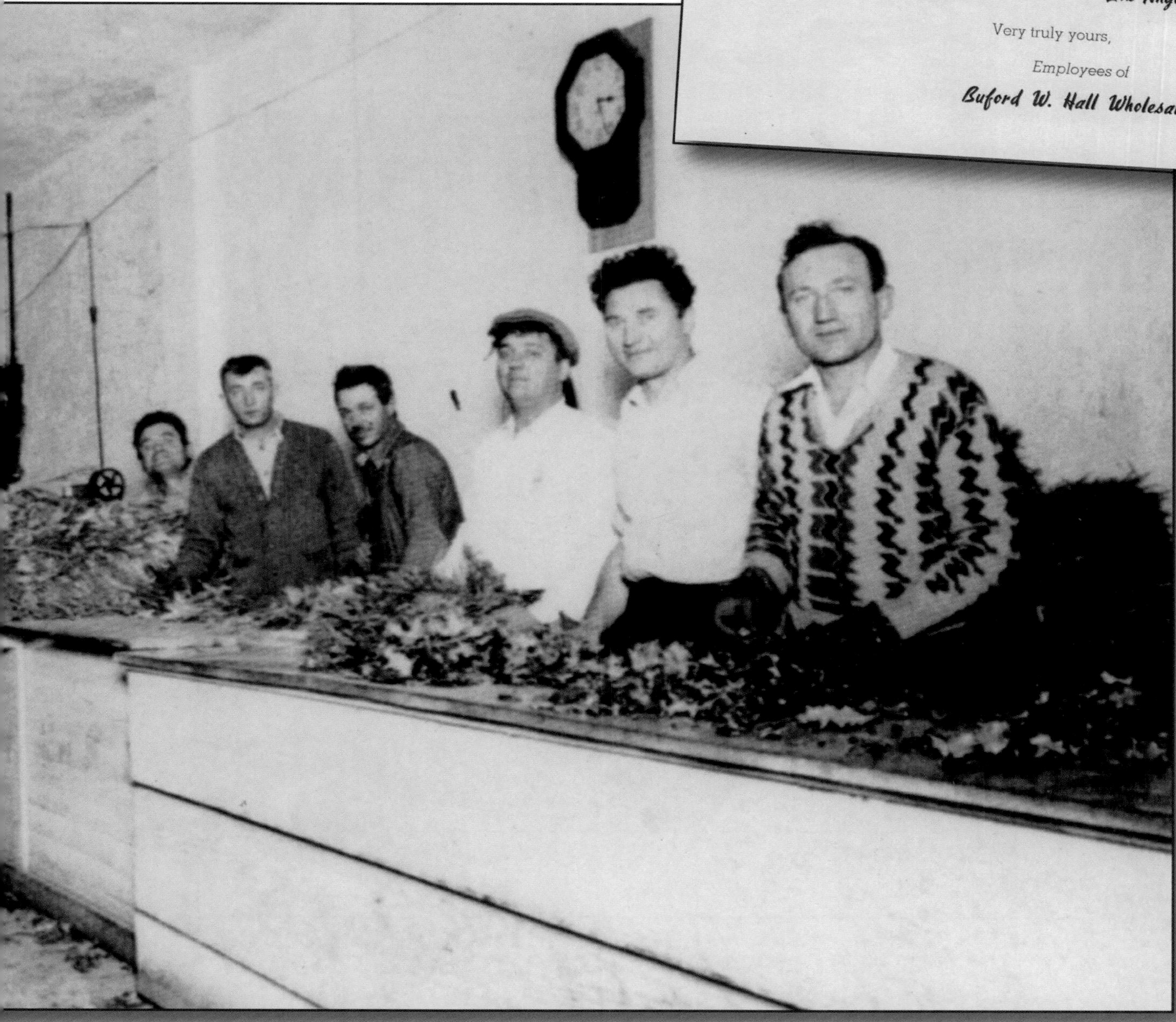

Left: Employees of Broadway Florist celebrate 20-year anniversary of Carrie Suhrer on October 2, 1938. From left around the table: Harry Hanson, unknown gentleman, Stuart Latham, Ray Nottke, Jerry Stathatos, Edith Greensleeve, Dan (Jr) Stathatos, Dan (Sr) Stathatos, Diamonda Stathatos, Carrie Suhrer, Evelyn Gilbert, Nel Ulmer, Tom Pappas, unknown and Jim Cavanaugh. ***Stathatos collection*.**

Bottom left: The crew at Buford W. Hall Wholesale Florists in the early 1930s. Back row from left, Dorothy Smith, Art Smith, Royce Chezum. Kneeling are Jacob Dekker, left, and Buford W. Hall. *Warren Hall collection.*

Below right: The Amling 600-feet-long greenhouses on Fifth Street in Santa Ana, after 1937, were used to grow the company's famous roses, shipped right from the field by Pacific Electric train to Los Angeles. *Amling collection.*

midwestern and southwestern states. Kevin Starr reports that by the middle of 1934, there were 142 agricultural workers for every 100 jobs. [7] Workers' living conditions suffered, benefits were non-existent and unions formed to come to their aid. In California, in the flower and vegetable fields as well as the fruit orchards, canneries and shipping docks, seasonal labor was essential for planting, harvesting and shipping.

California had been built with itinerant labor and the fresh, new ideas delivered by eager, enterprising immigrants. That arrangement had to continue for industry and agriculture to succeed. Strikes were common and politics were played at all angles. When it was all said and done, in spite of the violence and stressful years, the benefits and working conditions of thousands of farm and factory workers had improved.

Local Flower Business During the Depression

In the flower industry, Depression era reports and experiences were mixed. The profitability of farming dropped radically, which caused many landowners to divide and sublet small tracts to be farmed with more profitable cash crops. This chopping up of large farms placed a decidedly different countenance on the few wide open spaces that remained from Los Angeles to San Diego. The town of El Monte, just east of Los Angeles, was said to have transitioned overnight from a "little farm town one mile square" to a Los Angeles suburb.

Agostina Lugaro recalls receiving premium prices just after the Depression began to take its toll in Southern California. Italian immigrants, she and her husband Jack farmed chrysanthemums in Montebello. At 104 years of age as this book was written, Agostina recalled selling blooms from the trunk of the family car.

Floriculture continued to thrive, in selective locations and markets, in these difficult years. *Southern Florist & Nurseryman* magazine published letters and comments from many retail florists, among them:

> January 2, 1931 - Corsicana, Texas: Our Christmas sales broke all records.
>
> January 2, 1931 – Tulsa, Oklahoma: Surprised and delighted at the Christmas business… we went over last year's expectations.
>
> January 4, 1935 – Shreveport, Louisiana: Best Christmas since we've been in business with exceptional demand for nice roses.

The magazine's weekly reports from California seemed to support the states' retail reports:

> February 1, 1935 – Shipments from Los Angeles were heavy last week despite several frosts which caused a general scarcity of field-grown flowers. The market until the latter part of the week was comparatively bare.

It was during this period of continuing growth in the flower industry that Telegraph Delivery Services (TDS) was started by Edwin S. Douglas. Beginning in 1934 with under a dozen retail shops as members, its international arm was called Teleflora, the name by which it is known today. Douglas's goal was to offer a wire service membership with fewer restrictions than those imposed by FTD, which was well established since 1910. Both provided a valuable service of wire transfer floral orders and both expanded their services to their member florists substantially in the years that followed.

The commercialization of the cut flower and flower seed industries continued to mature and grow during the 1930s. Breathtaking blankets of color could be seen on the hillsides near towns along the coast, on the plains and in the valleys of the inland cities. They were popping up everywhere, from Lompoc to Leucadia.

As the flower business marched on and the Great Depression showed signs of evolving into war, public gardens and floral events and organizations continued to evolve.

In 1937 E. Manchester Boddy, publisher of the *Los Angeles Daily News,* purchased 160 virgin acres in a suburb called La Canada Flintridge. He cleared the land, built an elegant mansion overlooking 25 acres of live oak forest with a camellia-lined driveway and named the estate Rancho del Descanso. The property, along with additional acres later purchased, would become Descanso Gardens.

In 1938 the Los Floristas, Inc. association organized to conduct an Annual Headdress Ball, which became a large affair for Los Angeles florists in the years to come, attracting many designers and spotlighting a wide variety of flowers. This signature event still benefits the Los Floristas Handicapped Children's Center at Rancho Los Amigos National Rehabilitation Center and the Los Angeles County University of Southern California Medical Center. Like the Tournament of Roses and the Academy Awards' Oscars events, it became a major floral event in Los Angeles.

Even as war broke out in Europe in late 1939, California, the Golden Land for immigrants from both foreign shores and domestic states, was on its way to becoming the flower capital of America.

Endnotes

[1] *Los Angeles City Directory*, 1924, Florists

[2] [3] Sylvia Foltz interviews with Frank Kuwahara and Paul Ecke Sr

[4] *Los Angeles Times*, "Iced Flowers Go All Over Country," February 19, 1931

[5] *Los Angeles Times,* "Early Morn Presents Bright Scene on Street of a Million Flowers," February 23, 1931

[6] Padilla, Victoria, *Southern California Gardens, An Illustrated History*, University of California Press (1961)

[7] Starr, Kevin, *California: A History,* The Modern Library (2005)

The Southern California Floral Association

SCFA served thousands of members from its inception in 1931 until it merged with the California State Floral Association in the 1980s. It was supported by a staff whose offices were in the American Florists' Exchange at 766 Wall Street in Los Angeles, in the suite now occupied by the Los Angeles Flower District badge program.

The SCFA was formed initially as a nonprofit trade group to service the industry and became a for-profit corporation in 1950. Its members were florists, growers, wholesalers, floral delivery firms, floral supply companies and anyone involved in the floral industry of the region. After adoption of the California Retail Sales and Tax law in 1933, the Association became closely allied with the Los Angeles wholesale flower markets. Members and tenants were required to register their exemption certificates with the Association in

Continued...

Top: Leaders of the Japanese-American Flower Industry Association (forerunner to the Southern California Floral Association) pose for this May 16, 1936 photo. ***Seated from left are***: Yoshataro Matsushita, cut flower grower; W.J. Vander Bruggen, grower; Paul Yamamoto, grower and Bruin Flower Shop; William B. Williamson, general manager of Armacost & Royston; Mosatiro Kai, grower; Wall Godfrey, partner, Briggs-Godfrey Cut Flowers; Kametaro Akiyama, grower; Gebhard Prechtl, president, American Florists' Exchange; Akira Mori, owner, Mori Greenhouses.
Standing, from left: Takeshi Yagi, manager, Southern California Flower Market; James S. White, secretary, Southern California Floral Association; Shunichi Murata, owner, S. Murata Co.; Y. Yuzawa, owner, Vermont Florist; Paul Lambert, grower; C.J. Groen, owner, Groen Rose Company; H. Lijima, grower; William Zaima, owner, Figueroa Nursery & Greenhouse. ***Photo by C.J. Groen.***

Right: An early 1950s photo of the board of directors of the Southern California Floral Association. ***Back row from left***: A Santa Barbara route man, Charley Hum of Vogue Florist, general manager Walter Swartz and Ray Nottke. ***Front row from left***: Joe Shinoda of San Lorenzo Nursery, George Kubota, 1952 SCFA president Eddie Battistessa, Fred Miller of Monterey Park Florist, and Burbank florist Fred Fredenhagen.

Top: One of the many teams from the popular SCFA bowling league in the 1950s. Carl Hankemeier is second from right, kneeling.

Right: The Stamis Wildcats were one of the few bowling teams that represented flower growers, with most teams including wholesalers and commission men. In the back row from left are John Karavas, Cosmos Stamis and Dan Stamis. Front row: Brown Stamis, left, and Gus Stamis. As a kid tagging along with his father, Tike Karavas remembers the exciting ride in the pickup truck from Redondo Beach to Hollywood, to the Sunset Bowl. Tike's childhood heros, actors coming from their shows in the KTLA studio next door, often stopped by the bowling alley to watch the SCFA teams, who filled the entire bowling alley, a striking bunch in their chartreuse shirts. *Karavas collection.*

exchange for badges, putting the Association in the position of determining buyers' eligibility for wholesale status. (In 1965, the policy was reversed when the Association decided to issue auxiliary numbers to those who did not wish to become members but qualified for the exemption.)

The SCFA offered a number of benefits including credit union membership, a benevolent fund, a monthly newsletter, an investment club, legal services, flower design classes and an unending list of social groups and events including a winter cruise. In 1952 it sponsored an elaborately decorated float in the Tournament of Roses, which won the Sweepstakes award. Its annual Open House, Design School and Trade Fair was a popular affair that closed Wall Street for the day and featured entertainment, activities and the home cooking of market tenants.

In 1972, 71 percent (precisely 792) of the retail florists who were issued permits by the California State Board of Equalization were members of the SCFA. Another eight percent held auxiliary numbers.

Following are the presidents of the Southern California Floral Association from 1931 through 1988, earliest first with several individuals (Ebbo Dekema, Victor Levy, Nick Vander Bruggen, Jack Mayesh, Albert Znojil, and Art Dettweiler) serving two terms of office. A few later years' presidents' names were unavailable.

Donald Briggs, Wall Godfrey, Paul Lambert, John C. Hansen, Gebhard Prechtl, Kenneth Parker, G. Edwin Murphy, Harold J. Francis, H. Peter Raagaard, Ray W. Nottke, Fred C. King, Ebbo Dekema, Frank Fredenhagen, Edmund J. Battistessa, Fred O. Miller, Joseph Shinoda, Albert Znojil Jr.,

Top: Golfers show off their trophy after a 1950 tournament. Back row from left: Walter Swartz, Lennie Johnson, Eddie Battistessa, Mario Pozzo, Don Forsythe, Bert Johnson, Art Smith, Hank Marquis. Front row from left: Harry Francis, Joe Holladay, Jack Hauquitz, Chuck Hirata, Jack Reed, Fred Tayama. *Battistessa collection.*

Center: Dignitaries gathered for the Seventeenth Annual Open House on October 4, 1970. From left are Leroy Youts, Frank Kuwahara, E.G. Thornton, Art Dettweiler, Walter Swartz, Richard Nevin, City Councilman Gilbert Lindsay and Chiyo Tayama. *Photo courtesy Kirk Kirkpatrick AIFD.*

Right: Pictured at a Flower Market 1961 golf tournament are from left: Jack Reed (Market employee), Bert Johnson (gladiola wholesaler), an event hostess, Mike Cordova (Wilmington florist) and David Capilouto (Lakewood florist). *Bert Johnson collection.*

Tom T. Hide, W.J. Vander Bruggen, Charles R. Hum, Arthur B. Smith, Ray G. Miller, Ben Harmon, Paul J. Miller, Henry E. Sasajima, Paul F. Schaefer, Fred M. Tayama, Mel Cooper, Min Ioki, Charles L. Gibbons, Sam Applebaum, Victor Levy, Nick Vander Bruggen, Arthur T. Ito, Joseph Mayesh, William M. Riach, Arthur L. Dettweiler, Don Wakefield, David Y. Kitayama, Norman Yoshida and Art Bogad.

Many readers will remember the popular but strict Walter F. Swartz, who served as SCFA General Manager for many years and into the 1970s.

In the early 1990s, the Southern California Floral Association merged with the California State Floral Association, which had until that time focused its efforts on the Northern California floral industry.

Sources: (1) U.S. Department of Agriculture "Marketing Research Report 1042, An Analysis of Floral Wholesaling Facilities in Los Angeles, California," 1976; (2) The Bloomin' News (1970s)

Members and guests of the Southern California Floral Association enjoy a "Good Will Dinner" at the Biltmore Hotel in Los Angeles, November 18, 1949. *American Florists' Exchange collection.*

WordPix

Timeline: 1940-1959

1940	California growers ship almost 1,500 express refrigerator carloads of cut flowers, including 87,980 orchids sent by plane.
1941	FTD holds national/annual convention in Los Angeles in the Spring. California Association of Flower Growers and Shippers incorporates. Japan attacks Pearl Harbor on December 7. The U.S. enters World War II.
1942-1944	Southern California Flower Market member growers evacuated and their market facilities leased to non-Japanese growers.
1943	Japanese American grower incarcerations lead to lack of Easter flowers and plants. Ecke grows hydrangeas and lilies at the request of retailers. The invention in Great Britain of a programmable electronic machine used to crack codes in Germany's wartime orders lays the groundwork for the development of computers.
1944	The Second World War revolutionizes California's economy. Between 1940 and 1944, more than $800 million is invested in some 5,000 new industrial plants in the Los Angeles metropolitan area. A committee is appointed to consider establishing an arboretum for the Los Angeles area. (The Los Angeles County Arboretum in Arcadia is the result.)
1945	Japanese Americans begin to return home from the camps.
1946	Southern California Flower Market turned back to the Japanese American growers on January 1. Golden State Wholesale (a shipping company) starts.
1947	The wholesale value of flowers grown in Los Angeles County reaches $13,500,000. (*Westways*, June 1948)
Mid-to-late 1940s	Hollywood area experiences a boom time economically. Ecke's sales at the well trafficked Hollywood intersections skyrocket. Paul Ecke Sr. buys his wife a new Chrysler.
1948	The California State Floral Association forms. Floralife introduces Sno-pak, the first foam floral base that absorbed water. Lovell Swisher and Roy Wilcox meet at the Biltmore Hotel in Los Angeles to discuss starting a horticultural club for men.
1949	The Southern California Floral Association publishes the first issue of *The Bloomin' News* in October 1949. The International Flower Show is held by the Southern California Horticultural Institute. "Rudolph, the Red-Nosed Reindeer" makes his first appearance.
1950	Ayres-California Co. installs the largest deep freeze unit made by Frigidaire for the storage of wrapped ice ready for the packing cases of flowers shipping from California to other states. *Southern Florist & Nurseryman*, February 10, 1950 The Southern California Floral Association produces a 15-minute, educational movie titled, "The Gladiolus Story."
1951	Southern California Flower Growers Association, after reorganizing and transitioning from its non-profit status, becomes a profit corporation in order to expand into allied businesses.
1952	California Supreme Court finds California Alien Land Law unconstitutional.
1953	V.L. Smithers Laboratories introduces its moldable OASIS floral foam.
1955	George A. Berlin is first to sell to a major supermarket chain (Alpha Beta) Ken Short introduces the National Florist Directory Buyers Guide, nicknamed the "Red Book" Disneyland opens in Anaheim
1956	All alien land laws repealed by popular vote. The three San Francisco flower markets celebrate their new terminal at Sixth and Brannan streets with an Open House. Hundreds of flood refugees from Japan are allowed into the U.S. through the Japanese "nanmin" program, introducing more Japanese Americans to the flower industry in America. By 1956, San Lorenzo Nursery has more than one million square feet of greenhouse space in California.
1957	National Flower Week, October 20-27, is a huge hit as television and radio hosts and newspaper reporters plug the beauty of flowers. A formal ceremony is held at Los Angeles City Hall. The Soviet Union launches Sputnik 1 on October 4, the first in its Sputnik satellite series.
1958	It is estimated that more than half the flowers making their way through the Los Angeles Flower Market are shipped to out-of-state customers. (*Southern California Gardens*) The Dodgers play their first season since moving to Los Angeles from Brooklyn.
1959	On January 25, the Buford W. Hall Company becomes the first jetfreight shipper with American Airlines, shipping cut flowers on a 707 Jet Flagship to New York.

JDP Photography

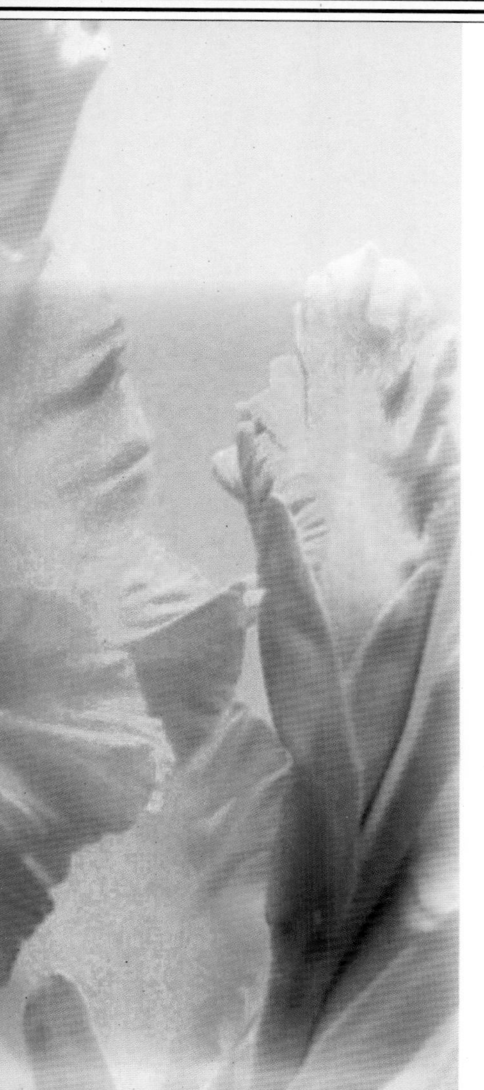

The Golden Years (1940-1959)

"Nor does that complete the saga of horticulture in the southland during the past fifty years. For here the ranunculus was made larger and more attractive; the freesias took on the colors of the rainbow; the gerberas became double; violets took on a new fragrance; the amaryllis was streamlined and the poinsettia became big business."

— John Graham, "Fifty Years of Horticulture," *Los Angeles Times* (1947) [1]

The Japanese attack on Pearl Harbor on December 7, 1941 propelled the United States into the war that started in Europe two years earlier. With the federal government spending billions of dollars in California, including requisitioning land in Rancho Santa Margarita which would come to be called Camp Pendleton, the state became an arsenal and a port of departure for thousands of military personnel. In the post-war years, more than one-and-a-half million Americans would move to California.

While the Second World War revolutionized California's economy, patriotism soared. Right after the Pearl Harbor attack, to help supply food, Bodger Seed Company in Lompoc converted its flower crops to vegetables, and continued in the produce mode for the rest of the war.

Flower growers around the country took steps to help the war effort. Many turned the spade in soil converted from flowers to vegetables, performing a patriotic service in the production of the Victory Garden, to reduce the pressure for food supplies to America and the troops.

The Japanese Americans, who by 1940 were farming (statewide) about 3.8 million square feet under glass, 2.4 million square feet under cloth and several hundred acres outside, had annual gross sales of nearly $4 million [2]. They faced a daunting challenge, as many of them were investigated by the Federal Bureau of Investigation, arrested, evacuated from coastal areas and forced to leave their businesses. The Southern California Flower Market was closed for several days as the FBI reviewed its books. Bank accounts of Japanese American growers were frozen, it became hard for them to get credit and many were forced to quit their businesses.

Japanese Americans who did not have connections or could not pursue employment in a "free zone" (several inland California towns and specified areas in mountain states, Chicago and the East Coast) were moved to War Relocation Authority camps. A February 26, 1942 *Florists' Review* article reported that eleven Los Angeles flower growers were included in the first evacuation district, with 26 more expected to move.

In San Francisco, leaders of the California Flower Market had the foresight in 1940, before the attack, to transfer ownership of their stock to citizen members and to elect U.S.-citizen board members of the America-born Nisei generation. The American-based ownership was helpful when government authorities later investigated their books but confiscated nothing. [3]

In Los Angeles, the Japanese Americans found their Southern California Flower Market closed briefly and then subleased to United Wholesale Florist, then under the leadership of Jacob Dekker, Art Dettweiler, Ebbo Dekema and Leroy Youts. [4]

Although the Japanese Americans took a great deal of verbal abuse, there were many Americans, especially European immigrants, who were sympathetic. Some tenants and wholesalers from the American Florists' Exchange came to the aid of the Japanese growers in the market across the street by offering to watch over their operations or help transfer ownership into other hands until they returned home.

Mori Nursery was able to retain its name, the only one to do so, during the war because their employee, a young French American named Fred Sarrazin, watched over the business while its owners were displaced.

Jacob Dekker, of the shipping firm United Wholesale Florist, leased the Flower Market properties of several Japanese Americans, as well as ranches and greenhouses, during their absence. One family, the Satows, found their checkbook returned to them by Dekker after their internment, complete with profits realized during their absence. Dekker became "Uncle Jake" to the Satow family. [5]

Paul Ecke Sr, a German immigrant who experienced his own share of prejudice in the United States, was asked by the government to help the war effort by raising fruits and vegetables on federal land. Ecke stored the machinery and belongings of several friends and customers of Japanese ancestry in his barns in Encinitas. For this act of kindness, rumors circulated that he was pro-Nazi. After his children were exposed to the malicious reports at school, Ecke called the FBI and requested an investigation of himself to prove his innocence.

Fred C. King of King Wholesale Florist tended a farm for a Japanese family. He paid the taxes on the land of several Japanese families during their absence.

Left: The patriotic floral flag first planted by Bodger Seed Company at Lompoc in 1942 has been re-introduced during recent times of military conflict and the 9/11/01 attack. The flag covered twelve acres and was composed of red, white and blue larkspur with the flagstaff of yellow calendula. It measured 456 by 260 feet. *Credit: Louise Bodger Whitman, House of Bodger, Bodger Seeds Ltd. (1981).*

Above: Patriot flag created by strategically planted flowers in the Ecke owned Flower Fields in Carlsbad. *Ecke Ranch collection.*

Sad to say, some of the commission men in the Southern California floral industry tried to build a propaganda fund that would enable them to take control of some Japanese American farms and to boycott the re-starting of those farms by their rightful owners. Those with conscience, including Paul Ecke Sr., refused to contribute to or participate in these efforts. [6]

Experiencing great losses were the Japanese American flower growers who were leasing their farmland and those who had to walk away from seeds and crops in the process of being hybridized. With new plantings just made, Spring was the worst time for the relocation. Growers' financial resources were in the crops and they could not hire people to take over. To complicate matters, when the official notice to move came in March 1942, the Japanese had to leave their homes within two days. [7]

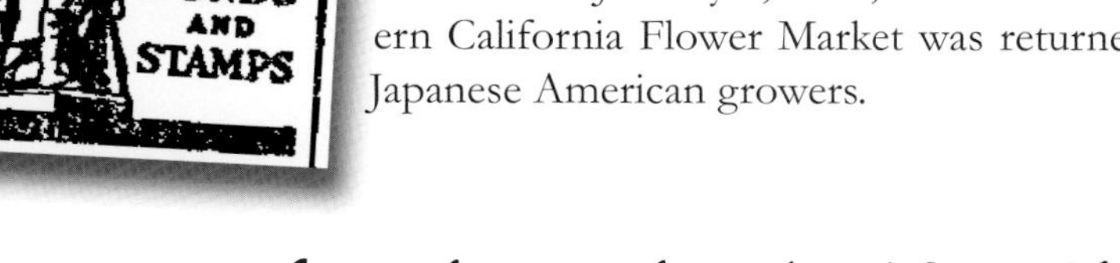

The wife and children of Morizo Yokomizo, "king of the ranunculus," carried flower seed packets in their suitcases enroute to the camp in Manzanar, California. The family doled out plants and seeds wherever they would best be appreciated and used. Manchester Boddy, a horticulturist and publisher of the *Los Angeles Daily News*, whose private estate eventually became Descanso Gardens in La Canada Flintridge, California, was the recipient of some of the Yokomizo camellia seedlings. (Boddy also purchased the Mission Nursery from Waichi and Mitoko Yoshimura.) Two lawyers with a passion for civil rights, F.D.R. Moote and Marion Wright, along with real estate manager Frank Kadletz, assured the Japanese that the Southern California Flower Market would be well taken care of in their absence.

A Mexican American family took care of Taka Goto's farm during the war. When the war ended, like many others, they turned it over to its Japanese American owners in excellent condition.

Bob Berry, who became a popular florist and designer with a Wall Street shop, enjoyed the friendship of many Japanese growers and decided he'd like to visit two of his friends in their camp. He made a special trip to see Tokuji "Tok" and Ichiro "Ich" (Jim) Yoshihashi in their camp in Santa Anita and later when they were moved to the Gila River War Relocation Center in Arizona.

> "So many people were so down on the Japanese and I had nothing but good things to say about them because I grew up with them and I knew them and I knew how faithful they were. The two boys that I went to see ... fought in the invasion of Italy, they joined the 442nd Infantry, which was an all-Japanese group, and they had 60 percent Purple Hearts." [8]

Homecoming in 1945 was bittersweet as many of the Japanese Americans, who were not fortunate enough to have their farms and businesses cared for in their absence, returned from the camps to find their properties neglected, rundown and in disarray. Racial discrimination was prevalent and even the children of the Japanese Americans were taunted. Although some decided to return to their homes in Japan, others remained in California, determined to rebuild. On January 1, 1946, control of the Southern California Flower Market was returned to the Japanese American growers.

Sacrificing for the War Effort

The war took its toll on families, as many saw their loved ones off to become soldiers and sailors on faraway shores. During and after the war, families and business owners found it difficult to get parts for machinery and automobiles and to buy trucks for their businesses. C.J. Groen, the rose grower, bought a 1947 Chevrolet stake pick-up truck with Army jeep parts in it. One of the first to come off the assembly line after the war, it saw more than its share of roundtrips from Montebello and Santa Barbara to the Los Angeles Flower Market. Replacing the engine in a truck made with Army parts wasn't easy.

Another handicap necessitated by wartime restrictions was rationing to help alleviate shortages caused by war needs. An A card entitled its holder to a mere three or four gallons of gasoline each week. B cards, issued to people working in military industries, got up to eight gallons weekly.

Gasoline rationing made it difficult for flower growers to make deliveries and for retail florists to get to the downtown wholesale markets. Enter the "route man," the delivery service person whose customer relationships spurred the growth of the industry over the next 20 years. These drivers introduced a delivery system that would make business run more smoothly for everyone, from grower to florist.

Old tires were donated to collection centers by Americans who then purchased tires made of recycled rubber. Drivers were asked to reduce usage of fuel and tires by driving no more than 35 miles per hour and not driving at night.

Giovanni Ghigo was stopped by police while driving his flowers to Market one night. He drove without lights during a blackout to honor wartime practices. Because he occasionally turned on the headlights to get his bearings, a police officer arrested him on suspicion of flashing signals to the enemy. Indeed, the threat of enemy attack was real. California had been fired upon, on February 23, 1942, when a Japanese submarine fired 25 shells across Pacific Coast Highway near Santa Barbara.

Diane and Johnny Mellano, whose parents immigrated to the United States from Italy, recall their families making arrangements to entertain Italian prisoners of war living in the detention center in Wilmington, California. On the drive to Wilmington, adults and children sat on hay bales in the open truck bed and sang while an uncle played the accordion. They delivered as many as 20 POWs and a guard to their home for the night and partied into the wee hours of the morning.

Hearing a knock at her front door one evening during the early years of the War, Maria Mellano opened her door to see FBI agents standing on her porch. She was home alone with her three children and frightened. The purpose of the agents' visit was simply to enforce the curfew, which Giovanni Mellano had broken by leaving home to visit friends after dark. The experience of having federal agents approach her home was nonetheless unnerving.

In 1943, between his junior and senior high school years, a seventeen-year-old Herb Tausch worked at the American Florists' Exchange loading and unloading trucks. Riding the Red Line street car from Sunset Boulevard to Wall Street, Herb started work at four o'clock in the morning. He was one of many young men who worked as laborers at the Market and would soon go off to war.

Greek farmers took over operation of many of the Japanese farms, especially those in the South Bay area. The custom of the day was for the men, regardless of ethnicity, to manage the business and their wives and daughters to work in the fields and packing sheds. As more labor was needed, other women were hired. Tike Karavas, who worked as a youngster in the Redondo Beach fields with his brother and his mother in the 1950s, recalls that Greek women worked in the fields with the local Mexican women, teaching them how to disbud, pick and package the flowers. Everyone pitched in to earn a few dollars, ethnic pride and labor side by side.

Victory!

Finally, in 1945, the Second World War ended. Over the next few years, soldiers were welcomed home in festive parades and celebrations, banks made money available for loans, veterans were able to buy homes at low interest under the Servicemen's Readjustment Act (the "G.I." bill) and consumers found they had money to buy flowers again. Southern Californians and the rest of the nation began to return to normal.

A Vibrant Floral Industry

The war years, as stressful as they were and in spite of reductions in farming acres [9], held promise for florists. Will E. Joy, president of Florists' Telegraph Delivery, made a bold projection at FTD's meeting in Los Angeles in September 1941. Joy said the wartime economic situation would result in more money spent for luxuries such as flowers because of the shortage of other merchandise.

Left: Italian soldiers enjoy dinner and party with the Mellano family and friends in Artesia, California in the early 1940s.

Above: C.J. Groen's original 1947 Chevrolet truck, made with surplus Army parts, in 2007. The truck is lovingly maintained in Whittier by Brent Anderson, C.J.'s great grandson.

Joy probably got it right, evidenced by San Diego County's fast-increasing acres of plantings of lilacs, tulips, stocks, asters, poinsettias and gladioli near the coast. In 1944, the first shipment of flowers to go by air lifted off from San Diego's airport bound for the East Coast.

The 1940s were full of energy, commerce and camaraderie at both the European-American and the Japanese-American flower markets. The Los Angeles Flower Market was a hub of activity, especially on Mondays, Wednesdays and Fridays ("Market Days") and just before holidays. Stars and celebrities loved to stop by for their photo opportunities among the colorful blooms. Growers trucking the day's harvest to Los Angeles often brought one or more of their children along. The youngsters enjoyed playing among the flower boxes and eating pancakes at the Rose Café, where wholesalers and growers passed the early morning hours before the route men showed up, and everyone met to socialize.

Where the Flowers Grew

Small flower farms from little plots to multiple acres now decorated the landscape from San Diego to Santa Barbara, many of them newly owned by immigrants and the first generation of their children. The bulk of the floral real estate of this great region was situated in the southern part of Los Angeles County, in the Torrance and South Bay area, but Montebello and its surrounding towns were large growing areas as well. Many landowners envisioned future profits from the sales of their properties. With urbanization encroaching on agricultural land, the value of real estate could not be overlooked. Meanwhile, flowers grew throughout the Southland:

- In the Blue Hills area of La Mirada and East Whittier, Frank Nakamura and his family, along with other families, grew Marguerite daisies, Marconi daisies, and their main crop, chrysanthemums. Frank and his wife Asaye quit flower growing in 1950 and opened Blue Hills Nursery on East Whittier Boulevard in Whittier, today a popular gardening center.

- Hermosa Beach, Redondo Beach and the Torrance area were home to hundreds of acres of asters, carnations and other flowers, grown mostly by Greek farmers (Dan Stamis, Brown Stamis, Peter Priamos, John Karavas, Gus Dimas, Jerry Defterios, the Stephanatos family, tulip grower Paul Lambert and many others). (Southern California seedsmen and breeders developed a wilt-resistant variety of the aster that extended its life, making it a more valuable and marketable product.) [10]

- The Amling family was famous for the roses grown in their Santa Ana and Westminster greenhouses.

Below: Early float builders the Miller brothers are shown on far left and third from left, with Frank Vescio, second from left and Fred Fredenberg of Burbank Florist.

Right: An early gathering of American Florists' Exchange members.

Bottom Right: Joe Shinoda, left, of San Lorenzo Nursery, with Frank Vescio, manager of the Los Angeles Flower Market.

Vescio collection.

Fifteen-year-old Nick Gandolfo working in the family's pom pom dahlia field.

Above: Angelo Capurro, brother-in-law to Nicholas Gandolfo Sr., operates the gasoline-fired hand cultivator used on the Gandolfo ranch, October 31, 1940.
Below: Ernst C. Amling in the Amling greenhouse in Santa Ana, California.

- Montebello, El Monte and the San Gabriel Valley were the growing fields for a wide variety of flowers, by dozens of growers, Montebello being known as the "City of Flowers." Gebhard Prechtl's Scotch heather field in Montebello was a bit of a deviation from the baby white callas, camellias, Easter lilies, chrysanthemums, stocks and other flowers there. Prechtl also grew broom flower and paperwhites in El Monte and melanthra heather and baby pink callas in Pasadena. Other Montebello area flower farmers included C.J. Groen, Roy F. Wilcox, John Polder and the Vander Bruggen family.

- Harold Pearson, former gardener for the queen of Sweden, tended a small gladiola ranch in Lomita, in the South Bay.

Paul Ecke Sr in the Ecke poinsettia fields, 1940s.

- In La Verne, Cecil Houdyshel, a pioneer in the commercial flower field, was growing bulbs, flowers and rare plants nationwide. His hybrid gladiolus, "Los Angeles," was a favorite among florists.

- The Guiseppe Franciosi, Guiseppe Gorini and Nick Gandolfo families all farmed tulips, daffodils and dahlias in Artesia, as did the Mellano and Ghigo families.

- Chris Colombo Brevidoro came to be known as the "lilac king" for bringing the fragrant cut lilac to Southern California. He founded the Colombo Lilac Ranch in Acton.

- In 1947, Bob Weidner bought Henson's Greenhouse in Buena Park. He would grow the nursery to great success before moving to Brea, and later to escape smog and traffic, to Encinitas.

- By 1956, San Lorenzo Nursery reportedly operated more than one million square feet of greenhouse space from Alameda County to the South Bay area.

- In Santa Barbara, C.J. Groen, owner of Groen Rose Company, teamed with Jacob Dekker, principal owner of United Wholesale Florist,

Top right: The home of Frank and Asaye Nakamura in the Blue Hills of La Mirada.
Center: Giovanni Ghigo picks daffodils, early 1940s.
Right: Carlo Lugaro, shown here, drove this 1947 tractor over surface streets when the family moved its farm from Montebello to Anaheim in 1953.

Top to Bottom: Joe Franciosi (Junior) potting tulips, 1955.

The Brevidoro men of Brevidoro Lilac Ranch: Steven (John's son), John, Chris, Robert.

Workers in Bob Stimming's stock fields in the 1950s.

A light moment on a Greek flower farm in Palos Verdes in 1949. Showing their gorgeous legs, from left are Natalie Hernandez, Dora Moreno, Henrietta Torres, Jenny Torres and Rose Camerino. *Alex Areyan Collection.*

to buy property for Groen's greenhouses and Dekker's field flowers.

- Growers in Marina Del Rey offered flowers fresh from the fields to florists and designers like Fred Gibbons and John Biestel. Their celebrity parties and blue book socials were elaborate affairs and the designers built their reputation for elegant celebrity parties on their gorgeous blooms and decorations.

- In San Diego County, Paul Ecke built a successful poinsettia cultivation ranch. G.A. Berlin contracted with the Edwin Frazee farm and other growers in Carlsbad, Oceanside and Encinitas to supply product for his commission business.

Sending Flowers to America

In his *Los Angeles Times* article, "Fifty Years of Horticulture," (*Los Angeles Times*, December 7, 1947) John Graham explained that Southern California's history could be written in terms of its horticulture. Graham described Southern California as a "trial garden" for flower lovers throughout the world, with its hundreds of miracle miles producing plants now flowering in all the 48 states and around the world. The exotic plants brought here by the early nurserymen and horticulturists had been hybridized and exciting new colors and sizes produced.

The Southern California cut flower industry grossed some $12 million annually from its approximately 4,000 acres of flower fields. As cultivation and irrigation methods improved, growing flowers became a full-time occupation, replacing the seasonal, part-time business.

By the late 1940s, air freight was carrying 30 percent of California's spectacular blooms to the far reaches of America. Even the somewhat remote Santa Maria area, north of Santa Barbara, had established air freight connections. Growers in Santa Maria as well as Los Angeles and San Diego shipped entire planeloads of fresh cut flowers weekly to Chicago, New York and Dallas.

Wholesalers and growers in other U.S. flower-growing states did not hesitate to pick up the phone to call their California connections to order flowers that were out-of-season in their areas.

- The Oklahoma Flower Market, started by William Hurley and his father Bert in Oklahoma City, ordered on a consignment basis until 1975 when its company ownership changed.

  "We placed all our orders by telephone and snail mail," says third generation owner Mike Hurley. "Most of our product was out of California and was flown to our various locations, up until the air traffic controllers' strike of 1981."

Kermit ("Knute") Hernlund's wife Eunice and children Eddie and Neola pose by the family's flower delivery truck, 1930.

Left: Groen Rose Company's farm crew in 1945 included Ross Nielsen (standing, fourth from left), Charles L. (Roy) Halsey (standing, rear seventh from left). C.J. Groen is seen standing in the rear, fifth from left.

Right: Tike Karavas and little brother Dan in 1945 in the family's flower field at 190th Street and Hawthorne Boulevard in Redondo Beach.

Below: Michael Mellano Sr, the smallest child, with Johnny Mellano, his older brother, and their father, Giovanni (John) pose with farm workers in their daffodil field at Artesia Boulevard and Marquardt in Artesia, 1940s.

Right: Gus Dimas stands in his Hermosa Beach flower field near Pacific Coast Highway and Artesia Boulevard. Note the other flower fields in the distance, early 1960s. *Karavas collection.*

Below: Victor Yack tends the flower stand which would become Victor's Flowers in Pomona, California, 1953.

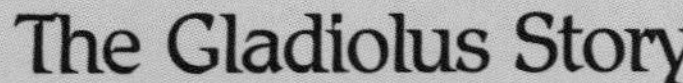

The Gladiolus Story

This 1950s professional documentary film produced by the Southern California Floral Association provided a behind-the-scenes look at how gladiolas are grown, packaged, shipped, designed and enjoyed. It includes a look at the planting of gladiola bulbs, harvesting and cutting and packaging, loading onto a jet plane, floral design, customer delivery and the use of gladiola arrangements in weddings, special events and at home. Complete with a demonstration about how to cut glads back as the top blooms wilt, the film offers design tips as well.

The film's planning committee included Edwin Frazee, Wall Godfrey, Arville G. Williams, Edmond G. Thornton and general manager Walter Swartz.

Participating in the movie sets and locations were Riverside Drive Florist, Vogue Flowers, Burbank Florist, the Lido Room in the Ambassador Hotel, Crossley's Flowers, Matchless Electric Home, Harold J. Francis Florist, the packing sheds of Vinson & Fortner in Vista, California, and the packing sheds of Pamplin's in Palos Verdes, California, Edmunds Wholesale Flowers and Wright's Flower Shop.

Participating floral wholesalers of the American Florists' Exchange included George A. Berlin, Briggs & Godfrey, Buford W. Hall Co., Inc., John A. Noonan, Harold Pearson and J. Ross Taylor.

Scenes featured in conjunction with the film's wedding event were filmed at Saks-Fifth Avenue in Beverly Hills, Cedric's, Broadway Florist and St. Mary's Church of Angels.

The film's production crew included executive producer Walter Swartz, John Parkinson, who wrote and researched the story, Dick Cutting, narrator, and Bernice Fay, music.

Thank you to Louis Alhanati of Parisian Florist, Hollywood, who provided the only known copy of this film.

This Annual Dinner of the American Florists' Exchange was held at the Royal Palais Hotel in Los Angeles on March 5, 1945. Mario Pozzo is seen at the left end of the lower seated row, next to an unidentified man, then Tom Trione, two unidentified individuals and Phil Herras

This christening party in honor of baby Dan Karavas took place on October 16, 1942, in the backyard of the Karavas family in what is now Watts, California. At this gathering, John and Bertha Karavas were persuaded by flower farming guests to try flower farming. Pictured are members of the Stamis and Stamatelatos, Karavas, Dimas, Kozakis, Ambatelos and other families. *Karavas collection*.

- Texas represented a large body of customers for the Los Angeles Flower Market. Wholesale shippers and some retailers journeyed annually from Los Angeles to the Texas state floral convention.

- Harrison "Red" Kennicott, today chief executive officer of Kennicott Brothers Co., Inc. in Chicago, remembers visiting the Market in Los Angeles in the 1950s and 1960s. He did business with Armacost & Royston's Bob Norton for cymbidium orchids, Dominick Tassano for stocks, Lou Lujan of Santa Barbara Flower Growers for novelty flowers including ranunculus and anemones (which were very hard to get in those days).

  Kennicott remembers his first exposure to route trucks was with the San Lorenzo Nursery, "the most dominant business on the Market" at the time, where he dealt with John Fukishima and Paul Shinoda Sr. He notes his association also with Encinitas growers, which "is probably another history project."

- In Wichita, Kansas, Jerry Yocum of Valley Floral Company recalls, "We started in 1941, primarily growing glads and gyp and storing in a small cave of sorts under one of the sheds in order to keep the flowers cool. As the business grew, so did the need to source California and Colorado."

- Valley Floral was joined by countless others including Southview in Chelsea, Michigan, Nordlie, Inc. in Detroit, Michigan, orders routed through organizations such as the American Bulb Company and others all the way to the East Coast. Supplementing locally-grown seasonal flowers, California blooms were filling vases in the offices, homes, funeral parlors, retirement celebrations, proms, award banquets and weddings of people all across America.

The Benefits of Association

In 1948, the California State Florists' Association formed (CSFA later changed the word Florists to Floral). Created to organize and unite all segments of the California floral industry at the state level, CSFA set the stage for the important part it would play in years to come. Addressing member concerns through government representation and encouraging professionalism in floral design through education, state competitions and certification programs, it has furthered floriculture consistently through the years. The Southern California Floral Association monthly newsletter *The Bloomin' News* always included CSFA news and events, along with that of other floral groups.

Other organizations evolved as well to bring like-minded florists, nurserymen, sales professionals and others together in their fields of interest. Special interest groups and councils also organized.

By 1948, a group of growers was meeting in North San Diego County regularly at the Vista Community Center, motivated by a desire to fight what grower Eugene E. Stuck called "a ruinous rate of taxation." They won a 66 percent reduction in the bulb tax and came to be known as the San Diego County Flower Growers' Association. (Today's San Diego County Flower & Plant Association.)

During the Korean War, the Society of American Florists formed a National Advisory Council to serve for the "duration of the war emergency." Presidents and representatives of the major national floral industry associations were invited to serve on the council to represent the floral industry to government agencies and be "on call" to respond when group action was necessary.

In Los Angeles in 1948, Charles S. Jones, chairman and president of the Richfield Oil Corporation and a "mover and a shaker" among the prominent men of the city, looked around and became concerned. Comparing the city with the gracious Old World cities of Europe and South America, he saw Los Angeles becoming slum-like. With its fast-growing population, mish-mash of architectural styles and little thought given to aesthetics, he noticed an "absence of beauty."

"Well, Charlie, if you were any good, you'd do something about it!," exclaimed his friend, prominent nurseryman Roy F. Wilcox. [11]

Do something he did. In the summer of 1948, Charlie Jones met with a handful of local floral and nursery leaders at the Biltmore Hotel. At the meeting were wholesale nurseryman Roy Wilcox, Manfred Meyberg, the head of Germain's Seed Company; Lovell Swisher, an insurance salesman;

Top: Casually posed in front of the American Florists' Exchange in July 1959 are, from left, C.P. Von Herzen, attorney, George Catlin, attorney, Paul Ecke Sr., Frank Blankenship and Kenny Foltz, son-in-law of rose grower C.J. Groen.

Center: Florists await the opening bell at the Los Angeles Flower Market, 1950s. Harvey Prechtl is shown at far left (facing page) with Ebbo Dekema to his left, both of United Wholesale.

Left: Retail florists await the 6:30 a.m. opening bell at the Los Angeles Flower Market, 1950s.

Los Angeles Flower Market collection.

Roy F. Wilcox & Co.
Beverly Blvd. & Wilcox Ave.
Montebello, Calif.
RAymond 3-3351
PArkview 1-2324
and
Get Coupons Here
81

John Armstrong of Armstrong Nurseries, Jack Bodger of Bodger Seed Company, William Hertrich, the Huntington Library and Gardens horticulturist; and Manchester Boddy, of Descanso Gardens fame. Although this was an enthusiastic group of about 40 men, nothing definitive resulted.

Jones was not dismayed. He and Swisher, Meyberg and Wilcox continued to talk about forming an organization until finally, at a meeting on June 15, 1950, at the California Club, the Men's Garden Club was formed. The organizing committee included Charlie Jones, Alfred Wright, Roy F. Wilcox, Manfred Meyberg, I.O. Levy, Ray Thomas, Samuel Ayres, Lyman McFie and Tom Ellsworth.

In the first half of the twentieth century, most business owners in floriculture and the nursery industry were men. The founders of the Men's Garden Club were unique and they represented many others who fostered an interest in the beauty of their surroundings. Many of them enjoyed hobby gardening and some displayed elaborate gardens around their homes. The Men's Garden Club's mission was to create value and encourage gardening among its members and their communities, which it continues to promote to this day.

Social Networking and Floral Occasions

In the 1940s and 1950s, those who sold through the Los Angeles Flower Market enjoyed a lively social life that was just about as colorful as their flowers. In the days before the public was permitted entry to the Market, those who worked and shopped there were a close community of friends and colleagues whose families socialized together and who enjoyed common activities.

Families of Market employees and members of the SCFA held backyard cookouts and took vacation trips together. Sports enjoyed by the men included hunting, fishing, bowling, golfing and gambling. Teenagers worked summer and after-school jobs in local flower shops and at the Market, learning the business and earning their own money for school and personal expenses.

Vern Vescio, son of American Florists' Exchange manager Frank Vescio, during the early 1950s, working for the Roy F. Wilcox cut flower business. *Vescio collection.*

Gambling was widely practiced at both the Southern California and American markets in the 1950s. During those dead hours between arrival and unloading of field greens and flowers and when the route men arrived to pick up their orders, many men stole away to the offices and back rooms of the Market to engage in a lively game of cards. A common practice in many industrial facilities and warehouses nationwide at the time, gambling had the unfortunate effect in Southern California of prepping younger men (and feeding the habit of older men) for local race tracks and the casinos popping up in outlying towns and in Las Vegas. Sometimes one man's winnings meant another man's loss of capital, a car or the dwindling away of his business.

Within the Southern California Floral Association to which the tenants, retailers and merchants belonged, a full agenda of social events contributed to friendships among members. Every Wednesday night, bowling league teams competed at the Sunset Bowl, near Sunset and Western Avenue. In the spring, a large family picnic was held at Elysian Park, near today's Dodger Stadium. There were regular golf tournaments, casual golf and baseball outings and planned and informal trips to Las Vegas.

Top: From left, Herman Seidler, Paul Ecke Sr., Gebhard Prechtl, Con Von Herzen and Carl Hankemeier, at the 1944 American Florists' Exchange shareholders meeting.
Center: From left, Jack Hauquitz, Eddie Battistessa of Edmunds Wholesale and Bert Johnson of E.H. Pearson Wholesale, all gladiola wholesalers.
Bottom: "Members" of an unofficial social club enjoy refreshments in the Rose Café. They are, from left: Gebhard Prechtl, Bob Ray, C.P. Von Herzen, Paul Ecke Sr., Bill Harris, and, in the back, Ed Hall, owner of the Rose Café until its purchase by Barny Barnhart.
Los Angeles Flower Market collection.

The Southern California Floral Association's annual Open House was a big affair in which all the tenants, vendors and suppliers of both markets participated. Wire services and suppliers exhibited, floral designers demonstrated and tenants displayed their freshest products and offered home-cooked food. Wall Street was closed to vehicular traffic that day, giving the area a private but festive ambience. Hundreds of retail florists, families of those working in the Markets and the public attended.

On a broader scale, the Las Floristas charity "Headdress Ball" attracted floral design contestants from the greater Los Angeles design community, who reveled in the opportunity to show off their talents and win awards in the prestigious, glamorous showcase.

At Hollywood Park, where celebrities and horse racing enthusiasts gathered daily during season, an annual Flower Show was the talk of the town. Floral designers Silverio Casabar, Phil Rulloda, Bob Berry and others, usually working in teams, designed large, extravagant floral pieces for the exclusive clubhouse clientele.

Although the occasion was one of sadness, the death of the widely known evangelist and media sensation Aimee Semple McPherson in September 1944 effectively emptied the Los Angeles and Southern California markets of their flowers. McPherson's passing drew sentiment from around the world, as her followers and members of the church she founded expressed their grief. Florists and wholesalers throughout the Los Angeles area were hard-pressed to fill all the sympathy orders from product of local suppliers during those few days of worldwide media coverage. Floral arrangements surrounded the Angeles Temple, where McPherson had conducted church services.

"The only epic event that I ever remember was when Aimee Semple MacPherson died," remembers Bert Johnson, American Florists' Exchange board member. "They cleaned out the Market. There was not one stem of flowers left in the market that day. My uncle said they were picking up leaves off of the floor ... There were no flowers left. I think that's the only time in the history of the Market where it was completely sold out."

In 1949, the Southern California Horticultural Institute created the International Flower Show, destined to become one of the largest floral exhibitions in the United States. The show was held each spring at Hollywood Park in the Inglewood suburb and became a showplace for ornamental horticulture. In 1957, well known entertainer Art Linkletter crowned Mary Acosta the Queen of the Show.

In October 1957, Los Angeles went all out to celebrate "National Flower Week." The Society of American Florists published a "Flower Facts and Fancies" booklet for the weeklong event, which was kicked off in the rotunda of City Hall on October 21. In attendance were the mayor, Norris Poulson, and Miss Alice Lon, the "champagne lady" of television's Lawrence Welk Show.

Working the E.H. Pearson Wholesale gladiola counter at the Flower Market around 1950 are Bert Johnson, left, and his uncle, Harold Pearson, right. ***From "The Gladiolus Story" documentary/promotional film.***

Other local events that involved many members of the floral industry in Southern California included the Academy Awards' annual Oscars presentation and the Tournament of Roses on New Year's Day. Such events, which continue today, came with a built-in need for florists and designers to decorate a multitude of private parties and receptions.

The Bloomin' News

In October 1949, following years of publishing weekly sales and information sheets for Market tenants, the Southern California Floral Association introduced a professionally designed newsletter called *The Bloomin' News.* The publication featured a flowery logo at the top of the first page and was printed in green and black on white smooth stock. It had the good fortune over the next 40 years of growing from its inaugural four pages to as many as 32 pages at times as its circulation grew, advertisers recognized its value and organizations and departments made use of its pages for disseminating their information.

In a 1948 Fiesta Days celebration that surely included flowers, couples dance on Pacific Avenue in Redondo Beach. Delfina Gonzales Reynaga, center right, and a military friend enjoy the occasion to honor the city's early Spanish and Mexican heritage. ***Reprint permission granted by Alice Buffington.***

It was a newsy, often gossipy, piece that both entertained and informed its readers through human interest stories, reports of the social activities of its readers, cartoons, jokes, photographs and floral industry and market-specific statistics.

Dozens of reporters contributed monthly columns for *The Bloomin' News*, informing readers of floral-related activities occurring in Orange County, the San Fernando and San Gabriel valleys, San Diego County and Riverside. There were updates from the wire services (FTD and Teleflora) and floral associations. When the annual Las Floristas Headdress Ball or any large gathering that displayed locally-grown flowers occurred, spectacular photos were published in *The Bloomin' News*. Contributing writers (including Rocky Pollitz and Gerry Prince Young) laid a foundation for future success with this industry publication. Others, like Bert Johnson in his "Brass Band" column and Charley Hum in his "Hum-ing Along," just entertained and kept readers reading.

One of the most successful newsletters ever published for any organization, *The Bloomin' News* ceased around 1990 when the Southern California Floral Association merged with the California State Florists Association. The American Florists' Exchange then introduced its Los Angeles Flower Market News, which assumed *The Bloomin' News* name once again around 1996.

Long-time grower and commission man Elmer Fisher said in 2007 that "I sure do like to have my finger in (the floral industry) and know what's going on." *The Bloomin' News* continues to be the medium that helps its readers do just that. (See *The Bloomin' News* sidebar, Chapter 6).

The "Please Omit" and "In Lieu Of" Challenges

In the early 1900s, newspaper funeral notices began to include the phrases "Please omit flowers," "In lieu of flowers" or "instead of flowers," followed by a suggestion to make a donation to a charity of choice or the charity formally listed in the notice. The practice represented a sincere effort to remove the burden of personal expense or to redirect funds to worthwhile causes, but it impacted the floral industry negatively and severely.

In the 1940s and 1950s, floral industry associations began a dialogue with the charitable organizations to discourage such memorial contributions. In 1951, as use of these phrases grew, the Society of American Florists and Florists' Telegraph Delivery Association raised $75,000 to support an awareness campaign for florists and funeral directors.

The Southern California Floral Association conducted a survey of death notices published in the *Los Angeles Times* and the *Los Angeles Examiner*, to determine if usage was increasing. Survey results for the months of July and August in 1950 determined the notices had increased by 2/100 percent.

The September 1950 *Bloomin' News* asked readers to go before their own clubs and organizations to state the principles on which the flower business functions. "It has been our experience that where our side of the story has been told that everyone is most willing to cooperate and to assist us rather than work against our better interests."

Usage of the "Please omit" and "In lieu of" phrases, which continue to this day, are viewed as a direct contributor to the decline of retail flower sales. The ease of writing a check, however, does not communicate emotion in the same manner as the presentation of flowers.

The Gladiolus Story

In the 1950s, the Southern California Floral Association produced a professional film (equivalent of today's documentary "video") about the growing, packaging, selling, designing and enjoying of the colorful line flower, the gladiola. Five active members made up the planning committee: Edwin Frazee, Wall Godfrey, Arville G. Williams, Edmond G. Thornton and general manager Walter Swartz. Months in the making, the story featured background music and narration and was produced under the leadership of Walter Swartz, SCFA manager.

The flower fields, retail shops, design rooms, packing sheds, department stores, churches and hotel lobbies featured in the film lent spectacular color, demonstrations and a sense of being with gladiolus in their natural surroundings. Although the gladiola fields have given way since then to condos and ballparks, this film still speaks to the heart of the flower industry and the Southern California people – throughout the chain from seed to sale – who built it.

AA

FIRST JETFREIGHT SHIPPER

In recognition of the part played in air transport progress by

Bufford W. Hall Co.

who, on January 29, 1959 *, shipped* cut flowers *aboard American Airlines 707 Jet Flagship on the first jet flight from* Los Angeles, California *to* New York City, New York.

March 9, 1959

Top: Buena Park Greenhouses' employees after loading their first truckload of begonias destined for a customer in Ohio, 1950s. *Weidners Gardens collection.*

Left: The certificate presented to B.W. Hall Company in recognition of the first jet flight from Los Angeles to fly cut flowers coast-to-coast. The 1959 flight of the Boeing 707 delivered flowers to buyers in New York City. Actress Maureen O'Hara attended the ribbon-cutting and presented roses to the jet's pilot. *Warren Hall collection.*

An Experiment with Surprising Results

In July 1951, the rose growers of Southern California agreed to a program that would let them pool their surplus roses and distribute them to florists for public relations purposes. To spur awareness and boost sales, the program allowed the florists to distribute the roses at no cost to banks, restaurants, radio and television programs and chamber of commerce special events.

Growers participating in the experiment included C.J. Groen, Amling Brothers, Elmer Amling, Albert Amling, Nakashima Nursery, San Lorenzo Nursery and Zappettini Company. Over the next thirteen weeks, 2,730 dozen roses were collected and distributed to Halchester's in Hollywood, Cedric's Flowers and Biltmore Flowers and Gifts.

Although retail results were inconclusive, the program's biggest drawback occurred as the supply of roses diminished due to urbanization. At the same time, the number of businesses in the downtown Los Angeles area increased.

"The surplus disappeared, and the growers were then forced to dig into their regular supply to fulfill the commitments they had made to the retailers in this test program," reported *The Bloomin' News* in November 1950.

How the Market Operated

While the American Florists' Exchange and the Southern California Flower Market continued their activities individually and were managed by their separate boards of directors, the Southern California Floral Association provided administration and enforcement of procedural rules for the Market as a whole. This umbrella organization introduced benefits, social affairs and policies and accounted for inventory and sales, reporting to its own board of directors.

Left: A 1950s promotion organized by Frank Kuwahara flew thousands of chrysanthemums to New Orleans to fill florists' Mother's Day orders. *Mellano collection.*

In the post-war years, the wholesale value of flowers grown in the metro area almost tripled. The wholesale value of flowers grown in Los Angeles County alone was more than $13 million. It is estimated that 95 percent of these, along with flowers from the other counties in the Southland, moved through the two Los Angeles flower markets.

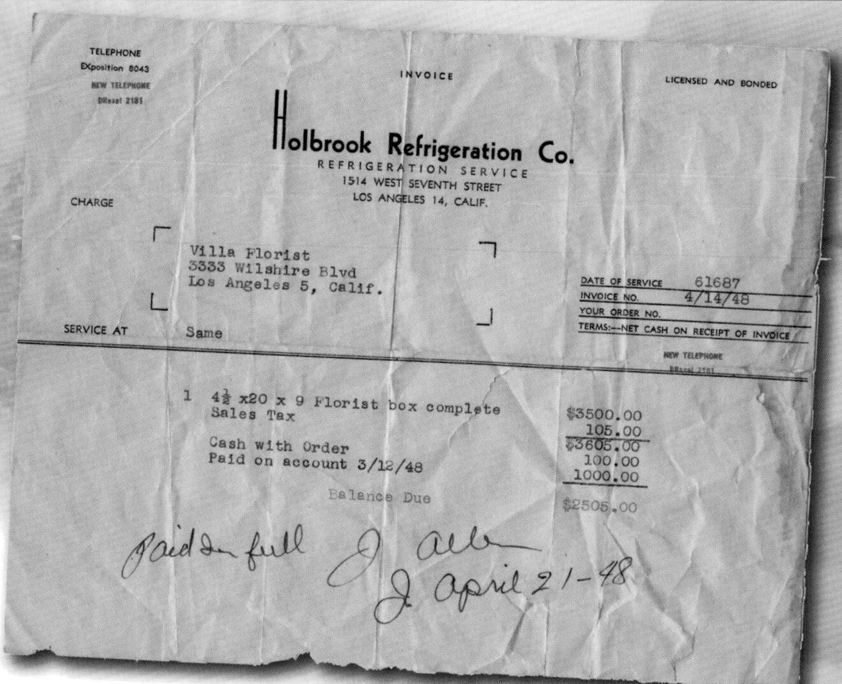

TELEPHONE
EXposition 8043
NEW TELEPHONE
DRexel 2181

INVOICE

LICENSED AND BONDED

Holbrook Refrigeration Co.
REFRIGERATION SERVICE
1514 WEST SEVENTH STREET
LOS ANGELES 14, CALIF.

CHARGE

Villa Florist
3333 Wilshire Blvd
Los Angeles 5, Calif.

DATE OF SERVICE 61687
INVOICE NO. 4/14/48
YOUR ORDER NO.
TERMS:—NET CASH ON RECEIPT OF INVOICE

SERVICE AT Same

NEW TELEPHONE

1 4½ x20 x 9 Florist box complete $3500.00
Sales Tax 105.00
$3605.00
Cash with Order 100.00
Paid on account 3/12/48 1000.00
Balance Due $2505.00

Paid in full J. Alb
J. April 21-48

Villa Florist receipt for its cooler, 1948.

Samuel Dutton Lynch, in his *Westways* article of June 1948, reported that the Southern California Floral Association, which incorporated and assumed management of the Market in 1952, was composed of 407 growers, 965 florists, 29 routemen and 22 shippers, with "a high percentage of them" swarming through Wall Street on market days. He added:

> "Not only do many nationalities mingle good-naturedly and cooperatively, but a man with a small plot of daffodils may have his stand next to the world's largest grower of stock, or the brilliant showroom of the world's largest orchid house. The small vendor who sells his flowers on a street corner rubs shoulders with the owners of exclusive shops, or shippers who deal in millions of blooms." [12]

Daily Routines

In the 1940s and 1950s, flowers sold at the Market consisted only of product grown in California, for the most part within a 150-mile radius of Los Angeles. Of course, what the local farms could supply was limited. Additionally, the public could not buy flowers at the Market, for it was open only to those with retail/resale licenses. These two facts led to the evolution of a unique transaction process and a somewhat colorful Market environment.

The three big "market days" (Monday, Wednesday and Friday) were based on the heaviest demand for cut flowers. This included demand from the southern U.S. states, which accounted for about 50 percent of the shipping volume from the Los Angeles Flower Market. This schedule dictated the personal and work activities of thousands of people connected to the Market.

Sunday, for example, was rarely a day of rest for growers, as they and their field crews were required to do their cutting, grading and bunching of flowers that day. They loaded the day's harvest onto their trucks on Sunday evening so they could be ready for transporting to the Market that evening or around midnight. Growers in San Diego County and in the Santa Barbara area left for Market around 10 or 11 p.m., to arrive by 3 a.m. on a market day. In the morning, while the grower was at the Market taking care of business, his crew was hard at work in the fields. The grower's holiday was Saturday, the only day not followed by a market day.

Growers unloading their trucks in the dark of night transformed the empty, warehouse-like interior of the Market as they stocked their shelves and counters and prepared for business. They loaded orders for delivery to special customers as well. Then some of them took a little break. Some caught a few winks where they could, others played cards, and some enjoyed breakfast at the Rose Café or any of the other three or four coffee shops on the street. By then it was nearly time for the bell.

The bell rang at 6:30 a.m., signaling the opening of the Market to the retail trade. In the moments before the bell rang, dozens of retail florists gathered outside the doors. Meanwhile, inside the Market, the growers and wholesalers, who were nearing the end of their work day having been there since midnight or earlier, prepared for business and packaged pre-orders for the routemen. Outside, the routemen waited in their trucks and vans, a parked caravan along Wall Street, ready to load their orders and take off to make their deliveries to up to 100 communities throughout the metropolitan area.

A little bit of cheating might have taken place on occasion, of course, as it is human nature to want to beat the bell, to get the best deal from your supplier. (With limited local supply, the best flowers went fast!) Retailers standing just outside the entry of the Market would shout to their supplier walking by that they were looking for ten bunches of orange gladiolas or long-stemmed tulips. The supplier would hold high what he thought his customer wanted, and the two would shout back and forth their further orders and requests. Multiply that exchange by dozens of others doing the same and the scene was hectic, noisy, exciting and something akin to the other Wall Street, that financial district on the East Coast, on a busy trading day. Here's how Bob Ayres of the Ayres-California Company, a floral wholesaler, so aptly described it in 1950:

> "... you might say that the Wall Street market during the early morning hours represents one block of rushing activity, bright lights, and helter-skelter push trucks transferring ownership of tons of brightly-colored flowers. By 8 or 9 o'clock in the morning when business people in adjacent areas arrive at work, Wall Street looks like any other business street. But the flower growers, wholesalers and buyers have already put in a full day's work." [13]

Deals were usually consummated with cash. Flowers were packaged in bundles wrapped in newspapers, as many are today, and laid on wooden tables or stuck in five-gallon oil tins of water.

Shippers, Route Men and Commission Men

Commission men occupied a large amount of space in the American Florists' Exchange in the late 1940s and 1950s, many of them representing large commission houses. These men, who arrived on each market day around 3 a.m. just like the growers, purchased flowers on a commission basis from growers, then resold them to the retailers, route men and shippers. In fact, the largest percentage of gladiolus sold through the AFE's Los Angeles Flower Market were handled by commission men.

Route men, on the other hand, delivered floral orders to an increasing number of retailers who did not wish to fight the traffic or had become accustomed to door-to-door deliveries during the War. The route men had to park their refrigerator trucks on Wall Street around 3:30 a.m. so they could place their orders, get on the road and complete their deliveries before the retailers' shops opened for business. Located in dozens of outlying towns, the buyers quickly came to appreciate the service these men provided. Early in his floral wholesale career, Johnny Mellano delivered flowers to florists in the Long Beach and Lakewood areas. He recalls his timing was such that the coffee would be hot when he arrived at Vic Levy's shop in Lakewood. Every shop was unique and every customer relationship nurtured.

And there were the shipping house buyers, usually arriving on Wall Street by 3 or 3:30 a.m. If a shipper was expecting delivery of an advance order, he would meet the grower as the grower backed his truck up to the shipper's door. If he was in a buying mode, the shipper would walk around to the arriving growers to place the necessary orders. In 1950, it was estimated that each of the approximately 30 shippers doing business through the Southern California Floral Association represented anywhere from a half dozen to 100 or more Eastern buyers and that 50 percent or more of the average day's sales were made by shippers.[14]

Retail Florists

The men and women who ran the retail shops that filled floral orders included florists all over metropolitan Los Angeles. From as far away as the San Fernando Valley and Orange County, they arrived at the Market just

Photo courtesy of Kim Randolph, The Enchanted Florist

in time for the 6:30 a.m. opening bell, lining up at the entrance just as they do today. They were easily distinguished from the route men and commission men by their more formal business suits, high heels, coats and ties, dressed for the workday. Here at the Market they could purchase product and supplies at wholesale prices that would make a profit possible.

Who Got the Leftover Flowers?

Badge-holding retail florist members crowded into the Market at the sound of the 6:30 a.m. bell in the 1950s, hoping to find top quality flowers after the shippers, route men and commission men had gotten theirs. By 8 a.m., the Market had cleared out and the retailers had left to stock their shops for the day.

Flowers not sold had several options. They were sold on consignment to commission houses, who sold them for whatever prices they could reasonably expect. There was also a group of independent peddlers who bought and resold the flowers on street corners. The rest might be refrigerated for street sales on the off-market day or taken back to the farm by the grower.

Commission houses remained open throughout the day and sometimes, when flowers were in abundance, retailers shopping later in the day found they could get great buys on flowers. Florist supply houses, such as Moskatels and Leonard Johnson's, stayed open during normal business hours as well.

Other Markets

Two other flower markets existed in the neighborhood around 1950. One was the Growers Market located in the middle of the block on Wall Street. The other was a group that occupied a large open lot at the south end of the block to sell their flowers. As the years went by, many wholesale floral markets and shops would serve the buying community in the nation's largest flower district.

The Delicacy of Pricing

Growers and buyers, whether they were wholesalers, commission men, route men or shippers, regularly argued over prices and quality of the flowers. It was part of the process, of course. Growers didn't want to sell or consign below production costs when sales were slow and wholesalers teased the growers with promises of higher-than-usual prices when demand was high. Some retail florists found their advance orders were not filled if before the scheduled pick-up date the grower was offered a higher price by another buyer. The retailer couldn't afford to get angry, but had to continue to nurture the relationship. Says Johnny Mellano, "You had to play liar's poker a lot."

Time Changes Everything

In 1952, two rulings by the California Supreme Court put an end to legal discrimination against the Japanese American community. The court struck down the Alien Land Law in two separate cases: Sei Fujii vs State of California (April 17, 1952) and Haruye Masuoka vs State of California (July 9, 1952). Both decisions based their opinions on the Fourteenth Amendment and both stressed the principle of equal protection for all.

Finally, in 1956, a state initiative for Proposition 13, sponsored by the Japanese-American Citizens League, successfully repealed the Alien Land Law, making it possible for Japanese Americans to own land. The initiative opened a world of possibilities for growers.

By the Numbers

By 1954 all of Southern California from Santa Barbara to San Diego was aglow with wide swatches of colorful flowers. Los Angeles County led the country in sales of nursery and greenhouse products, i.e., flowers, bulbs and seeds. More than 500 farms produced cut flowers, potted plants, florists' greens and bedding plants. Additional greenhouses produced roses and tropical plants, including orchids, gardenias, anthuriums and potted plants.

Montebello, just east of Los Angeles, was a hotbed of flower farming. By 1961, the Dutch growers there were shipping around a million of their exotic blooms to customers throughout America every winter, all sold through the Los Angeles Flower Market.

C.J. Groen and W.J. Vander Bruggen, Dutch growers in Montebello, pulled off a coup in 1956 that became legend in the annals of bird-of-paradise floral history. They booked passage on an ocean liner out of New York to visit their relatives in Holland but before departure, they shipped a thousand stems of bird-of-paradise, which many Easterners had never seen, to decorate the salons of the vessel. Then they invited New York City florists to see the unusual arrangements. It was such a spectacular display and covered so widely by the press [15] that by the time they returned home to Montebello, their businesses were booming.

In 1958, more than half the Southern California-grown flowers sold were shipped to other states. Around 70 percent were shipped by truck and train, while the remaining 30 percent went by air. The 650 growers of Los Angeles County accounted for $20 million annually in sales. [16]

It was not Los Angeles County alone that supplied the flowers to America, however, as growers began to migrate their farms out of the increasingly urban area and those farming in surrounding counties expanded.

In Santa Barbara County, the chrysanthemum, baby's breath and carnation crops enjoyed increasing popularity and robust sales as the county groomed itself to become California's top cut flower producer. The number of acres used to grow cut flowers reached 330 in 1957, up from 189 acres ten years before, with crops valued at $1,181,857. The county, particularly the Lompoc area, had also become a leader in the flower seed industry with 2,275 acres devoted to the growing of flowers for seed.

More than 750 acres in San Diego County were dedicated to the growing of cut flowers by 1958 and growers there were shipping some 400 boxes of cut flowers daily. With more than 30 different types of vegetation environments and what has been called the country's "most nearly perfect" climate, agriculture found an ideal home in San Diego County. For years, farms around the town of Encinitas produced more gerbera daisies than anywhere else in the world. In the 1950s, Edwin Frazee, considered the "Father of the Flower Fields" [17] introduced a special ranunculus with an unprecedented infusion of petals, making him the only U.S. commercial ranunculus grower. The Ecke Ranch, established in Encinitas, accounted for the burgeoning sales of poinsettias that helped put the county into a leadership spot in the flower growing industry.

Removed geographically from the challenges of urbanization, Ventura County's several hundred acres were planted with chrysanthemums, lilies, irises, lisianthus, stock, larkspur, delphinium and snapdragons, those specialty flowers that California would supply well into the next century to customers nationwide.

Orange County, on the other hand, was known predominantly for its citrus farms and increasingly, its nurseries, which were being built on land once occupied by rows of orange trees. Flower growing occurred on small acreages scattered throughout the county, including the farms of Jack Lugaro and Ted Ohara in Anaheim and the rose growing operations of the Amling Brothers in Westminster and Santa Ana. The county's prime real estate was forcing land values up to unaffordable levels for small flower growers, however, and it would not be long before many of the small businesses would sell out.

As urbanization crept closer it brought with it the problems created by polluted air. While city people from New York to Los Angeles dealt with soot-fall (the black residue or "industrial fallout" deposited on outdoor furniture and plants after several hours), those living in metropolitan Los Angeles were challenged by industrial smoke and exhaust fumes mixed with coastal fog, or smog. At its highest levels in history in the 1950s, it damaged the lungs of humans and made outdoor life miserable. Perhaps just as bad, air pollution put flowers to sleep, and that was yet one more challenge the Southern California flower farmers would contend with in the next decade.

These early 1940s Los Angeles Flower Market scenes depict the busy environment of the Market and the many people who made the Market a success. ***From the Mellano collection.***

Jack Reed of B.W. Hall Wholesale Florist massages his foot and reflects back on a successful day of selling flowers (notice the empty cans) at the Flower Market. *Herald Examiner Collection / Los Angeles Public Library*

[1] Graham, John, *Los Angeles Times*, "Fifty Years of Horticulture" (12/7/1947)

[2] Hutchison, Claude B., ed., California Agriculture, University of California Press (1946)

[3] Kawaguchi, Gary, *Living with Flowers*, California Flower Market, Inc. (1993)

[4] Hirahara, Naomi, *A Scent of Flowers*, Midori Books, Southern California Flower Growers, Inc. (2004)

[5] Nielsen, Paul, transcript of interview conducted by Jan Works (2007)

[6] Dutter, Vera E., *Poinsettia King*, Ecke Ranch (1975)

[7] Hirahara, Naomi, *A Scent of Flowers*, Midori Books, Southern California Flower Growers, Inc. (2004)

[8] Berry, Bob, transcript of interview conducted by Jan Works (2007)

[9] San Diego County crop records reflect some 400 acres of flowers being grown in 1941. That figure dropped to 200 acres in 1942 and rose back to prewar levels in 1946. Sales figures mirrored the trend. *Profiles in Flowers: The Story of San Diego County Floriculture*, by Robert Melvin, Paul Ecke Ranch Press (1989)

[10] Graham, John, *Los Angeles Times*, "Fifty Years of Horticulture" (December 7, 1947)

[11] Oguri, Kaoru, Ph.D., edited by George Brumder, *The Men's Garden Club of Los Angeles, An Informal History of the Early Years* (December 12, 2000)

[12] Lynch, Samuel Dutton, *Westways*, "Year-Round Flower Show" (June 1948)

[13] Ayres, Bob, *Southern Florist & Nurseryman*, "Operation of the Los Angeles Market – Part II-B, The Market Place – Wall Street" (February 3, 1950)

[14] Ayres, Bob, *Southern Florist & Nurseryman*, "Operation of the Los Angeles Market – Part 4-B, How the Market Works" (March 31, 1950)

[15] Taylor, Frank J., *Saturday Evening Post*, "The Flowers Known as Birds" (March 11,1961)

[16] Padilla, Victoria, *Southern California Gardens*, University of California Press (1961)

[17] In 1993, Paul Ecke Jr. and Mellano & Company opened The Flower Fields at Carlsbad Ranch to the public as an annual springtime attraction.

Wordpix

Timeline: 1960-1979

1960	The florists' wire service Florafax International is introduced. Goodyear is the first to cover a sporting event with a TV camera in the blimp (Orange Bowl).
1963	Southern California Flower Market completes $1 million facility. President John F. Kennedy is assassinated in Dallas, Texas.
1964	The Bracero Program ends. The Joseph Shinoda Memorial Scholarship Foundation is established by the California State Florists Association. President Johnson signs the Civil Rights Act of 1964 into law, making segregation in public facilities and discrimination in employment illegal. The Beatles make their first appearance in the United States.
1965	University research leads to artificial lighting of plants, affecting sales of potted plants. American Institute of Floral Designers, Inc. formed in Los Angeles by eleven local floral designers. Medicare and Medicaid are signed into law. American soldiers begin fighting in Vietnam. Rioting occurs in the Watts area of Los Angeles.
1960s	Some growers begin relocating from the heavily urbanized city to outlying towns, especially to the north (Carpinteria, Santa Barbara County) and south (San Diego County).
1967	Anti-Vietnam-war protests and peace rallies take place across the nation. The "Summer of Love" happens in San Francisco.
1968	Martin Luther King Jr is fatally shot in Tennessee.
1969	Flower farms begin to disappear from the local landscape, with farmers becoming wholesalers and imports gaining a foothold. The United States Department of Defense's Advanced Research Projects Agency Network (ARPAnet) and its installation of the first microcomputer by UCLA's Professor Leonard Kleinrock lay the foundation for today's Internet.
1970	American Floral Services (AFS) incorporates.
1971	Ray Tomlinson, a programmer for GTE Internetworking, successfully sends the first message between two computers, laying the foundation for e-mail communications.
1972	Twenty-nine firms occupy the American Florists' Exchange. President Nixon opens communications with China. Vietnam ceasefire is signed and troops are withdrawn. The U.S. military draft ends. The price of oil increases from $1.50 to $11.56 per barrel.
1974	Floral Marketing Association, the floral division of Produce Marketing Association, forms. President Nixon resigns during the Watergate scandal.
1975	Ken Short sells the National Florist Directory Buyer's Guide to Fred and Martha Jean Swindle. The Swindles start Redbook Florist Services the following year. War in Vietnam ends.
1976	The United States celebrates its two hundredth anniversary.
1977	Los Angeles Wholesale Flower Market Development Corporation started. (Disbanded in the 1980s). Some AFE board members are directors.
1979	Iranian students take 52 Americans hostage in the U.S. embassy.

JDP Photography

The Years of Transition (1960-1979)

"Ninety-five percent of the flowers sold at the wholesale market are grown in the Southland."

— Walter F. Swartz, general manager,
Southern California Floral Association,
in April 1968 [1]

By 1965, fewer than half the retail florists who purchased their blooms from the Los Angeles Flower Market actually traveled to the Market to make their purchases. They had come to rely upon the convenient, practical, door-to-door services of route men during the Second World War, when travel was restricted due to transportation costs, curfews and rationing. The route men, who included at least one woman [2], were the Market's earliest shoppers, arriving during the pre-dawn hours and hitting the road in their refrigerated trucks by 6 a.m.

About 125 different varieties of flowers and greens were displayed on the sales floor every day. All varieties of carnations, with some 21 natural colors, could be seen, along with thousands of daisies dyed in various colors to complement the current season. Flowers were sold by the dozen in bunches and bundles or by the hundreds or units. Almost all these flowers, purchased by route men, national and regional shippers or retail florists, were grown on the farms of Southern California.

The Floral Parade

The leading cut flowers of the late 1960s and early 1970s could be represented by these 1972 figures: Hybrid tea roses (16.3 percent of sales), carnations (11.6), pompon chrysanthemums (7.5), gladioli (6) and standard chrysanthemums (4.9). Potted plants accounted for 8.9 percent of 1972 sales; and florist supplies were 0.4 percent.

The per bloom price of carnations averaged $.08 in 1972. Standard chrysanthemums averaged $.21 and hybrid tea roses $.16. The per bunch price for pompon chrysanthemums was $.75 and for gladioli, $1.50. [3]

Bert Johnson, long-time American Florists' Exchange board member and a commission man who became a wholesale florist, recalls the cut flower prices of the 1950s-1960s offered by Pearson Wholesale:

> "We were selling gladiolas for 50 cents a dozen. Iris were 25 cents a dozen, and daffodils were $15 for a thousand of them. Bundles of stock were from one to two dollars."

Perhaps the best news for the California floral industry in 1971 was that reported by Victor Levy, president of the Southern California Floral Association, in January 1971: The State Board of Equalization had decided not to convert the sales tax procedures for Association members. Levy said the entire California floral industry would be indebted to the committee that convinced the State Board not to mess with the procedures. Committee members who represented the Association included Walter Swartz, Sam Applebaum, Victor Levy, Harold Francis, Tony Morales. They were joined by representatives of FTDA and the California State Florists' Association.

The State Board of Equalization did impose fees on the transmission of floral orders for retail florists, but abandoned its proposed tax on incoming orders.

Expansion of the Market

Beginning in the early 1960s, both the American Florists' Exchange and its neighbor, the Southern California Flower Market, undertook large construction and modernization projects. The AFE, serving a loyal clientele from its Los Angeles Flower Market on the east side of Wall Street, restored and refurbished its sales floor and constructed a building with 60,000 square feet on each of three levels on an adjacent property on its north side.

The ground level of the new building was leased to floral supply companies Moskatels (today owned by Michaels Stores) and the Pacific Coast Commercial Ribbon Mills (today's Floral Supply Syndicate). A doorway was constructed between the new wholesale suppliers' building that would allow shoppers easy access to and from the Market and floral supply merchants, but the doorway was never used because of security concerns.

Around the time the new three-story building was constructed by the American Florists' Exchange, the Southern California Flower Market demolished its well worn facility across the street and constructed a three-story building. With this addition and an entrance from Maple Avenue on the west side of their market, customers discovered they could walk through both markets easily. Entering from Maple Street on the west, they could walk through the SCFM, exit the east door, cross Wall Street and continue shopping in the American Florists' Exchange all the way to San Julian Street. The layout offered a customer-friendly convenience that encouraged shopping in both markets.

By 1972, the result of the new construction and improvements (valued at $429,420) to existing properties owned by the two markets meant that wholesalers occupied nine buildings containing around 205,000 square feet of floor

space, of which 18,000 square feet were refrigerated. The ground-level parking area totaled around 98,000 square feet and the assessed value of the land was $401,950. The Agricultural Research Service of the United States Department of Agriculture estimated the combined value of land and improvements to be around $3.3 million in 1972.

About this same time, the Fred King Building at 714 Wall Street was purchased by the American Florists' Exchange, adding to its real estate holdings and its ability to service customers.

The Flower Fields: Charming Californians for Generations

Ed Frazee recalled seeing ranunculus blooms for the first time in 1922 when his uncle Earl nurtured them along with the English peas he tended for horticulturist Luther Gage. That ranch, near Tamarack Avenue in Carlsbad, burned down a few years later and the Frazee family moved to Oceanside where Earl began growing freesia bulbs on leased land. In 1932, he added ranunculus and at age sixteen, his nephew, Edwin, quit school to work in his uncle's burgeoning flower farm.

Over the next several years, Edwin Frazee became adept at growing ranunculus. By the 1950s he had bred a superior ranunculus bulb with an unprecedented infusion of petals, known as a "double." Ed expanded to the coastal slope in Carlsbad overlooking the Pacific Ocean.

By 1975, Edwin Frazee retired, leaving the business to his sons John and Jim. Soon after, the flower fields moved a few miles north, just east of Interstate 5 at Palomar Airport Road. The land was a former poinsettia field owned by Carltas Company, the land division of the Paul Ecke family. In 1993, Jim determined the fields were not cost effective and asked Paul Ecke Jr. to terminate the lease.

The thought of closing the Flower Fields disturbed Paul Ecke Jr., who saw the spectacular, prominent blooms as part of the Carltas Company's plan and a landmark gateway to adjacent projects. In August 1993, Carltas secured a loan from the California Coastal Conservancy to keep the fields running for two more years. A venture to take over 50 acres of ranunculus was formed by Carltas with Mellano & Company, which farmed in the San Luis Rey Valley nearby.

At this important juncture, Paul Ecke Jr. persuaded Edwin Frazee to come out of retirement and provide the knowledge so necessary to grow the crop, which today includes the famous ranunculus as well as gladioli, watsonia, sparaxis (Wandflower), Oxalis (Blooming Shamrock), babiana and tritonia.

The survival and success of The Flower Fields®, now branded and supplying garden centers everywhere, represent the love and appreciation for their beauty by Edwin Frazee, Paul Ecke Jr. and the thousands of annual visitors who are awed and inspired by that beauty. The Flower Fields® has become a perfect synthesis of a robust working ranch and regional tourist attraction.

Reprinted with permission from
The Bloomin' News, *March 2003*

Left: Andy Kho won the 2006 photo contest with this spectacular view of The Flower Fields®. *Carltas Company collection.*
Above: Another colorful view of The Flower Fields.
Right: Aerial view of the popular Flower Fields at Carlsbad. *Carltas Company collection.*

Meanwhile, sales of California-grown cut flowers and foliage were strong and the business environment within the Flower Market was robust. The State Board of Equalization issued more than 1,100 permits to retail florists for Southern California in 1972. Seventy-one percent were members of the Southern California Floral Association and eight percent were auxiliary members.

Nearly 100 percent of the cut flowers and potted plants sold by retail florists throughout the five-county area (Los Angeles, Orange, Ventura, San Bernardino and Riverside) were supplied by the downtown wholesale flower market. [4] The two markets boasted a combined sales figure of $20 million per year, accounting for twenty percent of the national figures. [5]

Journalists and retail customers talked about the "Flower Market" and "Flower Terminal" (or "Depot") to describe the two large markets as if they were one. With the arrival of independently owned floral supply stores and retail shops on the arterial streets, a large flower district began to evolve. In the years that followed, this great flower district inspired story after story in publications including the *Los Angeles Times* and national consumer and trade magazines.

"By 2:00 a.m., from Torrance and Azusa, from Ventura and Escondido, from San Francisco and San Diego, the flower merchants begin to converge on Wall Street, the heart of Los Angeles' multi-million-dollar flower market, the largest wholesale flower market in the world," begins an article in a 1965 issue of *Westways* magazine. [6]

Whether the wholesale flower district was indeed the largest flower market in the world at the time, we cannot say. Most likely, in view of the size reductions of markets in San Francisco and New York in the 2000s, the Los Angeles Flower District can be considered the largest in the United States today.

The Fractured Face of America

History reflects the 1960s as an era of dramatic and in many cases, traumatic, change. In politics, global relations, education, finance and personal beliefs and culture, great shifts occurred that inevitably shook up households, revolutionized the country and shattered the sense that America was protected from the ills experienced in other places around the world:

The assassination of President John F. Kennedy in November 1963; Martin Luther King Jr's assassination in April 1968, followed just two months later by the assassination of Robert F. Kennedy. A drug culture that seemed to cast a spell over our youth. A sexual revolution. Radical feminism. Race riots in Chicago, Philadelphia and Los Angeles (Watts). Civil rights protests. And a war in Vietnam that led to organized protests across the country, some of them turning violent, and to sending our men and women to war.

Floral Industry Growth in the Face of Change

In the presence of the uncertainty and grief of the 1960s, people continued to buy flowers. Good things still happened. The baby boomers had babies, couples married, employees retired, the Southern California Floral Association held its always-popular barbeques and annual open house events, and volunteers conducted flower shows and the Las Floristas Headdress Ball. The California State Floral Association, Teleflora, FTD and regional flower associations held conventions and regional shows that involved the Flower Market. The Tournament of Roses and the Oscars entertained us with highlights and conversation. Southern Californians, we discovered, would use any reason they could to enjoy flowers, regardless of tragedy or transition. Life in the flower business went on, for some affairs, bigger and better than ever.

One such event, a 1968 Open House held across both Wall Street markets, featured the work of designers Kirk Kirkpatrick AIFD [7] and Gordon Schmuhl AIFD, of Flowers by Kirk in Van Nuys, along with Wayne Andrade of Andrade-McKee's Flower World in Newport

Beach, Sylvia Levy of Victor's Flowers in Lakewood and a host of other professional designers and commentators from across the country and around the world. Local florists and suppliers manned themed exhibit booths elaborately decorated with their florals. In addition to the Fall Open House, a similar expo was held each Spring.

A number of these designers, as well as, to name a few, Robert Berry AIFD of Los Angeles Florist, Richard Seekins AIFD and Scott Acevedo AIFD of Orange County, Fred Gibbons of Beverly Hills and many others, were invited to participate in the annual Las Floristas Headdress Ball, an award-winning social event held to benefit children's charities at Rancho Los Amigos National Rehabilitation Center in Downey, California. The Headdress Ball was such a large Spring event in the 1960s and 1970s that it created a very busy season for floral designers and event benefactors and volunteers. It was responsible for a large jump in flower sales as a dozen or more designers purchased carefully selected blooms for themed headdresses. The wholesale flower market and Las Floristas remained good friends for many years.

> "Because the industry is grateful that Las Floristas have chosen flowers as their medium," said Southern California Floral Association general manager Walter Swartz in 1968, "we give them a dollar's worth of flowers for every dime they spend with us." [8]

Frank Vescio, Market manager, left, with Flower Market visitors, 1970s. ***Vescio collection.***

In 1964, the California State Floral Association established the Joseph Shinoda Memorial Scholarship Foundation, honoring one of its founders, a man whose life was all about flowers. Shinoda, from Oakland, California, was well known as the president of San Lorenzo Nursery Company who led that company through remarkable growth. Arthur Ito, a floriculturist from Los Angeles, was appointed as chairman of a committee to oversee the foundation. Shinoda, who died in January 1964, had served the Southern California Floral Association as its president in 1954.

In 1965, a group of five Los Angeles area designers organized the American Institute of Floral Designers. Bob Berry AIFD recalls seeing the "AID" credentials on the badges of members of the Association of Interior Decorators at events for which he was floral designer. He, along with Beatrice Frambach, owner of Burbank Florist, Arthur Ito, Wayne Andrade and David Wittry felt the floral design industry should offer a professional designation, based upon the meeting of professional standards. The AIFD is a strong organization today that offers floral designers the opportunity to educate themselves while earning the AIFD credential. Wittry was with Crossley Flowers, Ito with Flower View Gardens and Andrade had been the florist for Disneyland and Disneyland Hotel while Berry had his Los Angeles Florist, Inc. retail shop.

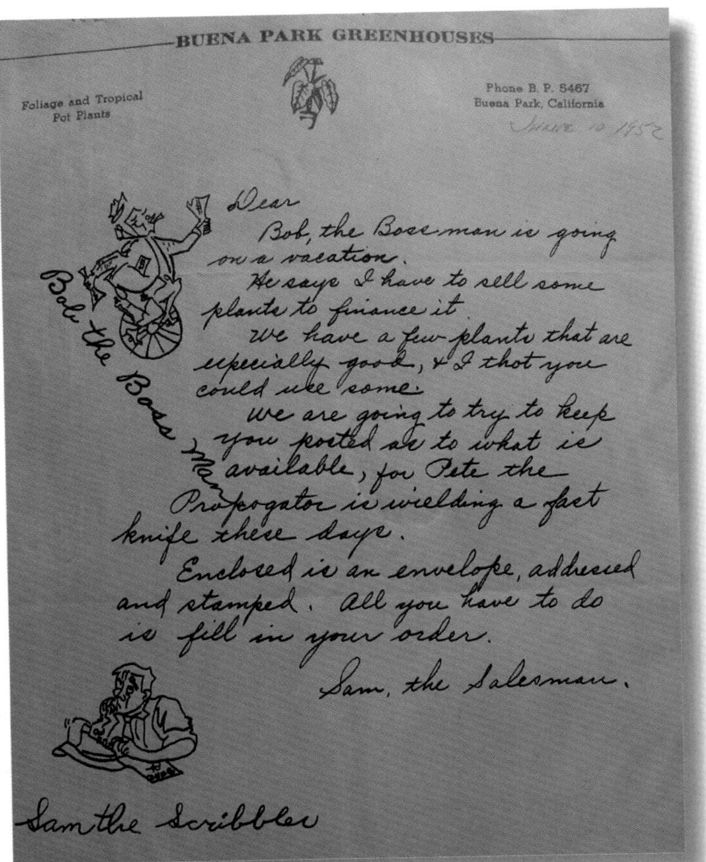

BUENA PARK GREENHOUSES

Foliage and Tropical Pot Plants

Phone B. P. 5467
Buena Park, California

June 10 1952

Dear
Bob, the Boss-man is going on a vacation.
He says I have to sell some plants to finance it.
We have a few plants that are especially good, & I thot you could use some.
We are going to try to keep you posted as to what is available, for Pete the Propogator is wielding a fast knife these days.
Enclosed is an envelope, addressed and stamped. All you have to do is fill in your order.
Sam, the Salesman.

Bob the Boss Man

Sam the Scribbler

A tongue-in-cheek (but personal) sales solicitation from Buena Park Greenhouses. *Weidner's Gardens collection.*

It was during 1966 that the California State Floral Association, the counterpart of the Southern California Floral Association, published its monthly newsletter as a center insert in SCFA's publication, *The Bloomin' News*. CSFA's *California Florist* broke away after a year, in order to distribute the magazine under its own identity as the voice of the statewide association and to offer expanded reports and articles.

As the 1960s rolled into the 1970s, floral organizations throughout the five-county metroplex enjoyed increasing membership numbers and sponsored their own floral design programs and flower shows. Morri Molho AIFD reported in a 1968 edition of *The Bloomin' News* the success of the Orange County Florists' Association's tenth anniversary celebration. Rocky Pollitz AIFD, president and FTD chairman, and West Covina florist Ray Tucker, names now familiar to our regional flower industry, helped organize that event and many more.

The flower industry experienced growth in the early 1970s in spite of major events taking place at home and abroad. Evelyn Weidner of Buena Park Greenhouses (now Weidner's Gardens) attributed the upswing to the hippies. These young folk of the era had a "flower power" mantra that emphasized the abandonment of all things "plastic" and espoused the use of objects and plants made of "natural" material.

An energy crisis, which had drivers sitting in their cars in long lines at the gas stations, began in October 1973 when members of the Organization of Arab Petroleum Exporting countries (OAPEC, consisting of Arab members of OPEC) announced that they would no longer ship petroleum to nations supporting Israel in its conflict with Syria and Egypt. OPEC-imposed price increases led to inflation in the economies of the involved countries,

C.J. Groen in Montebello greenhouses - 1946

Greenhouse Growing

The early greenhouse growers who supplied the wholesalers and retailers through the Los Angeles Flower Market would be amazed if they could see today's state-of-the-art high-efficiency greenhouses. From retractable roofs to radio frequency tracking of individual plants, the greenhouse industry has evolved to high yield production and streamlined operations.

Early structures consisted of cold and heated frames and hotbeds for the starting and growing of plants. Early 1900s "aster" houses were made of cloth. Houses supported by laths of cypress or redwood housed the growing operation for a number of plants. In the 1920s, "sash" houses appeared during cold weather, with heat supplied by simple piping systems.

During the formative days of the Southern California flower growing industry, horse-drawn wagons hauled including the United States. Supplies of fuel were limited and expensive. Flower growers in the northern and eastern United States, who had greenhouses to heat in winter, were especially hard hit by high fuel prices, and California greenhouse growers faced higher prices and lost much of the import business from the East and Midwest.

The war in Vietnam (AKA the Second Indochina War) was underway, involving thousands of American troops dispatched by presidents Kennedy and Johnson starting in 1965. The Watergate scandal was yet another ongoing news item. This series of illegal activities centered around a June 1972 break-in of the Democratic National Committee headquarters in Washington, DC in a hotel called The Watergate and attempts to cover up that crime. Investigations led to the August 1974 resignation of President Richard Nixon.

supplies of wood or coal to the greenhouses, to supply fuel for their heating.

Sylvia Foltz, daughter of C.J. Groen of Groen Rose Company in Santa Barbara, California, remembers that the irrigation system in her father's greenhouses used heating pipes insulated with asbestos.

In the 1930s-1940s, Albert J. Amling, an Orange County, California rose grower, built greenhouses with floors and benches of redwood and roofs of glass which he painted. He also installed a temperature sensor. It cost Amling around $25,000 to construct a 300-foot long greenhouse.

"Dad used to use bean straw as mulch in the benches between the roses," recalled Norman Amling in 2007. "They would build a bench four feet wide, about two or three feet deep, and a wood floor. Then they made a special wheelbarrow to bring the dirt from outside, because Granddad (Ernst C. Amling) wanted to recycle the dirt."

Hot water in the Amling greenhouses was regulated by a circulation pump and generated by a high-pressure boiler Albert Amling purchased from a Navy surplus store. The boiler heated the water to less-than-steam-generation level, eliminating the need for continuous operation and decreasing energy costs.

Greenhouse and growing methods evolved with technology. By 2007, greenhouse types included old, new and improved varieties: The lean-to, with one side attached to a building; even-span with roofs that feature an even pitch and width and straight sides; hoop houses made of bent tubular pipe covered with plastic; the ridge-and-furrow greenhouse with even-span greenhouses connected to produce more growing space, or a ridge-and-furrow house variation called a Venlo featuring narrow gable ends.

Continued...

Above left: C.J. Groen in the Groen Rose Company's Montebello greenhouse in 1946. ***Sylvia Foltz collection***

Right: Westerlay Orchids greenhouse of phalaenopsis orchids in Carpinteria, California, 2007, supplier to several Los Angeles Flower Market wholesalers. Featured are a mobile table system, mobile energy curtains, overhead micro-irrigation, heating pipes from a natural-powered boiler, hoses that dose waste CO2 from the boiler operation into the greenhouse for extra growth, and high-efficiency fans. Less obvious are the vent motors and misting system (used for cooling) and state-of-the-art computer system that controls all of this equipment. ***Courtesy Westerlay Orchids.***

Here Come the Imports

Flower wholesalers and growers in California began to notice cut flowers trickling into the area from South America and Europe. With recent improvements in transportation and technology, including refrigeration, packaging and computerization, imported products moved faster and retained their freshness longer. It seemed there was no longer a need to sell flowers from local fields within hours of harvest.

Some industry leaders made exploratory trips to other countries to see their growing operations for themselves. In the early 1970s, Frank Kuwahara, manager of the Southern California Flower Market, and Yoshimi ("Shimi") Shibata, proprietor of Mt. Eden Nursery in Northern California, organized a trip to Colombia, where it was alleged that roses enjoyed ideal growing conditions and could be produced on a large scale for exporting. Johnny Mellano and his brother Michael Mellano Sr. joined the group. Sure enough, they discovered, climate and growing conditions were ideal, rose growing operations were already in business and shipping by air was in place. Growing techniques still called for improvement, but labor and building costs were low, indicating that a profit could be made.

Other trips were arranged to the streamlined operations in Ecuador, Holland, Guatemala, Costa Rica and Mexico. In 1975, some members of the Southern California Floral Association traveled to Europe on another trip organized by Frank Kuwahara. Their exploration included visits to the flower markets in Holland, Germany, Switzerland and England.

Greenhouse Growing, continued

Today's greenhouse coverings are made of polyethylene, glass, structured sheets of polycarbonate, acrylic or fiberglass. Retractable roofs used by commercial growers allow the opening and closing of entire roofs, making an ideal environment for cut flowers that grow best outdoors but can't take early morning cold or rain.

Modern greenhouses include benches of expanded aluminum, steel, plastic or wood. Some have rolling benches for easy reconfiguring of the layout of the crop and expansion of production, which can increase growing space up to 20 percent.

The system used to control the environment inside the greenhouse is the challenge for today's commercial growers. They include thermostats, analog controls, digital controls and computerized environmental management. A computerized system with electronic sensors provides instant feedback and makes adjusting zone settings easy.

Heating systems may use forced air heat, steam heat, fans and infrared heating. Cooling systems use motor-

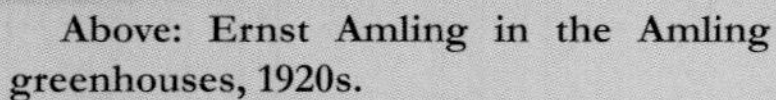

Above: Ernst Amling in the Amling greenhouses, 1920s.
Right: an Amling greenhouse under construction.
Far Right: Piers prepared during construction of the Amling company's early twentieth century greenhouses.
Amling collection.

Right: A pallet of Cymbidium Orchids, tulips and hydrangeas are readied for shipment to Mellano & Company at the Schipol Airport in Amsterdam, Holland in 2007. The flowers were purchased at the electronic auction and shipped by KLM 747 to Los Angeles.

Below: Imported flowers make their way through the cutting machine at Mellano & Company.

ized vents located along the sidewalls and ridge of the house. Recent new designs have led to the motorized ventilation of entire roof sections. Other growers use a system of fans that pull air from wet pads strategically positioned to cool the entire section.

Watering can be achieved through sprinkler systems, automated drip methods, boom watering for seedlings in plug trays, moist mats under potted plants, flooding of benches, systems allowing seedling trays to float on a nutrient solution and pulse watering.

With growers around the world seeking ways to reduce energy costs (up to 30 percent of greenhouse production cost), sharing ideas through trade journals and conferences is common. HortiWorld's *FlowerTech 2007* describes a competition to design a greenhouse that produces more energy than it consumes.

Radio Frequency Identification enables full automation and optimization of the growing process through an infrastructure of tags and readers to track environmental conditions and plant health and sort and route plants from seed to sale. Deployed on a large scale in Europe, RFID is making its way to California.

Large commercial greenhouse operations can expend up to 35 to 50 percent of their production costs on labor alone. High-tech greenhouse operations today can be operated by computer with robots doing the spacing of plants and benches being moved simply by pressing a button on the computer keyboard. Although not without impact on the labor market, advances in technology allow growers to reduce labor costs and produce better crops.

Sources: Greenbeam.com/GM-Pro (May 2007); National Junior Horticulture Association – www.aces.uiuc.edu/njha; HortiWorld.nl – FlowerTech 2007; RFID Update; BusinessWire, Greenhouse Grower – May 2007, The Bloomin' News – January 2006

Top: An early picture of the Leonard Johnson floral supply store on Wall Street. *Mellano collection.*
Right: Danny Temkin, left, with Eddie Battistessa in 1979 when Eddie allowed Danny to sell floral supplies from the Edmund's counter. Temkin's company grew to international status. *Courtesy Temkin International, Inc.*

At the flower auction market at Aalsmeer, just outside Amsterdam, the group witnessed thousands of cut flowers passing through a state-of-the-art, air-conditioned, humidity-controlled facility. This convinced the Japanese Americans in the group to move forward with the expansion and rebuilding of the Southern California Flower Market. It convinced every member of the group of the advanced growing, packaging and distribution methods already in place in Europe.

Increasingly, Southern California wholesalers began to make inquiries and enter into supply agreements with offshore growers. No longer were bulbs the only floral product entering the United States. Now American wholesalers and consumers were treated to freesias, liatris, alstroemerias and gerbera daisies from the Dutch; roses from Mexico and Ecuador; roses and carnations, shipped on a large scale from Colombia; and a variety of flowers from Canada which exported to the northeastern United States.

Floral imports were here to stay. The imports of the 1970s would be joined in the years to follow by exotic plants, tropicals and orchids. At the expense of local growers, the selection of flowers for designers and consumers had multiplied many times over.

In spite of political and economic changes, Southern California was traveling in high gear during the 1970s. Freeways were under construction, following on the success of the Arroyo Seco Parkway (today's Pasadena "710" freeway) and according to a master plan devised in the 1940s. Soon to criss-cross all of Southern California, from Ventura to the north to the Inland Empire in San Bernardino and Riverside counties in the east and San Diego at the Mexican border, freeways would connect retail florists and wholesalers with the center of commerce in downtown Los Angeles. The transportation bottlenecks so prevalent since the war years would, at least for a little while, become a memory. With the opening of the Santa Ana Freeway (I-5) in 1954, getting to Market became a little easier.

> "What do you think should be made our national flower?," a guest speaker asked his Garden Club audience in September 1964. The reply from a back seat in the room was, "How about the concrete cloverleaf?" [9]

Florists and event planners taking advantage of the new freeways continued to shop in the early morning hours at the Los Angeles Flower Market, and tenants and vendors continued to help family members and others coming into the business.

> "As a young 20-something-year-old buck back in 1979, I had decided to try and make ends meet by selling polypropylene clear and printed rolls directly to the florists, because the wholesalers would not give me the time of day. A friendly Eddie Battistessa from Edmunds Flowers allowed me, for a 'small fee,' to sit at his counter and sell my rolls … Eddie always made sure that I did a good job."
> – Danny Temkin, Temkin International

Camaraderie and a willingness to share knowledge, experience and sales space still characterized most of the wholesale Market.

Shoppers and sellers gathered daily in four restaurants to talk shop. The Rose Café, El Cato Japanese restaurant, Barney's and the small café in the Orchid Exchange were comfortable places for chatting, reading the latest *Bloomin' News* or *Southern Florist & Nurseryman*, *The Florists' Review* or any of a number of popular magazines and newsletters.

In October 1979, *The Bloomin' News* celebrated 30 years of providing local and industry news to the floral community. Gerry Prince Young, who regularly reported in a column about American Institute of Floral Designers' activities and submitted feature articles, wrote a series of briefs in the "What happened 30 years ago" vein, to celebrate the anniversary. The chatty, newsy publication had no editor, but published the articles and columns of as many as fifteen reporters every month.

In March 1979, the Society of American Florists' Endowment (SAFE) "Century III" $125 per person dinner was held at the Century Plaza Hotel in Los Angeles. The dinner event was chaired by Arthur Ito and held for the purpose of raising capital for an Endowment Fund to support floral and horticultural research.

Moving the Farms

"Carlo drove the tractor from Montebello to Anaheim" (a distance of around 20 miles by surface streets), recalled Agostina Lugaro in a 2007 conversation about the family's relocating its flower farm in 1953. Farming along the east side of Magnolia Street south of Crescent Avenue in Anaheim just blocks from Disneyland, they had Ted Ohara, wholesale flower grower and tenant of the Southern California Flower Market, for a neighbor, along with a number of other growers who sold through the Southern California Flower Market and the American Florists' Exchange.

Many flower farmers moved out to the less populated areas, where plenty of open land still beckoned, in Orange County. Among the strawberry fields and orange groves, the flower fields appeared in Buena Park, Orange, Anaheim, Brea, Santa Ana, Villa Park, Garden Grove and along the southern coast in Huntington Beach. Some new tenants of these leased acreages found they had to first remove rows upon rows of orange trees and then till and prepare the soil for the carnations and mums. Japanese growers like the Iwata family, who had farmed in the Blue Hills (now the site of La Mirada High School), discovered perfect soil for their Majestic Daisies in Buena Park. Less traffic, more land and only a short freeway drive to the Market in downtown Los Angeles: What could be better?

Moves to outlying towns became commonplace in the 1960s and 1970s, even as the city crept across the landscape to the suburbs and, farther, the exurbs as far away as Riverside, Encinitas and Lompoc. Before long, Anaheim's East Street no longer indicated the eastern edge of that city, as farmland gave way to residential developments and shopping districts appeared.

Johnny Mellano chuckles when he recalls that while his family lived in the small Los Angeles agricultural suburb of Artesia, the city had around 200 residents but 2,000 cows. Artesia and Norwalk were dotted with dairy farms and feedlots, most of which eventually moved out to Chino in San Bernardino County, or closed. The Mellano family moved its farming operation from Artesia to San Diego County, where in 1969 they purchased 80 acres of rolling hillside near the historic San Luis Rey Mission. In 1972, after their founder's death, the entire Mellano farming operation became established there.

"Our land on Marquardt in Artesia did not make a profit for its last three years," Mellano recalls. "If you owned your land, the taxes just kept going up, making it hard to make a profit. It wasn't until Prop 13 came along that taxes stabilized." [10]

Maria Ghigo crosses Wall Street during early morning shopping at the Market, late 1950s.

Las Floristas Headdress Ball: An Integral Part of Flower Market History

The Las Floristas Headdress Ball celebrates its seventieth year in 2008, no small feat for a charitable effort that at its peak was bolstered in huge measure by the Los Angeles Flower Market. For many years, the two entities worked as a team to produce a spectacular Ball with more than 800 people in attendance, to raise funds to benefit the Las Floristas Handicapped Children's Center at Rancho Los Amigos National Rehabilitation Center and Los Angeles County-University of Southern California Medical Center in Downey, California.

In the 1950s-1970s, Las Floristas was as big a floral occasion for the Market as Valentine's Day and Mother's Day, and its excitement in both the floral community and the media was contagious. Newspapers and television reporters consistently covered the build-up to the event, fueling the anticipation. It helped that Mrs. Conrad Hilton, wife of the founder of the international chain of business hotels, was the event's television chair. But it was the Headdress Ball itself that awed and rendered speechless even the most avid floral enthusiasts.

The Parade of Mannequins, called "Ticket to Paradise," at the April 20, 2007 Las Floristas Headdress Ball. *From the collection of Scott Acevedo AIFD.*

"Even in its most extravagant moments," wrote Katherine Bentley in the June 1971 issue of *The Bloomin' News*, "the real Broadway could scarcely have equaled the beauty and artistry ... The entire room was a bower of flowers with colossal Spring arrangements ..."

Fred Gibbons and Harry Finley created the décor that year, while Ray Noval's Orchestra musically announced the spectacular show and KCOP (Channel 13) broadcast the event in color. Floral wholesalers included San Lorenzo Nursery, Nakashima Nursery, Growers Wholesale Florist, Edmund's, Groen Rose Co., B.W. Hall Co., Ioki Floral, G.A. Berlin, Santa Barbara Flower Growers, Tayama, Kessler, United, Jack Mayesh, Dos Pueblos Orchid, Amling Bros., Puyallup Valley Floral and more.

In 1960 the ladies modeling the arrangements began to use back braces. At the bottom of the back brace was a pallet that fit into a pocket located in the

Mrs. Philip O'Neill, assistant flower chairman for the Floral Headdress Ball in April 1957, brings refreshments to florist Edmund Battistessa as he shows a bouquet to Mrs. Henry Paul Willis, Las Floristas president, February 15, 1957. *Herald Examiner Collection / Los Angeles Public Library*

Linda Nies as Cinderella with design by Richard Seekins AIFD and Scott Acevedo AIFD, winner of the Las Floristas Headdress Ball Sweepstakes and People's Choice awards in 1996.

John Corriveau, Keith White, Kirk Kirkpatrick AIFD, Gordon Schmuhl AIFD, Jim Brady, James Stephenson, Stan Matkowski, Claude Lecourt, Tony Lochetto, Wayne Andrade, Arthur F. McKee AIFD, Helen Gunsley, Roma Livingston and Anneliese Mahaljevic. Hundreds of others took the limelight in other years.

The success of the event can be attributed to the dedication of many volunteers in the Las Floristas organization and in the floral community as well.

In 1996, Las Floristas, Inc. won an AIFD Award of Merit Non-Industry from the American Institute of Floral Designers, for promoting floral design with the use of fresh flowers. But the real awards are those expressed by the designers, volunteers and the Market for whom the Headdress Ball and its charitable goals create lasting memories.

back of the "Merry Widow" the mannequins wore, so that all the weight was carried on the hips. At qualification, if the weight exceeded 35 pounds, the florist could remove flowers or framing or take a point deduction for being overweight.

Floral designers still compete in the centerpiece, Mannequin Parade and guest headdress contests. The spectacular arrangements feature thousands of fresh cut flowers intricately wrapped around carefully designed armatures to represent themes. Volunteers of the Las Floristas organization consider it an honor to model the elaborately designed headdresses in the event. Some of the 1971 designers included

"The wholesale flower market and Las Floristas have been good friends ever since this ambitious group of women got the idea of giving an annual Floral Headdress Ball as a charity benefit.
– "Flower Mart Blossoms While Rest of the Southland Sleeps,"
by Sharon Fay, Los Angeles Times, April 15, 1968

Flowers being moved by Frank Vescio, left, and Russell Eaton, center, are admired by Mrs. Frank H. Powell Jr., Mrs. William Schloen, Mrs. Wilfred Merrill and Mrs. Richard Schellenberger at the Los Angeles Flower Market, 1965. The ladies are shopping for flowers for the Las Floristas charity ball. *Herald Examiner Collection / Los Angeles Public Library.*

Paul Ecke's poinsettia ranch in Encinitas was well known among the growers of Southern California, so it did not take a lot of convincing to get some of them to move to Ecke's San Diego County. Edwin Frazee and Elmond ("Thorny") Thornton were other successful flower growers in the area.

> "From the farm at Encinitas, we took our cut flowers by truck (a little van of some kind) and sold them in the market in Los Angeles. We'd stop and get a sandwich on the way, then hop back on Route 101 (there was no freeway then). Encinitas was called the 'flower capital of the world' at that time." – Lewis G. Thornton in 2007. Mr. Thornton, now retired in Oregon, still lives along Highway 101.

The farms of Los Angeles County had all but disappeared by 1980. Some nurseries survived, able to thrive thanks to the ability to computer-schedule plants for a steady flow for wholesale distribution. Some continued to sell their flowers through the downtown markets. But many nurseries soon reduced their operations, closed or moved. Bob Weidner's large and well established Buena Park Greenhouses, which moved to Brea from Buena Park in 1956 because of freeway construction, moved again in 1968 to Encinitas in San Diego County.

The Van Wingerden family led the way for growers immigrating to the United States from Holland, to the farms of Santa Barbara and Ventura counties. Three Van Wingerden brothers (Case, Hank and Bill) left their homes and flower fields in Naaldwijk, The Netherlands to move to Carpinteria, California in 1967. They had learned through

Ray Winter, left, and his brother Duane, grandsons of Paul Ecke Sr. assisting in the Ecke Ranch's holiday sales area at the Market, 1971.

Where did all the flowers go?

Anaheim

Agostina and Jack Lugaro sold the southern part of their Anaheim property for the building of a golf course.

Buena Park

Both Giovanni Ghigo's flower ranch and Bob Weidner's Buena Park Greenhouses gave way to construction of the I-5 freeway.

La Mirada

The Blue Hills area farmed by the Japanese is the site of today's La Mirada High School and La Mirada Golf Course.

Los Angeles

The spot where Ralph Yack had his flower stand at Adams and Vermont became the site of the first Ralph's supermarket.

Montebello

Gebhard Prechtl sold 2.5 of his five acres in Montebello for the building of a school.

C.J. Groen's Montebello land made way for a large apartment complex.

Norwalk

Julius and Joe Franciosi's farm moved east about one mile when the Santa Ana (I-5) Freeway claimed three acres.

Gardena

Part of the Bodger Seed Company's ranch in Gardena became Bodger Park, a community of 804 homes. The corner of Prairie and Compton in Gardena became the home for a service station.

Redondo Beach

A McDonalds restaurant now occupies the field at 190th and Hawthorne where Tike and Dan Karavas worked as youngsters. A Taco Bell restaurant sits in the former field at Del Amo and Hawthorne boulevards. The fields at Aviation and Manhattan Beach boulevards gave way to construction of Aviation High School in the late 1950s, then became the Redondo Beach Performing Arts Center. The fields at Knobb Hill and Prospect Avenue became the Alta Vista School and Park.

There's a park at Blossom Avenue and 190th, a TJ Maxx store at 182nd and Hawthorne Boulevard.

The fields at Rindge and 190th, which supplied the flowers for Jerry Stamis who sold them as a teenager on Redondo Beach pier, have become a residential housing development.

Hermosa Beach

Vons Market now occupies the former fields at Pier Avenue and Pacific Coast Highway and a service station sits at Aviation and Grant. The flower fields at Prospect and 190th are still graced with a field of flowers.

Manhattan Beach

Real estate offices now occupy the fields at Artesia and Pacific Coast Highway, and a park can be enjoyed at Ardmore and Gould Lane. Over at Manhattan Beach Boulevard and Peck Avenue, the Pollywog Park and Manhattan Beach Museum beckon visitors.

Palos Verdes

Residences have been built where the flowers once grew at Calle Mayor and Pacific Coast Highway.

Santa Ana

The Amling company's fields at Fifth Street and Sullivan Avenue were replaced with a light industrial complex. A school now sits at the northwest corner of the intersection.

Torrance

The Del Amo Mall sits on the area once occupied by flower fields at Carson and Hawthorne boulevards.

The flower fields at Victor and Del Amo Boulevard are today a scene of higher learning for students of West Torrance High School.

Ventura

The site of Theodosia Shepherd's home and elaborate gardens, where the California flower seed business began, became the site of the Ventura County Library.

Our thanks to Tike Karavas for his assistance with this report. Other sources include House of Bodger by Louise Bodger Whitman and the families interviewed for this book.

research at their local university in Holland about the ideal climate, soil and water of this oceanside location. It was here that they established Dutch Brothers Nursery and began growing carnations, chrysanthemums, freesias and gerberas. Other Dutch growers soon followed.

A Market in Transition

In the early 1970s, leaders of the Los Angeles flower community and officials at City Hall buzzed with talk of a potential move by the wholesale flower markets to a suburban location. The Southern California Floral Association's membership had grown to more than 1,000 and business was on the upswing, but the antiquated buildings and facilities contributed to serious inefficiencies. The area around the market, populated with old garment industry buildings, had deteriorated and homeless people had found their way to the sidewalks along the Market. Personal safety had become a great concern, as evidenced by the mugging of wholesaler Dan Stamis as he sat in his small office doing the day's books, as well as various vehicle break-ins.

American Florists' Exchange directors were as concerned as those who frequented the Market and they began to analyze the situation closely. They commissioned an in-depth study by the United States Department of Agriculture's research arm. They hoped the USDA's research would provide an objective analysis of the past and the present and offer workable resolutions for the problems.

The U.S. Department of Agriculture's feasibility study, "An Analysis of Floral Wholesaling Facilities in Los Angeles, California," published in 1976, described the Market's history and current conditions. USDA researchers surveyed and spoke with hundreds of representatives of all levels of the local floral industry during the late 1960s and into the 1970s and summarized a few of the problems of the aging, ill-planned structures: Insufficient space, low ceilings, narrow doors and aisles and low door clearances located in inadequate multi-story buildings with antiquated elevators and wooden floors that had become unsound with age on upper levels.

The study pointed out the absence of truck docking facilities and the need to have large trucks and semi-trailers, once rare on the narrow downtown streets, loading and unloading at the market. It noted the limited space available for trucks turning and maneuvering through traffic, the need for forklifts in areas where no forklift platforms existed. It described the inadequate refrigeration facilities, the absence of canopies for protection during inclement weather, insufficient street-side parking space, inferior

Mayor Tom Bradley's Flower Market Advisory Committee, comprised of members of both Wall Street flower markets. Back row from left: Henry Nakajima, president Nakashima Roses, Bob Le Clair, manager, Amling Brothers, Jon Prechtl, Southern California Floral Association, Sab Shibata, owner, Sunnyside Nursery, Frank Kuwahara, manager, Southern California Flower Market, John Fukishima, president San Lorenzo Nursery, and Tony Chew, City of Los Angeles. Front row from left: Joe Mayesh, Mayesh Wholesale Florist, Mayor Tom Bradley, Mas Yoshida, president Growers Wholesale and Gilbert Lindsay, Los Angeles city council. *The Frank Kuwahara collection.*

lighting and finally, the inability of market management to provide adequate security because of the market's layout and location in a very public, highly trafficked area.

The analysis commented on the decline of shipping through the Los Angeles Flower Markets. It attributed the drop to the decision of shippers to consolidate deliveries directly to the Los Angeles International Airport for transport to distant markets. Substantial increases in retail sales were said to have offset the decline of shipping activities.

A special section of the USDA's report was devoted to market trends and projections. It was here that readers learned that the per capita consumption of flowers through retail shops had increased substantially from 1960 to 1970, in spite of the growing numbers of local supermarket chains that had begun to sell fresh flowers. Along with this came the USDA's opinion that most Southern California growers, averaging $64,000 in sales, did not have sufficient capacity to supply mass market outlets and preferred to sell to a variety of customers rather than become an exclusive supplier to one chain. The report surmised that both retail (special occasion floral orders) and mass market (impulse purchases) sales would continue to grow and could co-exist nicely.

Finally, the analysis offered its recommendations: Construct a 217,500 square foot enclosed building on "a 20-acre site in suburban Los Angeles." An artist's conception of the new facility and a proposed, detailed layout were included. The building would include all the amenities of skylights, automatic doors, wide door openings, tall clearances, large vendor units with sinks, 37 coolers totaling 280,000 cubic feet of refrigerated space, a central refrigeration system, an auxiliary cooler, proper insulation, robust heating and air conditioning system, docking and parking facilities with a central court for parking, overhead protection canopy, and heavy-duty paving to withstand truck use.

There is little doubt that the USDA study contributed to public reports of a pending move. The Los Angeles City Council discussed the issue at its January 10, 1971 meeting. Occasionally, stories appeared in the business pages of the *Los Angeles Times*, telling the latest news about the reported move. Locations said to be under the magnifying glass of Market officials included Carson, Pacoima, Santa Fe Springs and other areas close to freeway networks and rail routes. The City of Industry was also said to be under consideration; and the city of Bell hoped to develop a wholesale center that would force the closure of the downtown flower markets. [11] The nearby wholesale produce market was often included in the package reported by the media to be about to move out of the central district, as indeed, its leaders considered such a move as well.

Mayor Tom Bradley made an early morning visit to the Flower Market in 1976 to show his support of keeping the two markets right where they were. During his visit, he signed two consultant contracts totaling $120,700, aimed at developing plans for renovation. Revitalization, the alternative to relocation, was seen as the solution for both the markets and the city.

In their separate board meetings, directors of both markets discussed the research findings and the far-reaching implications of following the USDA's recommendations. Naomi Hirahara, in *A Scent of Flowers*, describes the reaction of the Southern California Flower Market directors:

> "The consensus of the Japanese Americans was to remain in downtown Los Angeles. Their fathers and grandfathers had created the market, and besides, moving further east would add travel time for those (growers) who had relocated to Oxnard and Carpinteria."

Councilman Gilbert Lindsay, at the lectern, recognizes the achievements of the Flower District at a Los Angeles city council meeting at City Hall. Standing are, back row, from left: Councilman Art Snyder, Darlene Kuba, Johnny Mellano, Frank Kuwahara and Ken Kamikawa. *The Frank Kuwahara collection.*

On the other hand, the pull to the suburbs was very strong for the directors of the American Florists' Exchange, who seriously considered a move to the City of Commerce. There, a former Goodyear plant (today's Citadel, an outlet shopping center) on 37 acres with one million square feet of building space, could have been purchased for $3 million – a large sum in the 1970s, but small in terms of its enormous potential and its value in today's real estate market. Johnny Mellano, manager of the American Florists' Exchange, saw possibilities for the center to include, in addition to a flower market, a garden center and bank.

In the end, with the Southern California Flower Market not willing to make the move to another location, the American Florists' Exchange decided to stay on Wall Street. Tenants, retailers, suppliers and wholesalers were best served if the markets remained together.

Interestingly, the large city produce market, which served the supermarkets and retail industry, also nixed the relocation idea it had floated to its operators. The operators could not be convinced that such an investment would pay off. Instead, it created a public-private partnership to build today's thriving Los Angeles Wholesale Produce Market.

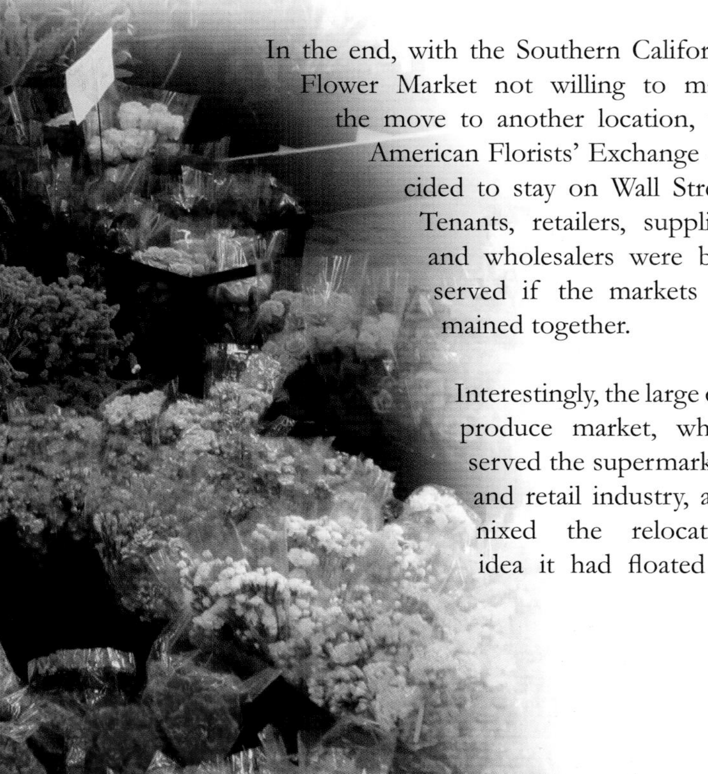

JDP Photography

After making the decision to remain in the wholesale district, both flower markets began extensive renovation projects, taking advantage of up to $3 million in public funds available as a low-interest loan. Leaders formed a nonprofit organization in order to qualify for the construction money.

In 1977, a group representing both markets created the nonprofit Los Angeles Wholesale Flower Market Development Corporation, which would exist into the 1980s. Its directors were Johnny Mellano of Mellano & Company, Bert Johnson of the American Florists' Exchange board of directors, Ken Kamikawa, president of the Southern California Flower Growers, Art Dettweiler of United Wholesale Florists and Frank Kuwahara, president of the board and chairman of the Mayor's Flower Market Advisory Committee. Legal counsel was George Catlin, the attorney for the American Florists' Exchange.

Over the next couple of years, the development group made its plans for redevelopment of facilities with the knowledge that keeping the two institutions together would continue to serve the overall flower district as it had for more than half a century.

The Southern California Flower Market was first to begin construction and broke ground on Monday, December 10, 1979. A public statement issued by SCFM president Tom Endow and general manager Frank Kuwahara said the planned construction, totaling $13.5 million, would preserve 7,000 jobs for the Central City. Market space would more than double, to 300,000 square feet.

The American Florists' Exchange would not be far behind, nor would the large-scale importing of flowers from South America.

[1] Fay, Sharon, *Los Angeles Times*, "Flower Mart Blossoms While Rest of the Southland Sleeps" (April 15, 1968)

[2] Rouleau, Art and Barbara, *Westways*, "Flower Merchants of Wall Street, Volume 57, Number 9 (1965), describe Mary Leggett, an attractive grandmother from Whittier who drove a refrigerated truck route for Mas Yoshida of Growers Wholesale Florist, covering a territory from Lynwood to Costa Mesa.

[3] An Analysis of Floral Wholesaling Facilities in Los Angeles, California, Marketing Research Report 1042, United States Department of Agriculture, Agricultural Research Service (1974)

[4] An Analysis of Floral Wholesaling Facilities in Los Angeles, California, Marketing Research Report 1042, United States Department of Agriculture, Agricultural Research Service (1974)

[5] Van Breems, Arlene, *Los Angeles Times*, "Market Open House Will Turn On Flower Power" (November 2, 1969)

[6] Rouleau, Art and Barbara, *Westways* "Flower Merchants of Wall Street," (September 1965)

[7] AIFD, a designation earned by qualifying under the rules and requirements set by the American Institute of Floral Designers

[8] Fay, Sharon, *Los Angeles Times*, "Flower Mart Blossoms While Rest of the Southland Sleeps" (April 15, 1968)

[9] *Bloomin' News*, September 1964

[10] Proposition 13, or the "People's Initiative to Limit Property Taxation," was a June 1978 ballot initiative that amended the State of California constitution and capped real estate taxes. It reduced property taxes in California by 57 percent (average) and required a two-thirds majority vote in both legislative houses for future state tax increases or revenue collected. It received a great deal of publicity throughout the country.

[11] *Los Angeles Times,* "Why Aid the Hijacking of an Industry?" (November 26, 1976)

Promotional photo for an upcoming Open House at the Flower Market, circa 1965. *Bob Berry collection.*

Wordpix

Timeline: 1980-1999

1980	Latinos begin to participate in the Flower Market as growers, wholesalers. Mt. Saint Helens erupts, sending ash into the atmosphere for hundreds of miles. The first all-news television channel (CNN) debuts.
1981	Phase I of major reconstruction of the Southern California Flower Market is completed. The first space shuttle, Challenger, is launched. The 52 American hostages held by students in Iran are released after 444 days in captivity.
1982	Fred Poland starts Carik Services with Carleen Poland.
1984	The Summer Olympics are held in Los Angeles.
1986	The space shuttle Challenger explodes just after take-off. The world's worst nuclear disaster occurs in Chernobyl, USSR. Haley's Comet is visible in the night sky, appearing only every 76 years.
1987	The nation's budget reaches the trillion dollar mark. On October 19, 1987, the Dow Jones Industrial Average plunges 508.32 points, losing 22.6 percent of its total value.
1988	Redbook Florist Services starts a wire service called TransAmerica Floral, for supermarket floral shops.
1989	On June 3, student protests in Beijing's Tienanmen Square leave thousands dead. The Berlin Wall falls on November 9.
1990	Iraq invades Kuwait; the U.S. sends troops to defend Saudi Arabia. The Hubble space telescope is launched.
1991	The Andean Trade Preferences Act becomes effective, introducing jobs in exchange for stricter drug policies in Colombia, Ecuador, Peru and Bolivia.
1993	Terrorists bomb a portion of a World Trade Center tower in New York City.
1995	Oklahoma City's federal building destroyed by a bomb made by homegrown terrorists.
1996	Downtown Los Angeles property owners launch a property-based business improvement program called the Fashion District Business Improvement District, including the Flower District within its 90 blocks. Director Kent Smith calls it the "creative heart of the city."
1997	Redbook Florist Services acquired by Teleflora, making Teleflora the world's largest floral wire service. The Los Angeles Flower Market's LA Flower Market Newsletter changes its name, bringing back the popular name of the former publication *The Bloomin' News*. The world mourns the tragic death of Princess Diana.
1998	The fledgling online auction called eBay goes public.
1999	The U.S. Women's Soccer Team wins the World Cup, captivating the hearts of the nation accustomed to seeing the laurels go to male soccer players.

JDP Photography

The New World of Flowers (1980-1999)

"Small, well-placed groups of traditional florists, freelance floral designers, and traditional wholesale florists shape taste, push innovation, and communicate changing consumer culture."

— Catherine Ziegler, *Favored Flowers: Culture and Economy in a Global System* [1]

It was a glorious New Year's Day! For months, flower farmers from Washington, Oregon and California to as far away as South America and Holland had worked vast fields of flowers for the harvest to be enjoyed by millions on January 1, 1980.

The freshest roses, chrysanthemums, gladiolas, tulips, strawflowers, orchids, irises, carnations and irises arrived just days before Christmas, allowing the farmers to finally relax and enjoy the holidays. Then, hundreds of volunteers went to work during "Dec" week – the days between Christmas and New Year's Eve - decorating skeletal parade floats with the beautiful blooms from around the world.

On New Year's Day, the Tournament of Roses parade becomes THE show of flowers, with its many fresh blooms displayed in living color everywhere. Millions of television viewers around the world and thousands who line the parade route in Pasadena see a flower show like no other. It is a show of flowers that for decades represented the flower growers of California.

Floral industry leaders hoped that California's beautiful floral vistas, the thousands of acres of flowers, would not disappear into memory, but it was a long shot. The flower growing segment that had represented such a substantial portion of the state's economy was fast giving way to imports and changing market trends as the smaller farmers gave up their farms. Still, a few flower farming operations could be seen in dense agricultural areas of the state.

Travel down Interstate 5 to Carlsbad in North San Diego County in the spring of the year. Voila! There's another testament to Southern California's floral industry: Spectacular floral vistas blanketing the gently sloping hillside facing the ocean's cool afternoon breezes. This magical place, The Flower Fields®, is something of a living proof that flower growing enjoys a natural and ideal growing environment in the coastal, semi-arid but irrigated rolling hillsides of the state.

As the new millennium drew closer, it was becoming clear that staying viable in the flower production business would require a shifting of the business plan.

Market Expansion

No business can succeed unless it embraces change. The American Florists' Exchange board of directors saw that truth clearly as it moved forward to create more space and improvements for its tenants.

In the early- and mid-1980s, the American Florists' Exchange enlarged and renovated its facilities, improving its ability to serve tenants and customers. The Southern California Flower Market's dedication in 1981 of a new building across the street, which expanded its market space to more than 300,000 square feet, complemented the AFE's expansion, transforming the district into a powerful center for floral commerce.

The main Los Angeles Flower Market building at 754 Wall Street became the focus of revitalization in the early 1980s. Counters, tables and shelves were repaired and replaced, in many cases, transforming 35-year-old display and work spaces. Walls, coolers and counters were painted. The $185,000 renovation of more than 10,000 square feet also included adding refrigeration, a module counter with a sheet metal top, fluorescent lighting, fire sprinklers, three- and four-inch drain feeders, a passageway between the Market and the Mellano building, a roll-up door along the main entrance on Wall Street and the construction of a large doorway between the Market and 766 Wall Street, which required relocating the stairway used to access the Southern California Floral Association's offices.

An upgrade of the property at 737 San Julian was completed as well, at a cost of $96,000.

In the mid-1980s, Mrs. Gebhard Prechtl and Paul Ecke Sr. sold the building they owned at the northeast corner of Eighth and Wall streets, occupied by Biaggi Evergreens, to the American Florists' Exchange.

On the north side of the Prechtl-Ecke building sat another building, this one occupied by Mellano & Company, Times Wholesale and Biaggi Evergreen's second location. Benifel Flowers occupied a tiny little building adjacent to this wholesalers' facility. On the north side of these was a parking lot with elevator access on its north wall to the second floor of the Flower Market.

Immediately after its purchase, the Exchange tore down the Prechtl-Ecke building and the wholesalers' and Benifel Flowers' buildings. It constructed a new building which became the home for Mellano & Company. Biaggi consolidated its operations into the former Mellano building. RDP Floral found a home in Biaggi's former location at Eighth and Wall.

Also during this period, the American Florists' Exchange purchased Wall Street property out of probate owned by Harold Lloyd.

A rehabilitation of buildings at 756 Wall Street and 728-738 Wall Street, the construction of a two-story building at 778 Wall Street and all the modernization and improvements in the Market building at 754 Wall Street were estimated to have cost the American Florists' Exchange just under $1 million.

The building of two stories at 778 Wall Street began upon the AFE's receiving a commitment from Art Dettweiler of United Wholesale that he would rent the lower floor; and the AFE considered Paul Ecke Jr's suggestion to add a second floor and lease space for a delicatessen in the building.

From left, Frank Blankenship, Bert Johnson, Johnny Mellano, George Catlin (attorney) and Paul Ecke Sr., mid-1980s directors of the American Florists' Exchange.

These improvements and additions, along with the new building constructed in the 1970s, with its 60,000 square feet on each of three levels to the north of the main Flower Market sales building, dramatically increased the ability of the AFE to serve its customers.

California's infamous earthquake of October 1, 1987, centered in the Whittier Narrows east of Los Angeles, took its toll on some of the older buildings on Wall Street. Most damage was minor, however, damage to the 750 Wall Street building, home to the B.W. Hall Company, was sufficient to require its rebuilding. The new facility was sold to Certified Florist Supplies.

During the time when the American Florists' Exchange made all these financial commitments, it also approved the payment of up to $4,000 to help pay remaining medical expenses for its faithful former manager Frank G. Vescio, who died in 1981. Vescio's position was filled by his son, Frank W. ("Wink") Vescio, and soon after that by Johnny Mellano, of Mellano & Company.

MARKET REPORT
SOUTHERN CALIFORNIA FLORAL ASSOCIATION
758 Wall Street, Los Angeles, California 90014
(213) 627-1201

PRICES & QUOTATIONS ARE FOR THE
DATE . of April 3, 1981
THIS ISSUE OF THE MARKET REPORT MAILED - April 3, 1981
TRADING ... GOOD

FLOWER
TODAY'S PRICES & QUOTATIONS

ALSTROEMERIA: S, eq, $4.50-$6.50 bun.
ANEMONES: fs, fq, 10¢-20¢
ANTHURIUMS: fs, fq, $4.50-$18.00 doz.
BIRD OF PARADISE: fs, gq, $4.00-$5.00 bun.
CALENDULA: gs, fq, $2.50-$3.50 Bdl.
CANDYTUFT: fs, gq, $2.50-$4.00 Bdl.
CARNATIONS:
SELECT: gs, eq, 16¢-20¢ each
STANDARD: gs, gq, 14¢-16¢ each
SHORT: gs, gq, 10¢-14¢ each
SPLITS: gs, gq, 6¢-10¢ each
ELEGANCE: gs, eq, $2.50-$3.50 bun.
CHRYSANTHEMUMS: BIG MUMS:
(Hothouse) gs, eq, $6.00-$8.00 Metric
DISBUDS: fs, gq, $4.00-$5.00
POMPONS: (Hothouse) gs,eq,$6.00-$8.00 Bdl.
SPIDER: gs, eq, $4.00-$5.50 Metric
CORNFLOWER: fs, gq, $3.00-$4.00 Bdl.
DAFFODILS: fs, gq, 10¢-12¢
DAISIES:BLACK EYE:fs,gq, $3.00-$3.50 Bdl.
GERBERA: gs, gq, $2.50-$3.00 bun.
MARGUERITES: gs, gq, $2.50-$3.00 Bdl.
MAJESTIC: fs, gq, $1.50-$2.00 Metric
KILLIAN: fs, fq, $1.50-$2.50 bun.
PAINTED: fs, gq, $3.00-$3.50 Bdl.
DELPHINIUM: S, gq, $4.00-$6.00 Bdl.
HYBRID: $3.50-$4.50 bunch of 5 stems
FORGET ME NOT: gs, gq, $3.50-$4.00 Bdl.
FREESIA: ss, gq, $2.50-$4.00 bun.
GARDENIA: ss, eq, $12.00-$18.00 doz.
MYSTERY: fs, gq, $18.00-$24.00 doz.
$1.50-$2.00 each
WORK GARDS: fs, $11.00-$14.00 flat 24
GINGER: RED: fs, eq, $12.00 doz.
GLADIOLUS: fs, gq, $3.50-$4.00 Metric
GYPSOPHILA:BRISTOL FAIRY:gs,gq,$2.00-$3.50

HEATHER:MELANTHERA: ss, fq, $2.50-$3.50 bun.
PERSOLUTA: gs, gq, $2.50-$3.00 bun.
IRIS: gs, gq, $2.50-$3.50 bun.
LEPTOSPERNUM: fs, fq, $2.50-$3.50 bun.
LILY: VALLEY: S, eq, $14.00 Metric
ENCHANTMENT: S, gq, $12.00-$18.00 bun.
LOVE LILY: fs, gq, $9.00-$10.00 bun of 5
CALLA LILIES: fs, gq, $4.50-$5.00 bun.
ORCHIDS: CATTLEYA:
(Color) fs, gq, $2.00-$3.50 each
(White) fs, gq, $2.50-$3.50 each
(Japhets) fs, gq, $1.25-$1.50 each
DENDROBIUM: gs, gq, $1.25-$1.50 each
CYMBIDIUM: gs, gq, $1.00-$1.50 each
(Mini Cym) fs, gq, $4.00-$6.00 per spray
PHALAENOPSIS: fs, eq, $1.00-$1.50 each
VANDA: gs, eq, $15.00-$18.00 per 100
PAPYRUS: fs, eq, $1.00 stem
POPPY: ICELAND: gs, gq, $3.00-$4.00 bun.
PROTEA: BANKSIA: $1.50-$3.00 per stem
PIN CUSHION: S, gq, $1.00 stem
OTHERS: fs, gq, 75¢-$1.25 per stem
RANUNCULUS: gs, fq, 10¢-16¢ each
ROSES: PREMIUM: fs, eq, $4.00-$12.00 bun.
BABY ROSES: gs, eq, $4.00-$6.00 bun.
SNAPDRAGON: fs, gq, $3.50-$5.00 bun.
STATICE: SEAFOAM: fs, fq, $1.25-$2.00 bun.
SINUATA: gs, fq, $2.50-$3.50 Bdl.
STEPHANOTIS: fs, eq, $5.00-$6.50 box of 25
STOCK: gs, gq, $3.50-$5.00 Bdl.
STRAWFLOWER: fs, gq, $3.00-$4.00 Bdl.
SWEET PEAS: S, gq, $8.00 doz. bun.
SWEET WILLIAM: gs, $4.50-$5.00 Bdl.
TULIPS: gs, gq, $1.50-$3.50 bun.
WAXFLOWER: S, gq, $2.50-$4.00 bun.
WILLOW: gs, gq, $4.50-$8.50 bun.

CODE-MARKET CONDITIONS:
P-Plentiful; gs-good supply; fs-fair supply; ss-short supply; S-Scarce; eq-excellent quality; gq-good quality; fq-fair quality; pq-poor quality; doz-dozen; bun-bunch; Bdl-Bundle; M-10's

AN EASTER MESSAGE TO ALL FLORISTS
Interested in upholding your flower shop image at Easter Time? If so, consider the lilies
of the field, see how they're grown---the double-stemmed ones! With our doubles, you'll be
one-up on the singles! Double-stemmed lilies in 6" pots with multiple blooms are featured
at SAN LORENZO this Easter. Our doubles will provide customer satisfaction, uphold the
flower shop image, provide easier and faster sales---all of which should add to your profit
margin. For doubles, call SAN LORENZO today. Singles in 6" pots, triples in 10" pots and
5-stemmers in 12" pots are also available.

Why is MICHAEL'S FLOWERS always sold out of lilies? Come see for yourself. We are now
offering nine different varieties of HYBRID ASIATIC LILIES - featuring PEACH BLUSH - a peach
colored lily with a pink tip; PICASSO - an orange lily with purple markings, reminiscent of
an artist's brush stroke; JULIANNA - a delicately formed creamy white Asiatic. Prices range
from $5.50, $10.00, $12.50, $13.50 & $14.00 - all 10 stem count. Your advance orders are
appreciated and are given priority. We also carry a full line of European cut flowers.
MICHAEL'S is constantly striving to find the most beautiful and exotic flowers to broaden
your design horizon. CALL: MICHAEL'S FLOWERS (213) 654-5774 - (Answering Service) or
(213) 623-1200 - Market.

OBITUARY

EARLY MORNING BULLETIN

OBITUARY

FRANK G. VESCIO, Market Manager of the Los Angeles Flower Market (American Florists Exchange), passed away Tuesday, March 31, 1981. He was 69 years of age.

Frank worked for Pacific Electric Railroad for several years prior to coming to the flower market in 1934. Frank worked as a guard in the early years, then in 1951 to the present time, he was the Market Manager. Frank had served the flower industry for the past forty-seven years.

Funeral services will be held Monday, April 6th at 1:00 p.m. at the Memorial Chapel at Rose Hills Memorial Park, 3900 S. Workman Mill Road, Whittier.

Frank is survived by his wife Jean L. Vescio, two sons - Verne and Frank W. Vescio, daughter Carol Stecker, nine grandchildren, two great grandchildren, brother John Vescio, sister Rose Farrier, three half-brothers - Fred, Joe and Jim Mancuso and two half-sisters Josephine Bruno and Ann Bower.

Frank Vescio was a member of the Benevolent Fund, Certificate No. 99, Assessment #274.

STOP BY TODAY--
AND HAVE SOME COFFEE & COOKIES WITH US AT
G M F L O R A L
AND TAKE A LOOK AT THE PROGRESS OF OUR NEW SUPPLY COMPANY UPSTAIRS
740 Maple Avenue .... (213) 489-7050

WHY IS MICHAEL'S FLOWERS ALWAYS SOLD OUT OF LILIES?
Come See For Yourself!!
We are now offering nine different varieties of HYBRID ASIATIC L I L I E S featuring:
PEACH BLUSH...a peach colored lily with a pink tip
PICASSO...an orange lily with purple markings reminiscent of an artist's brush stroke
JULIANNA...a delicately formed creamy white Asiatic lily
PRICES RANGE FROM $5.50, $10.00, $12.50, $13.50 & $14.00 - all 10 stem count
Your advance orders are appreciated and are given priority.
WE ALSO CARRY A FULL LINE OF EUROPEAN CUT FLOWERS. MICHAEL'S IS CONSTANTLY STRIVING TO FIND THE MOST BEAUTIFUL AND EXOTIC FLOWERS TO BROADEN YOUR DESIGN HORIZON.
CALL: MICHAEL'S FLOWERS - (213) 654-5774 (Answering Service)
or (213) 623-1200 (Market)

MEMBERSHIP

NEW MEMBER
RETAIL
5239. Secret Ray Flowers, 128 Old Topanga Road, Topanga 90290
(Megan W. Brand)
5238. The Petal Pushers, 503 Paseo Ganado, Anaheim Hills 92807
(Karen A. Grosso and Lizbeth G. DeSanctis)

CHANGE OF OWNERSHIP
60. Mission Hills Florist, 9146 Sepulveda Blvd., Sepulveda 91343
(Cliff & Ann Holcomb sold to William E. & J. Pylant)

MEMBERSHIP TERMINATED
238. Creations in Flowers, 1031 E. Elmwood, Burbank

Above: The weekly Southern California Floral Association Market Report displayed the prices of flowers (Sweet William, $4.50 to $5 Bdl; GS=good supply), along with advertising and announcements. It was available as a handout and was mailed to SCFA members.

Left: The Early Morning Bulletin offered Market-goers a bird's eye view of the day's specials and news. This March 1981 edition memorializes the Market's recently deceased manager, Frank G. Vescio. *Vescio collection.*

Growers' Challenges

The farms of flowers that blanketed the Los Angeles area landscape for decades were vanishing. In San Diego and Santa Barbara counties, where agricultural areas did not experience urbanization at the same accelerated level as Los Angeles and Orange counties, flowers still colored the landscape. There, small farms became big farms and corporations began to build flower-growing operations, preserving at least a portion of the floral displays and production. But small farmers were being edged out by foreign competition there just as in the more populated cities.

In Santa Barbara, the Groen Rose Company, with its greenhouses supplying many customers, analyzed the challenge presented by the foreign competition.

> "The only attempt to try to improve the situation would have been to reinvest in our nursery and grow roses hydroponically. The rose growing operations that exist today are all growing hydroponically with systems developed primarily in Holland." – Paul Nielsen, long-time manager of Groen Rose Company

At a time when about $47 million in imported roses were sold in the United States [2], Groen Rose Company's managers decided against the large reinvestment into their company, opting instead to lease their valuable greenhouse space to other growers.

Sylvia Foltz in the cooling room of the Groen Rose Company nursery in Santa Fe Springs.

As imported flowers became the norm, many wholesalers and growers doing business in the Los Angeles Flower Market shifted their thinking processes, tweaked their strategies and began to conduct their businesses differently. With hundreds of new colors and varieties now available, those determined to succeed embraced imports, cautiously at first, which allowed them to offer greater selections to their customers. Some growers realized profit by selling their land and moving elsewhere or reducing the size of their operations. Some became wholesalers of imports. Others, such as those growing carnations (supplied by Colombia to the tune of 40 percent [3] adapted by growing other crops specifically for niche markets.

Imports negatively impacted California growers in two other significant areas. First, offshore-grown flowers poured into the Eastern United States from Canada, the Netherlands, Israel, Colombia, Thailand and other countries. The buyers in the Eastern states were wholesalers and large retail florists who had previously bought from California growers and wholesalers.

Secondly, abundant, relatively cheap quantities of imports made it possible for mass markets to offer floral bouquets and potted flowering plants, creating a second major tier for retail sales, a tier that had not previously existed and which now drastically cut into the sales and profits of retail florists. Supermarkets sold pre-packaged and pre-designed bouquets and arrangements, making them ever so easy for consumers to grab while they shopped for groceries. Daily or weekly specials bundled several of these arrangements into a discounted price, making them even more attractive.

The bundling and pre-made bouquets were financed by some of the largest supermarket chains, discount stores and retailers in history, and the trend to sell flowers in stores other than retail flower shops hit the florists hard. Sole proprietors and small florist shops were no match for the Sam's Clubs and Home Depots of the world. Many florists found it impossible to continue using traditional marketing strategies. Some turned to Internet promotions (also highly competitive), some consolidated into smaller spaces or merged with other shops, and many closed their doors.

Smart growers, on the other hand, found they could diversify to meet the needs of specialty

JDP Photography Collection

markets or establish customer relationships with the supermarkets and discount stores. Jerry Defterios, of Delta Floral Distributors in Los Angeles, and others like him operated large production facilities for the assembling of bouquets destined for the grocery stores of Southern California. Those bouquets contain the blooms of imports as well as California-grown flowers.

Robert Thornton, a large, diversified grower in North San Diego County, saw the importing of thousands of flowers to California this way:

> "In California, there's a time to grow something better and cheaper than anybody else. So whether it be Holland or Israel or Kenya, Colombia or Michigan, Washington or Florida – we can avoid trying to compete with people who can produce something cheaper than we can … "[4]

Many growers followed Thornton's philosophy by changing or adding to the crops they were used to producing. Where once they grew carnations, now they also grew larkspur or field roses, appealing to the specialty markets. These were the special events, the weddings and celebrations whose planners and designers continued to seek flowers with large blooms, flowers, greens and fillers with heightened texture, and flowers with large, luxurious or unusual blossoms or design lines and shapes. The events themselves called for customization with colors and products uniquely appropriate for the occasion or individual.

In his November 1988 *Bloomin' News* column, Southern California Floral Association Executive Vice President Michael A. Bradley commented on the foreign imports. He reported that he had just fielded calls from both the French and Italian trade offices. Each wanted to arrange tours of the Los Angeles Flower District for growers from their respective countries. He offered this viewpoint about the possible outcome of their tours:

> "I welcome these visits as it gives me the chance to see and hear what is being produced in other parts of our shrinking world. Imports have been rather controversial especially with our Floral Trade Council of domestic growers, but these products have found a place in our markets and will continue to thrive. As long as imports meet our legal requirements and clear customs, they will keep increasing the consumption of our products as well as the outlets which sell them."

Imports and supermarkets were not the only challenges for local growers, who faced higher prices, tight fuel supplies and a changing workforce. A number of factors contributed to the rising cost of conducting a flower-growing or wholesale business in California and across the country. Labor costs had escalated; compliance with increasing government regulations required huge amounts of paperwork for reporting; and farmers forced to comply with new environmental regulations were required to evaluate the pesticides they used and make changes, if necessary, on a broad scale.

Shortages of fuel in 1978, fallout from OPEC's sweeping changes, resulted in gasoline and heating oil shortages across the country, which led to higher fuel costs into the 1980s. A greenhouse grower could not turn down the heat to save money or he'd lose his crop. He did what most business owners do when their costs rise: He raised his prices.

The human factor entered into the decision of some farmers to quit the business, and that was the reluctance of their children to continue to work in the business. The

Survey Says …

When asked during a mid-1990s survey if they believed relocation of the Wall Street wholesale market facilities would benefit the floral industry as a whole, 54 percent of respondents* answered no, 20 percent thought it would be beneficial, and 26 percent were undecided. When asked if they believed relocating the wholesale markets to new facilities at another location would benefit their particular businesses, sixteen percent replied yes, 61 percent no, and 23 percent were undecided.

The survey was conducted by the United States Department of Agriculture's Agricultural Marketing Service, Transportation and Marketing Division, with results reported in 1997.

*Respondents included 345 retail florists in the first year and 262 retailers in the second year of the survey; 64 wholesalers and 118 flower growers.

small family farms, hit hard by rising costs of labor and fuel, employed their children to cut, disbud and package flowers and to drive them to Market and unload them. By the time they were adults, the children had effectively paid their dues in labor and many made the conscious decision to find work or study for other types of employment. In some cases, the decision was mutual. It was the parents who, seeing how challenging business had become and how hard it was to realize a profit, sent their kids to college to learn a profession. Whether the college-educated children later returned to the family business was up to them. Those who returned did so with greater awareness of how the world of business operated in a modern society. A few came back into the family business with degrees in agriculture, horticulture and business administration, helping to take the family business into the future.

Retail Florists Adapt to the Changing Supply Chain

Not only were more retail florists using the door-to-door delivery service offered by their favored wholesale companies, other floral wholesale depots were springing up here and there, in Carlsbad just north of San Diego, in Orange County and within the Los Angeles Flower District itself. In 1989, Jon Prechtl, general manager for Mellano & Company, estimated there were some three dozen satellite flower-distribution warehouses outside Los Angeles. [5] Florists now had numerous suppliers, many conveniently located or willing to deliver,

Left: Battista Castellano with his business partner and brother-in-law Michael Mellano Sr, at the Mellano farm in 1998.

Opposite: Workers harvest white pom poms at the Mellano farm at San Luis Rey (Oceanside) in the 1980s. *Mellano collection.*

and wholesalers were losing long-standing accounts to the wholesale markets of Orange County and the San Fernando Valley. [6]

Although many florist members of the Southern California Floral Association visited the downtown Market on occasion, they did not always purchase the large volumes of flowers they had in the past. They chose instead to purchase only those products that could not be delivered or for which better pricing was not available from another supplier; or those specialty blooms that only certain suppliers at the Market could offer. They planned their trips and spread their buying power around. Some, who found their supply needs handled adequately in other ways, or were deterred by traffic congestion or the declining neighborhood in the wholesale district, rarely if ever set foot inside the downtown Flower Market.

Florists discovered that raising prices for floral arrangements meant no one would buy them. Flower arrangements, bouquets and cut blooms were still a luxury item, purchased from personal, discretionary funds. Consumers, already feeling the pinch of inflation at the gas pump, in the supermarket and at the department store, many times chose not to buy flowers. On the other hand, they might buy flowers they saw at the supermarket, recognizing the convenience of finding flowers where they shopped for groceries.

Florists were assured only that they had the niche and special events markets wrapped tightly in their hands. The young bride planning a flower-ful wedding would consult a wedding or event planner, florist or floral designer, not a supermarket for her flowers. That occasion along with others including retirement parties, proms and large, catered affairs required a personal touch and the ability to design a themed look for the event. A unique or exotic cut flower or an unusual arrangement was reason to visit or call the local flower shop.

The Internet Becomes the Floral Net

The Internet, with its millions of highly-focused websites, soared in popularity in the mid-1990s, making flower purchases as easy as clicking a few buttons at any time of the day or night. Consumers dove into online buying without reservation, enjoying the luxury of shopping at their fingertips.

The irony of the information-at-your-fingertips worldwide web was that it created a sub-culture of Internet-based flower peddlers who never touched a flower or set foot in a flower shop. These were "order gatherers" in business by virtue of the fact that they created thousands of links and bogus "florist" websites that displayed when users searched for local florists. Search for "retail florist +Seattle" and most likely you'd see links to floral search engines that offered dozens of (paid-for) links to Internet-only sellers. Sales commissions stacked up nicely for the online flower sellers, sucking business away from established florists.

Meanwhile, in the traditional world of advertising, non-retail florists placed ads in local telephone books as if they operated real flower shops in the cities covered by those directories.

Deceptive listings wreaked havoc on the bottom lines of authentic retail florists across the country. Organizations like the Society of American Florists and state floral organizations lobbied for state legislation to make it illegal to deceive shoppers about the advertiser's physical location. Efforts to push legislation against deceptive listings continued into the new century.

On a positive note, thousands of retail and wholesale florists and growing floral companies published their own websites in the 1990s, establishing a lasting and professional presence on the information superhighway. With this technical advancement connecting people around the world, larger firms also developed web-based facilities that enabled fast, private communications between the company and its suppliers and customers.

Tenants in the Los Angeles Flower Market soon learned to order their weekly roses or chrysanthemums using email or an instant messaging (IM) system. Potential customers learned of their history, products and services through their strategically-written web pages. Many growers and wholesalers published email newsletters ("e-zines") regularly to stay in touch with their customers and colleagues. They discovered that instant information and feedback streamlined their business process and helped them communicate their orders, problems with received products and more, speedily.

Web-based technology expanded for business purposes from the basic website and email to web-based software programs that streamlined the logging and processing of consumer orders. Teleflora, FTD and other major wire services had such programs in place by the year 2000.

The Bloomin' News

Except for a brief period, *The Bloomin' News* has bloomed almost continuously since October 1949. During those historic years, it shared the stories of births and deaths, war and peace, recession, boom times, flowers and fun.

The Bloomin' News stole its way to its readers' hearts right from its first issue. A potpourri of stories told about blue ribbons won at the Fair, floral design classes at Pierce College, the Orange County Floral Association's masked ball, association election results, the upcoming Open House, Kaz Minami's becoming father to a new baby girl, Hal Holm's report on a pending tax bill, Martha Gallagher's Sur Este Christmas party and the obituaries of Bill Groen, Sam Kolovos, Hacco Franco and others.

You could read the sales stats for the Market or all California growers or learn how a florist sold pre-made arrangements with a vending machine. You saw photos of the Headdress Ball, of starlets Ann Francis, June Allyson and others, taken at the Market; and the latest hunting trip and golf tournament.

THE SO. CALIF. FLOWER MARKET NEWS

VOL. 2, NO. 4 — 753 WALL ST. LOS ANGELES, CALIF. — JUNE 30, 1934

EDITORIAL

THE FUTURE OF THE FLOWER BUSINESS

"The future of the flower business." "What will it be?" "Is the business going to pick up?" These are the questions asked every day and are the most serious problems confronting us, especially the junior group who are starting.

The business is one of refinement and quality and it should be treated as such. On the growing end, we have the over-production of the same flowers year after year. Until a few years ago, we had less flowers and finer quality on the market. The growers' overhead expenses were not as large, and the selling prices was much higher. Now we have a tendency to grow acres of certain varieties like the seed farms, without giving the marketing a thought. After such a crop is raised and is ready to market, we find inferior grades due to lack of care because of too large acreage. We also find that there is market for only a certain or limited amount of the crop. Since this limited demand is such that it requires select grades, we have a surplus.

A surplus of the culls or inferior grades, then, instead of selling at a second price, we find ourselves selling for anything to anybody. In the end, the select customers are having a hard time competing their quality at a fair price against the people to whom we sold the inferior grades, at a low price. Then gradually the quality customers will buy less of the quality goods, and we find ourselves "loaded" with flowers which, rather than throw away, we sell for any available price. Thus we are in the condition we are today. No demand for quality at prices—no more select customers—no more stable prices so that we may be able to make a slight margin of profit, instead of which we find we are working for nothing or paying for the "privilege" of growing the flowers.

"What is lacking?" "What can we do to remedy such cases?" The answer is co-operation. Co-operation is something that heretofore has been lacking and that is the main purpose of the Junior Floricultural Society. So let's strive to realize our aims. As the saying goes: "If you succeed, it is my success also."

CONGRATULATE

The Junior Floricultural Society is proud to have as its member and vice-president, James Goto who was chosen as one of the two representative university students of Southern California to the Pan-Pacific College Conference in Tokio.

The entire group extends to him congratulations on his ability and good fortune, and also wishes for happiness, success, and a Bon Voyage.

* * *

Mr. and Mrs. Ichino, their two eldest daughters, and some friends are motoring to Loma Linda on June 17th to attend the commencement exercise of the College of Medical Evangelists. Dr. Wilfred Y. Hanaoka will be the only Nipponese graduate this year.

The Big Shot

Since the "Dai Nisei" became prominent in the activities of the market socially, economically, and politically, there has been a group that always want to be the "big shots". That is, getting the glory without working for it and using the other fellow's ability. These people may be the so-called big shots temporarily, but as you all know, most of the niseis are thirty years or younger. Success very seldom comes before forty to fifty years of age, so in the meantime they will lose all their prestige.

In the study of this question of big shots, there have been articles written in the newspapers that it is the result of the petty jealousies of the majority. They hate to see others succeed. This is not so, according to the study of the so-called big shots. There seems to be in their minds a thought that he is better than the rest; especially if that certain person is a tiller of the soil.

The majority of the niseis are glad to see any others of the same group advance. But anybody with any feeling of pride will oppose if he is told that he is inferior. For example, if you were working under a foreman and you had a better system than the foreman, he would probably disregard your suggestions for a superior system. In fact it may upset him enough to ask for your resignation. But if you asked him about your own idea, then he will listen and think for himself that your ideas may be better.

So if the group who have advanced a step farther will remember there will be less ill feelings and it may be better for himself, since the second generations' vocation depends on the prestige of the niseis as a whole because the first generation will be active for only a few more years.

STALE BUT TRUE

Bill Zaima and T. Kobata seen enjoying the exclusive and expensive atmosphere of the Italian Village Cafe during Bill's last night in town. He is or was at his extensive alfalfa ranch in Antelope Valley near Rosamond.

Seen at the Tennis Picnic were: Mrs. Tomita's supreme achievement, Aijii, and S. Kobata of the Gardena Kobatas, gazing at the wahines.

Sammy Muto industriously selling pop at the dance pavilion.

Strange but only "hana-ya" boys were seen at the picnic, the girls must have stayed home to pick flowers.

The San Gabriel Valley Citizens League hop also drew its share of farmers, yeah, even Fred Muto was there.

Miss Virginia E. Zaima was the dream seen dancing at the Blue Triangle, Melody in Blue held at the Beverly Hills Women's Club.

Tuck Kobata and Yuriko Umekubo were the first of the ten lucky couples to receive free airplane rides at the Jaycee Air Prom which was held at the United Airport roof gardens in Burbank.

Fred Muto was lamped steering Miye Fujioka around the floor.

This hop witnessed the debut of Mrs. Muto's bo-chan Takio into the realm of dancing circles.

Jimmie's store seems to be the mecca of all loafers since he has installed a new davenport. Contributions of a radio, ash trays, cards, tables, and accessories will be most gratefully and graciously accepted.

I see by the papers that Jimmie Goto, newly elected president of the Japanese Trojan Club of S. C. is one of the students selected to attend the American-Japan Students Conference in Tokyo, July 19 to 26. Lucky fellow.

All credit for the success of the recent anniversary hop goes to Miss Florence Zaima, "Lady Dependable".

This early newsletter (June 30, 1934), produced by the Southern California Flower Market, was a forerunner to *The Bloomin' News.*

The gladiolus convention and the undertakers' convention were covered equally. National Flower Week and Sweetest Day got their limelight. You might also learn that a bowling league member felt "crushed" by co-bowlers' references to his suspenders. Get acquainted with the new Association president through his bio on Page One. Or enjoy the tongue-in-cheek quips of Frank Riggio, author of "Curly Says." It might be gossip or it might be news, but if you had an interest in any topic, it was covered in *The Bloomin' News.*

Beginnings
First Issue: October 1949 (4 pages)
Frequency: Monthly
Phone #: Trinity 1201
Publisher: Southern California Floral Association

Transitions
1960s: CSFA's "California Florist" is part of *The Bloomin' News*
1990s: Ceased publication
1996: L.A. Flower Market Newsletter introduced
Editor: Marcy Young
Artist: Michael Wheary
Publisher: American Florists' Exchange

The Bloomin' News Resumes
1997: L.A. Flower Market Newsletter renamed to *The Bloomin' News*
1997: Publisher: American Florists' Exchange
1999: Peggi Ridgway becomes editor
1999: Michael Wheary continues as artist
2004: BloominNews.com website introduced
2006: Email notification list started
2006: *The Bloomin' News* begins printing in full color

The first issue of *The Bloomin' News,* October 1949, introduced the newly elected president of the Southern California Floral Association, Ebbo Dekema.

THE Bloomin' NEWS

Vol. 1 - No. 1 — October, 1949

OFFICIAL PUBLICATION OF THE SOUTHERN CALIFORNIA FLORAL ASSOCIATION

DISCOUNT SCHEMES CONSIDERED UNDESIRABLE

Reports from Walter Potter, secretary of the Glendale Merchants Association, indicate that a "high officer in the student body at Glendale College is soliciting Glendale business firms for a so-called "National Campus Club."

In commenting on the movement, Potter says:

"This is one of those discount schemes whereby he gets students as members of the club and sucker merchants sign up to give all members a discount.

"These discount clubs have taken on almost epidemic form and everything should be done to stamp them out.

"Why is the dollar of a J.C student any better than the dollar of any other good customer?

"This same thing applies to police, teachers, mail men, and every other class which might seek preferment.

"And isn't a student official who places the welfare of his school second, for such a promotion, about in the same class as the 5 per centers we read about down at Washington.

"We doubt if any of our members would fall for this deal, anyway, but these discount clubs are so undesirable we felt we should speak."

In his Merchants Bulletin last week Potter reviewed the situation for the benefit of members and in conclusion offered this observation to all merchants: "If my dollar isn't just as good as a mail man's dollar, then I'm trading in the wrong store. Others feel the same way."

"WALL STREET WITICISM"

We have no quarrel with those who sell for less,
They should know what their stuff is worth!

ASSOCIATION PRESIDENT

Introducing Mr. Ebbo Dekema, President of your Association for the coming year. Ebbo was born on March 15, 1918 in Banjuvangi, Java, Netherlands East Indies, he is the youngest of four brothers. At the age of two, Ebbo with his family was taken on a two year world tour which ended at their home in Holland. Ebbo was educated in Holland 'til the age of ten, then the family moved to Canada where they lived for one and a half years, before coming to Los Angeles. Ebbo completed his education in elementary and Junior High School and was graduated from Los Angeles High. During his scholastic career, Ebbo competed in track, cross country and light weight football, earning letters in all three sports.

Then, as is customary with all young men, Ebbo fell in love with the Miss Mildred Rae Overpeck, a graduate of Hollywood High School, they were soon married and now have a fine family of two boys, Johnny 7 and Mike 4.

During his off market hours he indulges himself in the very fascinating hobbies of collecting stamps, imported porcelain plates and figurines.

(Continued on Page 3)

State Board of Equalization Suggests Establishing System

Retail members need purchase invoices for flowers purchased from growers and wholesalers, when their U.S. Income Tax, State and City Sales Tax returns are audited.

Most growers and wholesalers give invoices to florists who buy on open account, however, many retailers pay cash, and these dealers likewise need purchase invoices to prove their flower costs for tax audit purposes.

To assist our Retail Florist Members, your Association proposes that all purchasers, whether by cash, or on open account, be given an invoice. These can be either your own invoice form or on the padded numbered forms, in duplicate, which your Association has on hand and will be glad to furnish to you at cost. The duplicate copy can be retained for a bookkeeeping record, and when paid can be filed in the customer's folder to form a record of that customers total purchases.

So far as your Association knows, ours is the only industry where the retailers have no invoice record of merchandise purchased, and your Association as one of it's services to you, wants to counsel and assist you in setting up voluntarily an adequate but economical accounting system for our retail members, before some governmental agency cracks down on you and prescribes a compulsory accounting system, which probably would prove to be more costly, and much less suited to our industry's needs.

"SPOT LIGHT"

From our observation, it appears that our industry is to be "written up" nationally. Kay Campbell, on assignment from Collier's Magazine, has been doing considerable research on Wall Street. When last seen, Miss Campbell was in the company of Fred King, making a tour of the growing area of Torrance and Gardena.

Continued...

Aileen Murashima's *Bloomin' News*

In the 1960s and 1970s, Aileen Murashima, secretary of Walter Swartz, Southern California Floral Association manager and *Bloomin' News* publisher, played a major role in production of the newsletter each month. Aileen took dictation of Mr. Swartz's announcements, transcribed her shorthand into typewritten text and submitted his stories, along with articles from writers and columnists, to a local printer for typesetting. All the stories were hand-typed using typewriters. Writers who couldn't type dictated their stories to secretaries and stenographers, or they hand-wrote their material for Aileen to type.

Today, Aileen remembers fondly the regular advertisers and writers like Frank Riggio who wrote the "Curly Says" ads, Robert Taylor, a *The Bloomin' News* writer and columnist for 25 years, and others. Back in the day, she and her office colleagues, including Cynthia Fujikawa and Ted Ruth, proofread and marked their stories for the typesetter, proofed the printer's galleys, submitted revisions and pasted the stories onto layout boards which the printer then photographed and converted to plates which were run on the press for printing. An Addressograph machine was used to imprint recipients' addresses on the mailing sections.

Today, stories are written and laid out using personal computers. California-based editor Peggi Ridgway works by email with artist Michael Wheary, based 3,000 miles away in Florida, who applies the automated styling made possible by a computer to Ridgway's text. The artist views his layout on his computer monitor. After the proofing and revisions are done, he uploads the electronic file directly to the printer's website. The printer's automated system informs Ridgway when the job moves from set-up to press to finishing/binding and shipping. Although research and editorial can require months, layout and printing are accomplished in less than two weeks. Dictation, transcribing, typesetting by outside services and the cutting and pasting of stories onto layout boards are but memories.

Aileen Murashima would really enjoy working with today's *Bloomin' News*.

NOV/DEC 1993 — of the American Florists' Exchange, Ltd. — VOLUME 2 N

MARKET SHARING

Newsletter Resolutions 1994

All you wonderful readers helped shape our editorial policy for the New Year. Thanks to your enthusiastic response to our survey, we've sent out your "wish list" of suggested article topics to our contributors and columnists.

Here's a sampling of what you want to see discussed in our publication: current business topics, tips for running a small business, techniques for building sales and improving operational procedures, more information about how to preserve cut flowers and how to better handle them in the shop, ideas for non-traditional arrangement techniques, and general tips on design.

Aside from the strictly business topics, you also want to know more about the history of the industry in Southern California, and you're curious to learn more about the vendors in the market.

Writing what you want ... should certainly ke... next year! And w... granting your news... the January issue, ... (Please ...

Ten Things You Can Do NO... To Make This Holiday Season More Profitable

By Marie Ackerman, AIFD, PFCI
AFS Director of Education Projects

Christmas seems to come around more quickly every year. It seems as though we just finish one Christmas and it's time for the next one. Being prepared for the holidays is not only important for your business, it is critical for your peace of mind. Here are some tips to help you prepare for the holiday season and to increase profitability.

...their appearance into a more fe... holiday look. Leftover containers... also be used at non-holiday ti... Generic containers also give your... tomers the best value for their m... because they allow you to use n... materials in the arrangement for... selling price.

RECIPE YOUR IN-SHOP SPECIALS

Write or type the exact ingredients of each of your shop's featured arrangements on 4"x5" cards and laminate them. Give each designer one set to be used when creating the arrangements. Not only will this help you control your cost of goods sold, it standardizes the...

HAVE A HOLIDAY TRAINI... SESSION

Teach your employees about the c... specifics of holiday plants and gree... Show them how to handle corpor... customers and how to upsell. Ke... each session informal and fun. ... some of the training time to bra...

Page Ten — THE BLOOMIN' NEWS

GAELIC GREETER

This cute colleen, Nancy McNamara made sure that St. Patrick's Day passengers aboard Union Pacific's "City of Los Angeles", got a proper touch of Irish welcome today when she distributed dozens of gay green carnations to the Paddy's Day travelers on the streamliner.
The Ancient Order of Hibernians provided their Fair Ambassador, and the Southern California Floral Association sent their tokens of this "Great Day For The Irish" to the trainload of passengers arriving in Los Angeles on this Day of Wearin' of the Green.

HERE AND THERE IN THE POT PLANT GROWERS ASSOCIATION

By Paul Boggus

On Monday, March 27th we met at Kaz Minami's place in Gardena and saw his houses filled to the doors with Easter Lilies. From there we drove over to the Kobata Nurseries and saw thousands of Easter Lilies, Hydrangeas and Calceolarias. George and Joe Kobata were the official guides for the tour and believe me we needed guides to get us through their place. Over a hundred thousand square feet of greenhouses and every inch filled with good clean plants, a sight well worth seeing, especially at Easter time.

A short walk from Georges and Joes took us to Tuck Kobata's Nursery and more Easter Lilies. Tuck, like all Lily growers, had a frown on his brow worrying about whether the cool weather would allow the lilies to pop at the right time.

A short business meeting was held in Tuck's garage, during which we discussed plans for getting more plants on Television shows. The meeting was continually interrupted by a whispering campaign between Tuck and his children and ending with Tuck digging into his wallet, which led him...

to observe that time an... are not in favor of a ... said that the wife and ... and receiving complet... long before the Lilies ... was just a little rough.

Around eight we al... the Colony Club to pi... rib that is) and Jim Bos... lost his appetite when ... started.

Due to an error in las... we failed to list Kaz M... our members. Kaz ... plants, such as Easter ... lett Roses, Cyclamen ... Sorry we missed you

Bob Boddy and Da... were two busy boys ... greeting their many ... Nursery business at ... Descanso Gardens.

Fellows please use ... or Vice President whe... Bostwick and Miles K... have worked hard an... Adams Nurseries and ... this honor and succe... Vice President in cha... Miles will be Vice Pr... of production.

Bill Cole of Pepper... just returned from ... where he called on ... that he has there. B... recently arrived fro... turned with him and ... Bill at his San Fernan...

Miles Kellum took ... plane trip to the So... cently. He visited N... Texas, New Orlean... Florida and Pittsburg...

Has anyone seen ... Weidner of Buena ... since his wedding d...

See you next mor...

Mother'... POTTED ... Star Nurse... 749 Wal... TUcker

Top left: Sometime in the early 1990s, after several years of *Bloomin' News* inactivity, the American Florists' Exchange introduced *The Los Angeles Flower Market* newsletter.
Above: An early story page.

Above: "Pictured above are Mr. and Mrs. George Johnson with their equipment that is used to haul flowers from San Diego County to the Los Angeles market. This is in keeping with the Association campaign number X24Q9Z3, that is, anyone that will put 'Say it with Flowers' on the side of their trucks we will be most happy to give congratulations and best wishes of success." -- From *The Bloomin' News*, January 1951.

Below: A 1999 holiday edition featuring retailer Suzann's Flowers and grower Paul Ecke Ranch.

Bloomin' News

A Bi-Monthly Publication of the Los Angeles Flower Market of the American Florists Exchange, Ltd.

November December 1999

Volume 8 ✦ Number 6

in this Issue

Editor Update 3

Los Angeles Flower District Badge Program 11 & 12

Suzann's Flowers: Three Generations Nurture The Beauty of Flowers

By Peggi Ridgway

Some years after playing in her parents' flower fields and working in their shop, Alma Mathis made a very natural transition into her own retail floral business. To hear her speak about her childhood is to know with certainty that those years among the gladiolus and pompoms trained her well. "I've known the flower business all my life," she says. "As a child, I made glamillias in the flower fields." Today her business includes Suzann's Flowers in Ontario and shops in Pomona, Upland

Continued on page 10 →

Suzanne's Flowers proprietor, Alma Mathis

Poinsettia Pride Began With Paul Ecke

developing the first poinsettia cultivar that could be grown as an indoor plant.

Today, more than 80% of all flowering poinsetties in the world get their start at Paul Ecke Ranch in Encinitas, CA. The current ...uction facilities span more

Bimonthly Newsletter
Volume 8, #6 • Nov./Dec. 1999

This newsletter is published every other month by The Los Angeles Flower Market of The American Florists' Exchange, Ltd. 754 Wall Street, Los Angeles, CA 90014

...ditor/Advertising Coordinator
Peggi Ridgway
714-228-1101

Printing/Design
Pinnacle Design, Santa Fe Springs

BLOOMIN' NEWS

...i-Monthly Publication of The Los Angeles Flower Market of the American Florists Exchange, Ltd.

May – June 2007 • Volume 16 – Number 3

Vases by Robert: Following the Dream

Robert and Alice Khosravian at their Vases by Robert stall at the Market.

Robert and Alice Khosravian's path to ownership of two retail/wholesale shops and a presence on the Internet represents the personal journey of many of the immigrant families of years gone by, who helped to found and build the Los Angeles Flower Market.

Starting with minimal inventory and little or no financial resources, with nothing but brains, determination and the motivation to press forward, early twentieth century immigrants, endowed with vision, built the foundation, even the very backbone of today's floral industry.

Robert and Alice are a modern-day immigrant success story and they inspire us. Back home in Iran, Robert worked in the screen-printing industry with his uncle, making a modest living. With the American Dream lingering in his heart, Robert decided to leave his country and set out to America. As Iranian-born Armenians, for two years, he and his wife dealt with the maze of administrative issues and paperwork required to obtain visas to leave their country and come to the U.S. Finally, they were able to immigrate to Spain, where another nine months transpired before they could move to the United States. Their arrival in the U.S. in 1988 signaled the start of their dream, which was highlighted with the desire for a good life for them and their children, Laranda and Chris.

Continued on page 19

...hat's INSIDE

The May/June 2007 issue (now in full color) featured AFE tenants Robert and Alice Khosravian, of the Market's Vases by Robert, in its cover story.

Immigration Labor Complexities

California's legacy is its ethnic diversity, evidenced by the fact that the workforce responsible for creating this nation-sized state was built by immigrants from around the globe. Many of the immigrants who landed in San Francisco, either during the Gold Rush or later, migrated south to Los Angeles. From the Gold Rush transplants and late 1800s visitors from the other states to the refugees from war-torn countries in the teens and 1920s, from the Germans, Greeks and Sephardic Jews to the Italians, Dutch and Japanese, they constructed the framework for California's thriving economy.

So it is bittersweet, this battle on the political front that pits Americans against each other on the subject of whether to grant public welfare, insurance benefits, educational opportunities, drivers' licenses and employment to "undocumented aliens" or to "send them all home." Clearly, it was not a battle about legally authorized immigrants but one about those who crossed the border, specifically the United States-Mexico border, without legal documentation. The heated discussion continued into the twenty-first century.

Another concern was security, tightened after the bombing of the World Trade Center in New York in 1993 and again after the domestic terrorist bombing of the Alfred P. Murrah Federal Building in Oklahoma City, Oklahoma in April 1995. But the terrorist attacks against the United States on Tuesday, September 11, 2001 [7], drove law enforcement and legislators to focus even more directly upon illegal immigration. Heightened awareness and high security levels became the practice at most public places, especially the US borders.

(The U.S. Customs and Border Protection agency reported that, in 2004, 262 million people attempted entry into the United States through 317 ports of entry; 600,000 were deemed inadmissible under current laws. Of that number, 399 travelers were apprehended for terrorism or national security concerns and 19,740 were criminal aliens.)

These concerns meant farmers and employers in the service industry would regularly be challenged to prove that their employees were fully documented and authorized to work in the United States. The legal status of the employees became hard to prove as copy experts, for a fee, created false drivers' licenses and birth certificates for the illegal immigrants. The employer had no way to verify the authenticity of the documents.

On the job and somehow getting word of the pending arrival of an INS inspector, field workers disappeared quickly from their work areas. Said one grower/employer: "You looked out upon the field where only minutes earlier you could see the workers picking flowers, and suddenly there was no one in sight." Even those who had been hired based on their false documents had scattered.

The effectiveness of the Braceros program [8], discontinued in 1964, had diminished after World War II when the federal government intentionally decreased the amount of imported Mexican labor so returning veterans could have those jobs. Since its end, illegal crossings had skyrocketed. Immigration would continue to be a hot topic.

Above: Charley Hum, right, with entertainer Lawrence Welk in 1958. Opposite: Paul Ecke Sr., left, and Edgar Engert, Ecke Ranch operations manager, load poinsettias to be trucked to the Los Angeles Flower Market, 1980s.

The Fashion District BID

In 1996, embracing a goal to turn a run-down, unsavory neighborhood into a vibrant, business-friendly and safe commercial and residential area, the Los Angeles Fashion District Business Improvement District was created. Its ensuing success led to consecutive five-year renewals and the expansion of its original boundaries to its current 90 city blocks. It reaches from the I-10 freeway north to Seventh Street and from Spring and Main streets east to San Pedro Street, encompassing the Flower District.

As part of the Fashion District, the Los Angles Flower District has enjoyed the benefits of the BID's improvements. In its first five years, crime in the area decreased 50 percent and more than $500 million was spent on development in the area. The security staff, or Safe Team, can be seen frequently, riding their bicycles through the area. Volunteer property assessments were replaced with state-legislated assessments. Signage throughout the area identifies the Fashion District.

The successful and highly visible Los Angeles Fashion District's BID program became a national model. It encouraged the renovation of old buildings and construction of new buildings as residential units, bringing thousands of new residents to the area.

The Market Opens to the Public

From the 1930s through the 1970s, the Los Angeles Flower Market had overwhelmingly dominated the wholesale floral trade in the metropolitan area. With that position changing so dramatically in the 1980s and 1990s, the Market found itself in dramatic transition.

Times were tough. Costs were high, budgets were stretched and the Market's retail florist customers were buying flowers elsewhere. In addition, the enormous influx of wide varieties of flowers from other countries created flower surpluses. In Fall 1996, Johnny Mellano and the AFE board, seeing the handwriting of the Market's future on the wall, took action that many Market tenants first reacted to with displeasure: They officially opened the Los Angeles Flower Market to the public.

The Los Angeles Flower Market of the American Florists' Exchange opened to the non-trade public with hours that began immediately after the wholesale/retail shoppers' hours, from 8 a.m. until noon on the busiest Market days, Monday, Wednesday and Friday; and from 6 a.m. until noon on Tuesday, Thursday and Saturday. The wholesale trade could shop from 2 to 8 a.m. on Market days and from 5 to 6 a.m. on the other, less busy three days.

In January 1997, after the public had shopped at the Market for a few months under the innovative badge program, the Tenants Advisory Board took several in-

formal surveys. Diego Ramirez, RDP Wholesale Flowers, who chaired the TAB, encouraged all tenants and retail customers to voice their concerns. The results of the surveys were that the "badge program" appeared to have strong support from the retail florists, many of whom had submitted positive comments. By September 1997, the badge program had more than 3,500 members. By December, some 80 to 90 percent of Flower District tenants supported the badge program.

"Going public" may not have pleased the tenants initially, but it attracted the crowds and has proved to be a business-building strategy which everyone now embraces. Today, one can shop the Market and encounter mothers and daughters, dads and sons and other do-it-yourself flower arrangers shopping for prom, weddings, Quinceanera and Christening flowers. Downtown residents of the trendy loft apartments and condos casually walk the aisles to find the latest, most intriguing color or exotic and unusual blooms, conversation topics for their coffee tables.

> "I lived in a loft two blocks from the Flower Market for two years and I loved to shop for flowers there every morning before I left for work," said one single man in his thirties.

In a city whose population had grown to more than three million by 1985, opening to the public was the key that unlocked and opened the door to a flood of new customers. Today, the Los Angeles Flower Market is a popular topic for regional media, especially during the winter holiday season and Valentine's Day, when thousands of shoppers converge in the 700 block of Wall Street to find their flowers.

The Mural on the Wall

During the 1997 year when the badge program was establishing itself as the public's ticket to beautiful, high quality flowers, the Flower District, that umbrella organization that operated the badge program, authorized the creation of a mural on the south wall along Eighth Street. The mural can be seen today in the artistic banner across the top of the District's website at www.LAFlowerDistrict.com, where characters painted into the artwork have been animated.

The Florists Delivery Service

Florist Bob Garren praises the creation of the cooperative Florists Delivery Service, born of necessity in 1981 to help florists save money on fuel expense and get their orders delivered across the freeway traffic jams with ease. As population and traffic increased and fuel prices surged, the "co-op" became a resounding success.

With a central meeting place in the fenced parking lot on San Julian Street, the co-op members, who numbered only a handful in the beginning, met to exchange their orders. Garren, of Flowers by Bob Garren in Huntington Park, was elected by the members in 1986 to manage the small but effective group. He and his assistant made sure that the number of arrangements brought into the lot matched those going out and that every one carried a delivery slip. Participating florists agreed to delivery by 4:30 p.m. to businesses and by 5:00 p.m. to residences. At the time, they paid $4 for each delivery performed and they were paid $2 for each delivery they made, with $2 deposited to the co-op's expense fund. Funds not used during the year were distributed to the members at their annual business meeting.

This nonprofit corporation licensed by the state of California provided a win-win arrangement for all its participating member florists as well as their customers. Florists reduced their delivery costs and the time it took to make deliveries. Their customers got timely delivery.

Garren, in a 2003 *Bloomin' News* article, was quick to praise the cooperative spirit of the drivers. "They take care of the flowers as if they were put together by their own shop."

The Florists Delivery Service started in 1981 still delivers flowers today.

Learning Floral Design

In the early 1980s, by arrangement with the Advisory Committee of the Los Angeles Flower District, Ray Tucker began teaching floral design at the Market. The Southern California Floral Association Design School held its classes on the second floor of the American Florists' Exchange.

The SCFA had sponsored floral design classes at local schools, but this time, it offered them downtown to the dozens of aspiring designers and florists who just needed a bit of a refresher. The classes were well attended and eventually they moved to a larger classroom on the second floor of the Southern California Flower Market.

Students had good instruction from Tucker, who also taught at Mount San Antonio College. He was an enthusiastic leader who inspired his class to do well.

Both flower markets actively supported the school, and Tucker served on the Advisory Committee along with John Rossi and Bob White, executive secretary.

In 1987, however, responding to changing demographics and needs, the Association closed the school. In 1988, Tucker started his own school at the Flower Market, called the Los Angeles Floral Career Center, which he ran until leaving for full-time design work with a local mortuary. Students sought out the Southern California School of Floral Design run by Phil Rulloda in Anaheim, a school operated by Elva May McLeod and several other floral design schools, community colleges and Regional Occupation Centers.

Flower Auctions of the '80s

The first domestic flower auction in the United States was started by the co-op of growers in San Diego County, the San Diego Flower & Plant Association. The co-op, started in 1980 by Encinitas carnation grower Phil Cancellier with early members Dave Pruitt, Anita and Bill Buerger, Spero Yianilos and Beulah and Pat Neal, launched in an effort to share the costs of marketing to increase consumer sales.

The co-op had a difficult time recruiting members, but it moved forward with plans to establish a flower auction. Early leaders, including Buerger and Pruitt, had seen firsthand the smooth-running auction at Aalsmeer, the Netherlands, and believed they could build a low-overhead, high-volume similar-type auction for San Diego County growers.

Finally, the San Diego County Flower and Plant Auction began in Fall 1982, the first innovation in floriculture marketing in the U.S. since the arrival of air freight in the 1940s. The auction, which moved to Carlsbad in 1985, was watched with interest by everyone in the industry. Some observers did not feel it made much impact, while others felt that auction-goers also frequented the stalls of tenants in the Carlsbad Floral Trade Center, thereby increasing business overall.

Mellano & Company, a San Diego County grower which participated in the auction at Carlsbad, made plans to develop its own auction on Wall Street. Its principals, too, had visited the grand-scale, highly-polished auction at Aalsmeer. So Mellano opened its privately-held, Wall Street-based Los Angeles Flower and Plant Auction on September 28, 1987.

The all-electronic system featured a descending clock auction. Information about the flowers and greens was displayed electronically as the lots of flowers traveled across the auction floor. Bidding began at a high number, and pre-qualified customers pushed a button to lower the bid or stop the clock to signify their desire to purchase the product.

Although a number of wholesalers in the Wall Street complex sold products through the private auction, many Market occupants did not endorse the concept. They saw it as negatively impacting their sales by attracting would-be business away from them, pushing prices lower and giving an unfair advantage to auction wholesale participants.

Auctions, which attract the larger retailer buyers, can represent "an efficient means of fulfilling the wholesaling function," said a 1997 USDA report which analyzed the Los Angeles Flower Markets. The report recommended education as a means to involving more retailers and wholesalers in the new concept.

Neither the San Diego County auction nor the Los Angeles-based Mellano auction survived. In 2007, the only clock auctions remaining in the North American floral industry were located in Canada.

Transitioning into the 1990s

In 1988, the Southern California Floral Association once again promoted the idea of moving the flower markets out of the inner city to a more easily accessible location where a state-of-the-art trade center could be built. SCFA Executive Vice President Michael Bradley, along with other Market leaders, strongly supported the move, or at least a study of its feasibility. A number of tenants believed their businesses were growing in spite of problems in the current location, however, and said they would not move.

"We are here to stay," was how Mas Yoshida, owner of GM Floral Company, expressed the feeling of many Southern California Flower Market tenants whose families had started their businesses there. And with that, the hope for moving the markets was tabled for another time and perhaps another generation.

The "Los Angeles Flower District" became the name that described the two markets, their tenants and merchants, badge members and the many auxiliary florists and wholesale storefront shops that had sprung up in the surrounding city blocks.

In the early 1990s, the Southern California Floral Association merged with the California State Floral Association. The SCFA's office space, on the second level of the Los Angeles Flower Market, became that of the Los Angeles Flower District badge program. In the first days of his employment as manager of the District's badge program in 1995, Frank Reyes recalls:

> "A lot of old-timers dropped by, and they asked if the Southern California Floral Association was back. I had to tell them it was now called the Los Angeles Flower District."

Top: John Noonan, background center, assists customers with gladiola purchases at the Noonan Wholesale Florist stall in the Los Angeles Flower Market, 1993.

Center: FTD president Charley Hum, right, presents flowers to First Lady Lady Bird Johnson in the White House Rose Garden, 1965. Also present are FTD executive secretary John Bodette, second from left, and FTD vice president Al Wilhelmey. FTD's Roger Passmore stands behind Charley Hum and the First Lady.

Above: Bob Berry designed the flowers for the equestrian events at Santa Anita Park during the Olympic games held in Los Angeles in summer 1984.

In 1997, American Florists' Exchange directors learned the results of a second AFE-commissioned U.S. Department of Agriculture study on the state of the downtown wholesale flower markets. The study pointed out the disadvantages of a "centralized" market in today's world of commerce. It also shared the candid comments and suggestions of 527 survey participants (345 retailers, 64 wholesalers and 118 growers). Although it offered few concrete recommendations for fixing things at the existing location, the authors of the report recommended that the wholesale flower markets establish regional markets in outlying areas:

> "Three or four strategically located regional markets … could provide retail florists with most of the economic benefits of a central wholesale market (numerous vendors competing on the basis of price, quality, and service), but without having to drive long distances, put up with congested freeways and otherwise waste valuable time." [9]

The report projected that regional markets would allow retail florists to charge lower prices and thereby increase sales. It suggested that domestic growers, facing increasing competition from foreign imports, shift production to "high-value specialty crops."

The data and recommendations from the USDA's report helped managers of the two flower markets to make their plans for the future.

In 1998, as the changing floral industry demanded a shift in the way floral markets conducted their business, the American Florists' Exchange made a tender offer to buy a majority of the growers' shares of the Southern California Flower Market, offering $6,000 per share. The Japanese American market, a faithful ally through all the shifts of the market during the 80 some years the two markets had shared the heart of the wholesale floral district, declined the offer.

The sands of time had shifted. Technology had advanced and imports, mass markets and urbanization had changed the lives of thousands of Californians in the floral industry. With such drama, the focus of the Market and the District changed as well.

Endnotes

[1] Ziegler, Catherine, *Favored Flowers: Culture and Economy in a Global System,* Duke University Press, 2007

[2] U.S. Census Bureau as quoted in "L.A. Flower Market Has Had Its Share of Thorns," by Jane Applegate, *Los Angeles Times*, February 13, 1989

[3] [4] Melvin, Robert, *Profiles in Flowers: The Story of San Diego County Floriculture,* Paul Ecke Ranch Press, 1989

[5] [6] Applegate, Jane, "L.A. Flower Market Has Had Its Share of Thorns," by Jane Applegate, *Los Angeles Times*, February 13, 1989

[7] Al Qaeda terrorists commandeered commercial passenger planes and rammed two of them into the World Trade Center towers in lower Manhattan, one into the Pentagon just outside Washington, DC, and one, in a failed flight to the White House, into a Pennsylvania field. Nearly 3,000 people died in the attacks.

[8] The Bracero ("strong-armed ones") Treaty was first enacted during World War II to bring agricultural workers into California by train during the short supply caused by the war. As a precursor to the 1940s program a similar program had been arranged between Mexico and the United States in 1920. Under this arrangement with Mexico, no worker was permitted to leave Mexico without a contract signed by an immigration official, which stated the rate of pay, work schedule, place of employment and certain conditions. With the advent of the U.S. Border Patrol in 1924, Mexican immigrants who did not meet these requirements were considered "illegal aliens."

[9] *Floral Product Marketing in Greater Los Angeles, California*, United States Department of Agriculture, Agricultural Marketing Service, Transportation and Marketing Division, April 1997.

CHAPTER 7

JDP Photography

Timeline: 2000-2008

2000	The Walt Disney Corporation wins the Award of Merit Non-Industry from the American Institute of Floral Designers for its outstanding use of floral displays. Americans become interested in the origins of the fruits and vegetables they eat and the flowers and plants they purchase, accelerating the "green" movement and creation of standards for organic and safe-for-the-environment farming.
2001	Southern California floral organizations co-sponsor a floral design event ("LA Fleur") at Los Angeles Flower Market. Terrorists take over four commercial passenger jets and fly two of them into the World Trade Center towers in New York City and one into the Pentagon. The fourth plane, intended for the White House but foiled by quick-acting passengers, crashes in a Pennsylvania field. Nearly 3,000 people die.
2002	The second "LA Fleur" floral design event is held at the Los Angeles Flower Market.
2003	The United States, United Kingdom, Australia, Poland, Denmark and other coalition members invade Iraq on March 20. Seventy percent of U.S. roses are imported from Ecuador.
2004	Wildfires ravage San Diego County resulting in more than $5 million damage to flower growing operations, while hurricanes pound the southeastern U.S. and impact the production of ferns and foliage.
2005	Hurricane Katrina destroys large areas in the city of New Orleans and surrounding areas in Louisiana and southeastern states.
2006	Dahlias make the list of million-dollar producers on the Santa Barbara County Agricultural Production Report. The California Foundation for Agriculture in the Classroom reports that California producers market cut flowers and foliage worth more than $330 million to the nation's 40,000 florists and 24,000 supermarket floral departments. Floral industry representatives present a plan for a national floral marketing funding initiative to be overseen by the U.S. Department of Agriculture. (The plan is later put on hold pending outcome of the Free Trade Agreement.) The final phase of Orange County's Measure M (half cent sales tax for transportation projects), widening of the I-5 Santa Ana freeway, begins its six-year project, some 50 years after flower farmers relocated to make way for the freeway's initial construction.
2007	Life expectancy for men is 75.5, for women 80.7. Apple, Inc. introduces the iPhone. The price of crude oil passes $100/barrel and consumers in California pay $3.39/gallon (average) for gasoline. The new federal minimum wage reaches $5.85/hour. The DOW Jones Industrial Average reaches 14,000. Crews of Atlantis and the international space station greet each other with hugs and handshakes – in space. In California, the legislature moves forward on approvals of a plan for a statewide high-speed rail system. The end of June records 2006-2007 as the driest year on record in Southern California. Raging wildfires devastate much of San Diego County, areas of Riverside County and Malibu Canyon in Los Angeles County, destroying thousands of homes and structures. A 20-year Colorado River water pact is made between California, Arizona, Nevada, Wyoming, Utah, Colorado and New Mexico to resolve disputes among water agencies, institute drought condition rules and commit states to negotiations on future controversies. Congress extends the Andean Trade Promotion and Drug Eradication Act to early 2008. Key trade associations meet to consider the creation of product identification standards for the global floral supply chain. City of Los Angeles engineers begin design of a new garden median at the well-known entrance to the Flower District at Eighth and San Pedro streets.
2008	The presidential race heats up with senators Hillary Clinton and Barak Obama vying for the Democratic party nomination and John McCain leading the Republications. The economy dips downward reacting to decreased housing construction, failures of sub-prime lenders and other factors. Dow Jones trading tumbles from its mid-2007 high of over 14,000 to under 12,000. On March 5, the U.S. Department of the Interior opens the floodgates of Glen Canyon Dam, releasing 300,000 gallons of water per second from Lake Powell into the Colorado River through the Grand Canyon, to restore its altered ecosystem. On March 15, 2008, the first professional (exhibition) baseball game is played in China between the San Diego Padres and the Los Angeles Dodgers. The first game ties 3-3; the Padres win Game 2 by 6-3. On the fifth anniversary of the start of the war in Iraq on March 19, protests are held across the country.

JDP Photography

Changing Neighborhoods

"Some things are certain: the Market has changed and will never go back to simpler times. As long as people fall in love, get married, have children and die, there will always be a demand for flowers."

— Gary Kawaguchi in *Living with Flowers: the California Flower Market History* (San Francisco)

The long-time Southern California grower, wholesaler or retail florist who meanders along the streets that line today's Los Angeles Flower District finds himself in awe in 2007 of the numbers of people and companies who have opened storefront shops to sell flowers and floral supplies. These new arrivals are not all members of the dynamic Los Angeles Flower District, nor do they all concern themselves with offering the high level of quality the Los Angeles Flower Market established over the years. But they are there, new sellers in a neighborhood that seems to be changing by the day, increasing the size of the "flower district" north from Seventh Street to Ninth Street and east from Maple Avenue to San Pedro Street and beyond. The public sees block after block of flowers and views the whole area as "the flower district."

Los Angeles is unlike other cities such as New York and San Francisco where flower markets have lately experienced reductions in size. Perhaps this attests to the highly diverse and entrepreneurial nature of Southern Californians and, not surprisingly, a spontaneity that springs forth to capture opportunity without the investment of strategic planning.

Ironically, in the midst of the dramatic changes in the floral industry that have occurred since 1960 throughout the nation, the Los Angeles Flower Market finds it is a magnet to new businesses. The proximity of available retail space to this nearly 100-year-old anchor of the district is a powerful draw, says a developer who in early 2008 opened a small wholesale flower mall a block away.

"Find me a small storefront space adjacent to the Flower Market" is the request developers and property owners hear. And there's plenty of room for all in the now mixed-use neighborhood.

With its mixture of predominantly South American and Mexican American store owners and a colorful but confusing array of street and storefront signs, floral products and displayed wreaths, the neighborhood has livened things up and attracted the bargain-seeking public. The downside is that the two "real" flower markets and their tenants and merchants are somewhat lost in the maze.

Will the public, who find this myriad of new shops open in afternoon hours, find their way a couple blocks west to the original flower markets during the markets' public (morning) hours? This is one of the challenges facing today's Los Angeles Flower Market.

The Changing District Neighborhood

Since the early 1990s, many of the factories and showrooms once used by the textile industry in the downtown wholesale district have been razed or renovated and converted to multi-occupancy lofts and apartments. Like many urban areas, the eclectic neighborhoods now attract people who work downtown and desire a shorter commute and a simpler lifestyle. As they've relocated to the now mixed-use wholesale-residential neighborhoods, restaurants, supermarkets, retail and entertainment venues have sprung up as well.

Industry Associations Through the Years

Since the 1700s, garden clubs, horticulture groups and flower event planning committees have brought thousands of people together to share the various aspects of growing, arranging, showing and enjoying flowers and flowering plants.

In the Los Angeles metropolitan area, *The Bloomin' News* reported in 1979 on the activities of the Sur Este Floral Association, the Orange County Florists' Association, San Fernando Valley Floral Association and Channel Counties Florists' Association, to name but a few.

On a broader scale, state and national associations formed that would ultimately educate and benefit the professional. Because of these organizations, research has accelerated and the flower industry has matured.

American Association of Nurserymen, Florists, and Seedsmen

The AANFS was born in 1876 at a horticultural society meeting in Illinois. During its first eight years, its members included florists along with seed and nursery professionals. The florists left in 1883 to form their own association, the Society of American Florists.

American Floral Endowment

This non-for-profit, non-governmental organization is a source for floricultural and environmental horticulture research and development funding in the United States. It publishes results of its research and finances scholarships and internships for students pursuing studies in floriculture. www.endowment.org

American Horticultural Society

Founded in 1922, AHS merged with two other major organizations over the years, including the National Horticultural Society, also founded in 1922, and the American Horticultural Council. This trade organization publishes the American Horticulturist magazine and other publications. www.ahs.org

American Institute of Floral Designers

The American Institute of Floral Designers, Inc. began in Los Angeles in 1965, organized by local floral designers. Art McKee was AIFD's first president; Wayne Andrade

The presence of residents in the blocks along the west side of the Southern California Flower Market has introduced yet another challenge: The noise of flower delivery trucks arriving between midnight and early morning hours.

Perhaps the greatest challenge in 2008, however, is the inability of the two flower markets to expand beyond the confines of their properties in a high-density neighborhood. In an area now considered "mixed use," meaning the co-existence of retail, wholesale and residential entities, re-zoning becomes essential to survival. The flower markets must re-invent themselves to embrace these growing trends.

Los Angeles Flower Market manager Johnny Mellano has worked tirelessly for several years toward new zoning for the Los Angeles Flower Market. Meetings with city officials and the study and preparation of plans and necessary documents are among the preliminary steps to zoning change. Zoning change will allow the Market to restructure, rebuild, sell selected areas and take any measures necessary to assure its continued success.

was vice president; Dave Wittry, treasurer; and Bea Frambach, secretary. The organization sought to upgrade the floral design profession through education. Now, each July, successful candidates for the AIFD designation are inducted into membership during AIFD's acclaimed National Symposium. Today's AIFD has more than 1,200 members and is headquartered in Baltimore, Maryland. www.aifd.org.

Association of Specialty Cut Flower Growers, Inc.

Formed in 1988, the ASCFG's goal is to united and inform the growers of specialty cut flowers. It publishes the *Cut Flower Quarterly*, conference transcripts and other publications. www.ascfg.org.

California Floral Council

Organized in 1959, the CFC serves flower growers through educational programs. (831 905-9753)

California Association of Flower Growers and Shippers

Incorporated in 1941 to aid San Francisco area flower shippers, CAFG&S (also known as NORCAL) is a non-profit trade association formed to enhance the floral transportation network and offer a variety of services for members throughout California. www.norcalflowers.org

California Cut Flower Commission

The California Cut Flower Commission funds research to improve quality and production of floral products. Its projects have included studies for alternatives to methyl bromide, disinfestation issues, pesticides and technology, controlled atmospheres and more. CCFC produces a newsletter and educational materials including a color chart and color flower guides. www.ccfc.org

California Ornamental Research Federation

CORF, the California Ornamental Research Federation, is a statewide partnership of growers, floriculture associations, allied industry and research educators whose mission is to identify and meet the research and educational needs of the California floriculture industry. Also see: Kee Kitayama Research Foundation. www.corf.org

Continued...

The Market "Waiting List"

While outsiders crowded into the wholesale area in the 2000s, the Los Angeles Flower District addressed internal demands for space. The procedure to replace an outgoing tenant in the Southern California Flower Market and the Los Angeles Flower Market is to seek a vendor who offers the same or similar floral product. An orchid wholesale tenant is replaced with another orchid wholesaler, and so forth. So the common belief that the Flower Market has a "seven-year waiting list" is true but not true. The waiting list may be specifically for a vendor of orchids or gladiolas or chrysanthemums.

Often, the outgoing tenant negotiates his own replacement, waiting until the deal is sealed before he gives his notice to District management, making it difficult for the next person on the waiting list to get in. To avoid having a tenant space unoccupied for any length

Market purchases make their way to retail florists' vans and shops, to be incorporated into the floral designs of the next few days.

Industry Associations, continued

California State Floral Association

The only organization representing all floral concerns statewide in California, the CSFA holds an annual and very popular Top Ten Design competition at its Calif Flora conference expo and publishes a semi-annual magazine. www.calstatefloral.com

California Women for Agriculture

CWA helps its members develop the knowledge and skills necessary to convey the mutual benefits of a vibrant agricultural economy and healthy rural communities to those who are in positions to impact the future of agriculture in California. www.cawomen4ag.com

Floral Marketing Association

This floral arm of the Produce Marketing Association is a nonprofit trade group started in 1974. It serves mass marketers and suppliers.

Flower Promotion Organization

The Flower Promotion Organization was launched in 2000 to promote flower consumption across the United States. Its radio, television and print advertisements are carefully and strategically orchestrated, with campaigns conducted in selected major metropolitan areas each year. The FPO has teamed up with the Society of American Florists in recent years to research the impact of flowers in the home and workplace.

Flowers For Kids

This innovative program increases the demand for cut flowers by teaming retail florists with local schools to educate children about flower care. The program is financed by Ecuadorian, California and Colombian flower growers with help from plant breeders, floral suppliers, importers, wholesalers and shippers. www.flowersforkids.org

Kee Kitayama Research Foundation

Founded in 1992 in honor of floral industry leader Kee Kitayama, KKRF is a source for floriculture research information. Since 1997, KKRF has worked with the California Cut Flower Commission to fund needed research in cut flower areas and plans to do the same for potted plants and ornamentals. In 1995, KKRF assumed the role of parent organization of the California Ornamental Research Federation (CORF) for the purpose of providing educational seminars for the ornamental industry. CORF also publishes CORF News. www.corf.org

Plantscape Industry Alliance (formerly California Interior Plantscape Association)

PIA enhances the professionalism of interior plantscapers and industry affiliates through quality programs, educational material and networking opportunities. The organization holds an annual conference and publishes a newsletter. www.cipaweb.org

of time, management must then review and approve the replacement or hustle to find another replacement quickly. In that case, the waiting list, if it includes a similar vendor, comes in handy.

This practice makes it difficult for business owners to enter the Market environment, sending many of them down the street to open their own shops or join one of the small flower malls springing up in the area. It protects the Market, however, retaining the integrity of the tenant and merchant family and guaranteeing the highest quality of the most in-demand floral products will be sold through the Market.

A Los Angeles Flower Market member, RDP Floral's prime location at the corner of Eighth and Wall streets is a marketing plus.

San Diego County Flower & Plant Association

Established in 1947 by Eugene E. Stuck, Donald Briggs Sr, Maurice Storm, Wilson Vinson Jr, J.G. Schilt, Herman Kanlunch and C.G. Hornung, this is a trade association of commercial cut flower and potted plant growers. The association works to pool growers and resources and present member-approved issues that demonstrate that the floriculture grower's agenda is positive for the economy and environment. The mission is to strengthen, advance and support the floriculture industry in Southern California.

Society of American Florists

Chartered by an Act of Congress in 1884, SAF was formed in Chicago by 21 members of the American Association of Nurserymen, Florists and Seedsmen. They created a new organization to provide hail insurance for members and invited retail florists across the country to become members. The next year, the Society had 400 members and by 1900, 533.

SAF is a vital national organization sponsoring programs that benefit everyone in the industry. It adopted the "Say it With Flowers" promotion in the early 1900s, helped popularize flowers for Mother's Day and initiated many other promotions to encourage flower purchases. It lobbies Congress, holds educational meetings and trade shows, publishes floral care information, gathers resources during times of national emergency and supports endowments and the recognition of individual and corporate achievement within the floral industry. www.SAFnow.org

Southern California Floral Association

Although no longer in existence, this organization served thousands of members from its inception in 1931 until it merged with the California State Floral Association in the late 1980s. Its offices were in the American Florists' Exchange at 766 Wall Street in Los Angeles, in the suite now occupied by the Los Angeles Flower District badge program.

Wholesale Florist & Florist Supplier Association

The WF&FSA was organized in 1926 in Chicago as the Wholesale Commission of Florists of America (WCFA). Through its annual conventions, seminars and publications and Young Executives program, it continues to meet its goals of advancing effective communication between floral industry segments and the education of industry employees and employers.

Events of Local and Worldwide Impact

The world celebrated the arrival of the third millennium and the twenty-first century on New Year's Eve of 1999. Elaborate, spectacular fireworks displays were viewed by millions through pre-arranged television staging. On New Year's Day, the Tournament of Roses held its one hundred eleventh Rose Parade. The B-2 "Spirit" (aka Stealth Bomber) arrived from Whiteman Air Force Base in Missouri to fly over the parade in celebration of the millennium. In the oldest and most prestigious of college football games, the Rose Bowl, Wisconsin beat Stanford, 17-9.

The year 2001 started off innocently but ended with the country facing the threat of war on far away shores. On September 11, 2001, Al Qaeda terrorists commandeered four jet planes and flew them into the two World Trade Center towers in lower Manhattan, a part of the Pentagon building and a field in rural Pennsylvania. Nearly 3,000 people lost their lives that day.

The Society of American Florists shifted into high gear, along with many other organizations and floral associations and thousands of American citizens. SAF reported that florists generously offered ribbons, carnations, bows and balloons, giving them away or selling them to give the proceeds to victims and relief efforts.

SAF coordinated efforts between the American Institute of Floral Designers, Teleflora, FTD and other industry groups. In one volunteer effort alone, florists sent buffet arrangements to the Spirit of New York, a harbor cruise ship serving 12,000 meals daily to Ground Zero rescue workers. Flowers were sent to family crisis centers and bouquets to the site where both the towers had collapsed to the ground. Florists volunteered to make arrangements for memorial and funeral services around the country.

Over the next few years, America would be engaged in a war in Afghanistan and Iraq intended to keep such events as the 2001 terrorist attacks and threats from ever happening again.

On the Flower Front

By the year 2000 producers were marketing California-grown cut flowers and foliage valued at more than $330 million (wholesale) annually to 40,000 florists and 24,000 supermarket floral departments, kiosks and other outlets. California retail florists alone employed around 11,000 people. [1]

Just as they did in the late 1800s, people continued to relocate to Southern California, sold on its climate and thriving and diverse business environment. A population of 59 million Californians was predicted by the year 2050 by the state's Department of Finance. All southwestern states, including Arizona and Nevada, were experiencing unprecedented growth.

San Diego County, which had for decades offered farmland to growers being pushed out by developers in the Los Angeles area, began to experience its own urbanization. A fifteen-acre piece of land in inland Oceanside near Fallbrook fetched $67,000 per acre, while smaller lots for homes along the coast sold for up to $250,000. One large Encinitas grower reportedly sold ten acres to allow the construction of 60 to 70 homes. Money from such lucrative sales was, some growers felt, the means with which to maintain and upgrade their greenhouse operations. [2]

Smog and dust from construction along with increasing population had their effects upon the flowers of the growers whose operations remained in the once predominantly agricultural areas. Dennis Turner, the principal planner for the city of Carlsbad, predicted the only survivor would be The Flower Fields®, which had become a popular Carlsbad tourist destination.

While growers confronted the problems of smog and development, nurseries seemed to enjoy unprecedented growth. Evelyn Weidner, who had moved with her husband Bob to Encinitas in 1968 to escape the citification of Brea, found her spacious gardens along busy Interstate 5 freeway to be perfectly situated. Across California and the nation, garden centers thrived.

As the price of gasoline climbed to four dollars per gallon in 2008, however, and foreign competition assumed a larger hold, greenhouse growers were saddled with increased costs. It now cost more dollars to keep product growing at ideal temperatures, and the need to use certain chemicals and to market products more aggressively added to the overall expense for doing business.

Bougainvilla and palms adorn a farm road in San Diego County.

Big competition for Southern California's small growers and florists came right to California's front door. Dole, the food manufacturer, began growing flowers in a large scale offshore operation called Dole Fresh Flowers. Gerald Stevens, started by Gerald Geddis, the brainchild behind the Blockbusters success story, and board chairman Steven Berrard, bought up small retail florists nationwide. It seemed the world was consolidating and the growers were getting bigger and they were serious about taking a big piece of the floral sales pie.

It was difficult to be profitable at the small retail florist shop level. Eventually, however, many of the big players exited the business, reduced the size of their operations or focused on supplying the large discount chains.

In 2007, the latest newcomer to California was Tesco, the United Kingdom and Europe's most successful retailer. Tesco built its first boutique grocery stores in Southern California, including cut flowers among its merchandise using the novel concept of a small neighborhood specialty market.

Local Floral Events of Note

On June 10, 2001, the "LA Fleur" floral design show took place across both the Southern California Flower Market and the Los Angeles Flower Market. The all-day event, which attracted more than 400 people, was led by San Fernando Valley florist James Lynch and was sponsored by the American Florists' Exchange, the Associated Florists of Southern California, the California State Floral Association and the Southern California Flower Growers, Inc.

Rich Salvaggio, AIFD, AAF, PFCI, vice president of floral publications for Teleflora, demonstrates floral designs for the upcoming holiday season at the LA Fleur event at the Los Angeles Flower Market, August 2002. *Bloomin' News collection*.

Phil Rulloda, AAF, AIFD, PFCI, and René van Rems, AIFD, PFCI, the featured designers, presented the spectacular designs for which they are so well known. Flowers and supplies for their shows were donated by Moskatels, Lion Ribbon Co., SOS Wholesale, Tropical USA, Tayama's Wholesale Company and Smithers Oasis®.

At this first floral design show at the Market in several years, Paul Ecke Jr. presented a prestigious René van Rems Award to its namesake. The Phil Rulloda Award was presented to Song Ki Yun, AIFD of Fontana. Cherri Mae Hoa took First Place in the design competition, qualifying for the statewide Top Ten competition.

On August 25 of the following year, Rich Salvaggio, AIFD, AAF, PFCI, vice president of floral publications for Teleflora, and Kim Morrill, AIFD, of Morrill Support in Seattle, Washington, took center stage in the second LA Fleur event. Their design shows presented color and design trends for the upcoming holiday season and were again enjoyed by several hundred attendees. The Phil Rulloda Award went to René van Rems and the Rene van Rems Award honored Rich Salvaggio, AIFD, AAF, PFCI. Donna Ha took First Place in the design competition and Doug Mayes won the People's Choice Award, qualifying them for California State Floral Association's annual Top Ten design competition.

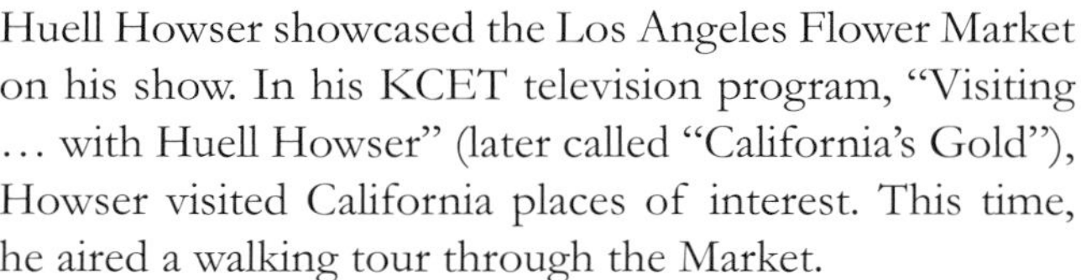

A large number of market tenants opened their businesses during both the 2001 and 2002 LA Fleur events.

In Spring 2004, popular television personality Huell Howser showcased the Los Angeles Flower Market on his show. In his KCET television program, "Visiting ... with Huell Howser" (later called "California's Gold"), Howser visited California places of interest. This time, he aired a walking tour through the Market.

In September 2006, the Los Angeles Fashion District Business Improvement District (BID) announced it had been awarded $10,000 by the Board of Public Works Office of Community Beautification to build a garden at the median at Eighth and San Pedro streets. The old eyesore with its broken concrete slabs would be replaced with a floral focal point, a perfect embellishment for the entrance to the Flower District. In October 2007, the construction of the new gateway not yet started, it was learned the project was still in the plans and the city's engineers would design it.

The entire Flower District becomes a popular media topic every year at Valentine's Day. In 2007, television crews from KABC, KNBC, KTLA, KTTV, KCBS, KCAL and KMEX were seen throughout the District, as thousands of shoppers browsed the spectacular floral displays.

Above and right: A few blocks from the Los Angeles Flower District, the Fashion District evolves into a recognizable presence in Los Angeles vogue.

Above and right: area businesses attract shoppers looking for floral bargains.

Standards for the Floral Industry / Going "Green"

By the beginning of the twenty-first century, consumers had become acutely interested in the origins of the vegetables they consumed and the flowers they enjoyed, which led them to seek out those products produced in a setting and using methodology which protected the environment and the human body. Organic farming experienced accelerated popularity as the trend grew.

Some flower growers achieved certification under the USDA National Organic Program for growing products using organic methodology. Others found the NOP restrictive, as it was developed with food production as its focus. In 2003, a group of North American flower growers and distributors asked Scientific Certification Systems to evaluate several sustainable agriculture labeling programs in use in the European market. SCS's findings led to the development of a sustainable floral standard for North America, which the group established as "VeriFlora." The VeriFlora standard became the template for a new national standard published by the American National Standards Institute under review in 2007. [3]

Some shippers, retailers and ornamental plant growers are pursuing certification also, as they meet VeriFlora's tough standards for agrochemical usage and developing a plan for organic pest management and soil fertility practices (adoption of some organic practices is a prerequisite). The standard also contains ecosystem and water quality protection measures, establishment of workplace social responsibilities requirements and proper traceability, product quality and chain-of-custody procedures.

Currently, VeriFlora, based on the Sustainable Agriculture Practice Standard for trial use, has more than 750 million certified stems in the North American marketplace. Many leading California cut flower growers and regionally-based floral distributors use the VeriFlora label, signifying products sustainably grown.

The demand for environmentally-friendly products fueled the "green" trend. Companies of all kinds began to "go green" by developing their products in environmentally safe ways that could be marketed as such, making their products, it was hoped, more appealing to buyers.

Global standards were being urged as well, as key trade associations met in June 2007 to discuss an industry-wide initiative to create product identification standards for the global floral supply chain. The technology of radio frequency identification (RFID), barcodes and electronic commerce had come of age and would help trading partners cut costs and gain better control of their products.

Above: The crumbling median at Eighth and San Pedro streets stands against the backdrop of newly-established fresh and silk flower and floral supply stores lining the east side of San Pedro Street.

Flower Quality and the Cold Chain

In 2005, Dr. Michael Reid [4], horticulturist with the University of California at Davis, and floral researcher Dr. George Staby released the groundbreaking white paper, "Improving the Cold Chain for Cut Flowers and Potted Plants." The paper emphasized the need to keep cut flowers at the optimum temperature of between 34 and 36 degrees Fahrenheit, speed the time from harvest to retailer and use proper handling practices.

With fresh flowers sourced globally, requiring more time to get from field to consumer, the demand for effective and speedy distribution increased. Millions of dollars were invested by growers and shippers in the 1990s and 2000s in equipment and technology to keep flowers at cool temperatures. As a result, flowers enter cool rooms within minutes after harvesting and most flowers transported to California from around the globe are kept in properly cooled environments with the temperature continuously monitored.

Above: The Coca Cola bottling plant built in 1937 stands a few blocks east of the Flower Market today as one of the finest examples of Streamline Moderne design. Designed by Robert Derrah, it resembles an ocean liner inside and out. Left: The Fashion District Business Improvement District's Clean and Safe Team poses for a picture. The security team is easily spotted in their yellow uniforms, as they dart in and out of BID neighborhoods on their bicycles. *Courtesy Los Angeles Fashion District BID.*

Keeping the integrity of the cold chain, which includes both timing and temperature, meant that flowers imported through the Los Angeles International Airport arrived fresh at the wholesalers' facilities and at the Flower Market. For retail florist customers who continue to maintain the cold chain requirements to their customer's door, this results in repeat business and loyal customers.

The pressure was on the industry, including floral design schools, to educate florists about speedy deliveries, sanitation and cool delivery vehicles. Drs. Staby and Reid emphasized that cool chain practices could mean the difference between increased business and flat sales.

The Trade Agreements

The Andean Trade Promotion and Drug Eradication Act was established in 1991 to discourage the exporting of drugs by encouraging the exporting of other agricultural products from the countries of Colombia, Ecuador, Peru and Bolivia. To a large degree, the ATPDEA was responsible for the overwhelming floral imports into the United States in the 1990s and 2000s.

Shoppers browse the weekly farmers market on Fifth Street outside the Los Angeles Public Library, summer 2007.

The South American countries pushed for extension of the ATPDEA to the United States Congress and the Act's existence was believed to have provided jobs to thousands who would otherwise have been employed in the drug trade.

Free Trade Agreements with the South American countries were pursued vigorously in the early 2000s by U.S. floral industry lobbyists. Representatives of both the South American countries and the United States pointed out the benefits of FTAs for U.S. floriculture. By February 2008, only the Peruvian agreement had been extended.

Other Legislative Issues

The highly controversial Comprehensive Immigration Reform Bill, debated, negotiated and lobbied for aggressively, failed to make the grade in June 2007.

"The broken immigration system absolutely has to be fixed," said Society of American Florists' senior director of government relations Jeanne Ramsay. She predicted that raids to apprehend illegal workers would increase, the borders would tighten and the labor shortage experienced by so many California growers would continue to worsen.

On a positive note, Ramsay said "the intense effort of the agricultural community including SAF" that fought for passage of the Immigration Reform Bill, helped another program called AgJOBS (the Agricultural Job Opportunities, Benefits and Security Act). The Senate approved AgJOBS as part of a large immigration bill it passed in May 2006, but the bill could not be passed into law until both the House and Senate approved it and the president signed it. The floral and horticulture industries rallied, led by the Society of American Florists, in October 2007 to let some 60 senators know of their support for the bill.

Weather, Water, Floods and Fire

Southern California with its myriad climates and terrains found itself increasingly vulnerable to Santa Ana winds, floods and drought situations. By the mid-2000s, the state had experienced substantially warmer temperatures and dramatically less moisture, and the impact from natural storms and extraordinary weather had worsened.

Fires of Compassion

Many are the stories of human compassion extended to victims of the October 2007 fires.

The Paul Ecke Ranch, its poinsettia crops never in immediate danger, took in 60 horses to assist neighbors. Families like Michael Anthony Mellano and wife Valerie in the heavily damaged Fallbrook area gave shelter to friends and neighbors made homeless by the tragedy.

John Frazee, of the Frazee family that grew field flowers and nurtured The Flower Fields® through the years, readied his mother's former home in Carlsbad as a temporary home for a fire-displaced family. In doing so, he came across a one-of-a-kind photo. The framed, laminated picture is of his father, Edwin Frazee, and Elmer Fisher, of the G.A. Berlin Company, at a presentation with Mayor Sam Yorty of Los Angeles. This picture, the only photo of Elmer Fisher which the authors of this book have been able to locate, appears on page 203.

Ironically, other states also experienced drought and floods, affecting California flower growers.

In October 2003, wildfires ravaged San Diego County, where more than $5 million in damage to flower growing operations and $2.5 million in damage to nurseries was reported.

In Fall 2004, Hurricane Charlie tore into the southeastern area of the United States, devastating communities and destroying large percentages of the fern crops in Florida. Charlie was followed by Frances, a hurricane that some said was the largest disaster the foliage industry had ever seen. It destroyed about 6,000 acres in an area of Florida that made up the primary point of supply of greens for the floral industry. Supplies of the familiar leatherleaf fern found in most floral arrangements were reduced. The ripple effect of these losses was felt by retailers and consumers in price increases and limited supplies across the United States.

In January and February 2005, the torrential rains that pelted Southern California combined with cold, icy air put a serious damper on the state's flower industry. Harvests were delayed, deliveries were cancelled due to mudslides, railroads cut back on services and rerouted some 90 trains. Again, the impact to the local economy and floral industry was severe.

August 30, 2005, was a day that will be long remembered by the residents of New Orleans and the towns of Louisiana and Mississippi. That day, Hurricane Katrina made landfall, breaking levies, washing away entire communities and creating devastation the likes of which had never been experienced before. Distribution of floral and agricultural products stopped. Flower growers experienced short-term financial burden due to the many transportation bottlenecks.

In June 2007, the *Orange County Register / Post* published the statement that 2007 had become "the driest year on record" for the area. Santa Ana, the article said, would end the 2007 rainy season (mid-summer the official annual cut-off) with just 2.2 inches, the least amount of rain since the city began keeping such records in 1948. Los Angeles wasn't in much better shape with its mere 3.2 inches for the year.

In Summer 2007, Governor Arnold Schwarzenegger declared a state of emergency for Riverside and Kings counties, saying drought conditions had reduced water supplies and caused some $4 million in crop losses. With such a declaration, state agencies could get the county's water agencies to drill new water wells or modify existing wells. But there was little time to make much headway before the annual fire season started.

The land in Southern California had become perfect kindling for fire. So it was no surprise that on Saturday, October 20, 2007, a fire that began in Malibu Canyon raced out of control, fed by Santa Ana winds which, powered by paths through deep canyons acting as wind tunnels, accelerated in speed and destroyed thousands of acres.
In fact, the Malibu fire would be the first of more than 20 reported fires during the next few days in Southern California, one set in Orange County by an arsonist, another set accidentally by a child and others ignited by sparks carried by gale-force winds.

At the end of the first week, with a large percentage of the fires under control, it was determined that Ventura County's Ranch fire had burned more than 47,000 acres. The Silverado fire in Orange County burned some 28,000 acres, the Buckweed fire in Los Angeles County nearly 38,000 acres. The Grass Valley and Slide fires in the San Bernardino Mountains burned 5,000 acres and in San Diego, more than 300,000 acres and 1,700 structures had burned. Nearly 2,000 homes were destroyed.

In San Diego County, 800 burned acres represented outdoor cut flowers, 45 greenhouses (but no greenhouse damage) and 750 acres of nursery stock. Farmers suffering the most damage were those growing the highly flammable protea, waxflower, lepto, banksia and eucalyptus. Damage to floral crops was in addition to that experienced by growers of avocadoes (the largest affected crop), palms and other field crops.

Complicating the situation for San Diego growers were two unfortunate facts. Those who had been evacuated could not return early enough to irrigate their crops, perhaps causing further losses. And these growers faced a mandatory 30 percent reduction in agriculture water supply beginning January 1, 2008, which would no doubt hamper their recovery efforts. The University of California's Cooperative Extension program, along with other agencies, planned to provide assistance.

For all these dramatic turns of event, the Society of American Florists and other floral organizations posted updates at their websites and in their newsletters. In these ways, they kept their members and the public informed and gleaned support of their efforts to help the afflicted.

Moving On . . . California Specialty Flowers Supply America

While the fires of October 2007 took their direct toll on California growers' operations, florists around the nation expected the availability of flowers they ordered from California growers would be reduced and the flowers priced higher. As far away as southern Florida, wholesalers and retailers expressed their belief that the flower supply for the 2007 holiday season would be impacted. Eucalyptus, protea, waxflower and some greens not grown in Florida during the winter months would be in short supply.

Johnny Mellano
Behind the Success of the Market

Today's American Florists' Exchange, Ltd. / Los Angeles Flower Market is a productive and profitable enterprise. A large part of its success can be attributed to the excellent job Johnny Mellano has done as the Manager of the Market.

For some 30 years, Johnny has managed the real estate and day-to-day operation of the AFE. Guiding the Market through the bureaucracy of city and state regulations, insurance, security and other business and property matters, he's simultaneously managed a changing mix of tenants and products represented in the Market, introducing in his early years as Manager a system of fairness to all tenants with regard to space and rent.

Preventive maintenance measures implemented for the physical plant and equipment have saved hundreds of thousands of dollars over the years and capital improvements such as refrigeration and lighting have enhanced efficiency. With the best interests of the Market and its tenants at heart, Johnny has lobbied continuously for safety and security and worked tirelessly with forward-thinking city planners toward re-zoning the property from Industrial to Multiple Use.

"You have to change with the times ...," Johnny explained in 2007. "We had to stay abreast of what's going on within the industry; the buying habits of retail florists have changed. And you have to change your product mix and your tenant mix to meet the demands of the customers coming into the market. We have done a good job with that." That awareness and willingness to flex with customer demand underlies the success of today's American Florists' Exchange.

Since his early years as Market Manager, Johnny has been a strong advocate of the local flower industry, helping to promote annual Open House events, flower shows and events like the annual International Flower Show at Hollywood Park. He enthusiastically opened the American Florists' Exchange for the "LA Fleur" events of the early 2000s, working with the Los Angeles Flower District, leaders of the Southern California Flower Growers, Inc., California State Floral Association and Associated Florists of Southern California.

Johnny Mellano and the Los Angeles area flower business grew up together. Born April 21, 1936, in Artesia, California, Johnny's family raised flowers on a six-and-one-quarter-acre ranch in Artesia and later expanded to larger farms in Southern California. Like others of his generation, he knew the physical demands of working in the flower fields, harvesting, loading and unloading flowers, driving them to Market and spending afternoons in the field after working at the Market since 1 a.m. There was no chance for this young man to keep pitching for his high school baseball team, but there was ample opportunity to learn the flower business. He worked on the farm and at a full-time job at the Market while attending Fullerton Junior College. Later, as Market Manager, Johnny learned from the examples of the leaders around him. People like Frank Kuwahara, manager of the Southern California Flower Market, became his mentors, contributing their wisdom and management savvy.

Johnny's Italian immigrant parents, Giovanni and Maria Mellano, imparted the value of hard, dedicated work to all their children in an era when leaders were self made. That work ethic served them well, evolving into a spirit of dedication, ability to see the larger picture, vision for what might be and innovative practices that, for the American Florists' Exchange, translated to success for shareholders, tenants and customers alike.

Johnny Mellano's management of the American Florists' Exchange / Los Angeles Flower Market is a major contributor to its long-term success.

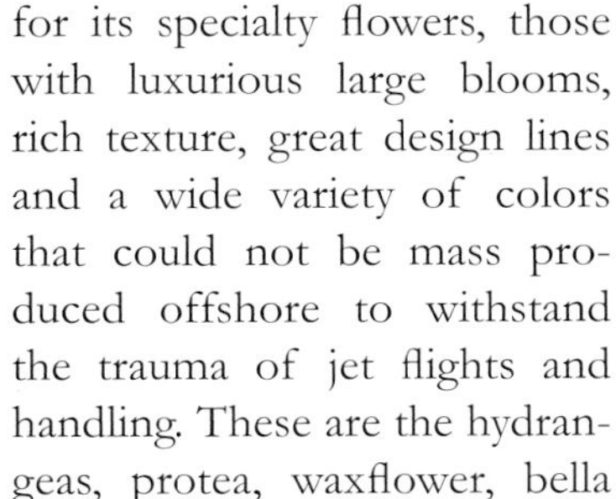

America looked to California for its specialty flowers, those with luxurious large blooms, rich texture, great design lines and a wide variety of colors that could not be mass produced offshore to withstand the trauma of jet flights and handling. These are the hydrangeas, protea, waxflower, bella donna (delphinium), lilies, asters, snapdragons and larkspur, the sweet peas and the small but spectacularly colored field roses that give a floral arrangement its aura of luxury, its feeling of opulence.

Retail florists across the United States continued to rely upon California flower growers for these specialty flowers for their most exquisite and custom-designed arrangements.

Toni Garner in Tulsa, Oklahoma has been ordering hydrangeas and field flowers from California wholesalers since the early 1980s, just as her parents did during their career as floral shop owners. Her needs for a weekend of 80 events and orders easily mirror those of many florists across the United States who will settle for nothing less than California-grown flowers.

Marketing Flowers

Moving into the new century, floral associations like the Floral Promotion Organization and the Society of American Florists invested thousands of dollars in public relations, marketing and advertising to inspire consumers to buy flowers. The results were positive and ongoing, with millions of impressions, articles and

Hustle, bustle and new projects surround the Flower and Fashion districts in 2007. From renovation of early twentieth century structures to new construction to support the growing Los Angeles fashion industry and downtown residential and shopping needs, 2007 was a busy year. ***JDP Photography.***

television coverage resulting in increased sales. In fall 2005, SAF reported that its PR Fund had generated dozens of articles and mentions in 120 local markets through the electronic media and exposed some 500 million readers to its message.

The California Cut Flower Commission spread the word everywhere about California flowers. Millions of people across the United States heard or watched cable television programs that focused on fresh flowers and their care and handling and demonstrated the design of floral arrangements using California cut flowers.

The American Floral Endowment released the results of its 2003 Ipsos Insight Consumer Tracking Study in 2005, which told us that people ages 40 to 54 represented 38 percent of flower purchases in dollar share. College graduates out-purchased non-college graduates by a large margin. Women far out-purchased men and, in dollars spent, cut flowers beat bedding plants, 38.4 percent to 35.7 percent. The total dollar size for the floriculture retail market was estimated at $19 billion. Cut flowers represented 38.4 percent.

Taking the pulse of the floral industry was disheartening, however, as sales continued to decline. Flower sales were not keeping up with surpluses caused by imports (some 70 percent of flowers sold in the United States). A 2005 report published by the Wholesale Florist & Florist Supplier Association pointed to a decline in the number

Below: the LA Fashion Center ("LA FACE"), a 650,000 square foot wholesale facility under construction at Fourteenth and South San Pedro Street, 2007. ***JDP Photography.***

of retail florists, who faced increased labor and fuel costs and decreasing profits. These reductions trickled down to wholesalers, shippers and producers.

In 2006, a group of floral industry representatives devised a plan for a nationwide initiative to fund the marketing of flowers through a cooperative national effort. To fund the program, domestic cut flower and greens growers and U.S. importers would be assessed by the U.S. Department of Agriculture at two percent of their invoice costs. They'd be expected to pass the cost along through the chain to the consumer. Twenty million dollars would be the initial funding for a nationwide marketing program.

Although most attendees at the 2007 information meetings recognized the need to pull flower sales out of the doldrums, others believed the cost would ultimately and unfairly be born by domestic producers and importers of record. Uncertainties of the Free Trade Agreement with South American countries, fluctuations in oil prices and the devaluation of the dollar vs the peso had a way of stalling what was, although sound in concept, a controversial plan. In the end, the proposal was tabled.

Change on the Horizon Once Again

No one knows the meaning of change better than the floral industry. Southern California flower growers started with one and five-acre plots of gladiolas and chrysanthemums in the neighborhoods of a little farm town called Los Angeles. They moved to the country to make room for developers. They became wholesalers of flowers imported from other countries. They held their breath as big corporations made inroads into the flower industry, changing the business environment. Change would continue, and growers, wholesalers and retailers would continue to adapt.

In the wholesale flower district of Los Angeles where the Southern California floral industry is so firmly rooted, change made itself known on every block. The neighborhood transitioned to one that served the public as well as the reseller. The Los Angeles Flower Market remained strongly anchored in the midst of the transition, finding a way to serve both the retail florist and the public.

Through all these changing environments, retailers, wholesalers, distributors, shippers and growers adapted to new, improved methods of conducting business and they embraced technology. Innovation, technology and continuous education became their way of life.

In many ways, the Los Angeles Flower Market of the American Florists' Exchange finds itself in the same position the early florists and backyard farmers found themselves when the city first began in the middle of the nineteenth century: On the frontier.

Every aspect of life in the young state of California was new then as it is now: opportunities, freedoms, the making of laws, the building of infrastructure, the need to respond to great challenges with custom solutions, and the enormity of the frontier.

Today, every aspect of the floral industry of the future beckons those who are willing to embrace change, respond early to market trends and innovate with enthusiasm.

Endnotes

[1] "Commodity Fact Sheet" compiled by the California Cut Flower Commission with information supplied by the California Foundation for Agriculture in the Classroom. www.cfaitc.org.

[2] Lau, Angela, "Acres and Pains," San Diego Union-Tribune, Signonsandiego.com, July 10, 2005.

[3] Crevoshay, Ralph, Vice President of Marketing, Food and Agriculture for Scientific Certification Systems, "The Sustainable Future of Floriculture," *The Cut Flower Quarterly*, Summer 2007.

[4] Michael S. Reid, Ph.D., pioneered the use of STS and the 1-MCP (EthylBloc) product developed to prevent the negative effects of ethylene upon cut flowers. In 2003, the Society of American Florists honored him with its Alex Laurie Award for Research and Education.

CHAPTER 8

JDP Photography

JDP Photography

Today's Los Angeles Flower Market / American Florists' Exchange

"A whole new industry is being opened up for southern California, which area more than ever will become the 'flower basket' of America."

— *Florists Review magazine*, 1944

The faces have changed, but the camaraderie and energy that characterized the Los Angeles Flower Market of the American Florists' Exchange since its start nearly 90 years ago continue. Tenants still mentor those with dreams of becoming flower merchants. Wholesale establishments, some now grown to national and international status, catalog the specialty flowers grown in the expansive agricultural lands of California as well as the trendy blooms imported from other countries. Although its countenance has become more defined and, in some ways, limited, the flower industry in Southern California remains strong. The American Florists' Exchange is the best demonstration ever of an enterprise flexing with its market.

American Florists' Exchange, Ltd.

The American Florists' Exchange got its start around 1917 to 1919 as an informally organized group of about 30 people who went on to incorporate the group in January 1921. The flower growers and florists who made up the Exchange had been doing business with each other informally in the small downtown floral and produce markets. They were inspired by the success of the Japanese Americans, whose Southern California Flower Market had been operational and incorporated since 1914. They were also motivated by the growing demand for fresh cut flowers and the ability to produce outstanding floral products in the most ideal growing climate in America. Based on a loan from his bank, Gebhard Prechtl controlled more than 50 percent of the stock. When it came time to fulfill obligations on other bank notes, he did some pretty smooth talking to convince those unsure of the AFE's future to buy shares at $50 each.

The first flower market operated by the American Florists' Exchange occupied space at Fourth and Winston streets in downtown Los Angeles. The AFE moved to its present 754 Wall Street location in 1923.

The AFE's Articles of Incorporation were signed in early January 1921 and the corporation was begun with $50,000 capitalization. Some 900 shares of common stock and 80 shares of preferred stock (of a total 1,000 available shares), were valued and sold at $50 each. The official name was "The American Florists' Exchange of Los Angeles." An amendment in 1931 changed the name to "American Florists' Exchange, Ltd." In January 1983, the name was again amended, this time to "American Florists' Exchange DBA Los Angeles Flower Market."

Capital stock of $50,000, of which $45,000 was common and $5,000 preferred, was difficult to sell at the time. The AFE's Los Angeles Flower Market was a fledgling enterprise having been tossed together by a group of European immigrants and citizens relocated from other states, who were still learning how to work with each other and with the varied topographies and inland and seaside climates of Southern California.

Individuals and companies who expressed their confidence in the future of the AFE by purchasing one share of stock each in the first year of business included Albert Goldenson of Los Angeles (who served as the first AFE secretary), Peter A. Priamos of Hermosa Beach, the Polder Brothers, by John Polder, of Montebello, George J. Hall of Los Angeles, H.N. Gage Company of Montebello, Peter N. Priamos of Torrance, Frank M. Warner of Inglewood, John Bodger & Sons Company of Los Angeles, Roy F. Wilcox and Company of Montebello, G. Rolleri of Los Angeles, Lowes Flower Shop of Long Beach, C.E. Schucan of Long Beach, C.W. Halton of Los Angeles, O.E. Burns of Calumet, Illinois, Robert Newcomb of Long Beach, C.J. Groen of Montebello and the E.C. Amling Company. Preferred stock was issued to the new board of directors. Based on a loan from his bank, Gebhard Prechtl controlled more than 50 percent of the stock. When it came time to fulfill obligations on other bank notes, he did some pretty smooth talking to convince those unsure of the AFE's future to buy shares at $50 each.

The first officers of the five-member board of directors of the American Florists' Exchange, Ltd. were Tom H. Wright, a Los Angeles florist (president), John C. Bodger, Montebello flower seed producer, Roy F. Wilcox, a leader in the decorative plant industry, Albert Goldenson, a Los Angeles florist, and H.N. Gage, a Montebello flower grower.

Gebhard Prechtl, a Montebello grower, and secretary J.S. Whyte witnessed the signing of the Articles of Incorporation.

The American Florists' Exchange presidents and the years they took office have been:

Tom H. Wright, 1921; H.N. Gage, 1921; Gebhard Prechtl, 1922; L.W. Hills, 1922; C.J. Groen, 1946; Paul Ecke Sr., 1957; Paul Ecke Jr., 1991; John Williams, 2002.

This information was gleaned from American Florists' Exchange documents, the transcript of a 1981 interview with Frank Kuwahara, general manager of the Southern California Flower Market, and conversations with individuals closely associated with the American Florists' Exchange through the years.

Guide to the Los Angeles Flower Market

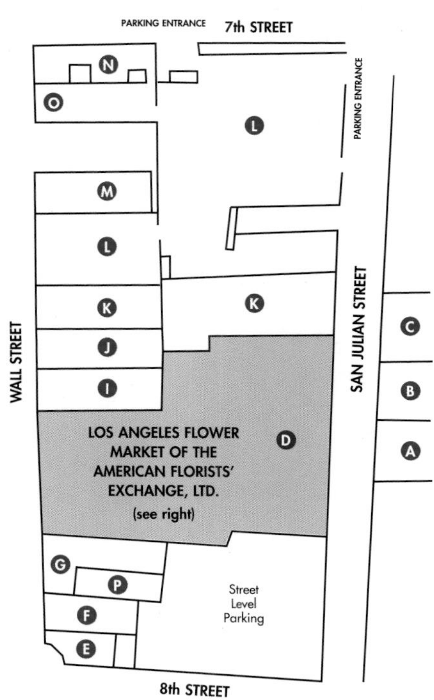

D
Enlarged to show market vendors

WALL STREET

SAN JULIAN STREET

Hours:
Trade/Wholesale: M/W/F: 2 to 8 a.m.; T/T/S: 5 to 6 a.m.
Public: ($2 admission weekdays; $1 on Saturday)
M/W/F: 8 a.m. to noon; T/T/S: 6 a.m. to 11 a.m.
For holiday and special hours, see www.LAFlowerDistrict.com.

● Restrooms ● Elevator

The Merchants of the Los Angeles Flower Market

- A. Dalsol Orchid Warehouse **213 614-1925**
- B. Floral Delivery Co-op .... **213 623.6974** **213 387.1357**
- C. Paul Ecke Poinsettias .... **213 622.8667** *December Only*
- D. See Inset
- E. RDP Floral, Inc.. .... **213 623.2514**
- F. Mellano & Company .... **213 622.0796** *Full Service*
- G. Mellano & Company Wholesale Florist. .... **213 622.0796** *Full Service*
- I. Dayro's Wholesale **213 623.4355**
- J. J. Dayro's Certified Florist, Inc. .... **213 623.5239** *Floral Supplies*
- K. Floral Supply Syndicate ... **213 624.3982** *Floral Supplies*
- L. Moskatel, Inc. .... **213 689.4650** *Floral Supplies*
- M. Stamis Wholesale .... **213 622.6770** *Floral Supplies*
- N. Floral Prop Rental .... **213 622.1700** *Floral Supplies*
- O. Abigail's Flowers .... **213 622.5041** Jay's Plants **213 612.0353**
- P. LA Flower District Association (Badge) **213 627.3696**

Los Angeles Market of the American Florists Exchange, Ltd.

- 1. JX Grand Tree Inc.. .... **213 833.0002**
- 3. William Sanchez Wholesale .... **213 627.6312** *Miscellaneous Cut Flowers*
- 4. Dan Stamis Wholesale . **213 622.6770** *Greens*
- 5. Blossom Valley........ **213 891.9320** *Roses*
- 6. G.M. Floral .... **213 489.7050** *Full Service*
- 7. Dayro's Wholesale..... **213 623.5177** *Roses & Cut Flowers*
- 7A. Flower Salad .... **213 624.1974** *Miscellaneous Cut Flowers, Greens*
- 7B. Dayro's Wholesale..... **213 623.5177** *Roses & Cut Flowers*
- 8. H.O. Norman .... **213 614.1031** *Floral Supplies*
- 10. Kim Brothers.......... **213 623.5922** *Miscellaneous Cut Flowers*
- 11. Eliseo's .... **213 627.4898** *Miscellaneous Cut Flowers*
- 12A. Kimura Plus **213 488.1620**
- 12B-13B RDP Floral............ **213 623.8069** *Roses & Carnations*
- 13A. Adriana's Wholesale... **213 624.0407**
- 14. Choice Flowers .... **213 489.4879** *Miscellaneous & Exotic Flowers*
- 17. Stelzner Wholesale .... **213 891.1514** *Miscellaneous Cut Flowers.............*
- 18. Sanvilla Wholesale .... **213 489-7089** *Greens*
- 20. Cal Pom Pons......... **213 623.6651** *Supermarket Florals, Rose Petals & Roses*
- 23, 33, 34 Mellano & Company... **213 622.0796** *Full Service*
- 24. Valle Wholesale .... **213 688.8810** *Full Service*
- 26. Gonzalez Wholesale ... **213 613.0756** *Miscellaneous Cut Flowers*
- 27. Abigail Flowers........ **213 622.5041**
- 28 29B. Ted's Evergreens....... **213 624.9510** *Greens*
- 29A. Vases by Robert....... **818 434.1512** *Ceramics*
- 30. Rosalios Wholesale .... **213 488.1876** *Miscellaneous Cut Flowers*
- 31. Balloons Away **213 683.8819**
- 32A. Gilbert Wholesale **213 689.9564**
- 32B. A Ruiz Wholesale ...... **213 622.3695** *Exotic Cut Flowers*
- 36 - 37 Tropical U.S.A.. .... **213 614.1915** *Exotic Cut Flowers*
- 39. J.D. Flowers........... **213 489.3234** *Roses & Cut Flowers*
- 40. S.O.S.. .... **213 896.0322** *Miscellaneous Cut Flowers*
- 42 - 43 Paraiso Flowers........ **213 488.0376**
- 44. Paradise Gardens ..... **213 488.5144** *Full Service*
- 45. Orchids Anonymous ... **213 623.4385** *Orchids*
- 50. Sanchez, Martin .... **213 629.4154** *Fruit, Candy & Stuffed Animals*

Johnny & Diane Mellano

Jim Mellano, right

Bob Mellano

Vince

Frank Reyes

JDP Photography

Gary, right

Federico

JDP Photography

William

Paraiso employees

Lourdes, center

Eliseo's

Jessie

Mrs. Park

Jorge

Julio

Lou Goitia and Johnny Mellano

Felix, Studio 8

Ruben Uluchyan

Ena Garcia

Raymundo

Elida

Wordpix

Victor

Kabir Abdul and Frank Reyes

Mabel, Amanda, Lydia, Elizabeth and Veronica

Armando

William

Ho

Ralph

Lou

Carla

Barry Veffer

Santiago

Hernan (right)

Debbie

Jose

Gloria de Romero

Gloria Sandoval and Willie Hernandez

Mario

"Junior" Ramiro Gonzalez (left)

Juan

Profiles in Progress
Wordpix

Wordpix

The profiles presented on the following pages barely come close to telling the full story of the growing, selling and shipping of flowers through the American Florists' Exchange. For while our authors devoted many hours to visiting with the people whose stories we tell here, there are many others – and many who have left the area or passed on – with their own unique experiences that, we regret, could not be captured.

Those who shared their stories gave us priceless anecdotes, opening their hearts and memories to the angst of growing and selling a perishable product before the days of reliable refrigeration or in a time of war or economic depression or as they experienced the growing pains of building a family or a business.

The wealth of information they shared comprises the rich and colorful tapestry of Southern California floral history presented here.

Stimming Flowers 1946 - 1985
The Stock King of the North

One year after World War II ended, flower farms comprised between three and four thousand acres of Southern California land and public demand for cut flowers continued to grow. Although some Japanese-American flower growers had not returned from the camps to their fields, many did. In Los Angeles County the only available land for new flower acreage was in the San Fernando Valley and Dominquez Hills. Local growers seeking new land on which to farm flowers looked south to San Diego County where there was plenty of wide open, if rugged, space.

Bob Stimming looked north.

Land in Ventura and Santa Barbara counties was fertile and the climate was pleasant. Local farmers grew barley, lima beans, sugar beets and strawberries, but no one grew flowers. Other growers at the Los Angeles Flower Market scoffed at Bob's plans and said that Santa Barbara and Ventura were too far away.

Bob grew up working in his father's floriculture business, so he knew all about the risks of growing flowers for a living. His father, William Stimming, was the largest grower of flowering Dutch bulbs from Holland in the state of New York. He had greenhouses in Ithaca and Newark Valley and was a founder and president of the New York State Flower Growers Association.

Bob had survived a mid-air collision in the Pacific Theater where he served as a B-24 command pilot during the war. After an 11-month stint in an Army hospital, unable to continue flying, he turned to the next thing he knew best – growing flowers. Realizing that he couldn't make any money working for his father in New York, he worked for a grower in San Fernando for three months before deciding he was better off on his own.

He started with 80 acres of stock in Santa Barbara. After a few years he moved south to Oxnard and began building a much larger farming and shipping operation. His growing fields included land in Santa Maria, where he farmed for 22 years, and another 50 to 70 acres in Lompoc, almost 100 miles to the north. Because his home was in Camarillo, he spent a lot of time traveling between his business interests.

Eventually Bob was growing cut flowers on 800 acres – most of it was land that he leased on a promise and a handshake which he said in a 2007 interview was all that was needed in those days: "I never signed a lease; if you messed up, your name was mud and you might as well leave the county."

Stock was his primary crop; he was the first grower to bring blooming stock to the Market out of its typical late winter/early spring season. Eventually his flower crops also included 50 acres of Dutch iris, daisies and 100 acres of gladiola.

Bob discovered that growing in California was completely different from growing in New York: "Everything was outdoors and you had the whims of the weather – the hot east winds, the floods and the rain. You could have a beautiful crop [one week,] and a week later you couldn't even pick it."

In the very early years of Stimming Flowers, Bob was occasionally broke: "I didn't know where my next loaf of bread was coming from, but it was okay because I didn't have any workers to pay."

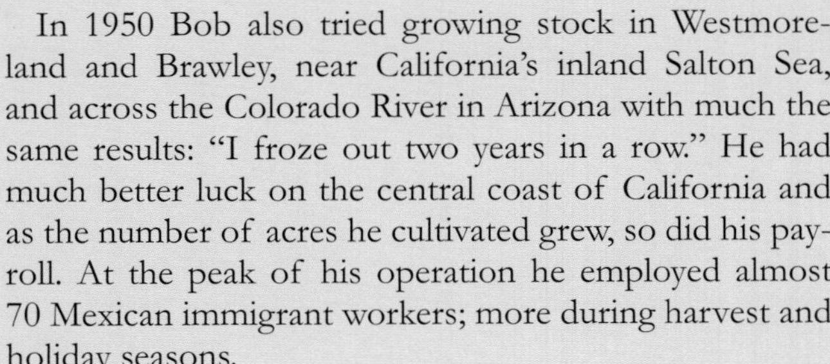

Above: Robert Stimming, 1960s.
Right: Bob Stimming always felt Jim Pamplin, pictured here in the 1960s, taught him everything he knew about gladiolas. Pamplin moved his glad fields from the Camp Pendleton area to Camarillo and Stimming hired him as an advisor on hybridizing. Stimming collection.

In 1950 Bob also tried growing stock in Westmoreland and Brawley, near California's inland Salton Sea, and across the Colorado River in Arizona with much the same results: "I froze out two years in a row." He had much better luck on the central coast of California and as the number of acres he cultivated grew, so did his payroll. At the peak of his operation he employed almost 70 Mexican immigrant workers; more during harvest and holiday seasons.

Like many other large growers during the 1950s and '60s, Bob contracted directly with a few of the chain grocery merchandisers to supply flowers for resale. Piggly Wiggly self-service markets in the South and Midwest were the first to get flowers from the Stimming Flowers' California growing fields in the late 1940s. He also recalls an Alpha Beta order that he split with Elmer Fisher of the G.A. Berlin Company that was "a bone-breaker ... 150,000 bunches of stock that I had to deliver in five days. Elmer provided the gladiolas."

Stimming Flowers' success in Oxnard and Lompoc was noticed down at the Los Angeles Flower Market. Growers discouraged by the negative effect that heat and smoggy air had on their crops began to think that perhaps Santa Barbara County wasn't so far away after all.

Among the first growers to follow Bob north were Jacob Dekker of United Wholesale and C.J. Groen of the Groen Rose Company, who together purchased 40 acres along the coast north of Santa Barbara. Bob put them in touch with a friend of his, a dentist who owned the land, and remembers that Groen and Dekker paid $1,000 per acre for the land in 1949. "I had the lease on that land and was just about to plant it in flowers until Mr. Groen decided to buy it. I knew it was a good piece of land," Bob recalled in 2007.

By the end of the 1960s several other Los Angeles-area flower growers had also moved their operations north – among them the Satow family, long-time carnation growers in Hawthorne, and the Kitagawa family, who had gardenia greenhouses in Venice dating from the 1920s. Wataru Kitagawa had purchased cuttings of a hybrid gardenia grown by Tom Wright, one of the founders of the American Florists' Exchange, and used them to develop an immensely popular gardenia variety called "Kitty's Mystery." Now the family was tired of urban crowding and needed room to breathe. They found new life for their gardenia business in Carpinteria in Santa Barbara County.

Local, then national, flower shipments

In the beginning Bob drove his flowers to the Market himself, three days a week. As his operation grew, he looked outside the Los Angeles area for new markets and

Robert Stimming's glad fields, 1960s.

began shipping from his fields to wholesale customers across the country with whom he dealt directly. He thinks he was the first grower to begin shipping flowers by air. "It was 1947; Rod McClellan, an orchid grower up in the Bay area, started about the same time I did."

The Flying Tiger Line and Slick Airways were the only transcontinental carriers who flew air cargo in those days. "United, TWA and American didn't want any part of air freight. Their attitude was they were making plenty of money on passengers and didn't want our business," Bob recalled.

Eventually the major airlines woke up and began chasing his air freight business, but by that time he was using Flying Tiger's C-47s (the military version of the DC-3 two-engine commercial aircraft) and Slick Airways' C-46s (equivalent to the commercial model DC-4 four-engine aircraft.) The planes flew into his airstrip and loaded at his packing sheds on the Oxnard Ranch.

In the mid-1950s, Stimming Flowers was shipping flowers six days a week. "We'd load 150 hampers and that would fill a DC-3," Bob says. "I'd write them a check for one-thousand dollars, and they would make five stops for me on their way to the East coast. Sometimes I'd send out three airplanes full of flowers, on the northern route, the central and the southern route. They would all end up in New York."

According to Bob, air cargo operators welcomed loads going east because while they had full loads coming from the east to the west, they usually had empty cargo space on the west to east leg. "In those days, before things were manufactured in California, they'd bring loads of clothing and other goods and swing by Detroit to pick up automobile parts. On their way back East, they really didn't care what our flowers weighed; they just wanted to fill up [the cargo bay.]"

Bob had no trouble lining up customers in other cities. He contacted the wholesalers to whom his New York-based father shipped flowers by rail. They ranged as far south as Richmond, Virginia, and west to Cleveland, Detroit, Chicago and cities in between. "They knew my dad and they knew me as a kid. He had a good reputation and that helped me get started."

When the major passenger carriers began offering cargo flights, Stimming Flowers used TWA, American and United. Their costs were lower because they already had terminal facilities and established routes across the country. Labor problems plagued Flying Tigers and Slick Airways; the two tried unsuccessfully to merge in 1954 to compete with the passenger carriers.

Having learned by trial and error the logistics of arranging and managing coast-to-coast air shipments for cut flowers, Bob was willing to share his knowledge with others. One growing operation that he helped was the Van Wingerden family – four brothers who moved with their families from Holland to the Carpinteria area in 1967 and established the Dutch Brothers Nursery.

"Fred Van Wingerden's mother could speak a little English and she came to me and asked if I would help them get started in the shipping business," he recalls. "They were growing carnations, pompons and mums and weren't having much luck in the local markets, so I gave them my list and got more lists from my dad, and showed them how to get started."

Forty years later the Van Wingerden name is still prominent among floriculturists in Ventura and Santa Barbara counties – many of the brothers' offspring are active cut flower nurserymen. "They've all thanked me, and we've been good friends since then; I've been invited to their weddings ... I'm just one of the clan."

Bob also had a relationship with Cal Poly's horticulture department on the university's San Luis Obispo campus, offering internships to graduating students and helping them get started on their floriculture careers.

His penchant for mentoring continues in retirement. In 2007 he is still in touch with a grower of stock whose horticulture career began as a nineteen-year-old flower picker for Stimming Flowers. "I made Joe [Ortiz] my

foreman and taught him the business. He's 66 now and farming five or six hundred acres of flowers in Santa Paula and in Lompoc on the land where I used to be, as well as in Brawley. I feel just like a dad to him."

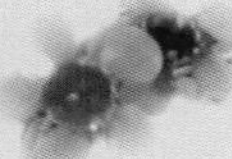

Bob Stimming hasn't lost his enthusiasm for the floral industry. He laughs often in remembering his years at the Los Angeles Flower Market and several friendships forged there that have endured the passage of time. One old friend is Eddie Battistessa of Edmunds Wholesale, from whom he bought a share of stock in the American Florists' Exchange so he could open a stall in 1946. He and Eddie are still in regular touch by telephone.

Bob kept that share of stock and maintained a stall at the Market until 1985 when he sold it to Mas Yoshida, a partner in Growers Wholesale Florist, and retired to Scottsdale, Arizona.

E. H. Pearson Wholesale Flowers 1920s-1980
Bert Johnson Wholesaler 1960-1970
Eighty-Plus Years of Swedish Persistence

Bert Johnson can still tick off the challenges of buying and selling flowers 50 years ago when the Los Angeles Flower Market was dedicated one-hundred percent as a venue through which growers could sell their products.

Only flowers that were grown locally were available unless someone brought in a shipment from San Francisco. In bad weather, when flowers were unavailable, business faltered. Retail florists had to "make do" with what local growers could provide. Public sales were not permitted.

So while wholesalers and commission men – of which Bert was one – could make money in those days, success hinged on their ability to read market trends and to cultivate relationships with the growers who provided their flowers and with the customers who bought from them. It was a balancing act in which the growers – and the weather – were in charge.

"A very difficult part of the business was that you were handling a perishable item," he says. "You had to know market prices and demand so you could sell what you had before it rotted. If you set the price too high, you were stuck with it. If you set the price too low, you weren't doing a good job for the grower."

Bert has been an American Florists' Exchange participant – an active one – for many years. In a 2007 interview, in his 40-plus year of service on the AFE board of directors and at the age of 87, he says he's always "the oldest guy in the room" at any AFE event.

Bert entered the U.S.A. through Ellis Island on his fourth birthday. His family was headed for the Los Angeles area, where an uncle had already found success growing flowers on a one-acre farm in Lomita. He also had a retail shop in San Pedro. The year was 1924.

E. H. (Eric Harold) Pearson's specialty was freesias. His first horticulture job was as a gardener for the Swedish royal family before he decided to emigrate to America in 1915. A freesia hybridizer on the East coast hired him to go to California where the new varieties of colored freesias could be field-grown.

Bert Johnson at the Flower Market, 1950s

Settled in the South Bay area of Los Angeles, Harold was undoubtedly happy to have family from back home in Sweden around him. He took his young nephew to the Los Angeles Flower Market, where he had a stall, for the first time around 1930. As was customary for immigrants, family members had first dibs on work when it was available so in 1942, when hired help was scarce, he asked Bert to come help out at the Pearson Wholesale gladiola counter. By that time, Bert was working full-time at the Bank of America. "I would go to the Market at 2 o'clock in the morning, work until 7:30 a.m., go home to change clothes and then go to my bank job."

It was, he admits, sort of a relief to join the U.S. Navy in 1944. "I bet I was one of the few people whose life was saved by the war," Bert says, recalling the terrible eating habits and exhausting schedule he lived as a young man so that when he entered the service, at six-feet tall, he weighed just 130 pounds. "I gave up two jobs for just one, and I got fed, too."

A broker for high-grade gladiola

Returning to Los Angeles in early 1946, Bert rejoined his uncle at the Market – this time it was his only career – and threw himself into learning the business of a floral commission broker. He worked side-by-side with Harold's wife Dena, who he describes as an incredible hostess that everyone liked.

Bert worked the Flower Market for his uncle for thirteen years, and then ten more on his own, specializing in gladiola brought in from Torrance and Palos Verdes in the Los Angles area, and from Vista in San Diego County. Some of the small Vista growers he recalls buying from were C. B. Robinett, E. P. "Pinky" Briley, Arville Williams, C. P. Loza, James Pamplin and Jack Merrill, and in Palm Springs – a wintertime growing area – Hector Ramsdale.

Shipments from San Diego were handled first by trucker Ben Wilson and then by gladiola shipper Vinson & Fortiner, but occasionally he made other arrangements with independent truckers. Bert recalls one incident when he seriously considered suing – but never did – the trucker who had placed flowers in the same truck with a load of refrigerators. "The refrigerators leaked their gas, and destroyed our entire shipment."

About 1960 Bert left his uncle's business so that his cousin Bob, newly home from Army service, could join his father at E.H. Pearson Wholesale. Bert opened his own counter representing two growers who switched their consignment to him with Harold's blessings. He added other bulb cut flowers to his line – including iris grown by James Ishabashi in Palos Verdes.

His customers included whole families whose members owned many flower shops – the Cohen boys, the Fisk boys and the Cordova brothers, to name a few. "In those days," Bert recalls, "your customers were all personal friends." Collection issues were non-existent: "If you had a problem with any one of them, you just spoke to their uncle – and you'd get the money."

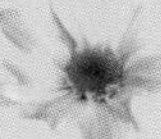

Perhaps the activity Bert is best remembered for by Wall Street's old-timers is the column he penned in the monthly *Bloomin' News* at the request of Market manager Walter Swartz. "Bert Johnson's Brass Band" was at its heart a chatty gossip column – chock full of the names of Market regulars, tongue-in-cheek digs and heard-on-the-street stories that ruffled more than a few feathers over the ten years it appeared. "Giovanni Mellano didn't talk to me for three years because I wrote that he always wore the same pair of pants to Market," Bert recalls with a chuckle.

About the time Bert opened his own counter at the Market, he also began seeking to own shares of AFE stock. "I hustled shares from growers willing to sell until I got a substantial number of them," he says.

Then, sometime in the 1960s, he joined the AFE board of directors and even when he left the Market in 1970 to join his wife Claudia in her real estate business, Bert stayed on the board. He was involved in the Market's successful acquisition of two important Wall Street properties in the 1970s.

Even with all of the changes he's witnessed and the tough decisions he has been part of, Bert regards his years working the day-to-day routine of the sales floor followed by his years of behind-the-scenes work on the AFE board with pride.

Like mother, like son

Just as Dena Johnson Pearson was an outgoing, fun-loving woman well-liked by her customers and remembered for her parties, so was her son, Bob.

Dena met her husband Harold not long after both had come to America from their native Sweden. He grew tulips, freesias and asters on a small ranch in Lomita and opened a counter at the Los Angeles Flower Market just as the Second World War was getting started. Bob began working for his parents at the Market at age fifteen, as the war wound down.

All three were hard workers – but Dena and her son, in particular, also played hard when the work-day was over. Bob recalls tagging along with his mother at age ten to watch the ponies run at Hollywood Park, Santa Anita or the Del Mar racetrack. It was an activity he came to enjoy, and it dictated his lifestyle forever as he indulged his passion for gambling.

Bob did his military service with the U.S. Army and after his discharge in 1953, was ready to join his dad full-time in the family business. His mother had died not too long before, and Bob jumped feet-first into the routine.

"On Sunday," he recalls, "I'd get up at midnight, go to the Market, get all the orders ready by 6 o'clock Monday morning, work the counter until 10 a.m., square everything away and be off to the racetrack or to Vegas by early afternoon. I was young, I didn't think I'd live forever, and three hours of sleep was plenty."

Soon after his son Bob began working full-time at the Market, Harold bought ten acres at Tehachapi, a valley at around 4,000 feet elevation surrounded by mountains about 110 miles north of Los Angeles, and began growing lilacs, peonies and tulips.

"When the season came in for tulips and peonies, just before Mother's Day, it would take three to four hours to drive up to Tehachapi to pick up a load from our ranch," Bob Pearson recalls. "The ranch crew had the flowers all picked and ready, so it took only half an hour to load up; and then three or four hours to return to the Market, where we put the flowers in water. By that time, it was 6 a.m. and time for the retail florists to stampede into the Market."

The Pearson Wholesale counter was the second one inside the back door of the Market, next to the Groen Rose Company. Bob sold it soon after his father's death in 1980, and says today that the almost 30 years he sold flowers to florists and route men remain the most memorable of his life.

Groen Rose Company 1917 – 1993
The Dutchman Who Grew Roses

Sylvia Groen Foltz remembers her father as a quiet and reserved man with a whole lot of patience. Undoubtedly, she was the beneficiary of that patience when, as an eight- or nine-year-old helper, it was her responsibility to place stephanotis in boxes of 25 or 100 flowers and tie several of the boxes together for transport to the Market. "I wouldn't always tie the string securely so when you picked them up, the string would break. I got told off about that," she recalls.

Still, growing up on a flower farm in Montebello, just eight miles east of downtown Los Angeles, was an idyllic childhood for Sylvia, the youngest of two sisters. Her father, Cornelius Johannes (C.J.) Groen was a major figure at the Los Angeles Flower Market, where his work on its behalf earned him widespread respect among other growers, wholesalers and florists.

C.J., or Con, came through Ellis Island in 1910, a young immigrant from Holland who left home at fourteen and headed for France to work as a circus roustabout. Then he went to England where he had his first brush with horticulture as a greenhouse apprentice.

Once in America, he worked on a private Long Island estate for a couple of years before settling in Montebello in 1912. With a few years of greenhouse experience under his belt, he went to work for the Turner Nursery, a predecessor of the Wilcox Nursery, and then into partnership with a couple of other Holland-born nurserymen, John and Walter Polder. They grew field flowers and bulb stock in fields that, beginning in 1917, also sprouted derricks pumping oil.

That was also the year C.J. married Lavina, a Swedish girl whose family had settled in Montebello, and struck out on his own as a flower grower. After completing military service with the U.S. Army, he leased a lot on Beverly Boulevard, planted carnations, worked hard to buy the land, and gradually focused his efforts on growing roses under glass. Over time he built several acres of glass greenhouses in which he grew the blooms that made the Groen Rose Company one of the major players in rose floriculture in Southern California.

Throughout his career C.J. promoted the flower industry and worked tirelessly for several industry groups. He was a charter member of the California State Florists' Association, one of the founders of the Southern California Floral Association in 1933, and a member of the national trade association Roses Inc. He was also an original supporter of the California International Flower Show, where he won an award for "Outstanding Display of Roses" in 1954.

By far his most important contribution to the Los Angeles floral industry was as one of the group of men who founded the American Florists' Exchange (AFE) and guided its early years. He even financed one of AFE's property acquisitions in 1945 with the help of Montebello banker J.S. Whyte, and served as AFE's president and treasurer from 1946 until his death in 1957. He was also remembered around the Market for the fedora he often wore.

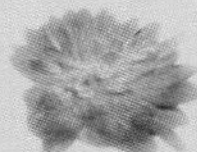

When you're eight, the age Sylvia was when she recalls playing on the carts used to take cut roses to the grading room, it's easy to imagine a cart as your own private "trolley car" by adding a few sticks and cloth drape. Younger by eight years than her sister Julia, Sylvia found her own entertainment in a world of mostly grown-ups and a teen-aged sister. She recalls her parents' parties at which everyone spoke in Dutch – an unfamiliar language because at home her family spoke only English. "The only Dutch I ever learned," she says now, "were all the Dutch swear words – at those parties."

Julia went away to college in 1936, and married Roy Halsey in 1940. Sylvia married Ken Foltz in 1947 after her college years, and worked for a while as a school teacher. Both daughters occasionally helped out in the Groen Rose Company office.

A Groen family affair

When C. J. Groen died in 1957, Sylvia and Julia helped their mother continue operating what was by then a flourishing enterprise with acreage in both Montebello and Santa Barbara.

"I don't know what Dad thought would happen to the business," says Sylvia now. "There were no sons, just two daughters, but we managed to keep it all going until 1993."

Their husbands also worked at various times for the Groen Rose Company. Roy joined the company in 1946 to handle sales at the Market and later opened his own business, Roy Halsey Wholesale Florist, which he sold to United Wholesale in 1950, and went on to open a restaurant among other business ventures. Ken then took over Groen's Market activity, and also worked in Montebello where the primary crops by that time were ferns and bird of paradise (*Strelitzia*). Rose production had been moved up the coast to Santa Barbara where the cool, moist climate was better for rose cultivation.

Beginning in the 1960s, Groen's Market operations were handled first by Jack Christiansen, then Casey Visser, followed by Mas Ogawa. Sylvia and Julia managed the office in Montebello, and in Santa Barbara, Ross Nielsen grew the roses. C.J. had hired Ross in 1937 to manage the Montebello farm. In 1949, when C.J. began moving his greenhouses to Santa Barbara, he incorporated his company and Ross acquired a percentage of ownership.

The city of Montebello continued to expand and in 1969 the Groen land was sold to a developer for a large apartment-house complex. "All of the 'birds' were dug out and loaded into large trucks to be transported to Encinitas, a less populated area, to be planted until they will again have to be uprooted to make way for progress," the *Montebello Messenger* reported on July 3, 1969.

Actually, roughly half of the birds stayed in Montebello and were planted beneath the Southern California Edison transmission lines. At one time Edison allowed that land to be leased inexpensively for agricultural and other purposes. Ken Foltz continued caring for the birds that were left in Montebello, and the Groen Rose Company moved its business office to Santa Fe Springs.

In Santa Barbara, Ross Nielsen's crew picked, graded and loaded the roses onto trucks that left the greenhouses in the early evening for the two- to three-hour trip to the Los Angeles Flower Market where they were sold throughout the night and early morning.

By the time Julia's and Sylvia's daughters – Linda Kirshman and Lori Anderson – joined the company, having raised their own children, it was the 1980s. Both did their share of two- and three-o'clock mornings at the Market, greeting the Santa Barbara trucks. The 1970s and early '80s were busy, prosperous years for the company.

Above: C.J. Groen stands in the back of the rose grading room, his son-in-law Roy Halsey to his left, late 1940s.
Opposite: The crew at Polder Ranch (C.J. Groen is third from right), around 1912. *Sylvia Foltz collection.*

When Mas Ogawa retired, Lori took over Market operations. In keeping with the Groen Rose Company's long-time support of the AFE, she served on the board of directors for three years, 1990-93, and fondly recalls the extravagant Open Houses, a full day of floral displays and camaraderie on both sides of Wall Street. "We always had two or three florists put together huge arrangements to show off all of our rose varieties," she remembers.

Groen Rose Company sold their product only at the Los Angeles Flower Market, supplying local wholesalers and florists. Occasionally they bought and resold roses from growers in Northern California, primarily during Tournament of Roses Parade season in Pasadena when a favorite customer was Isabella Coleman, one of the first float designers who pioneered an industry of professional parade float builders and for whom a Rose Parade Trophy Award is named.

"She was a wonderful lady and very particular about the flowers; she always wanted quality," recalls Sylvia, adding that the thrill of delivering their roses to the float construction area and seeing the colorful creations being assembled never diminished for her through the years. "I always had a wonderful time during Rose Parade season."

C.J. and Lavina Groen, 1954.

The end of a rosy era

The handwriting pointing to the eventual demise of rose cultivation in America began to appear on the wall in the early 1980s. Roses could be grown, harvested and brought into the United States from Colombia, Ecuador and other South American countries at lower costs that couldn't be matched by domestic growers.

The 220-plus members of the nonprofit national trade association Roses Inc. lobbied to protect the interests of its grower members against foreign imports. Sylvia, the first woman to serve on the board of the Michigan-based organization, went to Washington, DC to testify before a Congressional committee that was holding hearings on limiting certain foreign imports.

"We wrote letters by the dozens, trying to get some relief on trade and tariffs," she says, "but our little industry just wasn't big enough. We couldn't make enough noise!"

The Groen Rose Company was among the first to close its greenhouses, in 1993, a year after Sylvia retired. Domestic rose cultivation was concentrated at that point around the San Francisco Bay area. There were a few growers still operating in the East and Midwest, but their colder weather and higher heating bills meant they couldn't be competitive with imports.

Today, Roses Inc. has evolved into the International Cut Flower Growers Association to reflect the broader interests of grower members who have diversified into other cut flower crops for commercial production.

Groen's Santa Barbara rose producing powerhouse

C. J. Groen and Ross Nielsen made a great team: the first was an industry statesman and an astute businessman with an interest in horticulture and a flair for recognizing trends – such as the appeal of birds of paradise – before everyone else did. The second was an extraordinary manager who could make it all come together in the field.

Ross had worked for a Minneapolis nursery and, like many transplants from the upper Midwest, came to California to escape the cold winters. He worked for a while with Armacost & Royston, and then signed on to manage Groen's operations in Montebello in 1937.

After World War II the two of them realized that smog was starting to be a problem in the greater Los Angeles basin. Dirty air, plus Montebello's searing summertime heat, led them to look for some other location more conducive to growing premium roses yet close enough that they could still get their product to the Los Angeles Flower Market. They found what they were looking for in Santa Barbara County, between Hope Ranch and the University of California campus.

Jacob Dekker, who had founded United Wholesale Florist in the 1930s, was a good friend of C. J. Groen – they shared Dutch roots. In 1949 they purchased approximately 40 oceanfront acres together, and split the plot down the middle.

Dekker planted field flowers on his half and Groen began moving his greenhouses up from Montebello to the other half. Both men set aside land on which to build their own homes, and each moved a full-time manager up from the Los Angeles area to oversee growing operations – Henry Meyer for United Wholesale, and Ross Nielsen for Groen Rose Company. There was no financial connection between the two companies other than that they later purchased an additional 65 acres in order to secure well drilling rights, because there was no water on the original 40 acres.

Ross Nielsen's son, Paul, was nine when his family moved to Santa Barbara to build a home on two acres of land that C. J. deeded to Ross in a partial ownership agreement that also included shares of the newly incorporated Groen Rose Company. Growing up around the greenhouses – every year it seemed there were more of them being built – he decided early on that "I didn't want to be working seven days a week in the flower business like my father did."

So after graduating from UC-Berkeley with an engineering degree in 1962, he worked five years for North American Aviation in Los Angeles. "Then in 1967," Paul recalls, "my father came to me and said there was an opportunity for me to take over managing the greenhouse operation which employed 30 people in Santa Barbara. Dad's health wasn't good, and there was no one else in either the Foltz or Halsey families who was prepared to assume that responsibility."

Paul and his new wife Carolyn moved to Santa Barbara and he became his father's understudy in the nursery, taking on more and more responsibility over the years until Ross died in 1980.

Roses were the ranch's main product – 99 percent of the crop went to the Los Angeles Flower Market – but other things were also planted, including three or four acres of bird of paradise, a species that had done very well in Montebello but which did not thrive in Santa Barbara's cool ocean breezes. In the 1980s, the ranch diversified further by converting some of its older greenhouses to the production of potted plants.

"We were always able to sell all of our product at the Market and I think that was because people liked dealing with us – we were an established company with a good name offering choice merchandise," Paul says today. He remembers that soon after the company built an additional three acres of greenhouses in about 1980, all of the domestic rose growers began to feel the impact of imported product.

"By the early 1990s, when a huge portion of the market was being taken by offshore production, it seemed that the domestic growers who might survive would only do so by investing huge amounts of money to retrofit their greenhouses to grow roses hydroponically."

Paul's engineering training came in handy at this point. In 1990 the company converted four of its greenhouses to hydroponic production to test the feasibility of the technique, which had been developed originally in Holland. In 1992 he made a presentation to Groen's board of directors on what it would take to convert all of their greenhouses to a hydroponic system.

"The decision was not to invest that substantial amount of money in a venture that was so risky, because there was no way to know if, even after making the investment, we would still be able to sell our product competitively. It was too early to foresee exactly how South American imports were going to impact us," he says.

Groen ceased operations by early 1993 and leased greenhouse space to other Santa Barbara flower growers and nurseries. Paul himself became a broker and distributor of cut flowers. Over time his company evolved into the Central Coast Plant Company which today limits its business to potted plants and hanging baskets for the nursery and garden center trade. Its production facility still operates on the Groen Rose Company property.

Lewis Gardens 1931 > The Hobby That Grew into a Business

When Hubert Lewis died at age 97 and his wife died at age 98 in 2005, the couple had just celebrated 74 years of a truly special marriage.

Daughter Linda Martonik says Hubert and Helen worked together in their nursery business almost the entire three quarters of a century they were married, "side-by-side, and loved every minute of it."

Like many businesses, this one started from Helen Lewis's hobby — making corsages in the family's laundry room in Pico Rivera, California. When Linda was two or three years old, her parents opened a small nursery where they raised begonias, cyclamen, azaleas and Calceolaria crenatiflora (the "pocket book flower"). Linda remembers her mother lifting her up to sit on a bench and play while Mother worked. There she "played with the calceolarias and turned fuschia flowers into little ballerinas."

In 1946, when Linda was six, Lewis Gardens took a stall in the American Florists' Exchange. Later, when they opened a store across the street, they made history as the first Caucasian tenant of the Southern California Flower Market.

Lewis Gardens operated 25 acres in Whittier for many years and then began growing on 100 acres in Vista in San Diego County, from where they sent their potted plants to the Whittier facility for maturing.

After the move to Vista, Helen and Hubert Lewis let Linda have her own greenhouse to grow any flower she chose. One season she raised violets, another season it was ivy. At age four, she was growing coleus. She cared for the plants under loving parental supervision.

The Blue Hills of Mirada Hills

Lying just south of Whittier and east of the Los Angeles County line, the Blue Hills area of Mirada Hills (now La Mirada) included some of the expansive Orange County land holdings of the Irvine Land Company and the McNally Ranch. Blue Hills was a trade name the area's farmers adopted based on the spectacular blue lupine wildflowers that blanketed its rich adobe soil and gently rolling hillsides.

Although the Blue Hills soil was "sticky" after rains (vehicles sometimes got stuck in it), its nutrients fostered a growing agricultural community. Many farmers grew vegetables there, and chrysanthemums, daisies, asters and other flowers, creating a patchwork of colors across the hillsides. Their family names included (but were not limited to): Hagiwara, Hamano, Iwata, Kai, Mimaki, Mizufukas, Nakamura, Nakamichi, Nimoki and Takahashi.

C. W. Camp relates in his book, La Mirada: From Rancho to City, that in the winter of 1946 (after many of the Japanese-American farmers had returned from the World War II camps), "a whimsical nature briefly turned their hills into a frosty wonderland – snow covered the land, as it did elsewhere in the southland of California."

Although the farmers have long since moved away, the beauty of the Blue Hills and its gentle, sunny slopes can be seen today near La Mirada Boulevard and Foster Road in the La Mirada Regional Park, Municipal Golf Course and La Mirada High School campus.

Jacaranda trees in bloom in Spring 2008 at La Mirada Regional Park, formerly the Blue Hills flower fields.

Helen Lewis grew her hobby into a treasure that eventually supported the family and gifted each family member with experiences of a lifetime.

Blue Hills Nursery 1936 > From Frank and Asaye Nakamura's Dream

As a boy, Frank Nakamura worked with his siblings and parents on the family's flower farm in the Blue Hills area (see sidebar) of La Mirada (then called Mirada Hills), California, along with other Nisei (first generation Japanese American) growers who sold their blooms at the Los Angeles market. The earnest toiling of the earth was but a stepping stone to greater things for Frank.

Frank Nakamura left the farm with his family when the Japanese-Americans relocated to internment camps during World War II, and returned after the War, at around age 20, to farm for a few more years. Like the flowers, however, the little towns and villages were growing, first with housing developments, then schools, churches and commercial structures. One by one, the Nisei farmers were crowded out of Blue Hills.

In 1951, Frank and his wife, Asaye, started a tiny flower shop and nursery not far away, on the site of an old lemon grove on East Whittier Boulevard in Whittier. The modest garden center evolved over the next 60 years into a popular regional garden center.

The early Blue Hills nursery was in "the country." Frank hauled plant material in his stake-bed truck, and both he and Asaye worked in the nursery. A growing clientele came to place its trust in the couple who always sold them the best plants and answered their gardening questions.

As the Blue Hills Nursery grew, more personnel came aboard and Frank ventured to try new ideas. He planted seasonal colors in front of the nursery, leading customers to purchase similar plants. He opened a multi-retail complex at the garden center that attracted customers for its lawn mower shop, tropical fish, floral arrangements, art and custom draperies. For a long time, Frank operated a gift shop, managed by daughter Lisa, in the west end of the nursery building. Over the years, Frank took over those retail spaces but expanded the nursery. Today, the 15,500 square feet garden center is a popular source for gardening products for the region.

"People in this area have been tearing out their lawns and planting vegetable gardens," Frank Nakamura was quoted as saying in 1975. The *Home & Garden Supply Merchandiser* went on to describe how the gardening and indoor plant material boom of the 1960s and 1970s had "made a big change" in Nakamura's business. Frank and Asaye's nursery had flexed its marketing and merchandising muscles and kept up with trends.

Top: Frank Nakamura in an early photo of the garden center. Above: A recent photo of the Blue Hills Garden Center in Whittier.

Frank and Asaye still live near the garden center they built and nurtured, now managed by their son Stan, whose three children also work in the business. Their flower business has come a long way from the Nakamura family's flower farming days in Blue Hills.

Weidners' Gardens 1947 > Embracing Trend, Opportunity and Love of Flowers

Evelyn Weidner has weathered every trend from 1960s "flower power" to freeway construction. Southern California's dramatic growth trends had a direct impact on the Buena Park Greenhouses* business her husband Bob purchased in 1947. Construction of the I-5 freeway forced him to move the nursery, which he'd built into a thriving wholesale foliage company, from Buena Park to Brea in 1956. In the 1960s, facing the realities of smog, traffic and the need for more space, the couple took the opportunity to sell their property and move to Encinitas. Settled in Encinitas by 1969, the Weidners "embarked upon the glorious leisure experiment," says Evelyn, as they enjoyed retirement and travel. That was a trend that Bob Weidner never quite fully embraced, however, as, in spite of his years, the hard-working plantsman yearned to return to work.

The Weidners' Encinitas property on Normandy Street lay conveniently alongside the newly completed I-5 freeway, offering both visibility and accessibility. It just seemed natural to develop a Weidners' Gardens nursery. The pair parlayed their years of experience and renewed vision into quick success.

Bob Weidner. ***Photo by Tony Kranz***

Bob Weidner re-introduced the Boston fern as a popular house plant. He developed the new-plant-every-year marketing concept. Evelyn recalls that Bob "also brought Aechmea Fasciata, a bromeliad with a gorgeous pink flower that rises from the center, from Germany." Their years in the business also led to their pioneering the pre-finished plants concept, growing the plants to within three or four weeks of bloom before shipping them. And then one day, Bob's marketing brilliance really shone.

"Bob asked me how I'd like to have a patch of tuberous begonias as seedlings. I thought that around 50 for the yard would be nice. He said, Good, and then told me he's just ordered 25,000."

Evelyn Weidner says that when she picked herself up off the floor, Bob explained he'd ordered so many because he knew she loved begonias and he thought customers should be able to see a "big show" of the flowers. He also wanted people to dig their own plants when they were in bloom and ready for transplanting.

The Weidners suddenly found themselves in the begonia business. They posted Evelyn's hand-made sign along the freeway and distributed fliers to local shops. The words "Free Flower Show, Dig Your Own Begonias" drew hundreds of freeway travelers.

"I said I hoped we could sell $100 worth per day, never dreaming it would grow to thousands of dollars per day," Evelyn recalls.

Before long, the Weidners' dig-your-own begonias (and later, dig-your-own pansies) season along with sales of their other plants made Weidners' Gardens a full-time, no-longer-in-retirement business. Evelyn Weidner's horticulture industry and civic activities, along with marketing methods she and the Weidners' daughter Mary employed regularly, helped to grow the garden center. They embraced trends and opportunities with creativity and vision.

One year, a fuchsia basket the Weidners had hung for decoration drew so much attention that it became the next season's featured plant. The following year, impatiens took the stage. Eventually, the new plant-each-year concept was branded Proven Winners and evolved into an international marketing program.

Evelyn and Mary continued to grow the business after Bob's passing in 1988, building it into a destination and trusted source for customers across America. In 2000, Evelyn Weidner was inducted by the Kee Kitayama Research Foundation into the California Floriculture Hall of Fame.

Above: a Kiwanis Club lunch held in the Weidner Buena Park greenhouse in the 1950s. Left: Evelyn Weidner enjoys a typical sunny California day in the Weidners Gardens greenhouse in Encinitas, 2007.

***Bob Weidner bought Henson's Greenhouse in Buena Park, California in 1947, renaming it to Buena Park Greenhouses.**

The Flower Families of Montebello Carnations, Birds and Sweet Peas in the Beautiful Hills

It was an inspired publicity stunt that was, by any measure, successful. In 1956, two prominent Montebello-based flower growers, Cornelius J. Groen and Waandert J. Vander Bruggen – both of Dutch heritage, shipped a thousand bird of paradise stems to New York City to decorate the public rooms of the Holland-America ocean-going liner on which they had booked passage for a visit to their homeland.

Then they invited the florists of New York to come down to the docks and see the festive arrangements of the exotic bloom that, just four years earlier, had been named the official city flower of Los Angeles.

As reported in *The Saturday Evening Post** on March 11, 1961, in an article profiling the unusual flower and some of its successful commercial growers in Southern California: "Newspapers blossomed with stories about the exotic African flower that came from California. By the time the bird growers returned, their business had taken a decided upswing."

In the early 1950s, Groen and Vander Bruggen had played a role in the campaign to make bird of paradise the official Los Angeles flower, rather than the geranium that the city's mayor favored. The fact that commercial cultivation of "birds" was a California industry helped create the victory.

Groen and Vander Bruggen were long-time friends whose flower growing and wholesale operations were among the largest in Montebello, a community several miles east of Los Angeles.

Montebello, which means "beautiful hills" in Italian, had been an agricultural area since its earliest days when the community was called Newmark after one of the area's pioneering families. Flower growers and nurserymen established businesses in Newmark in the 1910s and '20s, drawn by its warm climate, fertile soil and abundant water from the nearby San Gabriel River. Newmark's large flower growing community included families of European descent, as well many Japanese-American families who leased or bought land on which to grow flowers or build greenhouses.

The Mori Nursery, in particular, operated in the same location from its founding in 1913 until it succumbed to urban sprawl in early 1973. As specialists in potted blooming plants, the two original Mori brothers – Akira (Fred) and Yoshiharu – were among the early nurserymen who bought poinsettia cuttings from Paul Ecke, Sr. of today's Ecke Ranch.

Frank Kuwahara's family grew narcissus and daisies in Montebello in the 1920s, and Frank began taking flowers to the Market when he was a high school sophomore: "I arranged my classes so I could take study hall the first period and if I was late, I didn't miss anything," he told Sylvia Foltz, C.J. Groen's daughter, in a 1981 interview.

Frank graduated from Montebello High School in 1930 and joined his father's business as expected, although he had hoped to study engineering at Cal Tech. He later became a leader of the Southern California Flower Growers, Inc., the entity that managed the Japanese-American flower market on Wall Street.

Other early wholesale nurseries in Montebello included the Howard and Smith operation (1905), which specialized in flowering plants, and the Turner Nursery, Henry Turner's hothouses for cut flowers on Beverly Boulevard, which eventually became the Wilcox Nursery and later, the A. A. Schnierow Nursery.

The Polder Brothers were two Dutch immigrants who grew bulb stock, carnations and other field flowers on leased land in Montebello. John and Walter Polder got their early agricultural training on private estates as apprentice gardeners before emigrating in 1912 and forming a partnership with fellow Dutch immigrant C. J. Groen, who went on to found the Groen Rose Company a few years later.

Montebello's first retail cut flower shop that was not primarily a nursery operation opened in 1930, a small sales stand on two acres devoted to growing annual blooms such as sweet peas, along with asters, caspia, chrysanthemums and stock. The farm and shop were run by the Goto family: parents Yasaku and Miyo and their eight children – James, Masae, Clyde, Michi, Echo, Taka, Toshi and Ray. The Japanese-American family spent several years during World War II in a camp and, upon returning, regained their shop and land and continued to grow flowers and nursery stock for sale at the Los Angeles Flower Market.

Most of the Goto children continued in the flower business with their spouses and children. Taka Goto and his wife Kay became the owners of Montebello's Unique Floral Shop. Jon Prechtl, working for United Wholesale in the 1960s, grew up in Montebello and recalls that Taka never forgot that Jon regularly set aside Marguerite daisies for him when they were difficult to find one season. Taka returned the favor from then on, continuing to buy Marguerites from Jon at the United counter twice a week for many years – and, says Jon, "Taka always paid cash".

Montebello's Polder Ranch workers around 1912. ***Sylvia Foltz collection.***

Masae Goto Nomura opened M's Flowers in Montebello along with husband Bob and children Rod, Ann, Duke and Jay. The shop is run today by son Jay, his wife Dorothy and their children Jill and Ryan. Duke and wife Karen with daughter Lindy run Commerce Flowers. Ann Nomura Morishita, husband Paul and daughter Robyn run M's Flowers in La Habra.

Echo Goto started a shop in Los Angeles called Centro Florist. In the early 1950s, Ray and Toshi Goto leased Calvary Cemetery Floral Shop. Ray also grew flowers on Bessho property and later moved to Las Vegas where he opened another shop.

In later years, Taka and Kay Goto and daughters Gail, Cheryll and son Kelly ran the Unique Floral Shop until around 2001 when Cheryll Goto became its owner. Cheryll now runs Unique Floral Shop with her daughter Kiku Goto-Berry and loyal employees.

Birthing the AFE

Montebello's flower growing community included several visionaries who conceived the American Florists' Exchange (AFE) as a wholesale market for the European American growers of flowers, and worked to make it a reality. Two of them, Roy F. Wilcox and H. N. Gage, signed the AFE's Articles of Incorporation.

Roy Wilcox grew azaleas and kentia palms in addition to roses on his expansive Montebello acreage. According to a manuscript entitled "The Men's Garden Club of Los Angeles: An Informal History of the Early Years" written by Kaoru Oguri, Ph.D. and dated July 18, 2000, Wilcox showed considerable initiative to keep his business afloat when the Depression of the early 1930s hit. He reportedly went to the Bank of America and asked for a loan to pay his staff and buy water and fertilizer. His argument that a cash influx would enable him to transplant his plants into one-gallon, then five-gallon cans within a year, and then into tubs and twenty-gallon containers – each year tripling in value – must have convinced bank lending officers that he knew his business. As the Depression eased, he was able to contract with organizers of the San Francisco Fair and with Hollywood Park, which opened in 1938, to supply all of their foliage plants.

Wilcox was a prominent figure on the regional floriculture scene for many years. He also served the California State Floral Association as president in the 1950s, and was instrumental in forming The Men's Garden Club of Los Angeles which had strong ties to the Los Angeles Flower Market through its influential members and advisors.

Montebello businessman H. N. Gage was another of the five men who signed the AFE Articles of Incorporation on the last day of 1920. He was apparently also a grower, but we know very little about him today.

Other Montebello floriculturists who were heavily involved in founding the AFE from its very earliest days prior to 1920 were calla and Easter lily cultivation expert Gebhard Prechtl, rose-grower C. J. Groen and bulb specialist John Polder. All three engaged in some aspect of planning, arranging financing, drafting incorporation papers and finding a suitable location for the Market.

We can only imagine the spirited discussions among members of Montebello's flower-growing community on their shared vision for a wholesale market that had their interests at heart.

***The Saturday Evening Post*, "The Flowers Known As Birds," Frank Taylor, March 11, 1961**

The Prechtl Family Pre-1914 > Three Generations Supporting the American Florists' Exchange

Gebhard Prechtl must have been a very practical man. He was, after all, of German heritage — a people whose tenacity, discipline and conscientiousness have been well-documented. As one of the men behind the start of the American Florists' Exchange (AFE) of the Los Angeles Flower Market, these qualities undoubtedly served him well, especially during the early years.

He must have believed wholeheartedly in the idea of a central market dedicated to the families of European-American flower growers. At that time they had nowhere else except the downtown produce market at which to sell their flower crops. The group borrowed money, leased a garage at Winston and Fourth streets near the new wholesale market for Japanese-American growers, and began selling shares to the growers and anyone else who could afford the $50-per-share price tag. Gebhard was not about to let their investment fail.

The financial crash of 1929 occurred just eight years after AFE's Articles of Incorporation were signed by two florists, a seed cultivator and two growers. Gebhard Prechtl had been president of the Exchange since 1922, its second year of existence. In its early years, the Exchange had difficulty selling its shares of common stock and by the end of the decade, he still owned 51 percent of them – no doubt a heavy personal financial burden, especially in the Depression years that followed.

That's when Gebhard's practical side came into play. His son Harvey recalled that because he couldn't pay the $500 taxes on all the property he owned, he decided to sell some of the shares outside the flower-growing community to Herman Seidler, who was a friend of Paul Ecke Sr., another of the AFE's "founding fathers." He also dug up his paperwhite bulbs and sold them to John Bodger of the Bodger Seed Company to raise money to pay his taxes.

Although Harvey, who passed away on April 6, 2008 at age 87, did not know the year in which his father arrived in New York City as an immigrant, he knew that it was prior to the First World War and that he arrived as a worker on a banana boat. Somehow he made his way to Coos Bay in Oregon which, said Harvey, "he left the first day it quit raining and headed for California."

Fortuitously, Gebhard's first job in the Los Angeles area was working for Henry Turner in Newmark, as Montebello was called then. Turner owned several large greenhouses on Beverly Boulevard where he raised cut flowers. His operation eventually became the property of Roy Wilcox, another of the founders of the American Florists' Exchange.

We can also assume that Gebhard was as ambitious and focused as he was practical. For example, he met his future wife, Hedwig, while working for the Turner Nurseries when he planted palm trees along the driveway at a large house in Santa Fe Springs where she worked as a maid for a German-speaking family. He convinced her to leave that comfortable employ. As Harvey recalled: "He wanted her to learn English. He told her that as long as they kept speaking German to her, she would never get anywhere."

Gebhard Prechtl in his lily field, early 1940s.

He must have been persuasive, because she did leave and went to work for a family in Pasadena in which no one spoke German.

Hedwig had been brought to America by a wealthy German family from Hamburg, arriving in February 1914, just months before the First World War broke out. She married Gebhard and they had two children, Hardwig (Harvey) and Erika. At some point they purchased five acres in Montebello, where Vail Avenue and Whittier Boulevard are today, and he began growing buddlelea and later, Easter lilies and baby white calla lilies. He also grew French heather and camellias in Montebello.

Harvey recalled that his father was "always big on buying property because it was the right thing to do" and eventually Gebhard also owned acreage in El Monte, where he grew genista, or broom flower, and paperwhites; in Pasadena, where he grew melanthra heather and baby pink callas; and in Walnut, where his attempt to grow lilacs failed because it was too hot there for lilacs.

Gebhard later sold half of his Montebello acreage to the city to construct a school, and moved his house across the street.

Early recollections of Wall Street

The European American growers of the Los Angeles Flower Market first began operating a small wholesale market on Winston Street in 1917, three years before filing official incorporation papers. We can be sure that Gebhard Prechtl and his colleagues were working behind the scenes drafting Articles of Incorporation, planning a financial structure, and keeping an eye on what the much-larger Southern California Flower Market, Inc. was doing.

When the Japanese-American wholesale market incorporated in February 1914, membership was closed to all but Japanese-American growers. That restriction was officially lifted about a year later, but Japanese-only sentiments continued informally throughout the 1920s and 1930s and greatly affected relationships between the two groups.

That was just one of the reasons Gebhard and the other founders of the Los Angeles Flower Market wanted a wholesale market of their own. Another was that the two groups of farmers tended to grow different types of cut flower crops. Realistically, everyone realized it was in both markets' best interests to be situated close by. When the Southern California Flower Market moved three blocks farther south to the 700 block of Wall Street in 1923, the Los Angeles Flower Market followed within the year, purchasing its first property across the street at 754 Wall Street.

We know that Gebhard Prechtl was instrumental in negotiating the purchase of property over time on behalf of the American Florists' Exchange in the Market area. "In fact," his son remembered, "all of the property they have now, with the exception of one or two pieces, he bought. He was a good negotiator."

Property records show that Gebhard and Hedwig Prechtl purchased two lots on San Julian Avenue, paralleling Wall Street one block east, in 1928 – one year before the worldwide stock market collapse. They held these lots for four years until the AFE was financially strong enough to buy them. It was AFE's second purchase in establishing a real estate foothold in the Market area; the deed was signed over in October 1932.

AFE's first building on Wall Street was an automobile repair garage on a forty-foot lot, and Harvey recalled his father telling him in later years that during the winter months, rushing deep water – often carrying fish! – ran down Wall Street, the result of periodic flooding from the nearby Los Angeles River before it was captured and tamed in a concrete channel. A diverting hump in front of the garage doors had been built to keep the water out of the building. As Harvey told the story: "The street was just like a river during the wintertime. You couldn't cross it when it was raining because the current was too swift."

Another original quirk of Market operations that didn't last long was how sales space was allocated to the shareholders. Space was assigned as it became available and vendors applied for the prime locations long in advance; how many shares they owned was a major consideration. "But in the old days," according to Harvey, "they used to draw for their stalls."

The Market owned the Rose Café, on the first floor of a building that was originally intended to house the growing Mellano & Company on its second floor. Next to it was an apartment house that Gebhard purchased for the Market from an elderly Miss Tomiko Minamiki. He arranged for her to continue living there rent-free. A few years later they decided to tear down the apartment building to widen the Market, and said Harvey: "They moved Miss Minamiki to a building that my dad owned together with Mr. Ecke and C.P. Von Herzen, the Market's attorney, that was on the corner of Eighth and Wall streets, and she lived there until she died."

The Depression years of the early 1930s were tough times at the Market. Gebhard and his board of directors were forced to take back shares from growers and commission agents who were unable to pay the rent on their tables during those bleak years. "I know some of those guys were mad at my dad because the Market took the shares back," Harvey recalled.

Those years were also when it became obvious that it was in the best interests of both Markets to agree on minimum wages, prices and Market operating hours. Otherwise, the federal government in the form of the National Recovery Act (NRA) would step in and do it for them.

The U.S. Congress passed the NRA in 1933 to stimulate the national economy by regulating business to ensure fair competition. "No one wanted that [interference] so we were forced to organize," Frank Kuwahara told Sylvia Foltz, C.J. Groen's daughter, in a 1981 interview recalling those years and how the Southern California Floral Association (SCFA), representing both Markets, came to be.

Frank Kuwahara was a young second generation Japanese-American who had been bringing his family's flowers to the Southern California Flower Market since 1928. Still in his early twenties, he had already shown an ability to overcome language and cultural barriers that kept the two sides of Wall Street in a constant state of misunderstanding. He was elected a director of the SCFA in 1936.

Frank Kuwahara already knew Gebhard Prechtl; they had been neighbors in Montebello. In fact, as a teenage driver, Frank had backed into Gebhard's car while leaving the high school's parking lot, across the street from the Prechtl family's driveway. "He wasn't happy about it, but I do recall he was fair," Frank told Gebhard's grandson Jon in later years.

Frank also told Sylvia how Gebhard Prechtl had given him some good advice later on, when both were involved in getting the two flower markets to agree on prices and operating hours: "He took me aside one day and said 'Frank, you are the first Japanese who has had guts enough to come over to our side and we appreciate that' and he said he would help me."

One of the tricks of forging productive relationships that Gebhard shared with Frank was to soften a discussion over a friendly drink: "But he also said to never get drunk, 'because if you do, you've lost it all' [he told me.]"

In the end, that famous German perseverance overcame most, if not all, obstacles to success. By the time Gebhard died in 1946, the Los Angeles Flower Market was completely full – all of the counters were rented. The two sides of Wall Street – European-American and Japanese-American – had learned to work together for the betterment of all, sponsoring joint events for the public and the trade. The Second World War had ended, and with it many of the feelings of distrust. The entire Flower District bustled with growers, shippers, wholesalers, commission men, florists from all over the Los Angeles area, and others engaged in the buying and selling of cut flowers and greenery.

Gebhard's son Harvey was always an early riser. Starting your day early is a difficult habit to break. Harvey worked for United Wholesale Florist, a shipping company with nationwide reach, for thirty-seven years, retiring in 1983. Middle-of-the-night and early morning work hours were his norm.

Harvey was born in 1921, the same year in which his father and his colleagues had seen the culmination of their dream for a Market devoted to the interests of the European-American flower growers of Los Angeles and environs.

When Gebhard Prechtl died in 1946, his son – who had already put in his war-time years serving with the U.S. Army in India – took care of the calla lilies for awhile, but soon realized he hadn't learned enough about the business from his dad to keep it going – "It wasn't my thing" – so he sold the land and looked to the Market for a job because he liked the flower business and wanted to stay in it.

Harvey's first job was sales for Frank Blankenship, who had farmed carnations on Osborne Avenue in San Fernando since leaving the employ of the Amling Brothers when the War began. Frank had assumed responsibility for farming the land of a couple of Japanese growers until they returned from forced internment.

After he worked the early morning hours selling carnations at Frank's counter, Harvey put in a few more hours at the B.W. Hall Company, one of more than a dozen shippers on Wall Street sending flowers from Los Angeles to flower shops across America. He recalled it was a busy scene: "The Railway Express used to have their semis parked up and down the street during the holidays because we had so many boxes. Each shipper had [their own] semi, and we'd just shove the boxes in the back."

He also remembered the procedure for packing the flowers for safe shipment: They were laid in boxes of either forty-eight or sixty inches length, on top of a pad and with a cleat nailed in place to keep them from moving around. "Then you'd put a piece of dry ice in the box with them, and ship it out."

After a couple more years working for two different Market entities, he went to work full-time for Roy Halsey. Halsey had started his own wholesale company as a consignment agent for many different growers after leaving the employ of his father-in-law, C. J. Groen, the rose grower. Harvey worked for Halsey until he sold out to United Wholesale a few years later.

Harvey remembered those late 1940s years at Halsey Wholesale for a couple of "firsts." Halsey was the first to sell stock out of season for Bob Stimming's Santa Barbara Flower Growers in Lompoc. They were also the first to sell the Murphy Seed Company's Bells of Ireland, an unusual-looking plant of bright green "bells" with tiny white clappers that eventually became popular for bridal bouquets.

When Roy Halsey sold his company to United Wholesale and headed back to service with the U.S. Army Air Force in December 1950, Harvey was the only Halsey employee that United's owners kept.

United Wholesale had been started by Jacob Dekker, who had previously been a partner at the B.W. Hall Company. "One of the guys who worked there, when he heard I was coming over from Halsey, was going to quit because he knew about the property dispute," said Harvey. He was referring to a situation years earlier when his father had been blocked from buying a lot that Jacob Dekker owned and that Gebhard Prechtl wanted to buy for the Market. That reluctant, loyal United employee was Leroy Youts, from Oklahoma, and he and Harvey became "good buddies" and friends.

Four days by rail to Chicago

In the 1930s and '40s, it took about four days for flowers from Los Angeles to reach Chicago by rail. Flower shipping folklore, as Harvey remembered it, was that when a very large shipment was sent to a flower shop customer in Chicago, it often foreshadowed a gangland murder that would soon be in the newspapers. Harvey chuckled as he recalled the tale: "The story goes that funeral flowers were ordered ahead of time, and when the shop owner would ask 'oh, is he dead?' he would be told 'no, but he will be.' So if business picked up a bit for the flower shop, it meant they probably had a funeral coming up soon."

Although air freight was available, it was expensive and United, like many of the shippers, used Railway Express which operated refrigerated cars and would accept the larger 60-inch long boxes while the air shippers would not. "They did a good job for us," Harvey said, "until they went belly up." Plagued by labor disputes and increased competition from trucking lines, Railway Express filed for bankruptcy in 1975.

Art Dettweiler and Ebbo Dekema were Jacob Dekker's partners at United Wholesale Florist. The three of them must have appreciated the hard-working young Prechtl because he moved up through the company over the years and became a buyer for five different routes delivering flowers to florists around the area. His daily routine was to go into work at eleven o'clock at night with a breakout sheet he had prepared earlier in the evening detailing orders from florists on his routes. After purchasing the flowers at the Market, he distributed them among the five route trucks, whose drivers loaded the flowers and then took Harvey's instructions for where to deliver them. By this time it was usually ten o'clock the next morning – a twelve-hour day that he worked for many years.

When his son Jon was age fifteen, Harvey began taking him down to the Market on Saturday mornings to work, as his father before him had done. Jon got a job selling stock at United Wholesale's counter in the Southern California Flower Market while attending college, and recalls many sleepy classrooms following a night working at the Market. He worked for United in progressively more responsible positions from 1965 through 1978.

In early 1979 Jon went to work for Mellano & Company, which was by then a major grower, wholesaler and shipper on Wall Street. He was Mellano's general manager from 1983 until 1990, when he left the flower industry – but not completely. Jon Prechtl has been on the board of directors of the American Florists' Exchange for many years, helping to care for and protect his grandfather's legacy.

Los Angeles Evergreen Company
1919 - 1935
Nick Gandolfo Wholesalers
1933 - 1975
The Flower Fields of Artesia

There was a time not long ago in parts of southeast Los Angeles County, not too many miles from Los Angeles' city center, when fields of flowers lay in colorful patchwork where today stand homes and shopping districts, streets and freeways, schools and hospitals. In 1940, in springtime, if you stood on 187th Street in Artesia, to the west of the small farming community's Main Street (now called Pioneer Boulevard) and looked south toward Orangethorpe Avenue (now called South Street in Cerritos), you would observe acres of flowers.

This land was the Gandolfo family's flower farm and in the 1940s, those blooms were tulips, iris, daffodils and other bulb flowers. In 2007, sitting in the comfortable home he built in 1953 just a few miles north of the land that had been the farm, Nick Gandolfo Jr., the family's only son, reflects that when his father's tulip and daffodil fields bloomed, the scene was so spectacular that public interest probably would have rivaled today's Flower Fields® attraction in Carlsbad, California. "But in those days we were in the country and only three, maybe four, cars passed by in an hour's time."

Standing in the dirt of 187th Street in 1940, you would also catch that distinctive aroma that says "cows are nearby – lots of them" because on this land, before the Second World War, large dairy farms co-existed with the fields of flowers, vegetables and fruit. Artesia had been a farming community since before the turn of the century; settlers were drawn to its rich soil and abundant water from naturally flowing artesian wells.

By the end of the war, land in Artesia and surrounding communities began to be more valuable to developers of housing for Los Angeles' growing suburban population than the worth of the crops it supported. People moved into the new neighborhoods the developers built and complained about the smell that emanated from the dairies and the dust of farming activity. Communities incorporated as cities and tightened restrictions on their agricultural neighbors. Over time dairymen moved their operations east to Chino and to the valleys of Central California, and the farmers sold their land for more than they had paid for it and sent their children to college, an advantage they hadn't had.

Earlier generations of Gandolfos lived in Sestri Levante, a district of flower farmers along the Mediterranean coast in northern Italy. Nick Gandolfo Sr. arrived in America around 1903 at fifteen years of age. He went directly to San Francisco where a cousin lived, and began working odd jobs: mining, washing windows and general labor. He earned enough to send money home for his widowed mother and his sister to immigrate to America, too.

When the 1906 earthquake hit the city, he was high up on a building washing windows. Family lore says that he put down his bucket and decided that would be the last window he would ever wash in San Francisco.

Nick had married an American-born Italian girl, Palmera, whose grandparents had settled in San Francisco in 1848 after sailing around the tip of South America. Nick and Palmera moved to Los Angeles at the urging of Nick's friend Bernardo Tassano, who was already working there and assured them that work was available. They lived in Boyle Heights where they began their family in 1920: two girls and then a boy.

About that time, Nick got involved in the local flower trade. His son thinks it was around 1919 that he set up a business with John Rainero to import evergreens from the forests around Santa Cruz in Northern California to sell to the floral trade. The Los Angeles Evergreen Company had its own building on Winston Street, the same street on which the still-forming American Florists' Exchange leased a garage.

By 1926 the business was extremely successful and had another partner: Giovanni Mellano, previously one of their providers of evergreens. Giovanni had visited Los Angeles on a whim a few years earlier, boarded with Nick and Palmera, and joined the company in 1925. He was godfather to Nick's second child, a daughter named Doris, born in 1923.

The Los Angeles Evergreen Company relocated to Wall Street about the same time that the other European-American flower vendors did: 1924, the year after the Japanese-American growers moved their market to the 700 block of South Wall Street. American Florists' Exchange principals felt it would be better for business if the two markets were located in the same vicinity.

Nick Jr., eight years old in 1933, remembers that the family never saw their father from November to Christmas, the busiest time of the year when evergreen garlands and wreaths were in demand for seasonal decorations at the downtown department stores and they had to be formed and tied by hand: "They used the real stuff in those days, nothing artificial."

Flora Mae Gorini and her mother, Aurelia, in the fields of daffodils and tulips on their Artesia ranch, 1937. Note the flower buckets. This is the truck they drove to Market.

Nick's dad (also Nick) with peach blossom trees in Artesia, 1940.

He recalls that his father also brought in lemon leaves, a popular filler in a lot of floral arrangements of the era, and that the greens came down from Santa Cruz on the American Express truck.

Nick Gandolfo and his partners kept Los Angeles Evergreen going through the Depression years, but by 1933 he had decided to try farming flowers in the same area where other Italian-American flower growers also had small farms. He sold his share of the business to John Rainero and Giovanni Mellano, and bought ten acres in Artesia. Flowers grew well in Artesia's fertile soil and climate of overcast mornings that don't clear until about noon when the sun comes out. "And every afternoon at around three o'clock there is an ocean breeze to cool down the temperature," says Nick Jr., still an Artesia resident.

Nick Gandolfo Wholesalers grew a variety of flowers at first and later concentrated solely on bulb crops. Nick took his flowers to the Los Angeles Flower Market in the family truck. After a couple of years, he hired two Mexican families to work full-time in the fields. Angelo Capurro, Palmera's brother, also worked on the farm as a general handyman. Nick Jr. thought of him as more like a sibling than an uncle.

As Nick's children grew older they helped, too. Doris Gandolfo Scholar recalls that she and her older sister Julia were responsible for disbudding the pom pom dahlias, an activity which blackened their fingers. "Everybody at school accused us of smoking," she said in 2007, recalling the onerous task. "My brother didn't have to do it because he didn't do a very good job anyway."

Nick Jr. was the baby of the family. When he was very young, he was also the only boy child among fifteen or twenty Italian families in their circle of friends. "Whenever we visited other families, I was spoiled rotten and my sisters hated it. I was a brat," he says now. He also recalls having "apple of his eye" status with Guiseppe Gorini, a neighboring flower grower in Artesia whose children were all girls, one of whom he eventually married.

As he grew up Nick also worked in the fields after school, and by the time he was a teenager he was going to the Flower Market during the summer with his dad. He still remembers the early morning, pre-freeway route they took into Los Angeles: north on Main Street (now Pioneer Boulevard) to Anaheim Telegraph Road, then Olympic Boulevard to Seventh Street. At the Market, he helped unload the truck and headed over to the Rose Café for his favorite treat, a hot roast beef sandwich – at five o'clock in the morning.

Flowers that did not sell were chopped up and dumped at the Market. Nick says they all called it "making soup" and growers often made soup during the hot summer months because the florists bought only what they needed for that day's trade. Keeping flowers cool during July, August and September was difficult. June was a good business month, Nick recalls, because of the wedding season, as was Memorial Day: "If you could get flowers to the Market the week before, you were set because everybody went to the cemetery."

The Gandolfo farm also had a stand of peach blossom trees – their branches were very popular around Valentine's Day, plus half an acre of hothouses and two large open lath houses planted with maidenhair and asparagus ferns in hanging baskets. But the major focus of Nick Gandolfo's business was bulb flowers: iris, daffodils, dahlias, daylilies and tulips.

In addition to a large contingent of Italian-American farmers, the local flower-growing community included many second-generation Japanese-American families. The two ethnic groups had different approaches to using the land to support their family. The Japanese grew chrysanthemums, carnations and other flowers that had seeds, and when the flowers were gone "they just plowed up the field and planted something else," Nick remembers. "Their land was constantly under cultivation. My dad thought it was better to grow bulb flowers because they had a higher value at the Market, even though we couldn't plow the ground until they died."

Open fields of tulips were subject to the elements of Nature, and Nick recalls one particularly bad hailstorm that bruised the flowers badly even though they had put up a cheesecloth cover. "That's the sort of thing you just had to live with," he says.

Nick also recalls his father recounting an incident in the early 1950s when a clueless agent from the Internal Revenue Service visited the farm. His sister Doris had gone to school to learn accounting and she did her father's books. One year they had a red spider infestation throughout the lath houses and used the repellant DDT to destroy the spiders. It worked, but it also meant they couldn't sell the ferns. Doris' income tax return showed a loss and the agent wanted to know why there was a big drop of income from one year to the next.

"He couldn't understand how a farmer could lose an entire crop and not realize any income from it, and as Dad was walking him back to his car, the agent asked 'How many ferns do you have out here?' Well, Dad just looked at him and said 'I have no idea how many plants are out there but there are five acres of them and you're welcome to go out and count them.' The agent just turned and walked away."

Nick Sr. retired when he turned 65 in 1953, and his brother-in-law Angelo Capurro took over the business and ran it as Nick Gandolfo Wholesale until he retired himself in 1975.

Nick Jr. and his sister Doris have kept their family's shares in the American Florists' Exchange although no one in the family has been involved in the flower industry for some time. Nick recalls: "In order to sell flowers at the Market, you had to buy shares in the Market, and my dad told me to never sell them."

Looking back on his youth, he reflects that "It didn't take much brainpower to figure out 'this isn't for me' and decide to do something else." After serving with the U.S. Army during the Second World War – he was a prisoner of war in Germany for six months toward the war's end – he came home and attended college on the G.I. bill. "I know my dad was pleased that I went to college. He was very strong, but he realized that [farming] was a hard life and he wanted something better for his children."

Nick earned a degree from Occidental College, married Flora Mae Gorini who he had known since childhood, and taught high school English and History in his hometown, Artesia.

Gorini Brothers 1922 - 1949
A Merger of Flower-Growing Families

When Guiseppe and Aurelia Gorini drove their flower-bedecked automobile down Artesia's Main Street in 1927 in a community parade to celebrate the advent of electric streetlights, it was undoubtedly a proud moment for them. They had decorated the vehicle from the wheels up with flowers to show off the fruits of their labors on the 25 acres they farmed along Orangethorpe Avenue (today's South Street in Cerritos).

Introducing the city of Artesia's new street lights presented an occasion in 1927 for a night-time parade. The Gorini family participated in their car decorated with flowers.

Guiseppe found success growing bulb flowers in Artesia, land of rich soil and readily available water. He bought his land after leasing a smaller plot called the Nuzum Ranch to see if he could support his family growing flowers to sell at the Los Angeles Flower Market. A previous venture with chicken ranching didn't pan out.

Guiseppe ("Pepo") and Aurelia moved to Artesia from Los Angeles in 1925 with their two young daughters, Matilda and Anna Lee. They were pleased to be part of their new community, and soon became American citizens.

Guiseppe owned a share in the American Florists' Exchange with his brothers, Bartholomew and Pietro; the three sold flowers at the Los Angeles Flower Market as the Gorini Brothers. At some point Bartholomew and Pietro left the business and Guiseppe continued alone.

Top: Aurelia Gorini (Flora Mae's mother) in the zinnia field, late 1920s.
Above: Guiseppe (Pepo) Gorini in the truck used to haul his flowers to Market, 1920s.

Guiseppe and Aurelia both came from Genoa in northern Italy. Each had followed older siblings to Los Angeles to find work and a better opportunity than Italy offered in the early 1900s. Aurelia's sister married into the Rolleri family which owned a high-end flower shop in the Los Angeles Athletic Club at Seventh and Olive streets. Although there is no evidence to support our assumption, it's easy to imagine that one of Aurelia's first jobs was working at the shop, and that observing the success of the Rolleris' business led Guiseppe to the notion that the flower business could offer a promising future for him and his bride. They married on December 28, 1912, at St. Peter's Catholic Church in Los Angeles.

There were plenty of little girls among the fifteen or twenty Italian-American families who grew flowers in the Artesia area in the 1920s but not many boy children. In a culture and an era in which women didn't do "men's work," we can imagine Guiseppe throwing up his hands and realizing it was "all hands on deck" to make a successful go of flower farming. In 2007, Anna Lee Gorini Gallizio's memories include working in the barn with her older sister Matilda putting tulips and daffodils in pots that their father would take to the Market early in the morning on Monday, Wednesday and Friday.

Flora Mae (Flo) Gorini was the third child born to Guiseppe and Aurelia – in 1929, four years after the family moved to Artesia. A neighbor boy peered over the crib rail at the newborn and declared: "She's going to be my wife." Nick Gandolfo was four years old when he made that prophecy. Twenty-two years later he did marry her, but not before proposing to her oldest sister Matilda – when he was seven and she was sixteen. Flo remembers that her sister kept the Cracker Jacks ring he gave her "for years."

The Flower Market was a magical place for Guiseppe's daughters in the 1930s and early 1940s when school was out for the summer and they were allowed to accompany their father to the Market. Flo recalls she never had any problem selling books of raffle tickets for church festivals there: "I hit all the stalls. They would pat me on the head and buy my tickets."

The Gorini Flower Ranch grew a wide variety of flowers on land situated between two large dairy farms. The largest crops were zinnias, snapdragon, stock, pompom dahlias and asparagus fern.

During the Second World War he leased additional land in La Mirada and grew sweet peas. Every Sunday morning before mass the entire family drove to La Mirada to pick sweet peas and get them ready to go to the Market early on Monday morning.

By the time she graduated from high school in 1946, Flo was the only daughter still living at home. She and Nick Gandolfo had been dating for about a year. In 1945 she made the first move by asking him to be her date for the junior/senior prom at Excelsior High School, and the following year he asked her father for permission to take her to a weekend house party that his Occidental College fraternity was hosting in Lake Arrowhead. Nick and Flo both recall the look of pride on her father's face when he saw a blossoming romance between the two childhood friends, although unfortunately he did not live to see them marry in 1951.

Guiseppe fell very ill and died in 1947 at the age of 57. Matilda had married John Vattuone; they lived in San Diego. Anna Lee had completed her nursing training in San Diego and came home to help her mother with the ranch. They kept it going for another couple of years, maintaining the three-days-a-week schedule of taking flowers to the Market with the help of Shorty and Vera Delgado. The Delgado family had worked for the Gorini family for many years. They decided to move on and Aurelia sold the Gorini Flower Ranch to Giovanni Mellano in 1949.

Giovanni Mellano, left, and Pepe Gorini fishing for barracuda on a barge off San Pedro, using live bait, 1940s.

Thus the productive acreage on Orangethorpe Avenue (South Street) went from one flower grower to the care of another, and a daughter married into a third family who was still growing flowers nearby. Both farms were thought to be "out in the country" as late as the 1960s because Artesia's downtown business district was several miles away. Artesia incorporated as a city in 1959. Suburban housing tracts continued to swallow up the land where vegetables, flowers and some of the region's largest dairy farms had once been so prevalent.

Mayesh Wholesale Florist: 1920s > From a Hollywood Flower Stand to International Operations

The first American entrepreneurial venture by Jack Mayesh was a hot dog stand at New York City's Madison Square Garden which his uncle, a New Jersey policeman, helped him obtain. But like many new Americans, Jack Mayesh set his sights on bigger goals.

In the 1920s, Jack discovered he could make a living in the flower business in Southern California. Selling flowers, which he did from a stand on a Hollywood street, required little inventory or capital investment. Jack quickly realized success by selling flowers to celebrities, who valued the quality they received.

"My dad had very limited resources," says Joe Mayesh; "so he would simply tell people he was booked and couldn't handle their order. The more he said that, the more they wanted his flowers."

Jack Mayesh started the wholesale flower business in the 1930s by bringing flowers and plants grown in Northern California to the Los Angeles market and flowers grown in Southern California to the San Francisco market. He was among the first to bring gladiolus from Florida by semi-trucks during the winter months to the Los Angeles market.

When World War II started and the Japanese growers were sent to interment camps, Jack Mayesh took over some of their farms and operated them in their owners' absence.

After World War II, Jack's son Joe, having completed his military service, entered the business, followed a little later by brothers Sol and Maurice. They operated the business at 744 Wall Street for many years.

In 1972, Mayesh acquired Kobata Brothers, today known as Kobata Growers and managed by Joe's nephews Harry and Jack.

Nearly a half century after its founding, Mayesh Wholesale Florist was sold in 1978 to Roy Dahlson, his son Patrick and associate Bobby Mitchell. Dahlson, who operated three flower shops and a wholesale route, used the Mayesh flower stall as a staging area while working for the Mayesh firm. The sale became a catalyst for growth.

"They've done a marvelous job," says Joe Mayesh today of the success the Dahlson family has brought to Mayesh Wholesale Florist.

In the 30 years since the purchase, the wholesale firm has expanded from its one modest sales location at the Market to several divisions and branches in other states, a nationwide distribution center by Los Angeles International Airport, a processing center in Miami, Florida, a company-owned transportation business in Ecuador and several hundred employees. Providing unique bouquets and consumer bunches for mass market accounts, the firm also offers bulk novelty varieties for events and fills the everyday needs of floral wholesalers and retailers across the United States.

Mayesh is the only floral wholesale company with its own custom-designed inspection area, located at its Los Angeles distribution terminal, where Department of Agriculture officers perform inspection, eliminating the need for long waits in U.S. Customs at the airport.

Perhaps the most amazing characteristic of the growth of Mayesh Wholesale Florist is that it has to a great degree been performed by members of the Dahlson family. The nine children of Roy Dahlson have served as the company's leaders and dedicated employees since the acquisition. Although responsibilities have changed and people have progressed, in the early 2000s son Roy led the technology area and daughter Cindie was operations manager (her husband Hans managed the facility at the Market). Son Patrick continues as president and chief executive officer and is involved in the flower industry statewide and nationally. Anthony managed the Orange County operation, Chris worked in the shipping/sales area and Richard as assistant manager at the Van Nuys facility. Pam headed the purchasing department while Ted handled local distribution. Steve worked special projects while nephew David managed special events and designed the company website. Daughters-in-law, sons-in-law and grandchildren are employed in the business.

From left: Sol, Jack and Joe Mayesh, 1950s. ***Photo courtesy of Joe Mayesh.***

As a 2001 *Bloomin' News* article so aptly stated, It doesn't take a flower scientist to see that all Roy's children helped grow Jack Mayesh's company to its place of prominence.

Floral Supply Syndicate 1939 > From a Local Hardgoods Distributor to a National Presence

The roots of today's nationally known Floral Supply Syndicate were planted in the first half of the twentieth century in a floral supply importing company run by a Maynard Adler in New York City. The floral pins and accessories Adler imported from Japan served the city's and surrounding area florists well, and all three of Adler's sons grew up learning all about the floral supplies, negotiating for their purchase with distributors and serving a growing customer base.

Sidney Adler broke away from the family business and followed his wanderlust to San Francisco in 1939 where, with partner Bill Rubin, he started the Sidney Adler Company in the city's Flower Market. In the early 1940s, however, Sidney was drafted into the U.S. Army and went to war to serve his country. Later, with the war and military service behind him and ready to try business ownership again, Sidney moved to Los Angeles.

In 1949, Sidney Adler started Floral Supply Syndicate, at 1145 South Wall Street, with Nate Rubin, the brother of his San Francisco partner. Although FSS was located three blocks south of the Los Angeles Flower Market, florists, craft merchandisers, interior designers, event planners and gift basket makers quickly learned of the wide variety of supplies offered at FSS. Typically florists would purchase their flowers and then stop by FSS to pick up ribbons, vases, baskets and decorative novelty items on their way back home.

Together, Sidney and Nate shared an uncanny and usually accurate sense about marketing. They firmly believed a product catalog would put their supply firm on the map, and they were right. The first FSS catalog was published in 1949 and was soon to be referred to as the "Bible of the industry." The FSS catalog evolved into a nationally recognized selling tool and reference guide for the hardgoods portion of the floral industry. FSS quickly became a major player in the business-to-business mail order industry serving the floral industry.

Fast-forward to 1978 and the arrival of a 26-year-old MBA student. Richard Kanner had formal retail management experience and was working in the manufacturing field, selling to distributors, while studying for a master's degree in business administration at the University of California, Los Angeles. His pure ambition motivated him to pursue a business that required him to be at work at 4:00 a.m. and which often he did not leave until 4:00 pm., but he recognized this as a great opportunity to build FSS into a national entity. With encouragement, support and financial advice from his father, he bought out retiring partner Nate Rubin.

"I got into the business to grow it," Kanner says. "I saw an opportunity in the floral industry and was able to bring a professional approach to selling the hard goods ... the goal was to grow the business using only profits derived from on-going operation and without ever leveraging or borrowing."

When Kanner bought Floral Supply Syndicate he also bought a shipping company. Now, between the firm's popular catalog and its new ability to ship anywhere, FSS was poised for growth on a national scale.

In 1981, with his partner Sidney Adler, Floral Supply Syndicate acquired Pacific Coast Commercial Ribbon Mills from then owner Thrifty Drug Company. The value was that it was centrally located in the Los Angeles Flower District. Soon after, the partners consolidated FSS and Sidney Adler Company, using the Floral Supply Syndicate name, at all three locations.

As Richard's energy and enthusiasm became more apparent, Sidney Adler decided to follow his former partner, Nate, into retirement. With the support and encouragement of Richard and his father, he sold out to brothers Larry and Dennis Shepherd in 1985.

Aside from the business aspects, Richard reflects that "the best part of working in the Los Angeles Flower Market was the people and the excitement of hearing the latest news as to who was doing the next grand party for a Hollywood or big corporate celebrity. Going to work was like going to a party where everyone was excited to see each other while sharing a cup of coffee. The Los Angeles Flower Market was a happening place!"

Two current FSS employees have their firmly-planted employment roots with the original two companies. Al Orozco, with 41 years' tenure, was with the Pacific Coast Commercial Ribbon Company; and manager Fred Tehrani started with Floral Supply Syndicate 28 years ago at its original location three blocks south. Fred and Al describe various and memorable booms and busts of the local economy that affected the business. One surprise occurred during the early 1990s recession when crowds of shoppers (the general public) swarmed downtown to "buy direct" rather than pay higher prices through retail shops. The sheer volume of vehicles necessitated the blocking of traffic on Wall Street. Street block then became a tradition for major holidays such as Valentine's Day.

Above left: Pacific Coast Commercial Ribbon on Paloma Street near Tenth and Alameda. ***Photo courtesy of John Amling, who managed the company for fifteen years.***
Above right: Long-time FSS employees Al Orozco, left, and Fred Tehrani in 2007.

Today's Floral Supply Syndicate has 21 regional warehouse locations across the United States, a high-tech, e-commerce website (fss.com), the expanding product catalog and a large mail order division with two major distribution locations: Camarillo, California and Charlotte, North Carolina.

Kermit ("Knute") Hernlund
1926 - 1974
A Master Plantsman

Old-timers may remember this Swedish plantsman as "Knute" Hernlund. Many will remember him for his uncanny ability to cultivate flowers and engineer techniques to streamline a farm into a mean, money-making machine.

Hernlund, like many flower growers, started his working career in an entirely different field. In 1926, the Minnesota transplant bought a rabbit farm in Riverside, California. When the heat killed his rabbits, he made good use of the land and manure by growing dahlias and other blooms, which he sold at the Los Angeles Flower Market.

The center of the flower business was a long commute from Riverside, and Hernlund moved his family, wife Eunice and five children, to El Monte. There, his crop of Transvaal Daisies froze one winter, yet Hernlund persevered, raising beautiful chrysanthemums, delphiniums and other flowers, and moving them through the downtown Market.

Knute Hernlund's knack for business led him into flower shop partnership in Pomona, which fit nicely into his delivery route. His crew picked the flowers and packed them for transport. The next day, his daughter Nicky Killion recalls, Hernlund delivered the flowers, with Nicky along for the ride, making stops at floral retailers all the way to Pomona.

Kermit (Knute) Hernlund around 1950.

In 1939, Hernlund went to work for Manchester Boddy at Descanso Gardens, tending camellias and the bread-and-butter cut flower crops, which he sold at market. When Boddy, horticulturist and *Los Angeles Daily News* publisher, sold some of his land to newspaper promoter Robert L. Smith, Hernlund went to work for Smith. Smith rose quickly to become the top combination flower grower-wholesaler-retailer in the nation, and Hernlund's part in this rapid success did not go unnoticed.

When the well known Signal Oil Company founder Samuel B. Mosher purchased Mission Flowers from Manchester Boddy and then bought the Los Pueblos ranch near Santa Barbara, he looked to Knute Hernlund for his expertise. As manager of Mosher's Dos Pueblos Orchid

Company, a 4,500-acre flower farm, Hernlund had his work cut out for him. From 1947 until he moved to Hawaii in the early 1960s, he traveled the world to buy stud plants for Dos Pueblos. He formulated different plant foods for baby and adolescent orchid plants, and, putting his University of Minnesota mechanical engineering degree to good use, he built innovative equipment and mechanized routines that put Dos Pueblos on the international flower production map.

Knute Hernlund was active in civic events and organizations throughout his career. He served as a vice president of Santa Barbara's National Horse Show & Flower Show and was appointed a director of the Nineteenth District Agricultural Association. But Hernlund, who died in 1974 after operating Island Orchid in Hawaii for a dozen or more years, was best known for his orchid and cut flower cultivation successes.

Dos Pueblos Orchid Company 1942 > Samuel Mosher and Kermit Hernlund: A Match Made in Orchid Heaven

The elegant orchid, visible everywhere today, was once a flower so unique that it was enjoyed only on special occasions. It was given on Mother's Day or by a suitor who needed to impress the young lady by his side attending theater or prom.

Samuel B. Mosher dreamed of making the orchid so common that it would appear on the dining tables of many American households. The revolutionary methods he employed to make it an everyday flower were frowned upon by old-line growers who propagated orchids, but they worked.

Mosher, who made millions in the oil business, started as a farmer in Whittier, California. He had studied agriculture (citrus) at the University of California, but in 1921, after five poor years growing citrus, he quit farming. He and another disillusioned farmer developed a "teakettle" condenser that would later save refiners of oil millions of dollars. He eventually bought out his partner, went into oil exploration and started Signal Oil Company. His wealth enabled him to finance the Flying Tiger Line air freight operation, a steamship line and a flower farm. Until he began air-freighting his blooms across the nation, he sold through the Los Angeles Flower Market.

In 1942, Mosher bought the historic Rancho de los dos Pueblos in Goleta, on the northernmost border of Santa Barbara where his 4,500 acres stretched from the ocean to the Santa Ynez Mountains. The ranch was semi-arid until Mosher's oil geologists discovered that the mountain behind his ranch was full of water trapped by hard rock.

The good news led Mosher to apply a popular oil industry technique: slant drilling to facilitate the flow of water to his fields, which he followed with the building of a reservoir and laying out of a grand farming operation.

In 1954, Mosher served as president of the Men's Garden Club of Los Angeles. He chose the orchid as his specialty and conducted his own research on the flower, which led to his growing orchids at Dos Pueblos. Carnations, stock and other flowers came before long, as Mosher expanded. His oilfield engineering came in handy again, as he devised a way to heat his custom-built carnation glass houses with gas from the ranch's oil wells.

Aided largely by engineer and flower grower Kermit Hernlund, Mosher built a very large orchid-growing operation on what Frank J. Taylor, in his January 1960 *Saturday Evening Post* article, called a "factory-in-the-field" scale at the Dos Pueblos Orchid Company (formerly the Mission Flower & Nursery) ranch.

Mosher and Hernlund reduced the orchid's seed-to-bloom time from seven or more years to just three summers. An orchid "baby food" and special foods for the "adolescent" plants were developed by farm manager Hernlund and were believed to be responsible for the orchids' accelerated growth, coming to bloom so quickly that they doubled the output annually.

Mosher built a chain of satellite orchid farms in Australia and Hawaii to assure a continuing supply of the blooms during California's off-seasons and to increase demand. His interest in the Flying Tiger Line and his marketing skill helped the mass production farm become a multi-million-dollar business.

Dos Pueblos Orchid Company's rich, heady days have been over for decades, succumbing to the shifting sands of time. Samuel B. and Margaret C. Mosher have been immortalized through their philanthropic ventures including the Samuel B. Mosher Foundation at UC-Berkeley.

Moskatels Early 1930s > Filling Floral Supply Needs for 75 Years

In the early 1930s, a young Leon Moskatel set up a retail flower shop on Wall Street just north of the also young American Florists' Exchange. In those formative years, the Market was a hotbed of opportunity for determined entrepreneurs, and Moskatel, who had immigrated to the United States from Istanbul, Turkey and spoke broken English, wasted no time putting his vision

The Moskatels store is dated by the 1959 Chevrolet. ***American Florists' Exchange collection.***

and business acumen to work for him. Leon had learned the retail flower business while working with his brother George Mosktatel in George's shop in Glendale, and he was eager to become a business owner himself.

Leon Moskatel's flower shop enjoyed a steady flow of customers, as he brought in fresh flowers from northern California, extended credit to customers and supplemented his cut-flower line with floral supplies. The floral supply line continued to grow as did his reputation as a source for the myriad of supplies his customers requested.

While Leon Moskatel was building his business, Sam Applebaum, who was born in the living quarters of his parents' country store in Murtaugh, Idaho, was getting his own lessons in business management and merchandising. After operating an auto repair garage in Idaho in the 1930s, he moved to Long Beach, California and worked in his uncle's flower supply business until he was drafted into the Army in 1941, where he served as a supply sergeant.

Sam Applebaum, a first cousin of Leon Moskatel's wife, Edith, was discharged from the Army and in 1946, he and Leon Moskatel formed the Moskatels company and formally changed its focus to that of merchandising floral supplies. Applebaum became active in the Southern California floral community, serving on the board and then as president of the Southern California Floral Association in 1970.

Through the years, Moskatels had become a creative's paradise, its shelves brimming with vases, floral foam, full-size trees, candles, interior design accessories, arts and crafts materials, seasonal and special event supplies and designed displays. Large hotels and resorts' event planners knew they could find large quantities of anything they needed there. Movie set decorators were known to create false forests with artificial evergreens from this store. Best of all, retail florists referred the general public to Moskatels for crafts and decorating supplies, lending power to word-of-mouth referrals.

After its original owners passed on (Leon Moskatel died on August 1, 1962, at age 59), Moskatels continued to thrive. Its prime location on Wall Street practically ensured its growth and a level of success which made it attractive to the Dallas-based Michaels chain, which acquired it in 1987.

With the exception of the Moskatels store located by the Los Angeles Flower Market, Michaels changed the names of most stores it purchased to "Michaels," and it positioned Moskatels in its Star Decorators Division. At the end of 2007, when Michaels closed three of its four Star Decorators stores, it kept the popular Moskatels store open.

Moskatels continues to serve Flower District customers' and many in outlying towns as it enters the twenty-first century.

Franciosi Brothers 1939-1960
A Family of Farmers Displaced by Suburban Growth

Two boys of about ten and twelve years of age, each wearing serious expressions and boxing gloves, circle each other, taking occasional jabs. Even on the grainy film that jumps irregularly in its passage through the 1940s projector, the pride in their father's expression is obvious as he steps in to referee.

A few frames later, the boys are helping their dad load cans of dahlias into the back of a stake truck, where a little dog watches. Behind them, a steady stream of automobiles passes in both directions.

The road behind them is Shoemaker, which ran in front of the family farm, the dahlias are red, and at 2 o'clock the next morning, Joseph (Joe) Franciosi, the youngest son, recalls at the age of 77, his dad Giuseppe will drive the truck to the Los Angeles Flower Market.

Guiseppe Franciosi came to the U.S. from Genoa, Italy around 1922, as a young man of seventeen. He went to work for his uncle, Angelo Tassano, who was already growing produce and later, flowers, in Artesia. In 1939 uncle and nephew together bought a 30-acre plot at Rosecrans and Shoemaker Avenues in an area that would, in 1957, become Norwalk, Los Angeles County's sixty-sixth city. They divvied up the land – eighteen acres for Angelo and twelve for Guiseppe – and farmed it until rising land prices, arrival of the new Santa Ana freeway and urban encroachment came together in the late 1950s to put them out of the agricultural business.

Guiseppe (Joe) Franciosi in 1985.

Toward the end of the Second World War, the local Italian American community of flower and produce growers was permitted to take Italian Service Unit members (prisoners of war who had agreed to support the U.S. war effort) from the detention camp in Wilmington for an evening of frivolity, potluck and back-home camaraderie with fellow countrymen. The Franciosis hosted some of the parties at their ranch. Joe remembers that their guests were fascinated with the farm machinery they saw: "This one fellow in particular had all kinds of questions about our tractor with the disc. I told him it tills the ground and chops up the dirt and then you get the plow and turn it under. They were used to doing it with a horse, I guess."

Not that everything on the Franciosi farm was mechanized; he also recalls working with horses and mules for cultivating, and the time when he was about sixteen that a swarm of bees came through. "I got to the end of the furrow, tied the horse to a tree and got out of there real fast."

Mules, in fact, were better than horses for field work, Joe remembers, because a mule will walk one foot in front of the other, while horses walk with a wide stride so that they stepped on the plants.

Guiseppe met and married, in 1927, an Italian girl who had attended Excelsior Union High School in the same freshman class as Pat Ryan, who later married Richard Nixon of Whittier. Guiseppe and Alice had two sons; Julius was two years older than Joseph. Both boys began helping in the fields at an early age. The family's flower crops included dahlias, buddleia, greens, ferns, tulips, daffodils and stock as a seed crop.

Joseph, born in 1930, says that the Depression years weren't as hard on his family as on some of their neighbors. He recalls that his dad paid just fifteen dollars for a pony for his boys, and only three dollars for a 300-pound hog – their owners needed money. When they had to hire extra labor to help out on the farm, the going rate was ten to twelve dollars per week.

Guiseppe, also called Joe, had shared a stall at the Los Angeles Flower Market with his uncle since 1926. In 1939, when he started his own business, he purchased his own shares in the Market. The routine of rising early to take his flowers downtown and then coming home to tend his fields eased as his boys grew up and took on more responsibility for getting the flowers picked, sorted and placed on the truck.

Son Joe recalls that the stems of dahlias were dipped in hot water after cutting to make them last longer. When, in the early 1950s, dahlias became less popular, they started growing bulb crops such as iris, daffodils and tulips. In 1953, a Franciosi display won "First Award for Tulips" at the cut flower exhibit of the California International Flower Show held at Hollywood Park in Inglewood.

The new city of Norwalk tapped their local flower expert, Guiseppe Franciosi, to chair the committee charged with building a float for the 1955 Tournament of Roses Parade in Pasadena. The float, which featured a large cornucopia, won second prize in its category; Joe remembers that there were five thousand roses on it.

The Santa Ana Freeway (Interstate 5) claimed three acres of the farm when it came through in 1949. The Franciosis moved both their home and their nursery over to Carmenita Road, about a mile to the east. Giuseppe began to slow down, moving toward retirement and knowing that his boys would soon assume responsibility for his flower-growing acreage. Both sons served stints in the U.S. Army during the Korean War. Julius was drafted in September 1950, and Joe was drafted the day after his twenty-first birthday in January 1951. Both went right back to the farm when they returned.

Julius and Joe added a few new things when they took over the business. They began growing gladiolas in 1954, and they added refrigeration to the nursery so they could begin shipping from the farm directly to florists and wholesalers across the country: stock to a customer in Minneapolis, bulb plants and some mums to a florist in Salt Lake City, and Esther Reed daisies to Oregon where they were in demand for the annual Portland Rose Parade.

Joe Franciosi's tulips took First Place at the California International Flower Show in Inglewood in 1953.

Franciosi potted tulips figured prominently in a 1950s special order when they were asked to make up twelve pots with a dozen red tulips in each for television comedian Red Skelton. Joe recalls that their potted tulips – dug up with the bulb and placed in clay pots – were very popular at the Market. Julius handled the sales end of the business, while Joe took care of the farming operation. During the fall and winter months they grew stock, candytuft and delphinium for seed crop.

Lady Luck served the Franciosi Brothers well in 1956 or '57 when a hailstorm moved through right after they had built a cloth house over a large plot of recently planted tulips. "We were lucky enough that the crop hadn't sprouted out of the ground yet," Joe says. "It took us four days to dismantle the wreckage and put it all back together again."

Luck had nothing to do with it when the farmland and dairies that surrounded them began giving way to new housing developments and more traffic, and the Market shifted as flowers were shipped in from outlying growing areas and other parts of California. Guiseppe sold the land around 1960, and the brothers opened two independent service stations that they ran for 27 years. Guiseppe died in 1997 at the age of 92. Julius died in 2004, and Joe – who always enjoyed farming – transferred his green-thumb talent to bonsai trees.

Brevidoro Lilac Ranch 1935 > Imagination, Hard Work and a Whole Lot of Luck

If you can imagine a happy-go-lucky fellow whose story-telling talents are legend, a man who laughed in the face of adversity, and whose devotion to his family and his chosen niche in Los Angeles' flower-growing community were steadfast, then you knew Christopher Colombo Brevidoro.

His is the classic tale of an immigrant who saw an opportunity to call his own. Along the way he encountered a loving family, a wide circle of friends, the respect of his community and success on his own terms.

The 120-acre Colombo Lilac Ranch is situated near the community of Acton in the foothills of the San Gabriel Mountains. It is high desert about 2,700-foot elevation, at the gateway to the Antelope Valley and fifty miles north of downtown Los Angeles.

It would be, Chris Brevidoro recognized immediately when he first saw the land in 1935, an ideal place to raise lilacs. He needed a niche to make a name for himself in the cut flower industry, and he had already identified what it could be. Now he had found a place to make it happen.

"He was always trying to find his niche," John Brevidoro, Chris' oldest son, explained in 2007, five years after his father died at the age of 99. John recalls his father telling him that he traveled as a young man in the flower business to Oregon, Nevada and throughout California on buying expeditions, with a double purpose.

"Dad had contacts with Italian growers of greens that he could bring back to Los Angeles, and he also looked for lilacs wherever he went," John said, remembering that his father also tried to grow heather.

In 1935, Chris was newly involved in a partnership with Giovanni Mellano. His role was to buy and sell flowers and greens for Mellano & Company at the Los Angeles Flower Market. Giovanni's role was to grow flowers on land he owned in Artesia, and get them to the Market. Both men were well-known as hard workers in the Italian-American community of flower growers.

Their business arrangement was that everything they purchased jointly would be sold and the proceeds distributed equally. For product that each grew or purchased individually, 90 percent of the proceeds of its sale went to the partner who brought it to the Market and the other ten percent to the other partner.

Chris realized that beyond procuring lilacs to sell, he could also grow them – a steady source of income at a 90-percent share. He had been buying lilac slips and planting them for sometime. They grew well in California's sunshine, but did not bloom. Lilac shrubs need at least one season of cold temperatures to set their aromatic blossoms.

Chris Brevidoro learned horticulture as a young man, age seventeen or eighteen, and newly arrived in California. He was born in 1903 in a little town that was part of Sestri Levante along the Mediterranean coast in northern Italy. This is the same region from which came Nick Gandolfo, patriarch of one of the families who grew flowers in Artesia beginning around 1933, and who had immigrated to America himself thirty years earlier. Nick sponsored Chris' entry into the country; in those days admission was easier if you had a sponsor who could help you find employment.

John recalls his father telling the story that he hadn't planned to immigrate but on the day before the ship sailed, an opening became available and his mother borrowed money from friends and relatives to pay for his trip.

The handsome young Italian lad was drawn quickly into the large community of Italian immigrants who were part of the fabric of Southern California life in those early days. "They were all entrepreneurs who had come here to work hard and make a life," John explains. "They weren't well educated so they couldn't get professional jobs. They were laborers."

Chris went to work for the Faustini family who owned and operated a vineyard in the Rancho Cucamonga area of the San Gabriel Valley. It didn't take him long to learn English and use it to his advantage. "Pop was a great embellisher. He would tailor his stories depending on who he was telling them to, so I do have trouble figuring out the exact history of his early years here," John explains, noting proudly that his dad could also speak Spanish, and he could play the accordion by ear.

First retailing, then wholesaling

Chris met his wife while he was working for a nursery in the Glendale area. Ida Ghio's parents were both Italian immigrants, although she was American-born. By the time they married in 1927 or '28, they were operating a flower stand on a street corner in Pasadena, their flowers displayed in containers along the curb.

In May 1967, Chris told a newspaper writer that he first saw lilacs when an elderly man came by on a bicycle and asked if he ever bought flowers. The article that resulted from that interview continues the story:

> "That year the late frost and snow had come down low from the foothills and the old man's cherished lilac bushes had burst into full bloom for the first time. Chris looked the bushes over and bought the crop for three dollars. He had no idea if the flowers would sell, for they were strange to him. To his surprise, before he could get the bunched flowers into the containers, they were sighted and purchased by eager customers." *

Pasadena was a city of fine gardens and large estates: an enclave of traditional East Coast culture in Southern California. Its moneyed residents missed their pale purple lilac bushes, so prominent back home but difficult to bring to bloom in California's climate. Chris saw their interest and began collecting and cultivating lilac cuttings.

When the Depression years arrived, Chris went into sales at the wholesale market because by this time, he and Ida had started a family. On Wall Street everyone knew him as a hard worker, but also a lot of fun. As John puts it: "He had a great gift of gab; people loved him."

Chris' industriousness and outgoing personality were noticed by Giovanni Mellano, who was looking for workers for his new business. He first hired Chris, then made him a partner. They made a great team, says John: "Pop was the brawn, and Giovanni was the money."

Together they began building the framework of a business that exists today as Mellano & Company, a Los Angeles-based floral industry powerhouse that still buys lilacs from the Colombo Lilac Ranch. According to John, Mellano & Company was one of the first at the American Florists' Exchange to lease its own building on Wall Street in addition to operating a stall within the Flower Market itself. And, says John Brevidoro, his father suggested they do that when an opportunity arose to rent a separate building that was attached to the Exchange's building. "I recall him saying 'we've got to do this' and it turned out to be a great move. It made them special, more than just another stall in the market because just like the other big guys, they had their own shop."

John was in junior high school in the early 1940s. In 1946, the Brevidoro family stayed at the Franciosi's farm in Norwalk to take care of it while the Franciosi family took an extended trip to visit relatives in Italy. The following summer the Franciosi boys stayed home when their parents went to Italy, Chris handled the Market for them, and John both helped out on the farm and worked for the B.W. Hall Company, a shipping firm on Wall Street.

Top: John Brevidoro's cherished photo of his dad, Chris, taken in 100+ degree heat in the lilac field. "This is my dad saying, 'We're doing it, but boy, it sure looks hopeless.'"
Above: Chris Colombo Brevidoro in his 80s, among his lilacs.

Chris Brevidoro, Giovanni Mellano and their friends were hunters, and they often went out for deer in the San Gabriel Mountains above Acton. They used to pack in on horses from a small farm adjacent to the forest and that is where Chris Brevidoro saw a wild lilac growing – and in bloom! – and knew what to do with the lilac wood stock he had planted and nurtured on a vacant lot across the street from his home in Los Angeles.

He leased the land in Acton with an option to buy in 1935, and began moving his lilacs to the first five acres. The bushes thrived, even after transplanting, and Chris purchased the entire 120-acre farm around 1940.

John cherishes a family photograph of his father standing in the hot sun between rows of knee-high lilac bushes, a hoe in one hand and a white flag in the other. He has a grin on his face. "This is my dad saying 'We're doing it, but boy, it sure looks hopeless' – it was probably 110 degrees that day," John remembers.

Every weekend the family drove up to the ranch, but Chris didn't put many demands on his two sons to help with the lilacs except during harvest season, a few weeks every Spring. They had their first harvest in 1944 or '45 and it was an immediate sell-out at the Flower Market.

"He did it basically by himself, with a little help from my Uncle Hugo and cousins on my mother's side, because he had no other family here," John says. "He was the hardest working man I've ever met in my life."

Finally at home in Acton

Chris gave up the Mellano partnership and moved to the ranch in 1946 when it got to be too much work to do both. He saw a future with his lilacs. His family stayed in the city so John could complete his last year of high school. After he graduated, they sold their home in Los Angeles and moved up to Acton permanently.

"My brother was distressed because he wanted to go to the same school I had, and my mother was distressed because she was a city girl," John recalls. During their weekends on the farm, Ida had to cook on a wood-burning stove and use coal-oil lamps for light and evaporative coolers for refrigeration. There was no telephone service at first and Chris had to build his own road to the property. Electricity came to Acton just one year before they moved there. "My father agreed to get my mother a television set, and that's how he convinced her to move to the ranch."

John joined the U.S. Navy and his brother Robert later volunteered for the draft and served in Germany with the U.S. Army. Both of them enjoyed farming but realized the Colombo Lilac Ranch would never support three families. John went to law school and practiced law for 28 years, and Robert became a teacher. During busy harvest seasons, they came back to the ranch to help their dad – more often as he aged.

Construction is expected to begin in 2008 on a new branch of the Los Angeles County Public Library at the southern end of Antelope Valley. The facility will sit on one-and-a-half acres donated for the purpose by the Brevidoro Family Trust. It will, John Brevidoro says proudly, be called the Acton/Agua Dulce Christopher Colombo Brevidoro Library, and the children's section is to be named the Ida Ghio Brevidoro Reading Area.

Things were tough for city-girl Ida in her first years on the farm, but she soldiered on, "a loyal wife," John remembers. He also remembers the day she announced that she would do no more canning of fruit from their small orchard. "She was an independent lady [who] would have loved to have been born [when] you're known for what you do and not for what your husband does."

Chris built packing sheds in 1953 and in 1954 they opened the lilac harvest to the public for the first time, placing ads in *The Los Angeles Times*. Ida helped wait on customers, and also helped care for the peonies Chris had planted alongside the lilacs.

"At one time we were the largest grower of cut-flower peonies west of Illinois, and selling them at the wholesale price of $15 a bunch," says John. "We were enormously successful with them for about five years, right after I got out of the service and moved back to the farm. But peonies are very susceptible to disease. We didn't know how to handle it and lost all of them." It was the early 1950s and drought had come to the Antelope Valley.

John admits that he, his brother and his dad made plenty of mistakes on the ranch. "None of us had gone to agricultural school, and we weren't trained farmers." They over-fertilized the high-desert soil and planted the wrong varieties of lilacs in the wrong areas. But lilacs are hardy shrubs, and many survived. The family's niche market continued to grow.

In 1949, Chris tried forcing lilacs to bloom early. Their season is only a couple of weeks, and he wanted to see if he could bring out the fragrant blossom earlier. He and Ida brought cut lilacs into the house and put their stems into buckets of hot water. Their efforts failed, says John wryly: "You just can't fool Mother Nature."

Wildfires have always threatened the Colombo Lilac Ranch. During one major fire in 1959, the Los Angeles Fire Department set up a command post at the ranch and used its reservoir to fight the fire, stopping it at the property line before it reached the San Bernardino National Forest. A fire in 2005 burned 10,000 acres all around the ranch but only burned four or five acres of the ranch itself. And a fire in 2007 came within a mile of the ranch, burning over 2,500 surrounding acres.

Chris and Ida settled into their community. They built a large home on a hillside overlooking their lilac fields. She joined the Woman's Club and later took adult education classes at Antelope Valley College. He served the local chamber of commerce as president for two years, donated land to the local water district for new wells, and also belonged to the Kiwanis Club.

The Colombo Lilac Ranch still produces an annual crop which it sells to wholesalers. John retired from his legal practice in 1992 and still works the farm. He maintains a small weekend home on the property, and has two full-time employees and as many as 25 helpers during the harvest season.

His younger brother Robert died in 2004. John's niece (Robert's daughter), Cathy, is John's partner in the family business. John's son Steven, daughter Angela and granddaughters Claire and Marjorie come up to the farm to help when they can. "We all love the flowers," John says.

So do their customers who today include, besides Mellano & Company, Choice Flowers, Mayesh Wholesale Florist and Holland Flower Market. The lilac blossoming season is a short window, just a couple of weeks for each variety, although the ranch does grow more than one variety now.

Reminiscing about the late 1970s and early 1980s, when Wall Street's then-major wholesalers and shippers bought their crop, John ticks off the names of their largest customers: "Joe Shinoda's firm, San Lorenzo, was big for us. B.W. Hall was a good customer of ours. Ed Battistessa, another Italian boy, used to be one of our customers. And Biaggi was a one-man operation who was good for us. Our crop is still a very niche market in the cut flower industry."

*** "Chris Brevidoro Story: 'Only in America'," Evelyn Moffett, *Antelope Valley Press,* May 14, 1967.**

The Stamis and Karavas Families 1946 > Dan and Brown Stamis Were Flower Market Staples

The colorful stories told by members of the Stamis family could fill a book of their own. Their tales of escapade, fun and adventure wend their way from the aster fields to the bowling alleys and casinos, and from the Greek flower market to the American flower market.

Michael (Stamatelatos) Stamis came to the United States around 1910 from the Greek island of Cephalonia with his wife Joyia (Julia) and their children Jerry and Dennis (Dan), processing through Ellis Island. The family settled in Redondo Beach where they followed in the footsteps of their countrymen who had established their own businesses in the land of opportunity. Daughter Bertha was born, followed by siblings Cosmos, Gus, Mary, Evelyn and Brown and they, like the older children, grew up weeding, cutting and packing the flowers from the local flower fields.

Dan Stamis Wholesale

Dan Stamis matured into a handsome fellow who, like many of the Greek immigrants, started his own flower business (Dan Stamis Wholesale). He was easily recognizable, this small man (5'7", 160 pounds at most), by his sport coat, slacks and suspenders and he bought his coats at the exclusive Harris and Frank menswear store. Dan was physically fit and a friendly, talkative, outgoing type who, although uneducated, was an astute businessman who loved people.

Dan quickly recognized trends and market demand and transitioned his small company from that of a flower grower to a wholesaler of greens. He went from growing King Asters in Hermosa Beach and Redondo Beach and wholesaling blooms he bought (and personally picked up) from Camarillo area farms to wholesaling leatherleaf fern and other greens.

"Someone sent my father some leatherleaf fern, and he fell in love with it," remembers his daughter Ellen Snow. "He eventually called himself 'the leatherleaf king.'"

Dan Stamis

Brown Stamis

Dan opened a counter inside the Los Angeles Flower Market (American Florists' Exchange) and leased warehousing space from the Market at 728 Wall Street. The phone number Dan Stamis started his Flower Market business with in 1946 remains the company's phone number today.

"He was quite a salesman," recalls Dave Snow, Dan's son-in-law and the owner of the business today. "The leatherleaf fern sold well. After that, he didn't handle flowers much. He started handling lemon leaf, huckleberry, cedar, curly willow, bear grass, brake fern."

It is unfortunate that on March 31, 1976, at age 72, Dan became the victim of a robbery and mugging as he sat in the little office in his warehouse, going through the day's receipts. His injuries were so severe that he had to crawl to the street to get help. The physically fit, friendly Dan Stamis was never the same after that, never returned to his work at the Market and was confined to a wheelchair until his death in 1986.

Brown Stamis Wholesale

In his early years, Brownie Stamis, Dan's younger brother, grew marigolds, asters and stock in Redondo Beach. Later, like Dan, he transitioned to wholesaling at the Market where he operated the Brown Stamis Wholesale counter for more than 35 years.

Around 1972, Brownie hired a young Mexican immigrant named Willie Sanchez, to help him with his Market operation. Sanchez, who had immigrated from Michoacan, Mexico at the age of sixteen, was eager and enthusiastic and quickly learned the value of hard, conscientious work, the routines of ordering, assisting customers and operating the counter, maturing into a capable business manager in his own right.

In the mid-1980s, Brownie Stamis retired and sold his business to his loyal employee, Willie Sanchez, one of the earliest Latino owner-tenants in the American Florists' Exchange. (Frank Regalado, a 1930s-1940s tenant, is believed to have been the first.)

Stamis to Sanchez and Sanvilla

Willie Sanchez brought his young children to help him in the new business he'd bought from his mentor/employer Brown Stamis, and taught them how to do the things he had worked so hard to learn himself. Eventually, after he'd devoted his career to the business, Willie took partial retirement. Son William entered the business and expanded it in 1995 to a second location across the street in the Southern California Flower Market, where Willie became manager and now operates under the William Sanchez Wholesale name.

William's sister Ivette became manager of the William Sanchez stall in the Los Angeles Flower Market in 1995. Other family members, including sister Cynthia, work in the business as well. In 2003, the partners changed the business name to Sanvilla when Ivette's new husband, Fernando Villa, whose family owns Villa Growers in the Southern California Flower Market, joined she and William as a partner in the business.

So even though its name has changed, Brown Stamis's business continues and it can still be visited at its original location in the Los Angeles Flower Market, right next to the Dan Stamis Wholesale counter.

The colorful Jerry Stamis

The very first job that Dan and Brown's older brother Jerry had was that of selling flowers from a cart on the Redondo Beach pier, and Jerry stayed in the flower business for a little while, growing asters in summer and stock in winter. Then he bought a gas station in Manhattan Beach. His nephew Costike (Tike) Karavas recalls that in those early years, a Greek fellow told Jerry of a nice girl in Pittsburgh, and Jerry just "got up and went to Pittsburgh and married her." The couple raised a family of three sons in California.

By the time Jerry had semi-retired, he'd bought a building just north of the Flower Market, which is now the Certified building. He then bought a small casino in North Las Vegas with his brother-in-law Jerry Lodge and named it Jerry's Nugget. The casino employed a number of family members, including Tike Karavas, who worked there for 30 years running bingo, food and beverage and the race and sports book, until he retired in his hometown of Redondo Beach.

Bertha Stamis marries John Karavas

Gus Dimas, a flower grower from Hermosa Beach, introduced John Karavas to Bertha Stamis, linking the families in the flower business. John Karavas grew the large King Asters for which the Greek farmers were so well known, as well as the other staples of the area's flower farms.

"One year, Pop had a price dispute with some wholesale florists who held out for the lowest possible price," remembers Tike Karavas. "My dad ended up dumping all the flowers at Wilderness Park – a pickup truckload." The story made the *Los Angeles Times* on August 8, 1950, and stated that "110,000 aster blooms were dumped on the hills above Redondo Beach."

John Karavas, left, with his partner Jimmy Farfoulos, late 1940s. Note the corn row planted to protect the young flowers from the wind.

John Karavas had a heart of gold and a soft spot for hard-working families and often cooked lunch-time barbeques for his employees. Shippers coming for their flowers timed their arrival so they could partake of the food.

When an earthquake demolished homes in his hometown of Karabados on the Greek island of Cephalonia, John Karavas, at age 49, sent one million drachmas for each of the families and collected donations around the Flower Market, which were then presented to Greece's Queen Fredericka during her visit to America. Karavas wasn't satisfied with these efforts so he sent a personal donation of the equivalent of $33 U.S. dollars to each of ten families which his sisters, still living in Cephalonia, named as having no other resources.

Dave and Ellen Snow

It just seemed natural when Erma, Dan Stamis's wife, asked son-in-law Dave Snow on the day Dan was injured in 1976, if he would enter the business and manage it. Dave had worked at the counter off and on for several years, helping out during holidays and seasons when florists and decorators' orders for greens made heavy demands. He knew the business basics and took up the challenge the very next day. In the years that followed that transition, Dave retained the Dan Stamis Wholesale name, making it one of the few tenants in the Market with recognizable longevity back to the 1940s.

Dave Snow, 2008

Ellen Snow, Dan's oldest daughter, has lent a share of expertise to the business as well, having worked for several years doing bookwork for her father.

Today's Dan Stamis Wholesale deals with a loyal following of florists, decorators, shippers and the public. Dave recalls a large customer who, until his company was sold, ordered 600 wreaths every year during the Christmas season, sending a bobtail truck to pick them up, 350 at a time.

Snow has expanded the Dan Stamis Wholesale counter area and added a cooler in the warehouse. Leatherleaf fern, although subject to price hikes, ice and freezes in its Florida growing environment, is still the main product. And there's Commodore (palm leaves), grown in Mexico and exported to Texas shippers.

The names and the faces may have changed, but the spirit of entrepreneurship and the eagerness to meet challenges head-on are ever present still in the businesses started by the Stamis family.

Ghigo Greens 1924 – 1983
An Italian Flower Market Family

Italians in America at the start of the Second World War were sometimes viewed with suspicion. The country, after all, was newly engaged in another world-wide conflict. Italy had joined with Hitler's Germany as an Axis power and declared war on America in December 1941. Non-naturalized Italians, especially those who lived on the West Coast, were thought to be potential "enemy aliens."

The close-knit group of Italians who grew flowers around Los Angeles had to deal with restrictions on their movements while going about their business, although none were interned in camp as the Japanese were. Giovanni Ghigo did spend one night in jail for violating curfew during blackout hours, and officers also came to his sister-in-law Maria Mellano's door one evening to make sure she was at home where she was supposed to be.

Giovanni, a hard-working farmer, was simply trying to get his crops to the Los Angeles Flower Market for the early morning opening. Driving during a blackout without headlights down a deserted street toward the city from his ranch in Buena Park/La Mirada, he flipped on the lights momentarily, just to see where he was going, and was arrested on suspicion of "signaling the enemy."

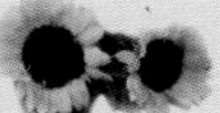

By the early 1940s, Giovanni Ghigo had been in the United States for 30 years. He grew up in Entracque, a small town in the mountains of northern Italy, and immigrated to New York in 1910. He didn't like working in the coal mines on the East Coast, and made his way to the Pacific Northwest where he joined other Italian immigrants who made a living picking greens for the floral trade.

By 1921 Giovanni Ghigo had moved to Felton, a small community near Santa Cruz in Northern California where Italians working in the greens business also congregated. He was engaged to marry Maria, a young lady who was also from Entracque. She traveled to America to wed her betrothed accompanied by her brother, eighteen-year-old Giovanni Mellano. The two arrived in 1921 after a long ocean crossing followed by cross-country train to San Francisco.

Thus the Ghigo and Mellano families' lives became entwined. Both Giovannis, brothers-in-law from the same mountain town in Italy, worked the evergreens wholesale trade in Northern California and eventually ended up in Southern California, owning flower ranches very close to each other. Both of them grew greenery and cut flowers, including zinnias and bulb-stock such as tulips and daffodils.

Ghigo, as he was called by family and friends, and Maria left the Santa Cruz area sometime within the next few years; Giovanni Mellano followed shortly afterward. By 1925, all three of them were living in Los Angeles.

In the mid-1920s, the Los Angeles Flower Market was just a few years old. The American Florists' Exchange had incorporated and purchased a building on Wall Street for $30,000. Shares of common stock were available for $50 each – a princely sum in those days. The privileges of share ownership appealed to these hard-working Italians; they desired to succeed in America and to be part of something bigger. Both Giovannis bought AFE shares and sold their flowers and greens in the Market.

The two families remained close. Nephew Johnny Mellano recalls that when his own three oldest sons were young, Uncle Ghigo liked to hand out quarters on the religious holiday of the Epiphany, January 6. Sometimes he slipped each boy a dollar bill instead, always admonishing them: "Don't tell your Auntie Ghigo."

More than one Market regular from the 1950s and '60s remembers Giovanni Ghigo's distinctive speech pattern that mixed his local Italian dialect, Spanish, English and even French. "He spoke the most broken English you've ever heard, but my father could understand every word he said," recalls Larry Bergez, whose father Emile owned one of the few retail flower shops on Wall Street in that era. Emile, a Frenchman, felt an affinity for the Italians; many of them were his good friends. Larry also remembers Giovanni Ghigo's industriousness: "His hands said it all; they were the beat-up hands of a hard-worker."

Giovanni and Maria Ghigo had two daughters, Doris and Inez. Both worked alongside their parents on the ranch and then went to the Market to sell what the family grew. Doris' daughter Inez Ayala says that her mother was the most hardworking woman she knows. Inez herself recalls being at the Market from a very early age: "I slept under the counter while my mom served her customers. As I got older I helped, too."

As the years went by, the Ghigo family's ranch, located about two miles from the original Mellano ranch, gradually lost ground to urban development. When Firestone Boulevard was paved, it split the Ghigo ranch in two pieces. In the early 1950s, the Santa Ana Freeway (Interstate 5) was built on a portion of the land.

Top: Doris Ghigo in the zinnia field in 1962.
Above: Giovanni and Maria Ghigo among their flowers, 1962.

Finally, around 1983 the Ghigo family quit farming when the city of La Mirada purchased the rest of the ranch to build an office and hotel complex at the junction of the freeway and Valley View Boulevard. Even then, Doris continued to go to the Market – the only life she had ever known – and sell greens to her customers from a small table.

Inez has happy memories of the Market's hustle and bustle: "I learned a great work ethic there. A day does not go by that I don't think of something that reminds me of the Market. It taught me invaluable lessons about business, life and beauty."

Vander Bruggen Family 1923 - 2003 Building a Legacy with Birds of Paradise

In the early hours of a Market day in the post-war 1940s, rats scurrying atop the rafters in the old Los Angeles Flower Market building were easy targets for eight-year-old Nick Vander Bruggen's BB gun. Those pre-dawn hunting expeditions were no doubt a "consolation prize" for getting up at two a.m. to accompany his granddad and dad into Los Angeles with a truckload of flowers.

The Vander Bruggens farmed flowers in Montebello, alongside other flower growing friends who had organized a market for growers of European-American descent on the east side of Wall Street. The family grew iris, calla lilies and bulb stock from Holland. "My grandfather and his friends were about fifteen years ahead of their time on the bulb stock because they didn't become very popular until later," Nick said in 2007.

Nick has good memories of growing up in the Flower Market. He recalls that Mike, the policeman who directed traffic in the crosswalk near the Market, always had gum in his pocket for him.

Like other sons of farming families, when he turned sixteen Nick began hauling flowers to Market in the family's truck by himself. By that time the family's fields included the regal bird of paradise, a tall thick stem supporting a beak-like bract from which pointed petals of bright orange with vivid blue tongues emerge.

The Vander Bruggens were one of several growers in Montebello who had taken a cue from brothers Elmer and Clinton Pedley and Donald F. Briggs, co-owners of California Birds, Inc. in Carlsbad, down the coast toward San Diego.

The Pedleys and Briggs, who also grew gladiolas, had invested the time necessary to bring bird of paradise from seed to fruition – up to seven years before their first blooms – and by the end of the 1950s were reaping the benefits. Every winter they sent more than one million stems to flower markets in the East and Midwest, reported The *Saturday Evening Post* in a March 11, 1961 article entitled "The Flowers Known As Birds."* The article's author also wrote that growers in Montebello shipped another one million birds through the Los Angeles wholesale flower market, and waxed poetic that "a brilliantly hued, top-quality bird is a dollar's worth of bloom in New York or Chicago on a dark wintry day."

Los Angeles selected the showy bird of paradise as its official flower in 1952 – a move heavily lobbied by local bird growers, most notably Manfred Meyberg, a prominent businessman, civic leader and a founder of both the Los Angeles Beautiful organization and the Men's Garden Club of Los Angeles.

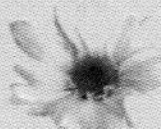

Los Angeles' official flower is not really native to California at all. Strelitzia blooms are commonly known as bird of paradise because their bright colors and showy features resemble an exotic South Pacific bird. Originally from South Africa, "birds" adapted quickly to Southern California's dry and sunny climate.

California's bird industry began several decades earlier, motivated by an enthusiastic amateur flower grower from Hollywood named Lovell Swisher. Swisher, an insurance executive and also a member of the Men's Garden Club, seized on the idea of cornering the Strelitzia market in the late 1920s. He planted hundreds of birds and learned how to hand-pollinate them and collect their seeds, then sold a lot of his seed to local nurserymen until both price and demand dropped as seed began to come in from Hawaii.

Swisher switched his allegiance to experimenting with orchids but his Strelitzia plants and seeds were the basis of plant stock for the majority of local commercial bird growers, including Don Briggs who had been talked into planting them on his expansive acreage by none other than Manfred Meyberg.

In the 1950s, Nick's grandfather, W.J. Vander Bruggen, and his friends in Montebello quickly realized the potential goldmine that cultivating birds represented, especially given the public's interest in the exotic blooms and their status as Los Angeles' official flower. Over time, W.J. focused his floriculture efforts on propagating, promoting and improving birds for both cut flower production and ornamental garden use.

W.J. was a native of Sassenheim, Holland, where he studied horticulture and began his career growing bulbs. In 1907 he decided to make a new life in America. After a few months working for a nursery in New Jersey, he moved to Chicago where, in 1909, he married a girl from his hometown in Holland. The following year the young couple moved to Richland, Washington, and W.J. found employment as a nursery manager.

They came to the Montebello area, at that time called Newmark, in 1914, most likely because a large contingent of Dutch immigrants also made their home there, and then to Santa Ana where W.J. worked as a park custodian until 1920. He also started a landscaping and nursery business at Main and Chapman streets in Santa Ana.

W.J. sold this business in 1923 and turned to what he knew well: growing bulbs and flowers. In 1925 he became a member of the young American Florists' Exchange, and took out a license as a commission flower merchant. He returned with his family to Montebello in the early 1930s and bought land.

Throughout his career W.J. took advantage of every opportunity to promote his chosen flower specialty. The November 1958 issue of *The Bloomin' News* features a photograph of several Los Angeles officials and civic leaders along with Walter Swartz, representing the Southern California Floral Association (SCFA), at city hall ceremonies opening National Flower Week. They are surrounded by some of the three hundred dozen birds of paradise that W.J. Vander Bruggen, who was winding up a year serving the SCFA as its president, had provided for the occasion.

W.J. won many trophies and prizes for his bird displays, and was a long-time member of the International Flower Show Committee at Hollywood Park. Other industry organizations of which he was a member were the California State Floral Association and the Society of American Florists.

His son and then his grandson, Nick, followed in his footsteps hybridizing and selling more colorful and longer-lasting varieties of the stately blooms, until imported Strelitzia stems from South America began appearing at the Market.

The reluctant farmer

"I didn't care if I ever went back to the flower business," Nick said in 2007. But family legacies have a siren call all their own and in 1968, after a five-year stint in the U.S. Air Force where he served as a flight engineer on missions around the world, that's exactly what he did.

Before joining the Air Force, Nick studied mathematics and engineering at East Los Angeles College and didn't want anything to do with the Flower Market. "I grew up on the farm and hated every minute, because while my friends were out having a good time, I had to work," he says. "In college, I was finally free."

Nick agreed to watch the farm for awhile so his dad could take a vacation. His attitude must have changed because he bought out his father and continued growing birds along with waxflowers, agapanthus and greens, and managing the commission business his grandfather had started on the American Florists' Exchange almost fifty years earlier.

Soon after Nick took over, urbanization claimed the original Montebello ranch and Nick moved his birds to land leased from Southern California Edison – land unfit for residential development because it lay beneath power transmission lines.

By the early 1980s, no longer able to compete with imported bird stems that sold for one-fifth the price of his, Nick accepted an offer to join GM Floral, a newly formed wholesale business with a large space in the Southern California Flower Market. "Mas Yoshida was a great man to work for; he let me continue growing and selling my own flowers to wholesalers while also handling GM Floral's greens business," Nick says.

Like his grandfather, Nick also served the SCFA as its president — in 1972, following three terms as a board member and then vice president. SCFA launched its credit union during his tenure. In 1970, he served as general chairman of the Wall Street Open House.

Nick was also involved in the association's dissolution in the late 1980s. "By that time, there wasn't a lot of support for it and growers and brokers were taking a heavy hit from inexpensive imports," he recalls. "Another divisive issue was the argument about allowing housewives to come into the Market. Some people, mostly growers, wanted a badge program; others didn't."

As the Southern California Floral Association ceased operations, Market leaders on both sides of Wall Street stepped into the void, creating a workable badge program that enables florists and floral-trade related businesses with valid resale certificates to enjoy shopping at both Markets.

Eventually, the bird of paradise was the only flower crop that remained in Montebello. The last two growers sold their birds independently to wholesalers. When Edison raised the cost to lease the land beneath their power lines, it became too expensive to compete with the imports.

Ken Foltz's Paradise Hill Wholesale went out of business in 1995, and Nick Vander Bruggen's Regina Farms, Inc., ceased operations in 2003. Nick sold his plants to several Montebello nurseries and retired.

******The Saturday Evening Post***, "The Flowers Known As Birds," Frank Taylor, March 11, 1961**

Harold Norman
Norman Seed Company 1942 >
Carrying the Family Tradition Forward

Harold Norman entered the flower seed business as a young man, working as a warehouse stock boy in Detroit, Michigan. He soon came west, desiring work with the Waller Seed Company in California.

In 1933 while at Waller Seed Company, Harold had a program on the local radio station, and he published a pamphlet of tips for households with hobbies of growing flowers in the garden.

Harold Norman harvests flower seeds in Lompoc, 1957.

In 1942 Harold Norman ventured forth on his own, setting up business as a distributor of flower seeds to the many flower growers coming through the Los Angeles Flower Market every day. He took a job with San Lorenzo Nursery, selling gardenias on the Market, while he got his business started in an upstairs loft there. He went full-time with Norman Seed Company in 1944 and, in 1947, he incorporated. In later years the family opened a warehouse in Costa Mesa.

Norman Amling remembers Harold Norman "walking around the Flower Market with his order book, taking orders for seed from the growers who had brought flowers to the market." On off Market days he traveled the coast from Half Moon Bay to San Diego servicing the needs of cut flower growers with seeds best selected to the local environment. Word of mouth produced sales to growers throughout the states.

Harold Norman contracted with large seed companies like Waller, Bodger and others including companies in Holland and France to supply his inventory. He also contracted with local flower growers who grew trial plots for him.

Harold Norman passed away in 1988, leaving a legacy of service and quality in the flower seed industry. Today the wholesale distributorship serves a loyal clientele, many of whom are located along the California coast. Farmers have developed new outlets for flower sales and many grow flowers to sell in local area farmers markets.

Family members carry on the Norman Seed business in Santa Ana, California.

Hollandia Flowers, Inc. 1978 - 1988

Hollandia Wholesale Florist's Decade in the American Florists' Exchange

As a grower shipper supplying wholesale florists across the nation, Art and Magda Overgaag, who founded Hollandia Flowers in 1970, recognized the chance to deal directly with area florists as a business building opportunity. With help from Bert Johnson and John Williams, Hollandia Wholesale Florist opened its American Florists' Exchange stall in 1978.

Specializing in cut chrysanthemums and gypsophilia, Hollandia provided premium quality flowers to greater Southern California florists via its Wall Street stall for more than a decade. Familiar names like Victor's, Toluca Lake Florist, Verdugo Hills Florist and Visser's, to name a few, were regular customers always looking for the highest quality at the best price.

Ellen Overgaag talks with employee, Nick, at the Hollandia stall in the American Florists' Exchange, early 1980s. ***Hollandia collection.***

Over the years, Hollandia's cut flower offerings expanded substantially. Alstromerias, calla lilies, iris, liatris, oriental lilies, roses and statice all accompanied the florists' all-time favorite, pom pon chrysanthemums. Hollandia operated on the big Market days — Mondays, Wednesdays and Fridays.

Ellen Overgaag, Art and Magda's oldest daughter, managed the stall through 1985. Gary Ahlmann staffed the booth from 1985 through 1988 when Hollandia exited the floral industry to expand into the blooming plant and fresh produce business. Today Hollandia is Hollandia Produce. The company markets its Live Gourmet brand of greenhouse grown premium vegetables to supermarkets and specialty retailers across America.

Edgar Engert: Supporting the Ecke Ranch and Local and Floral Communities

When Market tenants saw Edgar Engert walking into the Los Angeles Flower Market every September, they knew the Christmas poinsettia season was just around the corner. It was Edgar's job to manage the Ecke Ranch holiday sales area in the Market, and he always formulated his plan beginning with a cursory look at the area and reacquainting himself with other vendors in early autumn.

Edgar and Renate Engert came to the United States from Germany in 1958 with their baby daughter, and Edgar wasted no time finding work with Kurt Weiss's greenhouse operation. It wasn't long until he began employment with the Ecke Ranch, while he and Renate operated two retail floral shops in Del Mar, California.

"During the Christmas season," Edgar recalled recently of his breaking-in period, "I was sent up to the (Los Angeles) Market at midnight with a delivery truck. The Ecke Ranch area in the Market was run by Thorny Maurer, Mrs. Ecke's brother, and Thorny introduced me to customers – who yelled at me because we didn't have any more poinsettias."

That day, with poinsettias in great demand, Paul Ecke Sr sent Edgar back to the ranch in Encinitas with instructions to load all the plants from the greenhouses and drive them to Los Angeles. Edgar arrived back at the Market at 2 or 3 a.m., arranged with the employees to deliver orders to the route drivers parked and waiting along Wall Street.

"We pushed the carts of poinsettias to them so they could be on their way by 5 a.m. to deliver to the retail shops."

It became Edgar's tradition to spend at least one day at the Ecke sales area in the Market during every holiday season, working all day at the ranch and all night at the market ("to see how tough you were").

In 1988, Edgar took over Ecke Ranch's holiday sales area at the Market, beginning the habit of checking things out in September. Between that first visit and the beginning of the holiday season around November 10, he visited customers to get a feeling for upcoming orders.

Through the early 1990s, during the peak of holiday sales, Edgar stayed in a hotel during the week, hired helpers from Encinitas and trucked the workers to the Los Angeles Market. In subsequent years, he hired workers locally.

One year, strong, able-bodied Mormon workers from Utah filled the seasonal jobs. These young farm boys developed compassion for the homeless of the area and began to provide the less fortunate individuals with the huge, long boxes in which the poinsettias had been shipped, to use as sleeping cocoons. Lined up along San Julian Street, the locals came to calling them the "Ecke condos." Eventually, the boxes disappeared and the homeless moved to other streets, but Edgar and others remember those "condos" with a chuckle today.

Edgar with his uncle in New York City, one week after arriving from Germany in 1962.

In 2002, Ecke Ranch turned management of its Los Angeles Market enterprise over to Mellano & Company. Edgar Engert, who now runs the sales area at the Ecke Ranch in Encinitas, still visits the Market during the holidays.

Edgar's relationships with Paul Ecke Sr and Paul Ecke Jr are legend and both father and son inspired him. Paul Ecke Jr's goal was "to put a poinsettia in every home in America," Edgar says. He often rode with Paul Sr to the American Florists' Exchange board meetings and to visit customers. Paul Jr loved his contacts with people throughout the floral industry and the community and inspired Edgar to value his personal contacts.

Edgar's many involvements and contributions to his local community and to the floral industry have served him well. In the 1990s, he was invited to join the exclusive Men's Garden Club of Los Angeles. In September 2007, at the annual convention of the Society of American Florists, Paul Ecke III presented the "Golden Bouquet Paul Ecke Jr" award to him in recognition of his exemplary devotion to the profession, industry and community. (Paul Ecke Jr earned the award in 1992.)

Edgar has served as president of the California State Floral Association (2008) and Encinitas Chamber of Commerce, Parks and Recreation Commissioner for the City of Encinitas, and on the boards of many service clubs and civic and floral organizations. In late 2007, he and his wife celebrated their fiftieth wedding anniversary.

Soules Gladiolus Company 1938-1982
Tales of a Talented Gladiolus Hybridizer

Among the many growers of gladiola in its heyday as a popular cut flower, the 1940s and '50s, many would agree that Mabel Soules had a special talent. She was a hybridizer and frequent winner of national and regional competitions such as that held in 1950 by the Southern California Gladiolus Society. This event drew 11,568 enthusiasts over two days, reported *The Bloomin' News* in its July issue that year.

Mabel must have been called to the winner's circle many times at that show. Not only did she win a gold certificate in her class of small growers, she also won "Best Gladiolus spike in good condition with the longest flower head…" Her prize-winning bloom was a Marion Pearl variety, with a flower head that measured a whopping thirty-one-and-a-half inches. The judges also singled out this spike as the show's Grand Champion, winning for Mrs. Soules not only the local society's perpetual trophy, but also a silver medal from the North American Gladiolus Society, predecessor to today's North American Gladiolus Council.

The American Florists' Exchange also awarded trophies at the show. Mrs. Soules took home one of them for "best basket of 20 to 25 spikes of one variety" – a basket of the Sequoia variety – and one of her Sequoia blooms won the competition for the "largest individual floret." She also entered – and won second place – in open competition, with the Sweet 17 variety, for "best vase of six to nine spikes."

All of those prizes were undoubtedly repeated in the years that followed, so that by the time Mabel sold her Redondo Beach-based business to Jimmy Fernandez in 1963, 25 years after she started it in 1938, it was a successful operation and she had won quite a name for herself as a hybridizer of high-quality gladiola varieties, among them Pink Majesty, Janet and Heavenly Pink.

Jimmy Fernandez: continuing a prize-winning tradition

Jimmy Fernandez was no newcomer to the business of growing quality merchandise. He had been bringing aster, stock, chrysanthemum, hybrid delphinium and lilac to the Market since 1945. He had also worked for Fred C. King Wholesale Florist, which specialized in gladiolas, and then for Soules Gladiolus on and off for a couple of years. Jimmy kept the company name for its recognition factor, and Mrs. Soules continued to work with him as a consultant. Together, they continued to enter and win gladiola shows locally and elsewhere with Soules-originated and Fernandez-grown blooms.

In August 1964 they took top honors at the Western International Gladiolus Show held in Boise, Idaho. Spikes of their Pink Majesty variety displayed "many qualities desirable as a commercial cut-flower for marketing, as well as qualities desirable for use as an exhibition flower," *The Bloomin' News* reported in its September 1964 issue, an especially impressive achievement since the flowers had traveled over land from Los Angeles to Boise "for three days through 100 degrees heat" and had, at the time of judging, "carried ten, open, perfect florets."

Jimmy Fernandez retired in 1982 and sold the business to Ebbo Dekema. Then he and his wife Toni Ann began working for Don Bent, a builder of floats for the Pasadena Tournament of Roses Parade. Toni Ann was the daughter of Theodore (Ted) Katsogianes and his wife Mamie (Priamos) Katsogianes, so she knew her way around the Flower Market, too.

Toni Ann and her brother, Nick, were third-generation Greeks at the Market. They grew up working in their family's fields in Hermosa Beach until the 1960s. After Nick Katsogianes stopped growing flowers, he opened a wholesale commission house in the Market which he operated until his death in 1988.

Jimmy Fernandez died in 2002. "He was a fine man," said Nick's widow Dorothy Katsogianes in 2008. "Nobody ever had a bad thing to say about Jim Fernandez."

Defterios Family / Delta Floral Distributors, Inc., Early 1900s >

From Growing/Selling King Asters to Supermarket Bouquet Makers

In the early part of the twentieth century, thousands of new American residents extended a helping hand to their family members and friends, to help them immigrate, just as they had, to the United States. The Defterios family, from the Greek island of Cephalonia, was among them. Many of the immigrants landed in New York's harbor, processed through Ellis Island and worked their way to the Los Angeles area where they joined a growing community of European immigrants.

"You go where your countrymen are," remarked Archie Defterios in 2007. Archie said that "at one time, there were 30 to 40 families" that had come to the area's beach towns from Cephalonia.

Jerry Defterios, Archie's father, who liked California for its good weather, spoke no English but didn't hesitate to go into business. Following the example of other immigrants, he sold flowers at Seventh and Figueroa streets in Los Angeles. Now the fashionable "7th & Fig" shopping center in the Ernst & Young Plaza is located there, where dozens of restaurants and retail shops, including Paradise Florist, greet hundreds of visitors daily.

It wasn't long, however, until Jerry was growing flowers alongside his countrymen in Redondo Beach. Surrounded by flower fields and brushed with ocean air and sunshine, it sure felt like the old country of Greece. Archie remembers tagging along with his dad and hunting jackrabbits in the flower fields.

The war years arrived and as the Defterios family worked their flower growing business, they kept up on the news from Europe and family there. By this time, they were growing and shipping asters and Kosta Defterios, Archie's brother, and Jerry Defterios were now among the Greek compatriots who along with Italian, Japanese and other immigrants formed the backbone of the flower growing business in Southern California.

"I went to the Flower Market around 1 a.m. with a load of flowers with my dad, and people were celebrating in the streets – even at that early hour," recalls Archie of the memorable 1945 day when the war finally ended. "A sailor jumped up on the open truck and grabbed a bunch of our King Asters. When I told my dad, he said, 'That's OK; we won the war.'"

The years were good to the Defterios family, as they grew their business and branched into related areas. Shipping flowers to customers across the United States led them to use an early version of a "refrigerated" rail car: They drove the flowers by truck to the "Red Car" depot in Torrance, loaded and sent them to Los Angeles where they were transferred to a rail car carrying ice to preserve perishable cargo. Of course, the ice had to be replaced along the route as it melted.

The family was not involved in the American Florists' Exchange, but they did participate in the "Growers Market" built at 744 Wall Street, where an old hotel had been demolished, north of the AFE building. A sizable outlet, the Growers Market attracted the Greek, Sephardic, Filipino and other immigrant flower growers who were not selling at either of the other major markets on Wall Street. The Growers Market, owned by Jerry Stamis, Nick Pandalios and Jerry Defterios, ended in the early 1960s when its leaders retired and sold the property.

By then, Archie was in the School of Business at the University of Southern California and had some ideas of his own about how to grow his family's business. While a college student he worked three nights a week at the Market and then went to his 8 a.m. class. One day the professor asked why he was always falling asleep in class. Hearing of Archie's night job, the professor asked him to write a paper on "how you can better your business."

That was all the impetus the young, ambitious Archie Defterios needed. He wrote his paper about creating a business of arranging mixed floral bouquets (the business he's in today) to sell to supermarket chains. The business became a reality in the late 1950s when the Alpha Beta chain signed on as his first customer. He tested the then innovative idea, wrote the paper and got an "A".

"The professor's assignment changed my life," he says.

Archie's youngest brother Nick owned a floral business for years; and his brother Kosta went into the potted plant business in Ventura County, California, retiring just a few years ago.

Jerry Defterios discusses King Asters with a customer, 1950s-1960s.

Today, the flowers used by Delta Floral Distributors include a mixture of California flowers, which they used exclusively in the beginning, and imported flowers. The Defterios family, believed to be the first to import roses from Israel and several other places around the world, buys several essential bouquet flowers from California growers: stock from the Amling Brothers and greens from Mellano & Company, to name a couple. The company's relationships with growers in other countries have allowed Delta Floral to continue to grow the business. Archie has traveled "around the world a lot of times" in the flower business and takes "great pride" in the fact that he "can share a cup of coffee with flower growers worldwide."

Foti Defterios, Archie's son who works in company management, believes "the import flower supply helped the (flower) industry grow." Both Foti, who in 1984 earned a degree in Business Administration from USC, his brother Christo and sister Marianna have worked in the family business since their youth.

In 1991, complimenting the good work in the industry, the Fresh Produce & Floral Council named Archie Defterios its Floral Marketer of the Year.

Fred C. King Wholesale Florist
1920s - 1960s
A Giant Among Los Angeles Growers

Los Angeles-born Fred King, orphaned at the age of four and raised by an aunt, learned the lessons of hard work early on and applied them throughout his life to several business interests, all of them centered around the Los Angeles Flower Market.

Fred had many friends and admirers throughout the industry, probably because he helped more than one grower, commission man or florist get started. He also had a reputation for fair dealings, and he wasn't above jumping in as needed to work alongside the people who worked for him.

Fred King during his term as Southern California Floral Association president, 1940s.

Those people included his wife Elsie, who he married in 1918, and his children: Fred Jr., Edna and Lucille. The fields the King family tended were in Torrance and Gardena. By the time *The Bloomin' News* published an article about Fred's participation on the Southern California Floral Association's board of directors in March 1950 – he had served as its president two years earlier – he was said "to be the largest field grower of cut flowers west of Chicago. At times, having over 100 acres under cultivation."

Top: Fred and Elsie King amidst their gladiolas in Torrance, early 1950s
Above: Fred King, center, with colleagues at an Open House.

"My grandfather was famous for helping people out," said Fred's granddaughter Lucille (Eaton) Beach in a 2007 interview. "People would come to him and say 'Fred, I really need a couple of hundred dollars and I'll give you this to hold until I can pay you back' and he would always hand over the money." Sometimes Fred never saw his money again, and that is how he ended up with several useless plots of land located in ravines far from Los Angeles' fertile growing flatlands: "He ended up just giving them away."

Lucille recalls a carefree childhood in which she, her little sister Elsie and her cousin Chuck "helped out" but mostly played in their grandfather's flower fields. "That's how I learned to drive, in my granddaddy's truck in the fields." She could barely reach the truck's pedals, at age nine, she remembers.

The children were taught how to use the small ring-hooked knives to slice through the stems of gladiolas, and they learned to roll newspapers in tight rounds to stuff between the gladiola stalks in the water buckets to keep them from crushing. "Like pillows, so the glads wouldn't get smashed," she says. "We'd do them just for fun, until we got tired. Then we'd go off into the fields and find something else to do." One favorite activity was to catch frogs and put them in the five-gallon flower cans.

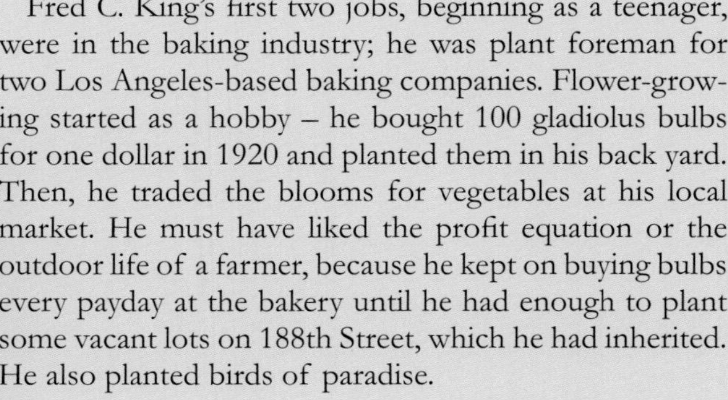

Fred C. King's first two jobs, beginning as a teenager, were in the baking industry; he was plant foreman for two Los Angeles-based baking companies. Flower-growing started as a hobby – he bought 100 gladiolus bulbs for one dollar in 1920 and planted them in his back yard. Then, he traded the blooms for vegetables at his local market. He must have liked the profit equation or the outdoor life of a farmer, because he kept on buying bulbs every payday at the bakery until he had enough to plant some vacant lots on 188th Street, which he had inherited. He also planted birds of paradise.

King joined the Los Angeles Flower Market in 1933. Over the years he won many awards for his floriculture skills, and developed two strains of gladiolus, a lavender and a red that was called "King Red."

During the war years, he told his Japanese-American farming neighbors in Torrance and Gardena that he would take care of their land while they were sent to the internment camps. His granddaughter, who was born in 1942, remembers the family stories that he grew flowers on the land, paid the taxes on it, and then returned the fields and some profit to their owners when they returned from the camps.

Fred King bought flowers from growers from San Diego County to Oxnard, with King Wholesale trucks covering a wide area from the 1930s into the 1950s. He also had a business called Southwest Bulb Company which shipped bulbs across the country, and was involved in a wholesale business in Chicago together with the San Lorenzo Nursery Company. And, he owned Southwest Tractor Sales, a large dealership that sold and leased Ford farm tractors, for many years. His son, Fred C. King Jr., worked at the Flower Market as a young man, then took over the tractor business on a full-time basis. In 1982 Fred's grandson, Charles King, opened a wholesale rose import company on the Market.

At some point in the 1960s, the King family's fields at the intersection of Hawthorne and Torrance boulevards became too valuable for growing flowers and the land was leased to a woman who built a trailer park, restaurant and gas station there. Before Fred King retired, he had helped his daughter Lucille opened a retail shop in the popular Farmer's Market venue, and had trained his daughter Edna's husband, Russell Eaton, in the finer points of flower selection, customer care and profitable wholesale flower sales.

When Fred King turned seventy – two years before he died – his long-time friend Bob Ayres of Crown Florist Supply in Phoenix, Ariz., penned a two-page tribute to "our contemporary for all the years most of us can remember" in the March 1970 issue of *The Bloomin' News*, saying in part:

"Like most of us salty pioneers, his successes, failures, reliance and sometimes bitter disappointment in his fellow travelers have all been part of the Wall Street game he played all his life."

Russell Eaton: Flower Man with a Heart

"Dad was a lot of fun, and a good man," says Lucille (Eaton) Beach about her father, recounting an incident when someone had thrown a puppy down the outhouse in the field. At the pleas of his eight-year-old daughter, he went down into the pit for the rescue.

Russell Eaton

Russell Eaton married Fred C. King's middle daughter Edna in 1941 while working for Union Oil. The two met as students at Gardena High School. Shortly afterward, he went off to military service in World War II. Russell, who had done a little boxing to earn money during the Depression years, had an adventurous spirit which came in handy when his combat unit came under fire. He and two other men blew up a machine-gun nest, and Russell came home with a Purple Heart and two bronze stars.

After the war, his father-in-law put him to work. He drove the trucks back and forth to Oxnard and also worked the fields, but his people skills and ability to quickly add sums in his head were utilized best at the Market where he both bought and sold product. "He never finished high school because he had to help support his family, but he knew flowers and their prices inside out," says Lucille.

In the mid-1950s, Russell broke his leg in five places in a motorcycle accident and wore a cast for eighteen months. When he returned to work, it was for Kessler Associates, one of the larger shippers in the Market at the time. He spent the remainder of his flower industry career at Kessler until he retired in 1986.

Russell's daughter Lucille says that one of her happier childhood memories is the sights, sounds and especially the smells of the Flower Market: "You can't find that anywhere else." She remembers her cousin Chuck pushing her around on the flower carts, getting yelled at for being in the way when a cart of flowers was coming through, and stopping by her granddad's flower cooling room to get a drink of ice-cold water from the dispenser there.

She also remembers hearing her father from time to time tell customers that "what we have isn't really that good, so you should go over to see so-and-so because their selection is better today."

Says Lucille: "I thought 'that's a good way to do business'. He told me it was in his best interests to take care of his customers like that."

When Russell's wife died, he started a new relationship with the proprietor of the neighboring sales counter, Amparo Rala, known to many at the Market as "Umpy". In his later years he lived with his daughter and her husband after suffering a stroke in 2000. He died in March 2007.

Buford W. Hall Wholesale Florists 1931 - 1987 One Family's Journey in the Wholesale Flower Trade

When Buford Hall arrived in Southern California in 1931, he must have realized that the local wholesale Flower Market, just starting into its second decade, offered tremendous opportunity for someone who had floral industry contacts in other cities. Buford had grown up in the flower business; previously he had a flower shop and greenhouse business called Hyde Park Floral Company in Austin, Texas.

In Los Angeles, he hung out his shingle as Buford W. Hall Wholesale Florists, with Jacob Dekker as his business partner. The company bought cut flowers from local growers and shipped them throughout the southern states.

"Dad was your typical Southerner; everyone was his friend," says Buford's son, Warren. "He could trade stories with the best of them; we used to say that if he were to talk to a brick wall, it would have no choice but to answer." Warren was a year old when Buford moved his wife Johnnie and son to Montebello from Austin; he recalls that the family's summer vacations were devoted to traveling throughout Texas and the South, calling on customers.

The company was originally located at the corner of Wall and Eighth streets. In 1939 Jacob Dekker left to start his own shipping firm, United Wholesale. Buford Hall moved into the old Armacost & Royston Building at 723 Wall Street, and took on two new partners, Arthur B. Smith and Royce J. Chezum, both of whom had worked for him since the beginning.

When Buford fell ill and died in 1944, his company was one of the most prominent wholesale florists on Wall Street. He and his partners had kept it going through the difficult years of the war, when railcar space for freight was hard to come by. Warren remembers that during the war his father bought ten acres on Garvey Boulevard in West Covina and grew tomatoes, potatoes and corn to sell at a roadside stand.

"The biggest shippers at the Market – the ones that shipped all over the United States – were United Wholesale, Buford Hall, San Lorenzo and Ayres Wholesale," Warren Hall explained in 2007. He joined his father's company in 1956 after four years of service in the U.S. Navy on a destroyer escort during the Korean War, followed by graduation from San Francisco City College.

After her husband's death, Johnnie Hall continued the partnership with Art Smith and Royce Chezum. The three bought the building at 824 Wall Street, across from the Los Angeles Traffic Court, to house their shipping operation, and also opened a gladiola consignment counter inside the Flower Market itself that Frank Riggio, who later worked for Milton Kessler, managed.

Warren and Beverly Hall

Stepping into the next phase

Even though he qualified by birthright as a partner in the business, Warren began at the bottom of the totem pole, labeling and tying boxes in shipping. Art and Royce were skeptical, Warren recalls: "They didn't know me; they only remembered me as a little brat running around the store years earlier."

But Warren had learned a useful lesson in the Navy and playing high school football, and that was how to follow instructions: "I found out that if you do what you're told, life is a lot easier." He applied himself in the shipping department and soon moved "up" to the gladiola sales counter in the Market. It didn't take long for the two older men to realize that, although his personality was quite different from his father's, Warren was a hard worker and could be counted on.

When asked in 2007 what he is most proud of over all the years he spent at the Flower Market, Warren Hall said, tongue in cheek: "Having Art call me 'obstreperous'; I had to ask my wife what it meant." Then he continued in a more serious vein: "I think we ran one of the most honest houses going. I sold the flowers like they were my own. My proudest thing is that most of my growers stayed with me for many years."

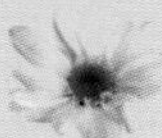

In the 1950s, the majority of the company's flower shipments went to the southern states, just as they had during Buford's time, but air cargo flights began to replace Railway Express. The advent of jet freight enabled California-based cut flower shippers to compete in markets on the East Coast. B.W. Hall Wholesale Florists was one of the Los Angeles Flower Market's first shippers to use commercial air freight non-stop to New York City, on an American Airlines' Boeing 707 in 1959. The company also sent flowers by truck to local customers from Bakersfield to San Diego.

Art Smith and Royce Chezum both retired sometime in the 1970s. Like other wholesalers in the industry, the company evolved to accommodate imported flowers. Commission sales became a major focus, since growers who continued to farm flowers in Southern California had started their own shipping operations. Warren rented a building to house the commission business in the middle of the block next door to the Flower Market, at 750 Wall Street, a building that he later bought.

In 1980 an arson fire damaged the building at 824 Wall Street that housed B.W. Hall's shipping operation. Warren decided to cease shipping, except to local customers, and focus on his commission business: "There was a certain satisfaction, and it wasn't monetary, if you could move those flowers out. We called our growers every day to tell them what we thought we could sell on the following day. My job was to move those flowers."

Busy holiday memories

The Christmas season, as busy as it always is, was Warren's favorite time of the year. A regular supplier was Mike Mushet of the Banner Queen Ranch in Julian, east of San Diego, who brought in flocked Christmas trees and evergreens including, one year, an unusual flocked okra bush that fascinated one visitor, Mrs. Gene Autry. "She called her husband to come down to the shop and see it; he spent most of his time there checking his watch and half-listening to his wife," Warren recalls.

Buford W. Hall Wholesale Florist building at 750 Wall Street during a 1983 Open House.

"Princess Pine" (a variety of evergreen pine) was one of Warren's biggest sellers for the Christmas holiday; he got it from Roy Hefley, the local representative of G.R. Kirk, a major supplier of Christmas greens and wreaths. Warren allowed Hefley to store whatever he brought to Market in his back refrigerator, even if it was destined for another wholesaler or shipper on the Market. They relied on the "honor system," a legal pad on which Warren kept track of cases he sold so Hefley could bill him later.

Warren's wife Beverly remembers that so much product passed through the store in the weeks before Christmas, she didn't see how they would have room for it: "The semis would be lined up in the street at one o'clock in the morning, and the chute was already full of greens. But they always found a place to put them. He never came home."

On weekends during the season she went to the Market to help, taking her two children and dog Shep with her. All three slept through the night covered with blankets in one of the lower bins where they laid up customers' orders. Beverly also handled the bookkeeping for the consignment business.

Warren's prickly wit aside, no one at the Market questioned his honesty. Not a particularly political man, he won appointment to the board of directors of the Southern California Floral Association in 1974, receiving the most votes of the growers and wholesalers that year, and served for two years. Other B.W. Hall people had also served the local industry group previously: specifically Art Smith who was elected president for 1959-60 and also served on its committees for open houses, market operations, and the annual flower show.

Warren remembers the Flower Market's manager Walter Swartz as a diplomat who was capable of bridging gulfs between the special interests of growers, wholesalers and retailers alike. "He kept order at meetings by treating somebody's smart idea or dumb idea the same. He simply said 'yes, I will take that into consideration' and then moved on to something else."

The building at 750 Wall Street was severely damaged in the Whittier earthquake of October 1, 1987. Warren moved his operation to what had been United Wholesale's building and stayed there for the better part of a year while he rebuilt. "That building was originally put up in the early part of the 1900s and the way it was laid out on the second floor, we were pretty sure it had been a whorehouse at one time," Warren said. When its reconstruction was complete, he sold the building to Certified Florists Supply and retired.

Lugaro Family Growers 1932-1962
An Industrious Couple Returns to Their Farming Roots

Giacomo (Jack) Lugaro and his wife Agostina were unique among the Italian flower growers of Southern California when they bought a farm in Montebello and started growing flowers in 1932. For one thing, they planted sweet peas and chrysanthemums their first year, modeling the crops that their Japanese flower farming neighbors grew. For another, both had expertise in other professions when they decided to become farmers instead.

Jack and Agostina grew up in a farming district near Genoa along northwestern Italy's Mediterranean Sea coast. Circumstances pulled them in other directions, until the opportunity to buy land and return to farming set them on a new course.

Agostina and Giacomo (Jack) Lugaro and their sons Carlo, left, and George.

The two came to America with the help of Agostina's cousin, Giovanni Puima, an Italian vice consul stationed in Los Angeles. Their immigration papers were delayed for a year and a half, but two days after their wedding they sailed for New York on the last voyage of an Italian liner named ironically, "America", for a sixteen-day crossing followed by six days on a train across the country. They arrived in Los Angeles in November 1923; Agostina was 20 years of age and Jack was 29.

Jack got a job in a metal-working foundry right away; it was a skill he had learned, and taught, in Italy during the First World War. Agostina trained to be a seamstress for a high-end dress designer in the Los Angeles garment industry. She worked on the thirteenth floor of a building at Broadway and Eighth streets.

Agostina rose through the ranks, sewing dress prototypes at first and then was assigned to go from department to department for the company's owners, inspecting and overseeing others' work. She earned top dollar for a woman in those days and was threatened physically by men who thought that her job rightfully belonged to a man. Her bosses, two German men, responded by hiring Agostina's husband to be her bodyguard. Jack had been forced to quit his job, suffering with health problems related to the hard work and noxious environment of the foundry.

From sewing to sowing

When the Depression hit the dressmaking industry, Agostina pleaded with Jack to move out of the city. "My husband thought he was going to start some kind of a business, but I say 'no, no, I want to go into farming' so we did," Agostina recalled in 2007, the year she celebrated her birthday four years past the century mark.

The Lugaros purchased ten acres in Montebello on which they built a house before cutting ties to the city of Los Angeles and moving to the farm. They went to the local Bank of Italy (now Bank of America) to introduce themselves. The banker in turn put them in touch with other local Italian farmers. One of the first flower growers they met was Angelo Tassano, who grew flowers with the help of a nephew, Guiseppe Franciosi. They were also from Genoa in Italy.

Angelo and his wife, known at the Market as Mama Tassano, had two daughters, Benita and Tuti. Agostina remembers that the Tassano family gave them dahlia and delphinium bulbs and seeds to help them get started. In the meantime, the Lugaros had also planted five acres of sweet peas, plus chrysanthemums.

Their first year of farming flowers, 1932, coincided with a downturn at the Flower Market. The Depression was in full swing. Agostina remembers that Jack took crates of beautiful 22-inch-long sweet peas to the Market and brought them home again, unsold. Sometimes he simply gave some of his flowers to beggars on the street outside the Market, usually young boys looking for a way to earn money just to get something to eat. One morning Jack came home especially discouraged because his earnings for the day amounted to just six dollars. He told his wife he thought he should quit farming and go back to his foundry job. Her reply was: "I say No; we won't go back. Don't worry; we'll make do."

And so Agostina, a strong-willed woman who was determined to stick with the farm life she loved no matter what, had Jack take her and the unsold sweet peas to the corner of Whittier Boulevard and Atlantic Avenue in East Los Angeles where she sold her flowers next door to a motion picture theater, a bank and a real estate office. That first day a woman from the real estate office came out to help because she had so many customers. Agostina made 30 dollars and so she came back the next day and the day after that, every day for three months. When her friends realized she was serious about selling on the street – and doing well with it – they built a bench for her and then a covered kiosk. Business at the Market picked up again, and the Lugaros gave the little kiosk to a couple of local boys they knew so they could make a living with it.

Friends help Agostina Lugaro, right, pick flowers, 1934.

In their second year of farming, 1933, they experienced their first frost and worked until two o'clock in the morning on a very cold night to cover their chrysanthemums with cheesecloth. Agostina remembers that a friend who owned a local flower shop dropped by the farm later in the day and was amazed to see that their crop had not frozen. She advised them the Market was empty, and they should charge a higher price because no one else had saved their crop. "I will never forget her," Agostina said.

Jack took their flowers to the Los Angeles Flower Market. Agostina went to Market with Jack only a couple of times, one of them in 1933 following the big earthquake, because she was too frightened to stay at home by herself.

Two sons carry on in Anaheim

Carlo was born in 1935. Agostina refused to go to the hospital until she had finished packing her sweet peas in crates for the Market, so the doctor dropped by the house to make sure she was okay. All he could do was advise her not to work too hard. Second son George appeared four years later.

Top: Carlo in the stock field, 1939.
Above: George and Carlos Lugaro and workers in the Lugaro field of stock.

Over the years the Lugaros planted other crops: rainbow asters, pompom dahlias, celosia, stock, ranunculus, calendulas and one acre of fig trees. The farm's fresh air became a weekend magnet for friends from the city who often came out on Sundays for large Italian dinners. The friends did much of the cooking while Agostina picked and packed her flowers for Monday's Market. And every week she delivered bouquets to her friends at the bank and the movie theater where she had sold her sweet peas in 1932.

The Lugaro family farmed for 26 years in Montebello until the city wanted their land for a school site. Jack and Agostina had already decided to retire and spent two years looking for land in a less populated community. They found what they were looking for in west Anaheim, seventeen acres of orange grove on Magnolia at Crescent Avenue, for $2,000 per acre.

They bought the ranch in 1952. The following year, eighteen-year-old Carlo drove their tractor all the way from Montebello and informed his parents he would like to continue farming instead of going to college. So the family worked together to clear out the orange trees. Their younger son George said: "As soon as they bought the land and put in a 500-foot well and a house on the corner, here came the city again, this time the city of Anaheim who told Dad they wanted his land for a school! He pulled out his bills and showed them he had invested a lot of money in that corner, so they went after other land nearby instead."

The Lugaro family planted the same mix of flower crops that had worked so well for them in Montebello. George graduated from high school in 1956 and joined his brother on the farm. He recalls many foggy just-after-midnight drives into the Market, straddling the white line in the middle of the road, driving straight and hoping for the best.

The Lugaros are best remembered by those who knew them for their hard work and pleasant character. "Carlo was very fit and strong, and he never had a bad thing to say about anybody," Johnny Mellano recalls. The Lugaro brothers' parents are remembered for their partnership throughout almost 68 years of marriage during which, Agostina says, "He liked to work and he liked me to go to work with him."

After a few years of farming, Carlo and George decided it was time to quit. They were tired of the hard work, and neighbors complained about their use of pesticides. They sold some of the land to a housing developer, and worked with the city to have some of it rezoned commercially. Then they moved their parents' house from the corner about half a mile south on Magnolia, and became partners in an auto parts business. George remembers being out in the field picking flowers during the transitional summer of 1961 while negotiating with auto parts warehouse salesmen. The brothers closed the farm operation that winter. Jack died at age 97 in 1991, and his oldest son Carlo died in 2006, at 71.

Agostina remains in touch with friends from the Flower Market, especially Joe Franciosi, who also farmed flowers in Anaheim in the 1950s, and with whom they split a Market stall.

Paul Ecke Ranch 1902 >
The "Christmas Flower" Family

Albert Ecke was already a successful businessman in Germany when he arrived in Hollywood with his wife Henrietta and four children in 1902, intending to grow fruits and vegetables because he was an advocate of a vegetarian diet. He had heard that California offered plenty of productive land in a good climate. By serendipitous good fortune, it was November – when a tall leggy shrub that grew wild on hillsides around the area began to turn bright red, just in time for Christmas.

The family's first farm was in Eagle Rock, northeast of Los Angeles; they grew vegetables, apricots, iris and a few poinsettias. Youngest son Paul Ecke Sr., eight years old in 1903, had picked up spoken English much quicker than his parents. In later years he often told the story of riding with his father by horse and wagon to the vegetable market at San Pedro and Ninth streets where he negotiated on Albert's behalf with customers.

The Ecke family in the garden of their home in Eagle Rock where they began their poinsettia business. Early 1900s.

By 1906 the family had sold the Eagle Rock property to real estate speculators and purchased two large lots in Hollywood on Hayworth Avenue, just south of Sunset Boulevard near Fairfax Avenue. Then Albert got homesick. His wife did not object when he announced that the family would return to Europe in April. They settled in Zurich, Switzerland, but within just a few months Albert realized that his children's hearts were more at home in America. He decided they would return to California, and they sailed from Bremen in October 1906.

Back in Los Angeles, Albert set about building a house on Hayworth for the family. He raised chickens and also planted poinsettias and chrysanthemums. He and his two sons hauled the flowers in bunches to a floral retailer downtown via the street car – at that time, the quickest way to get there from Hollywood.

Albert very likely had begun to realize the commercial potential of poinsettia cultivation, because he also leased ten acres bounded by Fairfax, Sunset, Ogden and Fountain for $150 a year and planted melons, tomatoes and more poinsettias. By the early teens, he had dropped all other flowers and produce in favor of growing poinsettias exclusively. In those days, poinsettias were sold primarily as cut flowers. Albert advertised in floral trade journals, and began shipping stems to San Francisco via American Railway Express.

Paul Sr. recalled in a 1981 interview that by the time his father died in 1919, they were selling poinsettias store-to-store locally as well as to a wholesale shipper, Los Angeles Floral, on Winston Street where the fledgling American Florists' Exchange had established a wholesale market two years earlier. The previous year, 1918, their Hollywood fields had produced a bumper crop, generating extra income that Paul Sr. used to purchase more property in West Hollywood for $500 per acre.

He had learned the value of owning land and the rewards of hard work in a variety of odd jobs growing up, including a paper route – he won a trip to Catalina Island in 1914 for sales of the *Los Angeles Times* – as well as on his father's small dairy farm adjacent to the family home on Hayworth. He milked cows and delivered milk to customers before and after school, first by bicycle and then using the four-cylinder Hupmobile he bought after he graduated from Hollywood High School in 1915.

Caretakers of California's poinsettia heritage

The three Paul Eckes who followed Albert in the family business have left their individual imprints on the company and the industry. Each dealt with the business realities of their time, showing a remarkable ability to chart a new course for the company as necessary. In their own way, each has contributed to building a stronger company with a distinct reputation as a leader in the poinsettia industry.

From left, Paul Ecke III, Paul Ecke Jr. and, seated, Paul Ecke Sr., in 1978.

"I remember those stories passed from grandfather to grandkids," said Paul Ecke III in 2007, "about how life is tough and you need to work hard, but if you work hard, you will prosper."

Reflecting on the differing roles his grandfather, Paul Sr., and his father, Paul Jr., played in establishing an international poinsettia industry with California roots, Paul III says: "I credit my grandfather with the original promotion of the poinsettia; he created the Christmas flower image. He created a market out of nothing, working with greenhouse growers and showing them how to reproduce their own plants.

"Then, my father took it to the next level. He was the showman who took the poinsettia story to the media – magazines, television and the movie studios. He loved being in the spotlight, and he was good at it. My grandfather liked working behind the scenes to make things happen; personality-wise, I am much more like my grandfather."

Hollywood's crimson fields

The showy parts of a poinsettia – red, pink, purple or white, depending on the variety – are actually modified leaves called bracts. The plant is native to southern Mexico and was brought to the United States by Joel Roberts Poinsett, the first U.S. ambassador to Mexico (1825-1829); hence the origin of the plant's popular name.

In the early days, poinsettias were crimson with dark green foliage and Paul Ecke Sr. was the first to grow them in quantity as a cut flower and later, a potted plant. His field packing barns in West Hollywood were never completely torn down. The old timbers can still be seen "as far as I know," says descendant Paul III, in the basement of the legendary Roxy Theatre, built later on the site in the 9000 block of the famed Sunset Strip.

After Albert died, Paul Sr. began switching in earnest from poinsettias as cut flowers to stock potted plants, although cut flowers continued to be major money-makers during the holiday season at retail stands on Doheny and at the intersection of Sunset and Sepulveda boulevards. The Ecke family sold poinsettias straight from the fields with the help of friends, many of them former neighbors and old school chums who signed on to work the harvest and roadside stand sales for a very busy two-week holiday period.

"One of our very best days was in 1924 when a windstorm wrecked all the flowers," Paul Sr. recalled: "We just cut the whipped red flowers and tied them in bunches. The movie colony came out and stormed us, just to get something for their houses. We blocked traffic for three-quarters of a mile on each side of our stand."

The "Santanas", or Santa Ana winds that blow hot and dry from the east, gathering speed as they funnel through mountain passes toward the coast, must have been fierce that year (1924) because they also took his first crop in Encinitas on the same day he set up to harvest them: "I did not get one cut flower. This was the first year I was down [in Encinitas]; I lost the whole crop."

He had purchased the land the previous year in sparsely populated Encinitas, 100 miles south of Los Angeles, because he needed additional growing fields and the cost of acreage in West Hollywood was rising. Still, there were incentives to continue growing in what is today the Beverly Hills area: "The Rodeo Land and Water Company gave me all the land I wanted to grow on free of charge just to beautify the community all through the 1930s." Hollywood's fields of bright red poinsettias attracted tourists and locals alike.

Windstorms were not the only threat to the Ecke poinsettia fields in the early days. "Your father didn't see how I could stay in business [with] the lickings I took with freezes," he told interviewer Sylvia Foltz, daughter of rose grower C.J. Groen, in 1981, describing the measures he took to protect his plants by covering them with dirt when a freeze was imminent: "If I planted deep enough the trunk underneath stayed dry and that salvaged me. If we covered them early and let the ground settle on them, it was fine."

Paul Sr. picked up the mission his father had begun: bringing "the Christmas flower" to the attention of the nation's floral trade. Traveling by train, automobile and later by commercial air, he packed bare rootstock cuttings on one side of his suitcase, clean shirts on the other, and called on commercial potted plant growers throughout the Midwest and in New York and Texas, assuring them that the seemingly dead sticks would produce beautiful red flowers in time to sell for Christmas. These annual trips usually took him away from home for three to four months at a time, and over the years he made many lifelong friends in the nursery business.

In 1931 Paul Sr. moved his family – wife Magdalena and their three children – permanently to Encinitas in time for his son to start school in their new community. Slowly the original ranch house, built in the 1880s, had been added on to and renovated. In 1936 a new two-story house was built nearby and the old house became the Ranch's offices. Paul Sr. continued to buy land in the local irrigation district and over time, recreated the stunning fields of bright red poinsettias that had captivated his Hollywood customers.

Werner Ecke, a cousin, took charge of the Hollywood fields; he had joined the business in 1929. When Werner died in 1954, Paul Sr. closed growing operations in Los Angeles completely.

The years of World War II were difficult for the Ecke family, as they were for all farmers who needed fuel and tires for their tractors and trucks. When his Japanese vegetable and flower grower neighbors were sent to internment camps, "he thought it was a travesty because he knew them to be just as American as he was," Paul Sr.'s granddaughter Lizbeth Ecke said in 2007.

With very little notice given to the uprooted families, he and Magdalena offered to store farm machinery, furniture and trunks for many of them in an unused barn. As a result, Paul Sr., a naturalized American of German birth, was investigated by the FBI as a pro-Nazi sympathizer during the war, even though his son was serving in the U.S. Navy. When the war was over, many of the displaced Japanese families did not return to claim their possessions, and Lizbeth says her mother remembers going through the trunks trying to figure out who they belonged to so they could be returned to the families.

Greenhouses and air freight

Every year natural mutations (or "sports") were cultivated, evaluated and if they appeared to be improvements over existing commercial poinsettia varieties, introduced the following year. New varieties kept the floral trade interested in seeing what the company would do to surpass the previous year's offerings. Softwood cuttings of the "mother plants" were shipped to nursery customers in the spring, and the company collected royalties on sales of the Ecke-developed varieties.

Paul Sr. and Magdalena began traveling to Europe in the 1950s through the 1970s, calling on growers, giving them cuttings to experiment with and showing them how to cultivate poinsettias as potted plants. Soon, in Europe just as in America, the potted poinsettia was the fashionable choice for Christmas holiday decorating.

By the time Paul Sr. sat down to talk with Sylvia Foltz in 1981, freezes and windstorms were no longer serious threats. His son, Paul Jr., had joined the company after earning a degree in horticulture from The Ohio State University in 1949, and at his urging they began building plastic greenhouses in the 1960s. The controlled growing environment produced a poinsettia that was more compact, durable, longer lasting and disease resistant.

The Ranch's business model also changed from bare rootstock plants grown outdoors to producing indoor bare rootstock cuttings for customers all over the world.

"They figured out they could build poinsettias from cuttings and my father realized that they could air freight cuttings to Europe," explains Lizbeth Ecke. Her brother, Paul III, remembers the arguments between his dad and his grandfather over tearing out field plants and moving into greenhouses: "When my grandfather did switch his thinking, he was very cute about taking credit for the greenhouses later on because when it worked it was his idea, whereas the real story is he was *vehemently* opposed at first."

Indeed, when Paul Sr. spoke with Sylvia, he described the broad scope of the company's business with pride: "We take care of customers all over the world with rooted cuttings; in Japan, Australia, New Zealand, Hawaii, every one of the Caribbean islands, in Colombia, Mexico, Venezuela, in Canada and in all of Europe from Norway down to the toe of Italy."

Paul Sr. received several industry and community honors. He served as president of the San Diego County Farmers, which named him their "Farmer of the Year" in 1968, and was president of the American Florists' Exchange / Los Angeles Flower Market for 34 years. In 1970 he was inducted into the Society of American Florists' Hall of Fame in recognition of his life's work creating one of floriculture's most enduring commercial success stories.

"It was exciting to be part of this interesting immigrant family that had done such wonderful things," said Elisabeth (Jinx) Kenney Ecke in 2007. As Paul Jr.'s first wife and mother of their three children, she has warm memories of raising her children in a rural environment of farming, animals and 4-H clubs, where her husband came home for lunch every day and worked in a business close to home.

Above: Celebrating the Silver Anniversary of Magdalena and Paul Ecke Sr.'s wedding in 1949 are from left Bill Dealy, Crix Dealy, Paul Ecke Jr., Magdalena and Paul Ecke Sr., Barbara Winter and Ray Winter.

Right: Magdalena and Paul Ecke Sr., as Magdalena prepared to visit her homeland, Switzerland, in 1950.

Paul Jr., "a born salesman" according to his daughter Lizbeth, boosted the poinsettia industry and the Ranch to international prominence using media coverage and the strength of his outgoing personality. "He never attended a function without bringing plants or flowers," said Peter Moran of the Society of American Florists which renamed its prestigious national award, the Golden Bouquet, in memory of Paul Ecke Jr. in 2002.

Every Christmas season, starting in the 1960s, Paul Jr. sent poinsettias to the White House and to the sets of local television newscasts and national shows such as "Bob Hope's Christmas Special," Johnny Carson's "The Tonight Show" and "Good Morning, America." He wanted television watchers at Christmas-time to see poinsettias everywhere. He also sent poinsettias to, and advertised in, the major women's magazines.

"My dad realized that women made the decisions about buying flowers. [He] was very interested in promoting the poinsettia and my mother was instrumental in helping him understand how you do that," explains Lizbeth Ecke.

Christmas sales season: a family affair

In the Ecke family, when potted poinsettias were coaxed to bloom in time for Christmas, the children of both Pauls knew their father would be working all hours of the day and night and they were expected to work, too.

Paul Jr. grew up helping his father in the fields and packing sheds on the Ranch, as did his sisters Barbara and Ruth, who was also called Crix. In the busy selling season, all three helped out at the wholesale market in downtown Los Angeles on weekends and during their holiday break from school.

Barbara handled Ecke bookkeeping at the Market in the 1970s during the pre-Christmas rush, taking the cigar box of cash to the drive-up teller before the bank closed at three o'clock. Every morning she drove into the Market from her home in Fullerton. She and her husband Ray Winter, a schoolteacher, used family summer vacations to make sales calls on nurseries throughout the Western states and Canada, taking their two boys with them in a camping trailer. They also called on customers during European trips in the 1970s and '80s, and visited their nephew Paul Ecke III, who was working in Switzerland, on one of their trips.

The Ecke family always celebrated Christmas on December 26, says Lizbeth Ecke: "My grandmother convinced her children from a very early age that Santa made a special trip to their house on the night of the twenty-fifth to bring their presents, because they were helping Santa with Christmas for everyone else and he understood that was their job."

During Christmas sales preparations, Lizbeth and her younger sister Sara helped their mother take coffee, hot chocolate and doughnuts out to the packing barn where workers were sleeving plants and dipping the stems of cut poinsettias into tin buckets of boiling water to stop the flow of white sap so they could take up water, a smell Lizbeth says she will remember for the rest of her life. Conveyor belts of potted plants were placed on trucks and taken into Los Angeles.

Left: Three generations of Ecke Ranch women in the late 1970s. From left are Elisabeth "Jinx" Ecke, Magdalena and Lizbeth.

Above: Paul Ecke Jr. in 2000.

The Ecke Ranch Christmas week crew at the Los Angeles Flower Market in 1971. From left, standing, are Bill Dealy, long-time employee Lyman Weaver, Paul Ecke Sr., Mike Tinch, Dave Slaughter, Dr. Bob Maurer, Paul Ecke III and Paul Ecke Jr. Kneeling at left is Ray "Bob" Winter and, right, Dr. Duane Winter.

Paul III drove one of those trucks beginning when he was sixteen, making deliveries to Forest Lawn Mortuary and to wholesalers on both sides of Wall Street. He also handled counter sales and recalls Pasadena florist Jacob Maarse with special fondness: "He was one of our best customers, a classy guy who always took time to talk to me."

Paul III first started going to the Market at age fourteen with Ranch employee Charlie McCarver, and remembers they stayed at the nearby Hotel Cecil ("a *total* flea-bag place that was an eye-opener for me.") The bustling Flower Market scene, with its upside-down hours, was educational for a kid who lived in bucolic Encinitas. "It's a tough schedule if you don't work at the Market 52 weeks a year; but I did learn a lot about customer service there," he said in 2007.

Paul Jr. served 30 years at the helm of the Paul Ecke Ranch. The breeding hybridization, genetic research, university internships, marketing, customer education and other programs he initiated on behalf of his beloved poinsettia put the Ranch on the international floriculture map.

One of the many industry honors he received was the Liberty Hyde Bailey Award, the American Horticultural Society's highest honor; another came from the Society of American Florists (SAF) which honored him with their Golden Bouquet Award in recognition of devotion to profession, industry and community. He was also president of the Los Angeles Flower Market.

Elisabeth (Jinx) Kenney Ecke recalls that when the SAF held its annual convention in San Diego in the 1970s, the local flower growers decided to host a luncheon in the Ecke packing barn, the largest one in Encinitas. She and Elisse (Mrs. Robert) Hall, who was Paul Jr.'s first cousin, decided they wanted to serve the group themselves. The only catered item was the main course, roast beef, which they ordered from a local restaurant. "We got matching aprons with flowers on them and put all the growers' wives, including my mother-in-law, and even the kids, to work cutting up thousands of pounds of fruit salad and bread, and serving tables." She says it was "a loaves and fishes day" because only about half of the 700 people who showed up for lunch had made advance reservations for the bus from the hotel, but they managed to make it work and the event was talked about at other SAF conventions for years afterward.

Above: The women of today's Ecke Ranch family, from left, Julie Hampton (wife of Paul Ecke III), Sara Ecke May and Lizbeth Ecke.
Right Top: The grandchildren of Paul Ecke Jr. in 2007. From left are Matthew Meyer, Vanessa May, Max Ecke, Corinne May, Polly Ecke, Lillie Meyer and Carolyn May.
Right: Max and Polly with parents Julie Hampton and Paul Ecke III, 2007.

Paul Jr. retired from the Ranch in 1991, the year his father died, but remained active in the industry, observing with pride as his son Paul III assumed the company's leadership mantle. When he died in 2002, Paul III said that the most meaningful tribute to his father would be to "send flowers to somebody you love, because he hated the 'in lieu of flowers' phrase in obituaries. He supported the flower business."

A family's service to AFE's Market

The American Florists' Exchange has benefited immensely from Ecke expertise in industry promotion and good business decisions. "For my entire lifetime, as long as I can remember, either my grandfather or my father was president of AFE," said Lizbeth Ecke in 2007.

Paul Sr. assumed the presidency in 1957, the year C. J. Groen died, serving until his death in 1991. Paul Jr. then became president and served until his death in 2002. Lizbeth then joined AFE's Board of Directors and continues her family's commitment to the Los Angeles Flower Market.

When the Market was just getting started, Paul Sr. was an original shareholder. He helped raise $30,000 to purchase its first building, the garage at 754 Wall Street, by selling $50 shares to other growers. Later, as AFE's president, Paul Sr. became passionate about the organization's real estate acquisitions on Wall Street. He firmly believed in the value of owning property and recognized that the Market would have difficulties expanding beyond its then boundaries without planning ahead to purchase more real estate.

In his 1981 conversation with Sylvia Foltz he expressed his concern about the need for more space and described the Board's strategies to procure contiguous space. Paul Sr. was the diplomat who persuaded Leon Moskatel to swap buildings with the Market in an even trade. The move freed up a piece of adjoining property the Market needed.

A life-long promoter of the Los Angeles Flower Market even after he moved to Encinitas, Paul Sr. persuaded other San Diego area flower people, including gladiola growers Thornton and Noonan, to purchase shares in the Market.

One of Paul Sr.'s childhood friends, Constantine (Connie or C.P.) Von Herzen served AFE as legal counsel for many years. C.P.'s family had been neighbors in Hollywood. As a young man he helped the family over the years with the dairy and later, harvesting and selling poinsettias. He became a prominent lawyer in Los Angeles, and was Paul's close friend and business advisor for the Ecke Ranch as well as on AFE legal affairs.

In 1981, when Paul Sr. had been AFE's president for 24 years, he told Sylvia Foltz that he didn't see an end to the floral industry's growth: "National publicity helps the trade, and the trend to use more flowers is all over the world. I don't see anything stopping it."

As soon as his grandson got a driver's license, Paul Sr. tapped him to be his driver into Los Angeles to attend AFE Board meetings. "Those meetings were my first real taste of the business," Paul III says. "I was clueless and semi-bored at sixteen, but I listened and it was interesting. Mostly I just liked hanging out with my grandfather, and he liked to be with me."

Above: Paul Ecke III, right, with wife Julie Hampton and late night television host Jay Leno in 1995. Ecke Ranch has decorated the set of "The Tonight Show" with poinsettias for many years.

Right: Lizbeth Ecke and Paul Ecke III at the Poinsettia Ball benefiting the Magdalena YMCA in Encinitas, California, 2007.

Today's company meets today's challenges

Paul III professes to be "just a farmer at heart" but his education and career path suggests he prepared well to take over the company's management and ensure its survival. He earned a bachelor's degree in horticulture from Colorado State University and a master's in business administration at Duke University's prestigious Fuqua School of Business. Then he went to work for Hewlett-Packard as a production scheduler in Palo Alto, Calif., and as production manager of the Hewlett-Packard factory in Malaysia until 1987, when he returned to the Paul Ecke Ranch as its data processing manager. He bought the Ranch in 1991, and retains 100 percent ownership.

With diversification and globalization, he has taken the company in new directions that have brought him industry respect. Paul III is pretty sure his grandfather would be supportive of his efforts to reduce costs while staying true to the company's mission of breeding quality floral products. A major step, in 1997, was to move cultivation of poinsettia starter plants, the cuttings that are the mainstay of the business, to greenhouses in Guatemala while retaining research and development, the activity that keeps the Ranch in the forefront as an industry leader, in Encinitas.

Poinsettias continue to be the Ranch's flagship product – but not its only one. In 2006 the Paul Ecke Ranch purchased Oglevee, a family-owned company in Pennsylvania that grows geraniums, begonias, impatiens, carnations and similar flowering plants. Both company's product lines are available through licensed brokers who buy cuttings from the company and receive extensive customer support from Ecke scientists and salesmen.

The Eckes also have licensing agreements and joint ventures with other strong growing entities, such as Mellano & Company to cultivate the Flower Fields® working ranch and tourist destination in Carlsbad on Ecke-owned land, a partnership with Ohio-based Yoder Brothers to develop and sell a retail line of home garden color plants under the Flower Fields name, and an arrangement with Armstrong Garden Centers to grow and sell Paul Ecke brand blooming poinsettias.

"We want to get closer to the ultimate customer," Paul III says about the Ranch's new direction. Unlike his father and grandfather, however, he doesn't have to spend weeks at a time calling on nursery owners and wholesale customers to accomplish his educational goals. The company's website provides information on growing poinsettias and caring for them at home, and even has an online diagnostic tool that growers can use to identify and correct problems they may be having with a poinsettia crop.

Ecke family business interests also include Carltas Company, a private land holding and asset management firm that oversees real estate the company owns in Encinitas and Carlsbad – land that Paul Ecke Sr. originally purchased for growing fields of poinsettias but that today is devoted to other uses such as housing, shopping, office space, recreation and The Flower Fields in Carlsbad. Lizbeth Ecke is currently the only family member working at Carltas Company and its various entities.

G.A. Berlin Company 1926 – 1986 An Honest Man's Work in Service to Flowers

It was the insurance underwriting industry's loss when Elmer Fisher realized in 1946 that he could make twice as much money working for his father-in-law, George Berlin, at the Los Angeles Flower Market. Elmer had married George's daughter Marian after completing his military service; they met when he was stationed in Santa Ana in 1941. Back in Pittsburgh, Elmer told the company that had hired him "No, thanks" and returned to California with his bride, arriving just in time for the Mother's Day rush in 1946. "I knew nothing," Elmer reminisced in 2007. "I couldn't even break the twine."

He picked up the flower business quickly. Over the next 40 years he earned a reputation for hard work, an easy-going honesty and savvy marketing moves, and built the company he eventually bought from his father-in-law into a Wall Street wholesale powerhouse. He also contributed many hours behind the scenes working on behalf of the floral industry, a tradition he continued after he retired.

George A. Berlin worked in greenhouses in Illinois and Ohio before moving to California in 1926 intending to grow roses. He got into the flower business as a commission broker instead and was probably the first wholesaler to bring gladiolas from San Diego County growers into the Los Angeles Flower Market.

There were many small gladiola growers in Carlsbad, Oceanside and Encinitas in the 1930s into the late 1950s. The Frazee family was one of them. They consigned their entire cut flower gladiolus crop to the G.A. Berlin Company, a practice that spanned more than 50 years, and eventually became the largest grower of glads in San Diego.

By the time his son-in-law joined him on Wall Street, George Berlin had been drawn back to farming, his first love; specifically, orange ranching. He had purchased a small orange grove in Garden Grove in 1927 and later, two more in Riverside. When George died in 1981, Elmer Fisher was just five years away from his own retirement from the company he still ran in his father-in-law's name. "I didn't feel right [changing the name] because he got me started in the business," Elmer says.

Gladiolas galore

Long-stemmed gladiolas were immensely popular at the Los Angeles Flower Market, and Elmer Fisher made them his specialty. He promoted glads heavily to the public and within the industry. One promotion he sponsored for many years was an annual gladiolus arrangement competition for floral designers; the winner received a G.A. Berlin Company trophy cup awarded at the Wall Street Open House.

Elmer says one reason glads received so much promotion was because there weren't too many other flowers available at the Market. "After the war the only things we had on a regular basis were chrysanthemums, stock, gladiolas and carnations, so that's what we promoted."

One of his more unusual promotions was when he teamed up with a dress designer who asked him to supply flowers in colors that she planned to feature at a fashion show. "Miss Elliott was her name," he says. "We grew the glads to match her gowns; it was interesting because she gave us the oddest colors to match." Elmer called on Edwin Frazee, his largest gladiolus grower and hybridizer, to develop the colorful hues.

Bob Berry was a favorite designer that Elmer Fisher used for many years to fashion gladiolus arrangements representing his product at Wall Street Open Houses, the Hollywood Park Flower Shows, and floral events at the Los Angeles Arboretum and other public venues.

Elmer's commission business depended on long-term relationships he developed with growers. As South Bay and Los Angeles area land where gladiolas grew became too expensive for flower farming, Elmer turned to the flower farmers in San Diego County.

John Frazee grew up in his father's business, Edwin Frazee, Inc. By the time he began driving flowers three nights a week to the Los Angeles Flower Market in 1963, at the age of 21, the company's gladiola production was substantial. "We had been using Weston Trucking to ship our flowers to the Market," John recalled in 2007, "but we got to such volume, it was cheaper to buy our own trucks and haul the loads ourselves." The Frazees started with small trucks, and bought their first semi in 1962. "A semi would haul a thousand cans of glads, and there were twelve dozen glads to a can."

The Frazee family's truckloads were matched by large volumes of mixed flowers trucked in from elsewhere and moving through the G.A. Berlin operation, including carnations and pompons from Carpinteria, ranunculus and freesias from San Diego, and stock and gladiolas from Bob Stimming in Lompoc. "We put up close to 300 standing orders three days a week for florists such as Art Ito, Harold Francis and Jeannette Carson who bought from us regularly," Elmer recalls.

When he got into the Rose Parade business (Fiesta Floats was his main account) Elmer insisted on bringing in local chrysanthemums and carnations from Carpinteria: "I never wanted to import product for the float builders because as a once-a-year buyer, I couldn't control the quality."

Touchy times

Eventually G.A. Berlin Company outgrew its space in the American Florists' Exchange. When Frank Kuwahara, manager of Southern California Flower Growers, Inc., offered him a prime location with parking in its nearly finished building, he accepted and moved across the street in 1963 although he still had a lease with AFE.

This created hard feelings among some AFE tenants who felt he was making a mistake. "But we just had too many flowers coming in, and needed more space," Elmer says, adding: "Bert Johnson, C.J. Groen, the people at Briggs & Godfrey, John Noonan and, of course, Paul Ecke Sr. – all the people I worked with there, were very good to me. I have nothing to complain about."

Above: From left, oceanside grower Edwin Frazee, Los Angeles Mayor Sam Yorty, Los Angeles-based fashion designer Miss Elliott and her manager-husband, and Elmer Fisher of the G.A. Berlin Company celebrate a late 1960s or early 1970s partnership in which Miss Elliott presented her new line of party dresses based on the colors of locally-grown gladiolas. ***John Frazee collection.***

John Frazee recalls that before Elmer moved, he tried to ease the delivery congestion that his heavy volume caused by arranging with AFE officials to allow trucks delivering to him to begin unloading at 6 o'clock on Sunday, Tuesday and Thursday evenings. "Otherwise, our unloading activities took up so much space they would have interfered with the other growers, consignment brokers and shippers who came in at midnight to get their orders ready. The Berlin stall ran down the center on the San Julian side of the Market. Whenever he got the chance to pick up more space he did, but he really outgrew that space."

Across the street, Elmer was given the same privilege to open the Market early for his deliveries. "We took up the whole parking lot with our truck and the volume of flowers we were unloading," John Frazee remembers.

Elmer Fisher had ruffled feathers on both sides of Wall Street as early as 1955 when he got the idea to approach the Alpha Beta grocery chain and ask if they were interested in stocking gladiola in their stores. They were, and Elmer came under fire from wholesalers and florists alike for encroaching on their markets. He did it, he says, because his growers were clamoring for higher volume sales of their flowers, and he thought he could tap the flower-buying public's inclination to pick up a bouquet for their home along with their groceries.

"I got called out about that for awhile, but florists didn't offer ready-made bouquets in those days and I thought there was room in the business for impulse flower buying. If people want an arrangement, they'll go to a florist to get it done and besides, I was still selling flowers to other wholesalers."

Brea and La Habra growers

To better service his grocery chain market, Elmer opened a warehouse in La Habra where Alpha Beta's distribution center was also located, and began having flowers delivered there. Eventually he provided floral product that went to 150 Alpha Beta stores throughout the Southland, and also to the Ralph's grocery chain. He also tapped growers in the neighborhood for product.

Paul Jaramillo, his brother Dave and sister-in-law Netty grew chrysanthemums, Killians and Shasta daisies in La Habra Heights and Yorba Linda, mostly for Elmer Fisher. His sister, Lita Nava, and her husband Manuel had several acres of carnations in Brea and first cousins, the Sandoval family, also grew nearby.

Paul's son Tino remembers that after Elmer opened his La Habra warehouse, his father delivered flowers there instead of driving them into Los Angeles. And when he needed product quickly, Elmer often dropped by their farm on Lambert Road, just around the corner, to pick up flowers.

Saluting the truckers

G.A. Berlin Company did not have its own fleet of trucks but relied on growers to bring product to the Market, and in turn sold product to shippers such as Edmunds Wholesale, Golden State and various independent route men who hauled flowers to Bakersfield and Las Vegas.

Before the war, Elmer says his father-in-law drove to Carlsbad and Encinitas to pick up flowers himself, "slapping his face to stay awake" on the drive back home. Then Ben Wilson, a San Diego trucker, began hauling flowers for as many as 25 San Diego County growers up to the Los Angeles Flower Market.

"That's how the growers were able to get their product up here during the war, when it was especially difficult with the gasoline shortage," Elmer explains. On the return trip, Wilson's San Diego-bound trucks carried newspapers – he had delivery accounts with three Los Angeles-area publishers – plus bakery goods and other freight. In the 1950s Ben Wilson sold his trucking company to Bob Weston, who had grown up in the commercial gladiolus farming business in San Diego County. Weston continued trucking flowers to and from the Los Angeles Flower Market and to other states for many years.

From the Market to other destinations, Elmer used other truckers, Dick Scott and Bob Prather in particular, who took loads of flowers to Las Vegas twice a week. Many truckers covered the Bakersfield market, Elmer recalls: "Not just little pickups either; they went out with bobtails full of flowers. Without those independent truckers, we couldn't have survived."

Time to quit

The floral wholesaling climate was in flux by the early 1980s, when the impact of imports on the Market was not yet clear. Elmer was ready to retire. The first individual he sold his business to went broke, so he took it back. He then arranged to sell out to a firm from San Francisco that was buying up floral wholesalers across the country. The day before the deal was to be signed, the company went bankrupt and the president disappeared with $40 million. "He had manipulated the stock market, and they never did find him," Elmer said in 2007.

He closed the business in 1986 without ever selling it, one year after his wife died, and moved to Solvang near his son Jay, a grower of flowers and greens in Lompoc. Overall, Elmer says, his memories of Wall Street are good ones. He was president of the California State Floral Association in 1975, and also served as president of the Joseph Shinoda Memorial Scholarship Foundation from 1985 until 1998.

"The floral industry – there's nothing like it," Elmer commented. "I still like to have my finger in it and know what's going on."

Frazee family: specialists in ranunculus and glads

The story behind the colorful Flower Fields in Carlsbad, as usually told, starts with ranunculus seeds brought from England by horticulturist Luther Gage in the 1920s. A local farmer, Earl Frazee, worked for Gage in Oceanside while his brother, Frank Frazee, raised beans. As the story goes, related by Frank's grandson John in 2007: "He was not making any money growing beans, so Luther Gage talked him into planting freesia and ranunculus together with his brother, and selling them on their own."

Gage put them in touch with Davids & Royston Bulb Co., a firm that was located at 825 Wall Street, one block south of the Flower Market. Davids & Royston was a partnership between Arnold G. Davids and Herbert B. Royston. Herbert had also worked for his uncle, Fred E. Royston, who had formed a floral wholesale company with Walter Armacost, the entity that became Armacost & Royston, Inc.

By 1933, Earl and Frank Frazee were the only commercial ranunculus growers in the United States. Later that decade, they added gladiolas to their crop mix and moved their growing fields to property leased from the U.S. government – land surrounded by what has become the Camp Pendleton Marine Corps Base – and to other pockets of land in North San Diego County.

Gladiolas were extremely popular through the 1950s and '60s at the Los Angeles Flower Market. "There were a lot of small gladiola growers in San Diego County," says John Frazee. He is the son of Edwin Frazee and a third generation farmer who says he would still be growing flowers if he thought he could make any money at it.

According to John, other major glad growers of the 1940s and '50s in San Diego County included Arville Williams and Don Hibbs. Over time the Frazee family became the largest gladiola grower in the area by picking up the slack as everybody else was getting out of the business. John recalls seeing a statistic that in 1955 there were 45 gladiola growers in San Diego County and that by 1965, only five of them were left.

One distinguishing characteristic of the Frazee family's business model was their loyalty to the companies that bought their product. "We sold bulbs to just one company, Davids & Royston, for about 50 years, and we did the same with the flowers – we stuck with G.A. Berlin exclusively up until the time that Elmer Fisher sold the business. They took care of us and I like to think that we did the same for them."

John Frazee gave up growing in 1982 and ventured into processing and packaging bulbs for other growers until he retired completely in 1998. His brother Jim continued for another ten years as Frazee Flowers Incorporated, growing a mix of other cut flowers and ranunculus during his last three years in business.

Jim Frazee leased his fields on Ecke-owned land in Carlsbad and when he retired in 1993, the Carltas Company, sister firm of the Paul Ecke Ranch, took them over and made them a popular springtime tourism attraction, The Flower Fields.

John Frazee never thought of doing anything else but growing flowers. "It's in my blood: Everything to do with flowers and farming. I'm still a farmer; I was born one and I'll be buried one."

Edmund's Wholesale Flowers Inc. 1945 > An Enduring Institution Selling Flowers

The man who founded Edmund's Wholesale Flowers in 1945 still has the dry humor and energy for which he is remembered at the Los Angeles Flower Market. Eddie Battistessa turned 95 years old in 2007, 27 years after he retired and sold his business to Brad Brown. Brad still sells flowers under the Edmund's Wholesale name at 756 San Julian Street, although the floral industry landscape in which he does business differs from that of Eddie's day.

The source of the flowers Eddie bought and sold, for example, was entirely domestic and ranged from California to Florida. At the beginning, he either bought flowers outright or took them on consignment from growers around the Los Angeles area and in San Diego and Santa Barbara counties. As the business grew, he frequented floral conventions in other states to make contacts with other wholesalers who might be talked into shipping him some flowers.

One of his major local growers was Bob Stimming in Oxnard, who supplied both stock and gladiolas. "I think I handled more stock at that time than anybody else at the Market," Eddie says. He remembers receiving shipments of stock three times a week; each shipment consisting of 100 cans, each can packed with four to six bunches of stock.

Another major difference was that Eddie shipped flowers across the country from Los Angeles starting in the early 1950s: "I shipped to the big wholesalers in all of the large cities. We had to have the flowers packed and down to the airport by 7 o'clock in the morning to catch all the early flights going to New York City."

The balance of Edmunds' flower sales were conducted at the large counter Eddie and his employees manned inside the Market: "More than half of my business was over the counter to local florists all over Southern California."

Sales to local retailers are still a big part of Edmund's Wholesale Flowers' business in 2008. The difference, says Brad Brown: "We deliver. I'd say about 20 percent are local deliveries and the rest is sales to others in the Flower District itself."

It's best to be the boss

Eddie Battistessa's first job at the Flower Market was working for his uncle by marriage, Tony Rainero, who with his brothers John and Caesar owned Los Angeles Evergreen. Eleven months later, he took his dad up on his offer: "If you have to work those hours, I'll support you!" and quit. His father worked for the Pacific Fruit & Express Company, which operated refrigerated railroad cars, so he knew something about the long hours and risks of a business devoted to handling perishables.

Eddie had already finished his education at Los Angeles City College and Oregon State. It was 1938 and he was still attracted to the flower industry. The first thing he did after quitting Los Angeles Evergreen was to go see Cedric Nelson who owned a flower shop on La Brea Avenue where he had delivered greens for his uncles. "I found some water lilies in an alley and just took them over and gave them to Cedric," Eddie recalls. "He asked me what I planned to do next, and then suggested I sell water lilies to florists like him."

Eddie Battistessa shows a bouquet to Mrs. Henry Paul Willis, president of Las Floristas, February 1957.

Cedric advised him how to get a business license and where to get water lilies. "I went out to see this fellow at Hines Nursery and he said I could come down and pick up some. He told me to sell them for whatever I could get and he would take half. I made more money my first day selling water lilies than I did working for my uncles, so I decided then and there I wasn't going to work for anyone else ever again."

Thus began Eddie's routine: he and his girlfriend Charlotte, who he later married, went to the beach at Balboa in the morning – Eddie was a surfer – and then dropped by the nursery in his station wagon to pick up the lilies. He had a delivery route on the west side of Los Angeles, and spent three years as an independent commission agent. Once, he even sent a Railway Express shipment of water lilies to a florist in New York City.

Looking around the Flower Market, he noticed there seemed to be plenty of buyers and not enough product to go around so he decided to try his luck with growers in Northern California. He rented a truck, hired a helper and set out for San Francisco. "It took three days to drive up there, pick up product and bring it back," he recalls.

Eddie enlisted in the U.S. Navy in April 1942 and spent his war-time service at the Los Alamitos Naval Base in Long Beach. When he was discharged three-and-a-half years later, he headed right back to the Flower Market. The Zappettini Company asked him to work for them, but he had already decided to see if he could get flowers from the San Francisco growers he had met before the war, and headed north in his station wagon.

"Those five growers were all happy to see me, so I bought some flowers and brought them down to sell at the Market." This was the official beginning of Edmund's Wholesale Flowers; the firm quickly became one of Wall Street's leading commission houses and shippers.

By the time Eddie was elected to the board of the Southern California Floral Association (SCFA) in 1950, he was known for the beautiful displays at his counter. His flair for presentation helped him move from a space at the rear of the Market to a more prominent location. "I kept asking for better placement," he recalls, "and I guess the big shots liked me – there were about five of them – because I ended up with a front counter."

Eddie's ambitious nature did not go unnoticed by others at the Market. "Personality" stories and gossipy columns in early issues of *The Bloomin' News* reveal that he took a lot of good-natured ribbing, mostly related to his athletic pursuits. Various nicknames assigned to him included "Muscles" and "Shoulders" which were apparently a nod to his physique. Eddie was, by all accounts, an accomplished golfer and also bowled on the American Florists' Exchange team in the Florists' Bowling League. A November 1950 *Bloomin' News* article mentioned his selection as the All-Southern California J.C. fullback when he played football for Los Angeles City College, and also noted that he was an "excellent" surfboard rider and skier.

In the fall of 1951, Eddie was elected SCFA president for the following year. He also served on several committees for Wall Street Open Houses, floral shows and elections in the 1950s.

At its largest, in the 1960s and '70s, Edmund's Wholesale Flowers had 30 to 32 people on the payroll. Refrigerated company trucks delivered flowers all over the city and to the airport for shipments across the country. Eddie's drivers went to San Francisco twice a week to pick up flowers from growers there, and he went up one day a week to pay his growers in cash for their flowers. According to Eddie, he was able to get product from growers used to dealing with San Francisco wholesalers who didn't always pay their bills promptly.

A mentoring role

Eddie became part of the personal business history of one young man in 1979: Danny Temkin who is today president of an international company that manufactures packaging supplies for many industries, including floral. Eddie allowed Danny to sit on his sales counter and sell rolls of polypropylene directly to florists "because the wholesalers would not give me the time of day," Danny said in 2007.

"Since I was not very busy, I learned how to tie flowers in newspaper and jute. Eddie always made sure that I did a good job. Now, 28 years later, I have an international company with over 500,000 square feet of production facilities and over 600 employees. I am a firm believer that the Los Angeles Flower Market was my springboard to a business that developed from Eddie's counter to what it is today."

Adapting with the times

Brad Brown shared Eddie's attraction to a career working with flowers. He first came down to the Flower Market as the buyer for Chris Conroy, founder of the Conroy's Flowers chain of retail shops. That's how he met Eddie: "We used to have coffee together three mornings a week. He asked me to come work for him and said he would like to turn over his company to me, but at that time I enjoyed what I was doing for Conroy's and declined."

Brad started at Conroy's as a part-time delivery person in 1974, when there were just three company-owned shops and two franchises. Chris Conroy talked Brad into quitting school and made him his full-time buyer. "As he opened more franchises, Chris encouraged me to start my own company with the idea that I would service his stores," Brad said in 2007. "I did that for a few months, and then I approached Eddie about buying his business." The sale was completed on April 1, 1980; Eddie was 68 years old and Brad was 24.

"In those days, there were a lot fewer wholesale flower companies operating outside the Market. If florists wanted product they had to come to the Los Angeles Flower Market," says Brad, describing one of the ways that flower wholesaling today differs from 1980.

"Also, we buy heavily in South America, and eight years ago I bought land in Baja, Mexico, so I could grow field flowers and have better control over supply. Sunflower is our main crop; we also have larkspur, Queen Anne's lace, stock, statice, seasonal things such as marigolds, and now we're testing carnations."

Mellano & Company 1925 > It All Started With Evergreens

Italians dominated the foliage business in California when Giovanni Mellano arrived at the age of eighteen in 1921. Families picked wild ferns, acacia and evergreen boughs in the forests of Northern California, and sent them by rail to the flower markets in San Francisco and Los Angeles. According to Giovanni's son Johnny, it wasn't easy work but it was secure because the Italian community made sure everyone in their circle had work to sustain them: "You didn't have to know English; you just had to have a strong back."

Many of the young men in Entracque, a small village in the Italian Alps where Giovanni hauled firewood to make a living, went to Argentina in search of a better future. The government there offered free one-way tickets to young men who would come and work. That sounded pretty good to Giovanni, but his sister Maria insisted that he travel with her to America instead, where she would marry her betrothed, Giovanni Ghigo, who was also from Entracque.

Ghigo was part of the Italian community foraging for ferns and evergreens in Felton, a small town in the Santa Cruz Mountains. He offered to pay for Giovanni's passage, if he would escort the bride-to-be to America. Putting thoughts of Argentina aside, Giovanni Mellano found what he was looking for – steady work and a sense of community among other Italian immigrants.

A year or so later, Giovanni's curiosity got the better of him. One day, after hauling a load of greens to the train station, he tied up the reins and kicked the horse to go home. Then he jumped on the railcar and came to Los Angeles to find out what happened at the other end.

And that's how he was introduced to the Los Angeles Flower Market where Italian-Americans sold evergreens, an exclusive commodity that was not commonly found at the nearby Japanese-American wholesale flower market. It's likely that was when he first realized the larger opportunities that were open to him.

Giovanni didn't stay in Los Angeles the first time; he went back to Felton for a couple of years to earn enough money to return to "the big city". By 1925 he was working for Nick Gandolfo and John Rainero at the Los Angeles Evergreen Company which had a table at the American Florists' Exchange. The following year he became their third partner. He was twenty-two years of age, and was known as a hard worker with an adventurous, fun-loving spirit.

In the spring of 1934, Giovanni returned home to Entracque to attend his youngest sister's wedding. While he was there, the youngest daughter of another family in the village caught his eye. Maria had been just a child when he left for America. Now she was eighteen, an attractive young woman who wasn't afraid to try something new. They married in Entracque and awaited Maria's U.S. visa, then returned to Los Angeles through New York six months later.

It's about 120 kilometers (approximately 90 miles) as the crow flies from Entracque to the French Riviera along the Mediterranean coast. When Maria was young, many townspeople annually traveled to the coast because work was plentiful there. They took the shortest route by foot across the high, rocky peaks of Italy's Maritime Alps.

Top: Johnny Mellano with his dad, Giovanni, in the late 1950s.
Above: From left, Bert Corgiat (Diane Mellano's father), Giovanni Mellano and Carl Hankemeier in a casual pose in front of the first Mellano facility at the American Florists' Exchange, mid-1960s.

Maria's father and brothers were experienced guides, leading others over the mountains into France where they hoped they wouldn't get stopped by the police and sent home because they lacked work permits. Maria was eleven when she went to France for the first time to work as a housekeeper. She also learned to weave flowering acacia branches into baskets for the tourist trade to earn extra income. Every summer she returned home to help her family plant and harvest hay and potatoes. In the summer of 1934, she also attended a childhood friend's wedding where she met Giovanni.

A Flower Market success story

When the newlyweds returned to Los Angeles in 1934, Giovanni had decided to end his partnership with Los Angeles Evergreen, intending to establish a wholesale operation of his own. He and Maria rented a house in Artesia and some land nearby on which to grow greens and flowers. He asked fellow Italian Christopher Colombo Brevidoro to partner with him at the Market. The new company was immediately successful because two of Giovanni's former customers transferred their evergreens business to them.

As his fledgling company grew, Giovanni looked to others for expertise he didn't have. He asked fellow grower Frank Blankenship if he could recommend an honest bookkeeper. Frank told him about his brother-in-law, Carl Hankemeier, who had managed sales at the Flower Market for the Amling Brothers, rose growers in Santa Ana. Carl Hankemeier became the third partner and stayed with Mellano & Company until he retired. His son, Terry, also worked for the company for many years.

Mellano & Company's cut flower and foliage farming and wholesale business continued to prosper. Giovanni Mellano was a generous and gregarious man with a strong work ethic. He fell naturally into his role as a leader in the Italian-American community at the Los Angeles Flower Market. By the 1940s, Mellano & Company was one of the major grower/wholesalers in the area.

In 1946, Chris Brevidoro left the partnership to concentrate on the lilac-growing ranch he had started in Acton, California. Giovanni invited two old friends and fellow Italians, Tom Trione and Bert Corgiat, to join the business. Before he married, Giovanni had boarded with Tom's mother-in-law and dated Bert's sister.

Bert Corgiat, a chef for the Union Pacific Railroad and after the war, for various hotels, casinos and restaurants in the Los Angeles area, had brought his own bride, Pierina, from Italy in 1933; the two had corresponded for seven years before marrying. When Bert developed a life-threatening allergy to seafood, his doctor advised him to look for another line of work. Giovanni must have thought his friend's outgoing personality would be a good fit at the Market because he offered him a job in his store starting on the 11 p.m. shift. Bert discovered he loved the work and the Market's camaraderie. He became a Mellano partner in 1948 and stayed until he retired in 1977.

Bert's daughter Diane and Giovanni's oldest son Johnny, playmates as children, married in 1958. Both recall the years of World War II when the local Italian-American community socialized regularly. Families took turns hosting as many as 100 guests, and the party often included members of an Italian Service Unit (prisoners of war) who worked in the local oil fields and lived in a Wilmington camp.

"Americans were allowed to entertain the detainees, boys a long way from home," Johnny recalled in 2007. "It was like going to the library and checking out a book – a reason to have a party. They had to bring a guard along to make sure the 'prisoners' didn't escape, but of course none of them wanted to. Dad put a chair for the guard by the door and gave him a gallon of wine and plenty of food. After the first party, the same American soldier requested 'guard duty' for our parties every time."

A Los Angeles County family farm

In 1936 Giovanni and Maria Mellano welcomed their first son, Johnny. That same year, they paid two thousand dollars for six-and-a-quarter acres on Marquardt Avenue in Artesia with a water well and a small house. The American dream was real: a home, a family, a business and their own land to farm. Their primary flower crops were daffodils, dahlias, amaryllis and hyacinths, and more than half of the land was under lath shade and devoted to asparagus plumosus, a variety of ornamental fern.

By then Giovanni's bride had learned English with the help of neighbors, including sister-in-law Maria Ghigo and the Gandolfo family. In a 2007 interview, Maria Mellano related stories of adjusting to life in America as a young woman newly arrived from Italy, remembering that "clothespin" was one of the first words she learned. Sharing a laugh with her daughter, Rose Marie Castellano, Maria recalled her daily routine: "Housework in the morning and in the afternoon, I used to go with the workers in the field and pick." She remembers how she pulled up daffodils and stacked them in bunches of 25 under one arm, three or four bunches at a time: "Oh, it was a lot of fun."

"In those days, Italian ladies stayed home and raised the babies," Rose Marie explains. "So Mom didn't go down to the Market except for social events. But at home on the farm she worked with and supervised the field workers until Dad got home after Market hours."

When America entered the Second World War in December 1941, Maria had not yet received her final citizenship papers. Johnny Mellano recalls a scary evening in the war's early years when the FBI came to their house with bright lights and a bullhorn. A suspicious neighbor had accused Maria of being an enemy spy. The investigation was short-lived and Maria was allowed to stay with her family, although she retained "enemy alien" status and was subject to travel restrictions. That meant she could not travel more than ten miles from home in daylight hours and not at all when it was dark – a curfew that lasted until the end of the war when she was allowed to complete the process of becoming an American citizen.

Maria Mellano with her boys, Johnny (the taller one) and Michael, in their field of daffodils in Artesia in the early 1940s.

In 1949, Giovanni bought an additional ten acres nearby on Orangethorpe Avenue in Artesia (now South Street in Cerritos) that another Italian family, the Gorinis, had farmed in flowers. Here he built a larger house for his family which by this time included another son, Harry Michael, and a daughter, Rose Marie. On South Street, primrose, caspia, sunflowers and eucalyptus were added to the crop mix.

Johnny and Michael grew up helping their mother disbud dahlias and pick daffodils. As they got older they also helped their father at the Market, especially on holidays. Mellano & Company had a counter inside the American Florists' Exchange building and also leased additional space in an adjoining building.

Maria and Giovanni loved to entertain, working together to create memorable parties at the ranch and during Open Houses at the Market. Bert Corgiat, a chef in his previous career, manned the barbecue grill while Maria and the other wives set out huge bowls of homemade potato salad and traditional Italian dishes for their guests. Those were the days of Wall Street Open Houses, Johnny recalls, when "everyone knew they could come to Mellano & Company for barbecued venison, and the line would be out the door."

Death Valley memories

In the 1950s, most of Los Angeles' mortuaries and the flower shops serving them and nearby Rosedale Cemetery lined West Washington Boulevard. The street was known in the floral trade as "Death Valley". Mellano & Company was the first wholesaler to run route trucks to Death Valley, delivering greens and ferns.

In 1956, after two years of college and six months of active military service in the U.S. Army at Ford Ord, California, Johnny joined his father full time at Mellano & Company. He worked primarily at the Market, but also on the ranch wherever he was needed. Immediately he saw that adding more delivery routes to other communities would be a sure way to grow their business.

"I could see there was money to be made in the route business," he said in a 2007 joint interview with his wife Diane, recalling the struggle to convince both his father and his future father-in-law that adding new routes would be a smart business move. "I kept telling him, but at that point in his life Dad wasn't looking to expand. He only wanted to protect what he had."

Persistence won. Giovanni eventually challenged his 22-year-old son: "So go buy a truck, start a route and show me what you're talking about."

Johnny knew he couldn't give up any of the other tasks that filled his day so he began a grueling routine: "I rose before midnight and went down to the Market to do what I was supposed to do there, then loaded up my truck. By 5:30 in the morning I was on the road to Long Beach. I read the obituaries to see how many funerals were planned that day in Long Beach, Wilmington and San Pedro. I dropped off what customers had ordered, made as many additional stops as I could, and then circled back to collect money from the earlier drop-offs. I usually got home around one in the afternoon, unloaded the truck – we had a refrigerator at the ranch – slept for an hour and then went out to pick eucalyptus or gather up what the field hands had picked and get it ready to go to Market. I came in at five o'clock, showered, ate dinner and was asleep by seven."

After he and Diane married, she called customers and took orders by phone for his next delivery day.

The young man's hustle lit a new spark in the company's wholesale operation and it continued to grow. As Johnny and Diane's five children grew up, they all were expected to chip in. Says Diane: "Every one of them at one time or another worked at the Market selling, packing, washing out buckets and sweeping the floor. We all have a special love for the family business.

"We're also proud of the fact that every one of Maria and Giovanni's grandchildren graduated from college, and that several of them earned more than one degree. In the Italy of their generation, children didn't go to school past the third grade."

Taking it to the next level

The entrepreneurial gene that drove Giovanni Mellano obviously infected both of his sons. First-born Johnny had a passion for the wholesale side of the business, and second-born Mike Sr.'s passion was clearly the farming operation that catapulted Mellano & Company into industry prominence during the company's second generation.

Mike, two years younger than Johnny, must have discovered his life's work growing up on the Marquardt Ranch. His chosen field of study was horticulture at Cal Poly in Pomona, followed by graduate school at the University of California in Riverside where he earned a Ph.D. in plant pathology.

Mike can't remember when he didn't work on the family farm with his mom and dad. As teenagers during Christmas seasons in the 1950s, both he and his brother Johnny also worked seasonal poinsettia sales for the Paul Ecke Ranch at the Market. For Mike, that is the extent of his experience working on the sales side of the flower industry. His expertise is farming.

In 2007, Mike named some of the foliage and cut flower crops that have come and gone in the almost 40 years since Mellano & Company moved its growing operation to the rolling hills of San Luis Rey along the southern border of Camp Pendleton Marine Corps Base: "When we started here we grew Marguerite daisies, Killian Shastas, asparagus fern and eucalyptus. Of those four, eucalyptus is the only one we still grow. We probably grow about 60 different crops here today."

The bottom line governs what the company grows, but there is one rule Mike says they have always followed: "If a plant company shows us something new, we'll try it. If a customer asks us for something specific and we think it's something we can grow, we do. If it makes money, we expand it; if it doesn't, we quit. We're constantly doing that and, of course, that results in the crop mix always changing."

Mike is very knowledgeable about the various methods of water conservation, drip irrigation, pest control, nighttime lighting and frost protection that have been tested, discarded, adopted and tweaked in the company's open fields and greenhouses over the years under his supervision and that of the company's third partner, brother-in-law Battista (Batti) Castellano.

Pilgrim in the land of opportunity

Batti, a fit and wiry man who retains the strong Northern Italian accent of his youth, was also born and raised in Entracque. As a young man he, too, traversed the mountains to seek work as a laborer in the flower fields in the South of France. Batti was twelve years old the first time he went and he recalls his number one goal at the time: to bring home a thousand-lira bill to his mother because she had never seen one. Several decades later, Batti's experiences seeking work in a country not his own helped him relate to the men he hired to work on the Mellano farm in San Diego County.

The years of World War II were hard on Entracque. The German Army established a command post in the town and took over a nearby mountain fortress as well. Entracque endured several Allied bombing raids, and Batti remembers that the local bridge was destroyed and not rebuilt for many years.

After the war, economic conditions in Italy slowly improved. Batti found a job at the Fiat plant in Torino, but never enjoyed working for someone else. During the 1960s, construction of a large hydroelectric dam brought thousands of workers to the Entracque area. Visiting his family on weekends, Batti realized he could make a good living by providing a taxi service. His was the only taxi in town, and that's what he was doing when the Mellanos returned to their home village on one of several trips to Entracque after the war.

Rose Marie, the youngest child and "princess" in Giovanni Mellano's family, was ten years younger than her brothers. Her involvement in the family business while growing up was serving food during Open Houses and helping her brother, Johnny, with Saturday morning bookkeeping chores.

In 1967, she was in her early twenties when she met Batti in Entracque. He had been working since he was a youngster, and his ambitious streak must have appealed to Giovanni because when he saw the spark between his daughter and the young Italian with the "go-getter" attitude, he offered him a job in America. On December 19, 1967, Batti arrived in California with only a suitcase and a gold necklace for Rose Marie. He spoke no English but was full of high aspirations: "A window has opened, I say to myself; but I'm gonna open a door, not just a window."

Batti recalls he was immediately struck by the expansiveness of farm land in Artesia compared to the mountainous terrain he was used to. He learned quickly how to manage the farm and its workers: "I learned Spanish before English because most of our field workers didn't speak English. I went to school at nighttime for English."

He also fell comfortably into the ranch's routine, where Maria prepared and served family-style Italian dinners on Saturdays and Sundays for family and friends and seemingly always had a meal on the table throughout the week. "I thought it was a restaurant; I never ate by myself," he remembers.

Batti and Rose Marie near their families' homes in Entracque, Italy in 1967.

Rose Marie and Batti married in 1968. Maria and Giovanni, who loved to entertain, hosted an engagement party at the ranch for 150 people.

Putting it on the line

Eighty acres of sagebrush and hard-packed dirt inhabited by rodents and rattlesnakes comprised the land near Camp Pendleton that eventually became the Mellanos' flower fields. Today, looking out across lush, green hillsides punctuated with patches of color in neat, even rows, it is hard to imagine the barren landscape that greeted them in 1969, their first year of farming in San Luis Rey.

Mike finished graduate school that year and joined the business full time with Johnny, who had bought out his father's interest in the company a few years earlier. While the wholesale side of the business was thriving, the farming side barely broke even. They realized that together they could build the company Giovanni and Maria had founded into something that would support all four families – but not in Artesia. They would need to buy farm land elsewhere.

New housing construction, high property taxes and the pressure of population growth made farming in Los Angeles County impractical by the end of the 1960s. Most of the neighboring dairy farms had already moved, and Johnny recalls the annoyance of neighbors stealing the light bulbs from the lights they used at night on their Shasta daisy fields in Cerritos.

"We could have gone anywhere in Southern California," Mike Mellano said in 2007, recalling the family discussions of those days. "We thought the weather down here would be better than up in Oxnard or Ventura, and it seemed to us that having flowers [to sell] in the winter was more important than the flower crops we might grow up north. We also guessed there would be better access to labor down here."

Paul Ecke Sr. had completely moved his farming operation to San Diego County over the previous four decades, and urged the Mellanos to do the same. The only dissenter was Giovanni. "Dad wasn't happy. He told us we didn't know what we were doing," Johnny says, "but I knew we could sell the product if it was good quality."

Giovanni was developing the early onset of dementia when the family decided to buy the land in San Luis Rey. Still, he lent them the $60,000 they needed for a down payment, even if it was with the attitude: "When you spend that, you can come back home."

They paid it back – and then some – by the time Giovanni died in 1972 at the age of 69. Mike had married Sharon and they were living in San Luis Rey. Batti became the third partner by purchasing Bert Corgiat's interest; he and Rose Marie lived in Oceanside until Batti decided he needed to live on the land where he could keep an eye on things. Batti ran the day-to-day farming operation, and Mike was the outside representative to the community and to the industry organizations important to their business, including the San Diego County Flower Growers' Association, the Society of American Florists and the California Farm Bureau Federation's San Diego branch.

On the farm in Artesia in 1962, a shirtless Mike Mellano Sr holds his nephew Michael Anthony. Mike Sr's brother Johnny, father of the two young boys, is pictured, standing, while Giovanni Mellano, father of Mike Sr. and Johnny, holds his grandson Jim.

Over the years they bought more land, cleared it and planted more crops, continually adopting more efficient ways to cultivate and get product to market. Sharon and Rose Marie answered the company phones in their homes, and Rose Marie did the payroll for the ranch until it got too big. Although the original plan was to take what they grew to the Los Angeles Flower Market, it eventually became more expedient to ship to customers directly from the farm.

The Fred Elmendorf influence

One constant through the years, and a link to the Market in Giovanni's day, has been Fred Elmendorf, a longtime Mellano employee, and one of its first in San Luis Rey. Fred grew up in the Los Feliz area of Los Angeles and began working at the Market while still in high school. His first job was as a counter helper for Ebbo Dekema when he was selling roses; Ebbo used to pick up Fred on his way into the Market three days a week.

Over the next dozen years or so, the personable young man moved up (and around) in sales and distribution for several other Market notables, namely Armacost & Royston, Jack Mayesh, and Sam Applebaum at Moskatels. Fred worked at the Market throughout his college years. It was the perfect job for a college student, he says: "Just three days a week, and classes didn't start until after the Market closed."

In 1970, Fred jumped on the opportunity when Johnny Mellano asked him to interview with his brother Mike in San Luis Rey. "And that's how the 'Casanova of Wall Street' ended up in San Diego County," says Johnny, with a grin.

In 2008, Mellano & Company employs approximately 300 people year-round. Its four wholesale distribution operations – in Los Angeles, Carlsbad, San Bernardino and Las Vegas – are no longer the primary recipients of product grown in San Luis Rey. Flowers from Mellano fields are picked, sorted, pre-cooled, packed and shipped on the premises to major wholesale florists and bouquet makers around the U.S.A. and Canada.

Carrying it forward

Giovanni Mellano's hard work and sharp business instincts laid a foundation on which the generations that followed him have created a family-owned and operated entity that is today the largest diversified grower of field crops for the floral industry, offering more than 60 varieties of foliage and cut flowers. Mellano & Company is a major importer, wholesaler and shipper of flowers and greens, and has introduced new methods of production, transportation and marketing that other growers emulate. Its wholesale operations include floral product imported from South America, Europe, Africa, Australia and the Pacific Rim to supplement the domestic crops.

Johnny, Mike and Batti have retired, although each is still involved in the industry. Johnny continues as the manager of the Los Angeles Flower Market, a position he has held for more than 35 years. The company's reins have been picked up by members of the third generation of the family. They include three of Johnny's sons (Bob, Jim and Michael Anthony), Mike Sr.'s son and a son-in-law, and one of Rose Marie and Batti's daughters.

Bob Mellano started in sales and now manages the company's wholesale operations and its mass-market bouquet division. He continues the company's active involvement in industry organizations such as the California Cut Flower Commission, the Society of American Florists and others. Jim Mellano was a stockbroker before he joined the business; he oversees finance and accounting for the entire company. Michael Anthony Mellano, like his uncle Mike, earned a Ph.D. in plant pathology and manages the company's growing operations – approximately 400 acres in San Luis Rey and Carlsbad, which includes the "Flower Fields" at Carlsbad, a joint venture with the Paul Ecke Ranch/Carltas Company.

Some of the employees in the early days of the Mellano farm at San Luis Rey, 1970, from left: Battista Castellano, Lupe, Fred Elmendorf, local grower Mrs. Johnson, another local grower and Mike Mellano Sr.

Michael Matthew Mellano, Mike Sr.'s son, joined the company after active duty in the U.S. Army; he handles distribution, which includes the company's cold chain innovations such as boxing and pre-cooling flowers immediately after harvest. Son-in-law Phil Kenney came from the paper industry; today he is sales manager in the company's San Luis Rey shipping operation. Both of them work at the business office on the farm's headquarters in San Luis Rey, as does Michelle Castellano.

Michelle oversees Mellano & Company's legal and real estate interests and also represents the company and the industry on an international level with farming issues such as the use of methyl bromide for pest control. Like her cousins, she has followed in Mike Sr.'s footsteps with her involvement in industry organizations such as the Society of American Florists.

"In the Italian culture of my mother's day, women were not involved in business except on a social level," Rose Marie says. "For me, it was a rare treat to go down to the Flower Market. I loved seeing the orchids and the roses and gardenias, because we didn't grow those, but it was definitely a man's world."

Several years ago, a consultant asked Michael Anthony what his vision for Mellano & Company's future would look like. He said it would be "a company that my grandmother would be proud of." At age 92, family matriarch Maria Mellano surely is pleased when she visits the San Luis Rey farm and reflects on everything that has come to be since she and Giovanni began their pursuit of the American dream.

Amling Brothers 1920 > A Flower Family With Deep Roots

The Los Angeles Flower Market has seen a lot of Amling flower men and women come and go over the years. Today's contingent, A. John Amling and Norman W. Amling, would be the first to admit that the Amling family tree can get confusing as it relates to the Market. After all, the family's floriculture tenure in Southern California has covered almost 90 years, plus two earlier generations in the Chicago area.

John and Norm, not exactly newcomers to the business of growing, selling and transporting flowers, embarked in 1992 on their own Amling Brothers business venture, continuing a family tradition shared by more than one set of Amling siblings.

Wooden spokes and "Say It With Flowers" speak for themselves in this 1920s photo of Amling Brothers trucks at the American Florists' Exchange. Courtesy Mellano family.

The first Amling in California's floral industry was Ernst C. Amling, described by *The Bloomin' News* in September 1957 as "one of the prime backers and mainstays of the American Florist Exchange." John and Norm are his grandsons.

It was in 1889 when Albert F. Amling, whose father Gottfried Amling, a farmer, came to America from Germany in 1850, formed a business with one of his brothers and built glass greenhouses for growing flowers in the Chicago suburb of Maywood. Ernst C. Amling, the oldest of Albert's five sons, and his brother Paul also had a greenhouse flower-growing business in Des Plaines, Illinois. In 1920 Ernst decided to try his luck in California; he bought land in Santa Ana, in Orange County, built five greenhouses and planted roses and carnations.

Ernst and Paul continued their partnership for several years until distance made it awkward to continue. They split up the business but each retained the Amling Brothers company name because it was already familiar at both the Los Angeles and Chicago flower markets. Carl Hankemeier was an early sales manager for the Amling Brothers on Wall Street in Los Angeles, and he later went to work for Mellano & Company.

Four generations of Amling men posed for a photograph when Albert F. Amling, then a prominent nurseryman in Chicago, visited his California-based offshoots. In the warm sunshine of a February day on the Amling Brothers farm in Santa Ana, Albert F. proudly held his great-grandson, John, born January 11, 1934, standing between his son, Ernst C., and his namesake, grandson Albert J. Amling. John was Ernst C. Amling's first grandchild.

Three generations. From left, Ernst C., his father Albert F., and Albert J., father of John Amling (the baby) and Norman Amling. February 4, 1934.

Seventy-three years later, John reflects on the twists of fate that although just eighteen years later a heart attack would claim his father at the age of 41, the family's involvement in floriculture continued as if predestined. In their generation, both John and Norm worked for some of the industry's biggest names in floral wholesaling.

Ernst Amling: an AFE champion

Ernst C. Amling and C.J. Groen died on the same day – August 27, 1957 – and the American Florists' Exchange lost two of its original leaders, both of them prominent rose growers. Side-by-side obituaries in *The Bloomin' News* saluted both men, noting that C.J. Groen was "one of the founders" and that Ernst C. Amling was not only an AFE "backer and mainstay" but also a life member of the Society of American Florists. He had been active in the Chicago Florists Club, a forerunner of the Chicago Allied Florists' Association, prior to moving to California in 1920.

Ernst Amling must have become involved with the men who were organizing a market for European-American growers in Los Angeles soon after he moved to Santa Ana. One can only imagine those early years when the businessmen who are today considered AFE founders and who, 30 and 40 years after the fact, were hailed as its primary backers, met to plan their fledgling organization.

They were businessmen desiring to improve the climate for their businesses. A couple of the founders and early organizers were retail florists in Los Angeles and Gardena, where the flower-buying public was concentrated. One was a man who had built a prosperous concern providing seeds to growers. The rest were nurserymen and a banker; all were prominent businessmen of some means. As far as we know, Ernst Amling and Paul Ecke Sr. were the only growers involved in those earliest, formative years whose acreage was outside the enclave of nurserymen who grew in Montebello.

The next generation of Amling growers

By the late 1930s, Albert J. Amling had three sons – John, Norm and Charles – and was working for his father as foreman of the Santa Ana greenhouses in which mostly roses, some stephanotis and gardenias grew. In the 1920s Ernst had shipped his product into Los Angeles on the Pacific Electric Railway that ran adjacent to the farm at Fifth and Sullivan streets, but when rail service ended, the flowers had to be driven into the city.

Both John and Norm remember accompanying their parents, Albert J. and Isobel, on early morning trips to the Los Angeles Flower Market. John recalls driving in with his father as a youngster of five or six and going to sleep under the counter, his head on a newspaper "pad" used to pack and ship gladiolas. Later, Norm went to the Market as a teenager, helping his mother with flower sales.

Sometime in the early 1940s, Norm and John's father, Albert J., and their uncle Elmer leased the greenhouses from their father and started their own business. Albert continued to manage the greenhouses, which by that time numbered more than five, while Elmer took care of getting the flowers to the Market. The third Amling brother in that generation, Johann, had moved to Los Angeles in 1939 to take a job with North American Aviation. At night he also worked for his father and then for his brothers at the Amling sales counter in the Market until he joined the Army in 1943.

When the war broke out, Albert and Elmer moved their families to Chino where they had purchased a dairy farm together. This allowed the family an additional agricultural exemption so that Albert could continue caring for the Santa Ana property on which their parents still lived. After the war, they sold the dairy farm and Elmer bought ten acres in Westminster where he planted outdoor roses. Johann moved to Portland, Oregon, in 1946 and started his own small greenhouse rose-growing business.

Ernst C. sold his greenhouses in January 1946 to his son, Albert, and one of his own brothers, Clarence, who moved to California from Spokane, Washington. Clarence Amling had been a Lutheran minister for 25 years, but when he read in *Florists' Review* magazine that his brother planned to sell the Santa Ana greenhouses, he decided to get back into the family business of growing flowers for wholesale.

Less than a year later, Albert decided to strike out on his own as the Albert J. Amling Company. He started from scratch on land he bought in Westminster about one mile from his brother Elmer's farm, where he built new greenhouses for roses and also planted roses outside.

Rose farmers in Westminster

For the next eighteen years or so, three separate Amling family businesses, the original greenhouses in Santa Ana and two farms in Westminster, coexisted peacefully at the Market in Los Angeles. Roses were as popular then as they are today, and the florists and shippers were eager to have whatever the growers brought in. "We can't help but notice the wonderful results Elmer Amling and Albert Amling have been getting with their outdoor roses," Bert Johnson wrote in his "Brass Band" column in November 1950 for *The Bloomin' News.*

Newly on his own in 1947, Albert needed a spot in the Market for his company but there were no open stalls at the American Florists' Exchange, so he sold his product through consignment broker Zappettini Company. According to Albert's son Norm, after about a year Frank Blankenship, who had worked for Ernst C. before the war, made room at his own counter for Albert and Isobel; and he found a share of stock they could buy to open their own sales counter.

Frank Blankenship had stepped in during the war to take care of the carnation fields of some of the Japanese farmers while they were away at the internment camps during the war, and he was still growing carnations in the San Fernando Valley. As a member of AFE's board of directors – he served several terms – he had the connections to bring Albert into the Market.

Early photo of the Amling Brothers workers. Courtesy Mellano family.

When their father Albert died unexpectedly in 1952, John was almost nineteen, Norm was fourteen and Charles was ten. With just one year of college behind him, John came home to run the farming operation, working side-by-side with foreman Emilio Garcia. Norm got his driver's license so he could help his mother take the flowers to the Market. He remembers the early hours: "We used to get there about 1 or 2 o'clock in the morning, but as years went by, they moved it up so we got there at midnight."

Elmer Amling had hired Vern Vescio, son of the Market's manager Frank Vescio, to sell for him at the Market. In 1949 Vern was nineteen years old and working two jobs: for the Edison Company and at the Market handling Elmer's counter. "Then he offered that I could live on his ranch; he would grow the roses and I would take them in and sell them. It was a good arrangement, so I quit the Edison job," Vern said in 2007.

As a teenager, Norman Amling's routine for many pre-Market Day nights started with going over to help Vern take the harvested roses out of the refrigerator, pack them for transport and load the truck. "This was about 10:30 at night, then I'd go home. My mother would be just getting up, and I'd help her do the same with our roses before we set off for the Market."

The original greenhouses

Clarence Amling bought out his nephew's interest in the Santa Ana farm and continued to operate on Wall Street under the Amling Brothers Wholesale Florists name and as Clarence Amling Roses, Inc. (the greenhouse business.) He persuaded his son-in-law, Jack Dexter, married to his oldest daughter Eunice, to come to California and work for him as general manager of the greenhouses on Sullivan Street.

The Dexters arrived in Santa Ana in March 1946 and Jack worked on the farm until rose-growing ceased. The land on which the greenhouses had stood for so many years became more valuable as commercial real estate. The greenhouses were torn down in 1978, four years after Clarence Amling died.

Gloria came home after two years of college to work for her father in the office at the ranch and also at the Market. When her father objected to her driving in the early morning fog from Anaheim, she got an apartment in downtown Los Angeles with another girl who also worked at the Market. Her younger sister Carol worked the summer months at the Amling counter.

Above: Model T Fords, 1920s.
Right: John Amling in the greenhouse at Westminster, around 1953.

The Amling Brothers Wholesale Florists sales counter at the Market employed between six to eight people in its heyday, Bob LeClair recalled in 2008. He and Gus Hall managed the Market operation for Clarence Amling. Roses that did not sell were sometimes returned to the Santa Ana greenhouses, and Jack shipped them to their Amling family contacts at the flower market in Chicago where they were turned into rose blooms preserved inside glass globes by the Bowl O' Beauty Company, a popular gift item at the time.

Bob also remembers that the Amling family came down to help out on busy holidays, a memory that Eunice shares: "I went in along with my dad, my mother and both of my sisters; we would all be there for Christmas and Valentine's Day and Mother's Day."

The other two sisters, Gloria and Carol, both worked at the Market for their father regularly in addition to holidays. Gloria recalls that at Christmas they would bring in over 100,000 roses in a very short timeframe. It took a lot of planning and pinching and light control to get them all to bloom at just the right time – not too early and not too late.

The roses were packed in long rectangular wooden boxes with lids: "They looked like coffins," she recalled in 2008. "We sold the roses by the stem, from eight-inch for the shorts up to fourteen- and sixteen-inch stems which were the most popular for trimming to make a bouquet."

In 1950, Clarence Amling spoke at the monthly meeting of the Pacific Rose Society in Pasadena. His topic was "My One Hundred Thousand Children" – his children being the rose plants in his 600-foot-long greenhouses in Santa Ana. That same year he served as president of the California State Floral Association. He had made a successful transition from minister to floriculturist.

Patents and the Amling-DeVor partnership

The Amling family name is on several patents for rose varieties, all of them bred in the Santa Ana greenhouses. The first was the "Red Talisman" hybrid tea rose that Ernst Amling and his son Albert J. developed and patented in 1931. They were the first Californians to apply for a rose patent.

Clarence Amling successfully bred and patented two rose varieties: the first was a petite pink he named "Carol Amling" for his youngest daughter in 1953. The second, introduced in 1971 to mark the fiftieth year since Ernst Amling had moved to California from Illinois, was "Robin Sue," a hybrid tea rose named for Jack and Eunice's daughter. In a letter to customers, Clarence described his new creation as "an iridescent flaming orange rose with the elegant look of shimmering satin, the feel of velvet on a young woman's cheek, a fragrance that is delicate, fresh and alive …"

Patented roses were the focus of another successful nursery business that Clarence got involved with in the 1950s: the Amling-DeVor Nursery in Livermore,

California. When Paul DeVor and his father George, a foreman for Jackson and Perkins rose growers for many years, wanted to start their own company, Clarence and his brother Walter provided the funding. The nursery's business model was to supply rose plants to greenhouses; the budding stock was grown in Arizona. "My dad was a good salesman," Gloria said in 2008. "He called on greenhouse growers regularly to sell them patented rose stock for commercial cut flower sales."

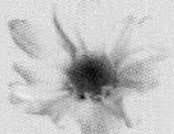

In 1964, Isobel Amling retired and sold her Westminster property and greenhouses to chrysanthemum grower Tom Hide, a Southern California Flower Market tenant. She eventually remarried, in 1982, to Albert Znojil, a Pasadena florist whose family had immigrated from Czechoslovakia. Al and Isobel dated for 20 years, seeing each other at the Market, but neither wanted to give up their respective homes – he lived in Pasadena and she in Orange. "Then one day they snuck away and got married," says Norm's wife, Carol.

Clarence and Pauline Amling at their Los Angeles Flower Market counter in the 1950s.

Al Znojil's father, also named Albert, had worked at Siebrechts Flowers since 1916. When Al got out of the service in 1948, he and his father bought the shop together. It was located on Colorado Boulevard, along the Tournament of Roses Parade route, which made it a popular gathering place for friends on New Year's Day. Al served as president of the Southern California Floral Association in 1955 and again in 1957, and also held several board positions with the Florists Telegraph Delivery (FTD) Association's local unit over the years.

"When I was about twelve or thirteen, I took the Red Car down to the Flower Market to buy flowers," Al recalled in 2008. "When I got back to my stop in Pasadena, the conductor helped me unload them."

After his mother quit the business, John went to work for George Cohen ("one of the finest gentlemen I've ever been associated with") at Pacific Coast Commercial on Paloma Street, buying and selling floral supplies, ribbon and decorative items. After fifteen years there, during which he ran operations and supervised a workforce numbering 20, he left the floral business altogether.

Norm stayed at the Market and worked for growers Jimmy Fernandez and then John Noonan briefly before moving to Oregon where he owned a dairy farm for ten years. In 1975 he returned to California and went to work for the San Lorenzo Nursery in Santa Ana for awhile, and then became a full-time truck driver while keeping an eye on what was happening in the floral industry.

In the early 1990s, it seemed right for John and Norm to take up the flower business again when they were presented with an opportunity to supply the product and transportation needs of supermarket bouquet makers. Operating as the Amling Brothers, they started out growing desert flowers such as sunflowers, larkspur and statice, but today they grow only stock on land they lease in the Coachella Valley. In 2007, they purchased Newport Wholesale Floral, Inc., which operates out of the San Diego International Floral Trade Center in Carlsbad, California.

Norman, right, and John amidst their stock flowers in the Coachella Valley desert, 2002.

Ahead of his time in greenhouse design

When Albert Amling built his Westminster greenhouses in 1947, he decided to try something different to heat them: hot water circulating continuously through pipes around the side walls, much like a hot water heater. Until then, glass greenhouses were heated using boilers to make steam; the boiler had to run constantly to maintain a high temperature. Energy costs were going up, and boilers had maintenance and safety issues. Immediately following the 1933 Long Beach earthquake, Albert went out to the greenhouses in Santa Ana to turn off the high-pressure boiler.

For his Westminster glass houses, Albert purchased a Navy surplus boiler, put in piping systems with a circulating pump, and heated the water to 200 degrees, below the steam-generation level. "The idea was to use hot water, and it was much more efficient," says Norm.

It was the boys' job to check the temperature in the greenhouses every evening, after their parents had gone to bed, especially if the next day was a Market day. "We had to write down what the temperature was at each end of each greenhouse, and what time we recorded it," John remembers.

Another technical innovation in the Amling Westminster greenhouses was an automatic temperature-sensitive switch; as it got colder during the night, hot water flowed through additional water lines situated overhead. John and Norm recall that it cost their father about $25,000 to build just one of their 300-foot-long glass greenhouses, half the length of the ones their grandfather had in Santa Ana.

Less-expensive alternatives for indoor growing long ago replaced glass greenhouses, and hot water systems for heating them are routine, but there are still some families around who recall the days when commercial growing "under glass" produced beautiful roses.

Thornton Flower Growers 1930–1990s John Noonan Wholesale Florist 1948–1995 San Diego County's Glads and Visionaries

Elmond G. Thornton's introduction to commercial floriculture was as a hired hand on the gladiolus ranch of Encinitas-based grower Donald Briggs in 1928. He must have shown an early talent for flower farming because four years later, when he was 21 years old, he and his boss agreed it was time he tried to make it on his own. It was the depths of the Depression and Briggs apparently felt he couldn't pay the young man a proper living wage, so he staked him to $38 worth of bulbs and wished him luck.

The gamble paid off. Over the next two decades E.G. "Thorny" Thornton built a company that became one of the largest shippers of fresh flowers and bulbs in San Diego County. He is considered one of the area's floriculture pioneers; in 1947 he helped launch the San Diego County Flower Growers Association.

Thorny's oldest son Lewis recalled in 2007 that he and his younger brother Robert went along with their Dad to the fields from an early age, and that summer vacations always included a trip to Oregon where he got his bulbs: "He would see what was blooming and check out the latest colors. All the growers up there knew him, and he was often invited to judge gladiolus shows in Oregon."

Lewis and Robert were working in the business by the mid-1950s. The Thorntons grew gladiola and other field flowers on more than 300 acres at that time, and began shipping flowers out-of-state by rail and truck, and then by air, in earnest. Before that, they loaded their cut flowers into a small van-style truck and took them to the Los Angeles Flower Market themselves. "We'd stop and get a sandwich on the way. There was no freeway then – just Route 101 along the coast," Lewis recalled.

The Thorntons shipped their own product as well as other growers' flowers, and they were the first to use refrigerated trucks to send fresh cut flowers out of state. For many years Thorny actively lobbied the trucking and airline industries on behalf of the flower industry, seeking fair freight rates, as a member of the Society of American Florists' transportation committee.

Cut flowers grown in Thornton fields evolved over time to include many other varieties besides gladiolas as the public's taste in fresh flowers changed. "Dad sold only to wholesalers, and he found new customers at conventions of the Wholesale Florist & Florist Supplier Association around the country," Lewis says. "Or, he would go visit the wholesalers he already knew. In just one call, he could sell a big lot of flowers."

From left, Bill Coffin and his son Dave, both route men serving Market wholesalers, with John Noonan in 1995.

Thorny officially turned the business over to his sons when he retired in 1978. Robert continued the growing operation which by 1989 consisted of more than two dozen field and greenhouse crops planted on 250 acres that the company owned or leased. Forty-five of those acres were assigned to birds of paradise; he also had ten acres in roses.

Lewis maintained the sales and shipping division, called Thornton Blue Pacific, which handled tons of fresh flowers daily from his brother's fields as well as for other growers. "We shipped between 200 and 300 boxes of flowers to out-of-state customers every day,"

Thorny died in 1984; both of his sons are retired.

Bold Baja adventure

If the weather in Encinitas, renowned as "the flower capital of the world," was ideal for growing flowers, Thorny rightly assumed it would be even better farther south, on the peninsula of Baja California Sur, Mexico. In 1948, he formed a partnership venture with another of San Diego County's pioneering gladiola growers, Arville Williams, whose fields were in Vista, California.

They leased 25 acres near La Paz, on the peninsula's east coast, flew in some bulbs and planted a crop of winter glads. As the story is told in Robert Melvin's *Profiles in Flowers: The Story of San Diego County Floriculture*, published in 1989, the only hitch in their plan was transportation – everything in or out of La Paz had to go by sea or by air because the road was generally impassable.

The two men contracted with a Mexican air freight company that flew DC-3s, the twin-engine prop "workhorses" that flew troops and cargo so reliably during World War II. But the planes were aging, slow and not refrigerated. The flowers had to be quickly harvested, bundled and loaded for the long trip to Los Angeles.

One hot morning, Thorny and Arville were aboard with their load of flowers and engrossed in a poker game when they realized that the lone pilot had left the controls on autopilot to visit the rear latrine and locked himself out of the cockpit. The tale continues: "When Thorny later told this story to farm advisor Seward Besemer (he never did tell his wife), he confessed that right at that moment nobody was thinking much about getting good glads to market. They hadn't forgotten that one of this same outfit's planes had recently gone down in a remote Baja bay, never to be seen again."

The pilot eventually got the cockpit door open and we can assume that everyone breathed a sigh of relief. But the glad growing venture in La Paz was short-lived: "Try as they might over the year and a half the operation lasted, the partners could not consistently deliver a top-grade product to the Los Angeles Flower Market. The planes were just two slow and Baja too hot."

Still, Lewis Thornton (a teenager at the time) recalled, they had grown outstanding flowers in La Paz, proving the climate theory correct. A plus was that La Paz offered superb fishing and diving; Thorny caught a marlin on one of the trips. The venture, if not profitable, had just about broken even when Thorny and Arville pulled the plug on it.

Early truckloads of glads to Los Angeles

Arville Williams Sr. was one of several early gladioli growers in San Diego County who sold their crops to the commission brokers and wholesalers at the Los Angeles Flower Market. While Donald Briggs, E.G. Thornton, E.P. "Pinky" Briley and Edwin Frazee grew their flowers along the coastal areas of south Oceanside and Encinitas, Arville Williams ventured inland to farm.

The family arrived in Vista, California, in 1927 and purchased twenty acres of land in what is now downtown Vista, seven miles inland from the Pacific Ocean, east of the coastal town of Carlsbad. Arville had been a cement contractor in the Los Angeles area; he decided to try San Diego floriculture instead. He and an uncle, Jim McClain, planted gladiola.

According to *Profiles in Flowers*, half of their first crop froze, but then their luck changed and they were the first commercial glad growers in the Vista-Fallbrook area. Arville Williams went on to lease additional acreage and became the inland area's largest glad grower, sending truckloads of flowers to the Los Angeles Flower Market. Also a founding member of the San Diego County Flower Growers' Association, Arville Williams died in 1958.

Eugene E. Stuck was another gladiola grower who farmed inland fields and relied on the commission brokers in Los Angeles in the early days. His fields were in Mira Mesa, California. He was also a writer and "the resolute voice of the grower in an industry that often seemed run by everyone but the farmers," as *Profiles in Flowers* noted. He wrote on issues affecting growers, such

as unfair tax assessments on bulbs, for industry publications such as *Southern Florist and Nurseryman and Florists' Review.*

At the Los Angeles Flower Market Gene Stuck wrote for *The Bloomin' News*, reporting on San Diego County growers at first, and then throughout the late 1940s and 1950s he wrote a regular feature as "Picardy Pete, the Flower Grower from the Far West." The Picardy was a popular glad variety of the time. "Always written from the grower's point of view, there was little that escaped Picardy Pete—from the woes of the flower field to the audacity of the Los Angeles commission man," said Robert Melvin in *Profiles in Flowers*; he included several examples of Picardy Pete's "thorny satire and easy humor" from his popular column:

- "You can tell who's who in the floral industry by looking around their offices for aspirin. A shipper always has a full bottle, a retailer half a bottle, and a grower no bottle at all. The grower never has time to take them.

- "Pete on grower types:
  Conservative: He will drive 40 miles and wait three hours in line to save 89 cents.
  Moderate: Knows everyone is out to cheat him so he cheats first.
  Liberal: He invented saving money by spending it, and knows that for every dollar he spends he somehow saves fifty cents. He's often tinged with frustration.

- "As everyone knows, a commission broker is a man with sixteen bosses and no place to hide. He is hounded on the south by a grower, on the east by a shipper, on the north by a retailer and on the west by the Pacific Ocean.

- "And now, a Merry Christmas to all; and just remember that being fresh is one of the nicest things a flower can do."

John Noonan Wholesale Florist

E.G. Thornton also partnered with two other Encinitas-based gladiola growers, Val Noonan and his brother Norman, in a gladiola farming entity called Thornton and Noonan Company. As early as 1935, fellow Encinitas flower grower (and poinsettia specialist) Paul Ecke Sr. urged the three of them to purchase a share in the Los Angeles Flower Market. At that time, the Market was the only local wholesale outlet for San Diego County growers.

John Noonan assists a retail florist customer in 1989.

Val Noonan had two sons, John and Keith; both were involved in the flower business as commission salesmen. Thornton and Noonan opened a wholesale stall at the Market in 1948 with John as its manager. In 1953, John purchased the wholesale business and it became John Noonan Wholesale Florist. His brother Keith, who also grew stock in Encinitas in the 1980s, eventually joined his brother in the wholesaling effort. Mike Mellano, Sr. remembers that the Noonan brothers moved a lot of product from San Diego through the Los Angeles Flower Market: "They were hard workers."

Jon Prechtl, who also worked in floral wholesaling, first for United Wholesale and later for Mellano & Company, recalls that Keith always brought some of the nicest carnations into the Market from San Diego growers.

John Noonan retired in 1995; he and his wife Eleanore live in La Canada Flintridge, California.

Florists & Designers

JDP Photography

Designing with Southern California Elan!

This potpourri of Southern California floral designers is far from complete, as there are many talented individuals who have left their floral print on our flower market and the region. We could not begin to write all the stories of creative people like Wayne Andrade, Mori Moho, Arthur Ito, Scott Acevedo, Richard Seekins, Bob Gordon, Sylvia Levy, the Conroy's stores and designers, and the dozens of others who flower shops have been, as *Flower Confidential* author Amy Stewart calls them, "green spots of nature in the city" and whose spectacular arrangements have been viewed as works of art.

We share these highlights of a few whose work has come to our attention during the production of Sending Flowers to America.

Silverio Casabar, AIFD: A Child's Talent Inspires Many

This respected Palm Springs designer got his start as a young boy assisting in the flower shop of the Royal Hawaiian Hotel in Honolulu. Casabar's father, Bill Sutton, was a former Navy man who worked as a gardener for Matson Company, the hotel owner. Sutton and his wife, Silverio's adoptive parents, recognized his son's abilities and continually encouraged him.

Silverio Casabar, on ladder, is assisted by his stepfather Bill Sutton, left, and Vincente Gorospe. They are adding the finishing touches to the famous hibiscus tree, made of 300 blossoms from the hotel's garden, in the lobby of the Royal Hawaiian Hotel. The year is 1952. ***Rulloda collection.***

At age ten, Silverio Casabar designed his first floral arrangement. As a young teen, he coordinated a large Matsun company party and created all the affair's floral arrangements. With nowhere to go but up, he learned to knock out arrangements quickly and with sensitivity.

The family moved to California and established a nursery. With Earl Tonyan providing recordkeeping services, they opened the retail flower shop, Bill and Silverio's Flowers by the nursery. Silverio continued to excel, taking the gold medal for large window display at the International Flower Show at Hollywood Park at age eighteen, followed by Tournament of Roses float design and Las Floristas headdress awards.

"Silverio is 'the magician,'" says his long-time admirer Phil Rulloda. The two have worked together to create many arrangements and large displays through the years.

Silverio traveled the design circuit for many years both in the United States and abroad. His shop in Santa Monica closed after fifteen years, and in 1976 he opened a floral shop in Palm Desert. He has been semi-retired since 2002 and now, in his early 80s, is still associated with the shop. He works every day and plays tennis weekly.

The Flowers

Color and scent are the distinguishing features of cut flowers, which are usually categorized as line flowers, mass flowers and filler flowers.

- Line flowers (gladiolus, snapdragons and curly willows are examples) are tall and give your bouquet height, width and balance.
- Mass flowers supply an appearance of weight or mass. Typically round and full-faced, they become the focal point of color and interest and usually have only one flower on the end of the stem. Examples are roses, carnations, gerberas, sunflowers, lilies, daffodils, tulips, irises, chrysanthemums, freesias, zinnias, alstroemerias and proteas.
- Filler flowers and foliage are stems with a lot of little flowers and foliage that round out the bouquet and give it a soft, full look. Examples are baby's breath, Queen Anne's lace, ferns, heather, eucalyptus and asters.

Source: California Cut Flower Commission and the California Foundation for Agriculture in the Classroom.

Leo's Flowers: The Multi-Retail Concept Becomes a Key to Longevity

Today's Leo's Flowers at the corner of Santa Monica and La Cienega boulevards in Los Angeles began in 1938 on a spot now occupied by the prestigious Beverly Center shopping mall near Beverly Hills and Hollywood. Getting from "there to here" took a whole lot of love and vision.

Leo Alkana had emigrated from the Greek Isle of Rhodes, worked as a huckster in New York City, and arrived in California in the 1930s with ten dollars in his pocket. He made friends quickly and soon partnered with Eli's Wholesale Flowers, then opened his own flower shop.

It wasn't long until the young, single man set his eyes on a beautiful blond-haired singer named Margaret and fell in love. One morning in 1948 after they had dated for a while, Leo told Margaret to "Buy yourself a nice suit; you're going to the Flower Market with me."

But as they left the Flower Market that day, Leo headed his car east, away from the city.

"Where are we going?," Margaret asked.

"We're going to Vegas to get married!," Leo replied.

Margaret Alkana, 2003. *Bloomin' News collection.*

And so begins the story of today's Leo's Flowers. Much to Leo's delight, Margaret spent the next few years learning the flower business and the two of them worked it together for many years. She took over the shop after Leo's death in 1961, continuing the business as Leo's Flowers. When the Beverly Center came in and needed the land the shop sat on, Tony DeMario, a realtor friend, found the current, prime location in the midst of a busy retail area.

There was a beautiful magnolia tree at the front of the property, surrounded by a parking area, in which Margaret saw visual appeal. But it was not to be.

DeMario made a suggestion that put Leo's in good stride for years to come. He recommended Margaret build a "mini-mall" on the property as insurance for future income. Taking his advice, Margaret constructed the mall with five retail stores, which because of their diversity have since helped her weather economic downturns that severely impacted other florists.

In 2007, after Leo's Flowers had long been successful as the focal point at the front of the mini-mall, Margaret would drive up La Cienega Boulevard and see Leo's name on the building. She'd smile and say, "Leo, how do you like what I'm doing?," knowing Leo delighted, that nearing the age of 90, she was still in the flower business.

Kirk Kirkpatrick, AIFD: Frequently Featured Commentator and Designer

Kirk Kirkpatrick AIFD, now enjoying retirement in Hawaii, is a charter member of the American Institute of Floral Designers and a past AIFD president with a long, colorful history as a floral designer in the Los Angeles area.

A frequent featured designer at Flower Market open houses and design shows, he commentated and demonstrated at flower shows across the nation, often sponsored by FTD, Teleflora, Florafax or a state floral association.

Continued...

Kirk Kirkpatrick AIFD, right, added animation to the floral display he and Gordon Schmuhl AIFD operated at the 1975 Open House. Their trio of schnauzers was dressed in coordinated outfits matching their own.

Retail Floristry Fixtures over the Years

The list of retail regulars who worked, competed and played with their Los Angeles Flower Market comrades through the years is long; their shops were local purveyors of blooms in neighborhoods all over the Southland.

Some shipped their flowers in wider distribution, either using one of the telegraph (and then telephone, then computer) services or doing it themselves. Their contributions are remembered by today's "old-timers" and in the archived pages of *The Bloomin' News.* Some names on the roster of not-to-be-forgotten retail luminaries include:

Charley Hum

Charles R. Hum at one time owned five different flower shops around the Los Angeles area, beginning in the 1930s until 1980. He was, by all accounts, very well-liked at the Market, his popularity no doubt boosted by his extra-curricular activities on its behalf. He served on planning committees for many of Wall Street's open houses, various sales and management conferences for florists, design schools and the California International Flower Show at Hollywood Park.

Charley's older brother, Harry, managed the Pierce Brothers Mortuaries, which had five or six locations around Los Angeles, so he had the "in" to furnish their floral needs. His first shop was inside the Pierce Brothers location at 720 West Washington Boulevard. He eventually moved to 845 West Washington, and also had another location at the Pierce Brothers in North Hollywood, both of which he operated under the Vogue Florists' name. In 1961 he purchased the venerable Wright's Flower Shop at Fourth and Spring streets downtown from Ray Nottke's widow Louise, and in 1968 he purchased Biltmore Flowers and Gardener's Flower Shop, also on Washington Boulevard.

His son John, who worked for his dad during his high school and college years, recalls to this day the color-coded system they used to identify phone lines as they rang in each shop so that they would be answered by the appropriate name: "The green line was 'Vogue

Continued...

Kirk was president of San Fernando Valley Floral Association and Teleflora's Southern California Unit. An occasional media guest, his design work for the popular "tussy mussy" bouquet earned him a spot in a floral design book. He was also invited to design headdresses for Las Floristas Headdress balls, which earned him several awards.

Flowers by Kirk, which Kirk and partner Gordon Schmuhl, AIFD, opened in Van Nuys, California in 1959, was a place of spectacular color and energy, as the designs created by Kirk and Gordon adorned the premises. Holiday open houses there attracted many loyal customers and friends. Kirk eventually moved, then downsized to a smaller shop. He and Gordon retired to Hawaii in 2002 where they continue to participate in floral events, in fact, displaying 25 fully decorated Christmas trees in their Maui home in December 2007.

"If we are to live the life of a florist, not merely a vendor of flowers, we must be creative artists, on the leading edge of both fashion and design. Our apprenticeship in this profession is for a lifetime. We must use all the tools and skills available to us to gather a vast understanding of all art forms and techniques; thus we can bring a broader knowledge to the service of flowers." **– Phil Rulloda, Tropical & Contemporary Floral Design**

Gordon Schmuhl, AIFD: Designing for the Floral Industry and the Media

Co-owner with Kirk Kirkpatrick, AIFD, in the Flowers by Kirk retail shop in Van Nuys, Gordon Schmuhl, AIFD, was a floral designer, gift buyer and interior designer for the store. His work took him to many areas of the country and beyond.

A floral design instructor with the Los Angeles Unified School District's Adult School Classes, Schmuhl was a president of the American Institute of Floral Design and served as an AIFD director, vice president, program and symposium chairman. He judged many fairs and competitions and demonstrated floral design in events across the nation, showed Western floral style and headdress design in Japan and created headdresses for Las Floristas Headdress balls, which earned him many awards. His arrangements were featured in wire service magazines and catalogs and he was always a popular designer at Los Angeles Flower Market events.

Since retiring in 2002, Gordon Schmuhl, AIFD, has continued to teach floral design and acrylic painting to senior citizens and groups throughout the Hawaiian Islands.

Bob Garren: A Lifetime Spent Pushing the Envelope

Like that little pink battery-operated rabbit, banging on his drum, Bob Garren personifies energy and longevity, not to mention a slightly irreverent take on a life in flowers. Now in his 70s, he shows little signs of slowing down the pace at which he attacks the business of serving his many long-time customers and involvement with several Market-related organizations.

Bob has seen a lot of changes in floral retailing since he began helping out as a young man in the Huntington Park shop he eventually bought. He's been influential in a few of those changes himself, such as the flower shop delivery cooperative he helps organize and the floral supplies buying cooperative he helped launch in the 1970s. He would be the first to agree that he tends to "tell it like he sees it" and has never been afraid to try something new if he thinks it will be an improvement over the status quo.

Bob values his many long-time friendships in the floral industry. He enjoys visiting the Los Angeles Flower Market very early in the morning to pick out the freshest blooms, just as he always has, and regrets that many of today's florists don't share his enthusiasm for greeting other regulars and old friends at the Market. He also mourns the passing of Sur Este and the other regional associations of florists who met regularly for dinners, workshops and parties: "I miss the closeness we had, and the fun things we used to do!"

Recalling the activity of Market days when only retailers were allowed in the door, and before

Top: Bob Garren made this floral replica of Gene Autry's palomino horse "Champion" at the behest of the horse's breeder for Autry's memorial service at the Autry Museum in 1998.

Above: Bob Garren's flowers for the set of "Hour" Magazine, a syndicated Los Angeles talk show hosted by Gary Collins in the 1980s.

route men started delivering flowers to retailers' doorsteps, he describes the scene as "…like a bunch of ants going every which way …'I want this! I want that!'… it invigorated me!"

More than one Los Angeles florist can claim Hollywood celebrity connections; Bob is one of them. His niche in the 1970s and '80s was floral arrangements for the sets of locally-produced live television programs hosted by Dinah Shore, Gary Collins and others. Television kept him very busy and he recalls those years as "…fun and exciting! Some people did parties; I did TV shows. The phone was ringing all the time for something new to do."

In 2007, reflecting on the almost 50 years he has owned his shop, Bob explained his philosophy on how retail florists like himself have survived the changes in their marketplace: "We have to remember that we're in the service business. You have to do beautiful work for your customers, or they will go somewhere else for their flowers."

Bob Garren

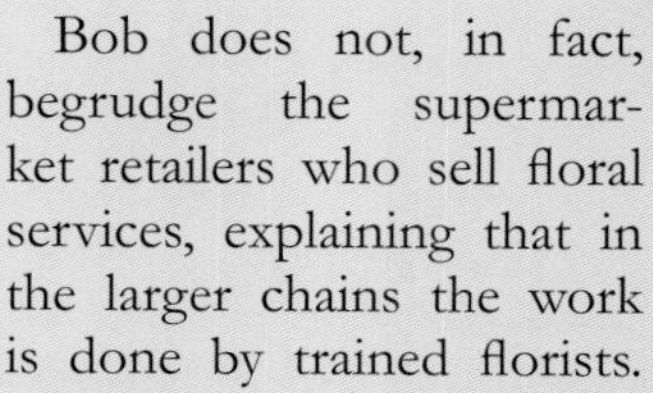

Bob does not, in fact, begrudge the supermarket retailers who sell floral services, explaining that in the larger chains the work is done by trained florists. "What standalone florists like myself offer is style and consistency. We know what our customers like."

Flowers by Bob Garren/Southeast Flowers is situated on a corner in what used to be called a streetcar suburb of Los Angeles, Huntington Park, just a few miles southeast of the Flower District. The shop's first owners, Jack Vliss and his mother, sold fruit and vegetables when it opened in 1925 as an open-sided stand on the street with a lot of foot traffic. As the neighborhood changed Jack added flowers to the mix; eventually the shop became devoted solely to flowers.

As a young man, Bob worked for the Los Angeles City school system as a finance manager. A Vliss family friend, he was also a customer. He began spending his Saturday mornings helping Jack in the shop, and it wasn't long before he realized that owning it might be a good way to get more time on the ski slopes – because it employed a delivery man and designers. He bought the business in 1960.

He added "Flowers by Bob Garren" to the business name once he got into local television in order to get screen credit under his own name. His first exposure to "television folk" was when the producers of "Dinah's Place" called asking for help with floral set decorations. He remembers that it was just before Christmas and he was dismayed at their late inquiry; he only went over to

Continued...

Retail Luminaries, continued

Florists', the brown line was to be answered 'Wright's Flower Shop' and the blue line was 'Biltmore'."

Charley met his wife Fern in the early 1930s because she worked for Pierce Brothers. The two of them were regular participants at many industry events as Charley took on more responsibilities in service to the flower industry. In October 1958 he was elected president of the Southern California Floral Association, having previously served two terms as a Board member, beginning in 1951. In the 1950s he penned a column "HUM-ing Along" for *The Bloomin' News,* and also served on the board of the Society of American Florists.

Charley campaigned successfully for president of the Florists Telegraph Delivery (FTD) Association with the support of many friends at the Market in 1965. He had already served the national FTD organization as vice president, treasurer and director. He was also active politically in the California floral industry as a director of the California State Florists Association.

His many extracurricular interests included the Florists Bowling League and golfing with fellow flower people. He also enjoyed the camaraderie of fishing and hunting expeditions with the fun-loving group of Italian-Americans at the Market. Johnny Mellano recalls the story of one deer hunt in Acton and how prankster Chris Colombo Brevidoro pulled off a practical joke on Charley:

"The group had finished for the day and was sitting around camp on the Brevidoro farm drinking wine and reliving their successes. Charley hadn't gotten a shot off all day. So Chris slipped away and got a stuffed deer head which he propped up in the bushes nearby without Charley noticing. Someone pointed it out and Charley picked up his shotgun and fired three or four times; it didn't move. 'I know I hit him!' Charley kept saying until he realized he'd been had. Dad said that although he was madder than hell at the time, Charley told that story for years afterward."

Emile Bergez

"Frenchie" – as he was known at the Market – had a shop at Wall and Eighth streets which was one of the only retail stores in the area during the war years into the 1950s.

Continued...

see what they needed because the referral came from a friend of his, Rock Hudson.

"I told them 'you already have a florist' and they said 'but he's so busy' and I said 'what do you think we all are at this time of the year?' and Dinah said 'please, Rock Hudson would like you to do it' ... so I did."

Thus began a long friendship. Bob arranged Dinah's flowers for the rest of the years her shows aired, as well as for the Jim Nabors Show, a short-lived Regis Philbin show (before he moved to New York) and for a Los Angeles-based syndicated talk and news show called "Hour Magazine" hosted by Gary Collins 1980-87.

More than once, Dinah and Rock joined him on an early morning trip to the Flower Market. "We'd meet at a restaurant in Hollywood and then go to the Market," Bob recalls. "They both loved flowers and felt absolutely comfortable there. I remember one lady asked me 'why do you have him pushing your cart around?' And I said 'because if he's going to come to the market, he's not going to just stand around' and I put him to work for me!"

Bob Garren and Dinah Shore on the set of "Dinah's Place," early 1970s.

Besides television set dressing, he has been the personal florist – the one they always call – for Peggy Lee, the Everly Brothers and several other Hollywood personalities. The most unusual request he ever filled was to construct a life-size, pompon-covered and cotton floss-maned replica of Gene Autry's palomino horse for the singing cowboy-turned-baseball-executive's funeral service in 1998. "We had to rent a truck to get it to the Autry Museum," Bob recalls.

At one time Bob was also in the wedding chapel business, a complementary activity for a florist. He performed as many as 30 or 40 weddings every month in a chapel he owned near his flower shop in Huntington Park, and recalls one wedding in particular: "I was the minister for one couple who had been together for a long time but had never married. Their children, grandchildren, great grandchildren and great-great grandchildren all attended the wedding; and it was fabulous!"

The workload- and profit-sharing advantages of cooperative ventures must appeal to Bob, because he was involved with organizing two of them on the local flower retailing and wholesaling scene.

Certified Florist Corporation began as a collective buying organization for floral supplies in the 1970s and has since evolved into a real estate holding company owning properties on Wall Street as well as other properties around the city. And since the early 1980s Bob has been responsible for the day-to-day administration of the co-op Florist Delivery Service, which offers retail florists a less costly way to extend their geographic reach in metropolitan Los Angeles by "sharing" delivery tasks.

Bob also served on the advisory board that developed the Los Angeles Flower District's badge program in the mid-1990s. "It's one way to control the door and keep the public out while the florists are shopping. Can you imagine what it would be like if everyone was allowed in at five a.m.?"

As long as he can shop early to avoid the crowds, Bob is not opposed to allowing the public into the Market. He understands why housewives, event planners and floral designers alike are drawn to the Market to select the raw materials for their artistic expressions.

"The Market offers so much variety! Flower lovers work in the season, and I love it. What other industry does that except the clothing business, and they're always eight months ahead of it. Poinsettias ... gourds ... pumpkins ... spring bulbs and other season-specific delights; it's just a wonderful thing!"

Haley's Flowers & Gifts: Weathering the Storms of Life to Serve the Community

Frank Haley didn't start out to be a minister, a radio DJ, a clothier or a florist, yet he's been all those things and more. With an entrepreneurial spirit that began as a child selling snow cones in Texas, this humble man has excelled in all his careers through the worst of conditions.

The Watts Riots of 1965 occurred three years after he opened a clothing store on Main Street in the South Central area of Los Angeles, but Frank hung on there for 22 years more. In early 1992, ready for a break from the fast-changing fashion world, he sought divine guidance and became the owner of a flower shop at Forty-Seventh Place and Broadway, near his old clothing store. Again, the area came under siege as riots erupted and violence filled the streets. And again, Frank Haley, who learned floral design from a friend and by astute observation, weathered the human storm. In the following months, as major retailers and banks moved out of the neighborhood, his flower shop remained a beacon of light and beauty.

"We've had more ups than downs," Frank says, rejoicing and smiling. As both the proprietor and designer, he receives many thank-you notes, which adorn the wall of his shop.

Frank Haley in his shop, 2002.
Bloomin' News collection.

A frequent shopper at the Los Angeles Flower Market, he says that, "Early on I learned to let the wholesaler be my warehouse." He is blessed to be located only fifteen minutes away.

Frank Haley also hosts a Gospel music show on radio and serves in a ministerial capacity in his church, so he is known throughout the community. It is this local floral landmark and the florist within that families trust with their flower orders for milestone events and loved ones' funerals.

Mario Del Fante: Floral Retailing, Italian Family-Style

It seems a foregone conclusion that Mario Del Fante would make a career, as his father did, in the retail floral trade. The lessons he learned about "making do" and customer service from helping out in the family's Los Angeles flower shop as a youngster in the 1940s have served him well. Sixty years later, greeting visitors to his own busy shop in West Covina, his easy-going, friendly demeanor feels comfortable and genuine. Most of his employees have been with him for many years.

Continued...

Retail Luminaries, continued

Emile came to Los Angeles as a boy in 1906. In 1916, when he turned eighteen, he joined the French Army and served in Europe until the First World War ended, then took a series of flower industry jobs for retailers such as George Hall, Peter Brown and Dan Stathatos at Broadway Florist, all retail shops located downtown in the 1920s. In 1932 he started his own business, a flower stand at North Main and Workman streets, an area largely populated by Italian and French families. He moved his shop to the Flower Market area in 1941.

Emile's wife Mildred and their three children all worked in the flower shop. His son Larry recalls that he and his brother Raymond took the bus downtown after school: "It stopped right in front of the store. We lived in Montebello but we were raised down there on Wall Street."

Larry grew up knowing the Goto family of Unique Floral in Montebello; his dad often sent him over to help out in their shop. When Taka Goto was sent to an internment camp during the war, he left his new car with Emile to care for it until he returned.

Frenchie's friends at the Market knew they could go to his shop any time to get a sandwich; his refrigerator was always stocked with wursts, French bread and wine alongside the flowers. One regular visitor was Bert Corgiat, a partner at Mellano & Company. Says Larry: "Bert was a character; he used to tell us stories of when he worked on the railroad, and he always sharpened Dad's knives for him."

Larry Bergez worked for his father until Emile retired in 1974, and then went to work for his uncle, Milton Kessler, who was one of Wall Street's major shippers at that time. "Milton was my mother's brother, and Dad got him a job right after the war working for the B.W. Hall Company. Buford Hall was a good friend of my father's; he always said that Buford was one of the finest people he ever met. I didn't know him because I was just a child when he died."

Larry was one of many floral designers who worked for Bob Berry, beginning in the 1970s: "I'd be bone-tired after working all night for my uncle, but Bob would come and find me when I got off and convince me it would be only for a few hours. I'd end up being there all day." Larry also worked on Bob's major floral installation crews at Santa Anita Park, the Jonathan Club and the California Club. "Bob is one of the finest florists around, and an honorable man. It was a privilege to work for him."

Continued...

Although Mario acknowledges the flower business has changed quite a bit over the years, he continues to enjoy his work combining retail and flowers, especially the opportunity to design memorable displays for weddings and the other special events of people's lives. He appreciates the wider variety of cut flower blooms that are available at today's Los Angeles Flower Market, especially in contrast to the years before and during World War II when product selection was limited.

Like other florists in those days, Mario recalls his father used lettuce leaves discarded by a nearby restaurant to form the base for single and double sprays of gladiolas for funerals. He also remembers how the labor shortage of the war years affected the retail flower business, then considered a "non-essential" industry. "If Dad did one of those big Italian funerals, he might have 20 to 25 pieces to do. There might be flowers in the fields, but no labor to pick them and bring them to the Market."

Ben Del Fante with customers in his shop on North Broadway in the Lincoln Heights area of Los Angeles, circa 1940.

His father's solution, Mario recalls, was to go to the flower fields, pick the flowers himself, pay for them on-site and bring them back to the shop. Another shortage of the war years that affected the floral industry was a lack of wire for making arrangements. "We had to buy rolls of wire about fifteen to twenty inches across," he reminisces, "grab about one inch diameter, cut the length you wanted, pull on one end and then pound it against the concrete floor to straighten it out."

Mario was about eight years old when he began going to the Market with his father before school. He recalls his fascination watching the workers at Mellano's greenery business assemble and tie bundles of lemon leaves, huckleberry and other loose greens. "It was interesting because they obviously enjoyed their work, sitting together in a circle on empty buckets turned upside down. Carl Hankemeier always had a big cigar in his mouth."

Benjamin Del Fante's first stop in America after immigrating from L'Aquila in central Italy was Seattle. He was fifteen when he joined his father, already working there. Employed (unhappily) in a macaroni factory, he took a second job at a large florist shop, Rosai Brothers, as a salesman. Because he was just five-feet, two-and-a-half inches tall, they called him "Little Ben" and taught him floral design because he obviously had a knack for it. By 1923, Ben had his own shop in downtown Seattle.

In 1931 he heard through the Italian grapevine that a boatload of marriage-eligible Italian girls would soon arrive in Los Angeles. Ben traveled south, met his soon-to-be bride Gina, and never looked back. As an unknown in the local floral industry, he took part-time jobs at several flower shops around the city and then decided it would be best to open his own shop. He found a place on North Broadway In Lincoln Heights, across the Los Angeles River and about three miles from the Los Angeles Flower Market. His "Little Ben" moniker followed him to the Market, where he was a popular customer, building a thriving retail business.

He moved from his first location to another on the same block, until a new post-war landlord served an eviction notice. Mario recalls his father's desperation until a realtor showed him how he could purchase his own building nearby, just around the corner on Daly Street. "That was a blessing in disguise," Mario comments today, "because property ownership in California was then, as now, a good thing."

The family moved into an apartment above the shop. Mario and his older brother, both in high school, also worked in the flower shop. In 1951 the Korean War pulled Mario into the U.S. Navy; when he left the service,

Mario Del Fante works with a holiday arrangement at a late 1960s Christmas Open House at the Los Angeles Flower Market. His display was sponsored by Buford W. Hall Company.

he was married and had started his own family. He needed a job, and his father had one for him. Over the next few years, Mario picked up more floral design expertise from the other designers his father employed, working twelve-hour days from early morning trips to the Flower Market through night classes at Los Angeles City College after work. He knew he would eventually have to strike out on his own and he wanted to learn as much as he could about floral design and retailing.

Ben Del Fante first soloed as a florist in Seattle in 1923

When the opportunity to go to work for another well-known Los Angeles retailer, Darling's Flower Shop, came along, Mario snapped it up. He recalls that his new boss, John McCormick, cut a distinguished figure when he went to the Market to select the day's product: "You might think he was a doctor or something because he always wore a suit, heavily starched collars and a tie. And he never carried the flowers himself; his driver always picked them up."

Thus Mario absorbed a bit more knowledge about a life devoted to buying, styling and selling flowers. A few years later he went to work for Kathleen and Lowell Miller at their shop in Covina, where he had moved his growing family. Finally, in August 1965 he opened his own business and promptly put the oldest of his eight children to work on Saturdays and after school, making nosegays and corsages. His wife Doris Ann made the shop's deliveries in the family station wagon, packing the smallest children in with the flower arrangements and, says Mario with a grin, occasionally having to "stop at another flower shop to buy a flower or two to replace those that the baby massacred" before the delivery was made. As the business grew, he hired a part-time driver and designer. Eventually, his wife became a great designer, teaching herself through observation and practice.

A self-described workaholic, Mario also worked as a stylist for Bob Berry, helping assemble major floral displays at the Santa Anita Park's Turf Club. "That was

Continued...

Retail Luminaries, continued

Larry met his wife Rachel Villaruz, at the Flower Market through her sister, Amparo Rala. Amparo and another sister, Connie Songcayauon, were married to Filipino flower growers; they came to the Market to sell their husbands' product. Although she had been a schoolteacher in the Philippines, Rachel worked for Edmunds Wholesale when Amparo introduced her to Larry. He says he had his eye on her for a couple of years before they met. Larry's floral career ended after five years with Kessler & Associates, and he went into a business that offered more normal working hours: "Dad always told me I should find another line of work. 'A flower shop is a good job for a slave' he used to say, because we often worked 70 to 80 hours a week."

Frank Fredenhagen

Losing sight in one eye in an accident as a two-and-a-half-year-old youngster didn't impair Frank's passion for "giving back" to the communities in which he worked and lived.

Frank, the owner/operator of Burbank Florist, was an active participant in numerous civic organizations such as Masonic Lodge, Moose, Rotary, Toastmasters, American Red Cross, Elks and the Burbank Chamber of Commerce. In the floral industry, his contributions are also many: he was elected president of the Southern California Floral Association in October 1950, following six years of service on the Board. He also held offices with the California State Florists Association and was a regional director of the Florists Telegraph Delivery organization.

An Idaho native, he came to Los Angeles at the age of fourteen to live with his aunt. He first worked for a flower shop at Fourth Street and Vermont Avenue, then eleven years for Lewis Flowers at Wilshire Boulevard and Vermont, before purchasing the Burbank Florist Shop in 1944.

Frank's reputation for expertise in building and decorating floats was no doubt enhanced by his long-time service to the Burbank Tournament of Roses Association.

The Francis Family

"Of the famous family of florists named Francis" is how a front page article in *The Bloomin' News* of December 1950 portrayed Harold John Francis when he was profiled as

Continued...

Certified Florists

In the mid-2000s, the California State Floral Association and Master Florists Association introduced a program designed to certify florists and demonstrate their creativity, knowledge and expertise.

A California Certified Florist (designation of CCF) has met basic qualifications and passed written and hands-on examinations. Practical experience and self study are considered.

Those who meet the qualifications of the five-year program receive the California Certified Florist (CCF) designation. See CalStateFloral.com or MasterFloristAssn.org for more.

interesting work, on tall ladders, because sometimes the displays were twenty feet up in the air," he recalls. Mario is just one of many who consider Berry a mentor in the business of designing large scale floral decorations. He eventually had to give up working with Berry as his own business took off: "On Friday nights we'd often work until two or three o'clock in the morning and then I would go right from there to my shop and start cranking out my wedding decorations for Saturday."

Del Fante family ties to the Los Angeles Flower Market are still strong in Mario's memory. His favorite vendors included "Elmer Fisher of the G.A. Berlin Company, Bert Johnson for gladiolas, Gibo and Harry Sakai over on the Japanese side of the street for carnations, and B.W. Hall for miscellaneous flowers. I also enjoyed the two or three years I did design demonstrations in the Buford Hall Company's display at Market open houses."

Phil Rulloda, AAF, AIFD, PFCI: The Teacher's Lessons Go Before Him

He dreamed of playing semi-pro tennis, mowed lawns in exchange for flowers, studied to become a psychologist, worked in the grape and lettuce fields and walked up to five miles a day to sell watermelons and deliver newspapers. Today, Phil Rulloda is one of the most respected floral designers and instructors in the nation.

Phil Rulloda's design work for an event in Kalihi, Hawaii.

"I saw flowers as a way to involve my family," he said in a 2001 article in *The Bloomin' News*. His mother took flower arranging classes and had Phil as her devoted helper.

Determined to excel, he worked in a retail flower shop after college, then opened his own shop in 1968. Before long, with his sister Sharon and brother John, he owned ten shops in Arizona and a floral design school in Santa Ana, California. Then he took a much-deserved break, semi-retiring in Sedona, Arizona.

If you know Phil Rulloda, you know he's not suited to retirement. It wasn't long before he and Cathy Hillen, AAF, AIFD, opened a shop together in Fullerton, California, then married and in 1988 started the Southern California School of Floral Design in Anaheim. Phil became a well-traveled floral commentator throughout the United States and Europe.

Two men converse at a flower stand at 1186 West Adams Street in Los Angeles, circa 1925. Carnations are advertised on special at four dozen for 35 cents. *Security Pacific Collection / Los Angeles Public Library*

He designed for special events and places including the Las Floristas headdress balls, the International Flower Show at Hollywood Park, the 1984 Los Angeles Summer Olympic Games, Christmas at the White House, and the Benz Gallery of Floral Art at Texas A&M University.

Top: Phil Rulloda competes in the Europa Cup in Athens, Greece, 1974, representing FTD and the United States. He took sixth place.
Above: Phil Rulloda, center, works with his students in 2007.

Through the years, Phil's designs have earned him a host of prestigious awards. Holding special meaning are the AIFD Distinguished Service to the Floral Industry Award presented to Phil and his wife Cathy Hillen Rulloda AIFD in 2007 at the annual Symposium of the American Institute of Floral Designers in 2007, for contributions made to the industry through their design school and educational programs around the world; the 2004 Tommy Bright Award he was awarded by the Society of American Florists' Professional Floral Communicators – International (PFCI); the FTD America's Cup he won in 1974, and the AIFD Award of Design Influence in 1991. Also in 1991, the Associated Florists of Southern California presented him with its first Phil Rulloda award.

"There is not a person who has taught, inspired and mentored more floral designers than Phil," said Ardith E. Beveridge, AAF, AIFD, PFCI, CAFA, in 2005, a member of SAF's PFCI board of trustees at the time. Beveridge's comment goes along with something Phil

Continued...

Retail Luminaries, continued

an SCFA board member. Indeed, more than one Francis family member – several of them named Harold – owned flower shops around Los Angeles' neighborhoods and suburbs.

They all descended from Frederick Francis, a grower in Victoria, British Columbia, who tried the climates of Seattle, Oakland and San Diego before settling in Los Angeles in 1920. Frederick bought a retail shop at Daly Street and North Broadway in the Lincoln Heights neighborhood, and began sending his youngest son, 14-year-old Harold John, to the Los Angeles Flower Market on the street car to purchase product for the shop.

A few years later, Frederick Francis bought a store at 36th Place and Vermont Avenue that had an attached greenhouse, "the tradition as it is practiced in the East and to a very small degree presently here in Los Angeles," *The Bloomin' News* noted. Young Harold John was assigned duties for planting 500 Lily of the Valley each week to sell in the shop and to other florists nearby.

Eventually Harold J. opened his own shop, and made his mark at the Los Angeles Flower Market as the first retail florist who was elected to the SCFA Board. He also served two terms as SCFA president in the 1940s, and in 1937 he won election to his first of two terms as the district representative of the Floral Telegraph Delivery Association.

Other Francis family members who at one time operated retail flower shops in the Los Angeles area include another one of Frederick's sons, Harry, who bought the Vermont Ave. store from his father and also opened a shop on Washington Boulevard at Fifth Avenue. Harry had two sons who were also in the business: Gordon, who owned Alhambra Florist, and Harold E. Francis, who owned the Inglewood Flower Shop. In his 90s in 2008, Harold E. shared memories of his service to SCFA as its vice president and treasurer. He was also an original member of the Certified Florists Corporation.

Ray Nottke

Ray was a retail business manager extraordinaire who rose from the ranks as a bookkeeper to become the owner of one of Los Angeles' oldest flower shops. He was also an active supporter of the floral industry – a founding director of the California State Florists' Association and twice president (1947 and 1949) of the Southern California Floral Association.

Continued...

Rulloda himself said in May 2001 when he was selected as a featured designer for the first annual LA Fleur event at the Los Angeles Flower Market:

"The best way to spend your life is in doing something that will outlast it."

Fred Gibbons: Planning a World of Floral Events

This country boy from Arkansas showed us how to plan and arrange a world class event clear across the world. Starting with a part-time floral shop job as a college student, Gibbons moved on to assist Viggo Larsen work a large event in Texas, taking over with his partner Harry Finley when Larsen became ill. From there, the celebrity connection led to acting lessons and a stint in Hollywood where high profile events and socials were the norm. He and Finley opened their floral design business in 1958 while Gibbons continued to act.

Fred Gibbons enjoys setting the mood for Carnival in Venice, Italy.

One day, while decorating a party for actress Greer Garson, Gibbons recalls that a gruff voice commanded him to "come down off that ladder." The voice belonged to gossip columnist Hedda Hopper, who advised him to forget acting and focus on what he was really good at: exquisite floral designs that were fast becoming the talk of the social elite.

Gibbons' career quickly advanced as a designer and planner for large, elegant parties until he was being hired to arrange affairs in Rome, Paris and London as well as Beverly Hills and Las Vegas. For a while he planned events for Starlight International's multi-level marketing incentive trips. In the 1990s, he opened the Treefrogs floral and antiques studio (wife Gail, a designer, manages the antiques), which is now his Beverly Hills base for designing for the stars and star-studded events everywhere.

René van Rems, AIFD: Educating and Inspiring a Worldwide Floral Community

Dutch born floral designer, entertainer and educator René van Rems has delighted thousands of people over the more than 20 years he's conducted educational seminars, workshops and stage programs for the floral community, in California and around the world. A favorite and frequently featured designer, van Rems has taught at the University of California at San Diego, is a National Speakers Association member and was director of promotion for California Cut Flower Commission.

René van Rems works his design magic before the Columbine Garden Club audience in Phoenix, Arizona in March 2007.

A California resident since he arrived as an exchange student from Amsterdam, Holland in 1978, René apprenticed starting at age thirteen with shops in Amsterdam. He studied floriculture/horticulture at the Rijksmiddelbare Tuinbouwschool and art and interior architecture at Rietveld Academy of Arts.

Anita and Bill Buerger, owners of The Orchid Farm in Encinitas, California, sponsored René during his exchange student days, providing a comfort zone and sharing his passion for floral design in a way that empowered him to branch out on his own. He owned a floral studio in Encinitas for more than ten years, where he offered event décor and design.

René Van Rems' work for California Cut Flower Commission helped strengthen the connection between California flower growers, wholesalers and retailers, while he brought visibility to CCFC and California-grown flowers. He is the author of the book, *René's Bouquets...a Guide to Euro Style Hand-tied Bouquets* and has been recognized many times by the industry:

The American Horticultural Society honored him with its Francis Jones Poetker award. In 2001, René was honored at LA Fleur at the Los Angeles Flower Market when he was presented the first René van Rems Award by Paul Ecke Jr for design education excellence. His work has been spotlighted in museums, magazines and on television, particularly for his European influence on American floral design.

Now offering management consulting, design and marketing for every area of the floral industry, René's floral design demonstrations for Teleflora, CCFC, state floral associations and other industry groups continue to inspire thousands.

Verdugo Hills: From Patient's Therapy to Flower Business

Jens (Jim) Knudsen's Verdugo Hills Floral Company and the floral business owned by his daughter Peggy Lee had their roots in the cultivating of African Violets by a patient recovering from a mental breakdown.

Jim Knudsen was a male nurse in 1939 and tending Charlie, the recovering patient. To help Charlie develop his hand and mental functions, Jim had Charlie spend part of every day setting leaf cuttings into flats of sand and, as the plants sprouted, Charlie cut the leaves away from the developing plants and planted them into little pots. Later, they were transplanted into bigger pots and offered for sale.

The number of plants in Jim's greenhouse multiplied and he found himself selling them through Wright's Greenhouses, just north of the Los Angeles Flower Market in the building which later housed Zappettini and San Lorenzo. He worked with Cornelius Bout at his booth in the Market.

"I sometimes went to market with Dad," Peggy Lee recalls. "It was like putting an extra day in the week. I loved it."

Continued...

Peggy Lee, daughter of Jim Knudsen and proprietor of Peg's Flower Shop, is shown in this March 27, 1950 clipping from the *Herald Examiner.*

Retail Luminaries, continued

Ray arrived in Los Angeles in 1919 as a young man, a United States government employee assigned after World War I to help dismantle the Ross Field Balloon School in Arcadia. He stayed in California, and took a job in 1921 as the bookkeeper and, a year later, manager of the original Broadway Florist store downtown.

After 23 years at Broadway Florist, Ray purchased Wright's Flower Shop, together with Mary Mumpower, in 1944.

Cedric Nelson

Cedric's Flowers, on the northwest corner of Wilshire and La Brea, was one of the largest retail shops in Los Angeles in the 1950s and '60s. Its flamboyant proprietor, Cedric Nelson, had a "large" reputation to match. Many people at the Market remember him for his larger-than-life personality, generosity, flair for promotion and most of all, his love of playing the ponies at Santa Anita and Hollywood Park. Win or lose, he loved to boast about how much money he'd either picked up or dropped at the track.

Cedric decorated some of the biggest parties and events around Los Angeles in his time, including major Hollywood film premieres at Grauman's Chinese Theater. The display area of his shop was, by all accounts, a treat to visit and amazing in its variety. At FTD conventions, Cedric's parties were always the most popular; everyone looked for an invitation.

Bill Visser, who founded Vissers Florist in Anaheim in 1956, worked for Cedric when he first immigrated to the U.S. from Amsterdam as a young man. Bill actually slept on a cot in an upstairs room at the shop, Stella Berry recalls: "Personality-wise, they couldn't have been more different."

Stella's husband, floral designer Bob Berry AIFD, worked parties and national conventions for Cedric in the 1950s as a freelancer, learning the ins and outs of arranging themed floral decorations for major events that he later applied in his own business. One almost-catastrophe Bob recalls was a Chinese-themed party at a trucking convention in Phoenix that was to feature a very large Buddha statue he had trucked over from Los Angeles. "But he hadn't measured the doors, so he couldn't get it into the hotel and had to set up the entire party outside."

Another catastrophe not so easy to recover from was when the wading pool Cedric had set

Continued...

Knudsen enlisted in the Navy and served until the end of the Second World War as a pharmacist's mate, leaving as a chief. In the meantime, Peggy went to work at the Forest Lawn Flower Shop under James Murphy. In 1946, she bought out Verdugo Florist (owned by Velma Zitto) in Tujunga, changed its name to Peg's Flower Shop and started making her own trips to Market. Sometimes her father drove.

"My badge number was 592," she says. "In 1946, I was one of maybe only four or five women buyers at the market. I can remember two of them were Tillie from Whitford's in Pasadena, and Mrs. Hahn from a shop in West Los Angeles."

Lee retired from the business in October 1988.

Roberta Sutton, Natalie's daughter, models her floral headdress at the Hadassah Headdress Ball held at the Castaways in Burbank on May 27, 1962. The "Around the World" theme, specifically "Under the Mediterranean Sea," was Roberta's idea. Swimming fish on spring steel wires swam around as the model walked.

Natalie Sutton: Wood Fiber Flowers were Just the Start

The Flowers by Natalie shop, opened in 1953 by Natalie Sutton in Van Nuys, was home to free classes in which Natalie taught the craft of making wood fiber flowers. When the popularity of wood fiber flower making faded, Natalie invested in a small refrigerator and became a student herself. She attended Verne Jackson's floral design school classes at night.

Natalie then began to carry a small supply of cut flowers which she bought at the Los Angeles Flower Market, driving to the Market during "several early dawns a week for what I thought I could sell," she recalls now at the age of 91.

Natalie Sutton in her Flowers by Natalie shop in Van Nuys, 1955.

Roy Dahlson, who later purchased Mayesh Wholesale Florist and whose family grew Jack Mayesh's company into a national company, became one of Natalie's routemen, eliminating the need for her several trips a week to the Flower Market. George Nakano, representing San Lorenzo Nursery, was another.

Natalie Sutton and her floral design crew won the Sweepstakes trophy for their design entry in the Hadassah Headdress Ball one year. They also designed for the Las Floristas Ball extravaganza. The crew included daughter Roberta, a fine artist in her own right who went on to become a floral designer, and her little sister, Betty, who became a florist in Florida.

"We had others in our crew by this time... We all pitched in whether it be for a wedding or a funeral; we all worked well together."

Natalie, who sold her shop in 1973, now resides in an assisted living home in San Luis Obispo.

Hasson/Villa Florist: The Flower Shop with Deep Mid-Wilshire Roots

As a young man of 20 in 1926, Victor Hasson had been working on the streets of Los Angeles since immigrating with his family around 1915 at the age of nine. Originally from the island of Rhodes, the Hassons had come to America on an Italian passport.

Victor started out as a shoeshine boy downtown. Then, like many other European immigrants without a trade, he turned to retailing – produce, flowers, whatever he could buy easily and sell quickly.

By 1926 Victor was selling flowers to residents of Hancock Park, an affluent community west of downtown along Wilshire Boulevard. Just one of many flower peddlers working Los Angeles' streets, he was approached by wealthy banker G. Allan Hancock with a business proposition.

Would Victor, Hancock wanted to know, be willing to open a permanent flower shop on the front lawn of his imposing Italianate villa on the northeast corner of Wilshire and Vermont Avenue?

Hancock was the son of Mexican War veteran Major Henry Hancock who had once owned much of the land that today comprises Hancock Park and the Wilshire "Miracle Mile." He had recently moved out of the brick castle-like house his mother had built in 1913. The younger Hancock wanted to circumvent a legal log jam that prevented the City of Los Angeles from allowing commercial zoning in Hancock Park.

Victor Hasson at his Villa Park shop.

He thought he could force at least partial commercial rezoning by allowing a business on his property. The city would be obliged to sue its proprietor for operating a business in a residential neighborhood. That happened and when it did, Hancock took over the suit and won it.

"Only by a series of legal maneuvers in which small business structures, such as the tiny flower shop set in the Hancock lawn, were placed on properties while the residences remained, were the owners able to break the old restriction," reported the *Los Angeles Evening Herald* on February 12, 1938, recalling the events that led to early commercialization of the area.

Victor's son, Ron, doesn't know how his father and G. Allan Hancock came to be friends. He only knows that their friendship lasted for many years, even after Hancock moved his family north to settle the community of Santa Maria and his dad moved his shop, now called Villa Florist, to Wilshire Boulevard and Catalina Avenue in 1932.

Continued...

Retail Luminaries, continued

up in a restaurant sprung a leak and gallons of water gushed over the floor about an hour before the doors opened. "He was fond of using pools and water features in his displays; I remember he rented huge bronze fountains and other unusual props. He was always able to sell them when the event was over because he was such a good salesman."

Bob also remembers when promotion-minded Cedric had the contract to provide the dozen long-stemmed red roses that were presented to winners of the weekday television program "Queen for a Day" broadcast from Hollywood: "He used Armroy roses from Armacost and Royston, and his name was always on the credits for providing the roses."

Cedric Nelson was 100 years old when he died in 2002.

Don Wakefield

Don Wakefield brought his retail flower shop experience with him from Dallas, Texas, when he arrived in Los Angeles in 1962. He spent a couple of years freelancing as a designer and then joined the staff at the Statler Hilton Hotel Flower Shop downtown. He purchased the shop in 1969 from Charles Futterman and renamed it Don Wakefield Flowers & Gifts.

In 1978, when he was elected president of the Southern California Floral Association to serve the following year, he sold the shop but retained a consulting role and co-ownership of the lease with the Hilton Corporation.

Don had an unusual career path to the floral industry. He held various legal positions for several Dallas companies, including a title insurance company, a life insurance firm and a railroad before buying a florist shop in 1954. He must have found his footing in flowers, because he served as area president of the Dallas-Fort Worth unit of Telegraph Delivery Service, and traveled through the United States and Canada on its behalf before deciding to cast his lot in the Golden State.

The Rolleri Family

The flower shop at the Los Angeles Athletic Club was owned and operated by members of the Rolleri family from 1916 until it was sold in 2004 by the only remaining family member.

Continued...

Association Sends Flowers to DJs

In the week before Mother's Day, 1950, the Southern California Floral Association sent each of 43 Los Angeles area radio disc jockeys two dozen roses with a card suggesting the roses would put them in the mood to play Al Jolson's recording of "Remember Mother's Day." Jolson's recording was played more than 20 times and the local florists enjoyed a healthy sales volume. Participating growers and wholesalers included Nakashima Nursery, Armacost & Royston, William Zappettini Co., C.J. Groen Rose Co., Albert Amling and Amling Brothers, Inc. – *The Bloomin' News*, May 1950.

Villa Florist thrived in that location, across the street from the Ambassador Hotel. Victor's wife, Rose, worked with him every day building a flourishing trade with an upscale Mid-Wilshire clientele. But as his father's health declined in the early 1960s, Ron became more involved in the business, eventually taking on more responsibility once he'd graduated from UCLA in 1961. Victor died in 1969 at age 63.

Ten years later, Ron moved the business further east. He bought property near Lafayette Park and built a large store of 3,300 square feet with expansive French doors, large green awnings and brick façade for walk-in traffic appeal. The building became a venue that attracted the advertising and movie-making crowd who found a ready-made "flower shop set" perfect for filming and print ads.

The May 1981 issue of *The Bloomin' News* reports on an insurance company's television commercial being filmed at Villa Florist in a "unique use of a flower shop."

Ron, a gregarious and friendly man who wouldn't know how to be anything but out-spoken and direct, recalls going to the downtown Flower Market with his dad beginning when he was thirteen or fourteen years of age, during school holidays.

The Market was a conglomeration of old structures, before the new building was constructed, he recalls, and he sharply remembers the frenzy that erupted when the morning buzzer sounded: "When the rushing started, you could almost stand on top of people."

Like all the other florists at the Market in the 1950s, Ron and Victor competed to buy the limited supplies brought in by local growers: "Whatever was available, we were appreciative to have it. Especially if the weather was bad, like in January, February or March, when it rained."

Ron recalls that large bunches of stock sold for 48 cents, and florists used it to make up funeral work when nothing else was available. Everything in the Market in the 1950s was grown in Southern California, except for anthuriums that were shipped in from Hawaii.

Designers compete in the always popular Top Ten competition at California State Floral Association's Calif Flora event, held in October 2007 in Oakland. *Bloomin' News collection*.

By the 1960s, some wholesalers and growers began to look for other sales outlets, such as the supermarkets. Villa Florist, as a retailer, was an early participant in that movement, because the original main store in the Ralphs chain was about six blocks from the shop at Wilshire and Catalina and ordered bouquets from Ron to sell in the store on holidays. Eventually the chains began to go direct to the large growers to get their floral product.

An incident in the mid 1960s – unfortunate for the grower who put all his eggs in the wrong basket, Ron says – was when a large nursery operation in the San Jose area turned down Ron's early November request for a large order of poinsettia plants. "Sorry, Von's and Safeway have already got my production," he was told.

But by late November, the grower had called to say he had some extra poinsettias he could sell him. "I don't need them now," Ron informed him. Then the grower admitted that the grocery chains had cancelled their orders. And, says Ron, the same thing happened to him the following Valentine's Day, Easter, and "by Mother's Day, the grower was out of business."

The Los Angeles Flower Market has always been a major supplier for Villa Florist. Ron moved the business once again in 2006 to a building just a few doors from the Market at 720 Wall Street. Today, he focuses on commercial accounts exclusively.

In the late 1960s and early 1970s, he seized the opportunity to promote "Secretary's Day" as a major workplace observance that brings millions of dollars during the last week of April to the floral industry nationwide. Villa Florist jumped on the bandwagon and began pushing the idea among corporate customers. "It succeeded beyond my wildest expectations." Today the week-long event is sponsored by the International Association of Administrative Professionals, and businesses are expected to recognize their support staffers with gifts of appreciation – often, it's flowers for their desks.

Villa Florist's largest project for a corporate account was in the mid-1970s when a Los Angeles-based architectural firm asked Ron to provide the floral arrangements for the opening of a major hospital they had built in Saudi Arabia. "We sent all California-grown flowers – gladiolus, carnations, roses and stock. Even in those days it was unusual for a retail florist to be involved in something that large. These days, it would never happen."

Like many Market veterans, Ron recalls the camaraderie over the years fondly. "There was fighting, there was constant bickering; you yelled at the growers and at the gatemen, yet it was a very close group. We were unified, just like our country was during World War II."

And, as in those war-time years when gas rationing led growers and florists alike to share delivery tasks, Ron was one of six florists who in March 1981 joined forces to form a non-profit co-op Florists Delivery Service for the Los Angeles area, an idea proposed by Marc Granovitz

Continued...

Retail Luminaries, continued

The club was founded in 1880 and built its twelve-story building on the corner of Seventh and Olive streets in 1912 – notable at the time as the first building in Southern California to have a swimming pool on an upper floor. The proprietor of its flower shop, Jeronimo Rolleri, was born in Italy in 1879; it is unknown when he came to Los Angeles but he apparently lived in San Francisco first where he formed a personal friendship with Amadeo Peter Giannini, founder of the Bank of Italy (it later became the Bank of America.)

Family lore as related in 2007 by one of Jeronimo's lone descendants, his grandson Ronald Lord, tells the story of a day immediately following the devastating San Francisco earthquake of 1906 when Jeronimo sat next to his friend in the city's North Beach Italian neighborhood. Banker Giannini was handing out money from a makeshift office of his two-year-old bank to people who had lost everything and needed credit to begin rebuilding their lives, and Jeronimo added his own money to the supply of available cash.

In their prominent Los Angeles shop, the Rolleri family employed the sister of a niece who had married into the family. Aurelia Gorini and her husband Guiseppe later farmed flowers in Artesia, California, and were early shareholders in the American Florists' Exchange.

Ronald Lord was raised by his grandfather Jeronimo after his mother, Rachel Rolleri, died when he was just a year-and-a-half old. Ron remembers hearing his grandfather say that his badge number at the Los Angeles Flower Market was 34, and that he used to drive to the Market in a horse-drawn buggy.

Ron says he did not intend to enter the flower business but when he was discharged from military service in 1958, his grandfather said to him: "Ronnie, they need help at the shop." Since selling the business in 2004, he has worked for Cheryll Goto at the Unique Floral Shop in Montebello, another long-time family flower business.

James L. Lynch, AIFD

In his more than a quarter century of working in the floral industry, Jim Lynch, whose death in 2006 saddened the Southern California floral community, made a name for himself that evolved into a synonym for excellence. Owner of Fleur Design Concepts in Tarzana with partner Keith Kemp, Jim served as presi-

Continued...

of Boulevard Florist in Lawndale. The co-op still operates with more than 25 florists participating, and Ron has been the group's treasurer since its start.

As a long-time buyer on both sides of Wall Street, Ron has seen many people and institutions come and go. He recalls the Market's Benevolent Fund: "Every time somebody died, you put in a dollar or two – you were billed for it. Then when you died, your family would collect. The Japanese call it 'koden' – money in an envelope for the deceased. It was a nice thing, but by the time my mother died in 1992, the Fund was long gone."

The Singing Flower Man

The March 1974 issue of *The Bloomin' News* told the delightful story of Joe Richards, a public relations professional turned street-vending florist, who bought his flowers at the Los Angeles Flower Market and then sang his way into the hearts of shoppers.

Richards designed and built a special flower cart which he parked just outside a store called Judy's in the Century City Shopping Mall on Wednesday through Saturday each week. Dressed in white slacks and colored shirt, he set up his wrought iron cart with yellow, gray and white striped awning trimmed with ball fringe and, using a tape player for musical accompaniment, he sang his musical numbers.

"When I sing, they really become aware of me," said Richards. "They smile, or stop and talk, and buy my flowers."

Selling carnations, baby roses, daisies and other in-season flowers, Joe Richards grossed around $20,000 a year. Some customers who complimented him on his "natural" singing ability were stars of stage, screen and television.

Richards thanked a number of Flower Market tenants for helping him get started, including Ogawa and Casey Visser, Nick Katsogianes, John Holub, Jibo Satow and Sus Yokomizo.

Ron also recalls the news sheet printed and handed out every Market Day under the stewardship of Walter Swartz, the Market's manager. The one-pager informed Market-goers what was available that day, general pricing, who was ill and who had died. He especially remembers fondly the Market friends – Tony and Gloria Morales and Charley Hum – who jumped in to help him on short notice when his father died in 1969. "It was three days before Mother's Day, but they spent all night long helping me make flower arrangements for his funeral the next day."

Both Hassons were involved with The Southern California Sporters fishing club, a popular activity for many Market people that had begun in 1954. "Dad was their photographer in the 1960s and he used to go on all their trips." When the group's organizer, George Kobata of Kobata Wholesale, fell ill in about 1978, he asked Ron to take over the club and make the charter arrangements. "It was mostly growers and wholesalers but included a few retailers, too. We had wonderful camaraderie then."

Broadway Hits for All Occasions

The saga of the Stathatos family and Los Angeles' historic Broadway Florist reads like a Horatio Alger classic – the realization of the American Dream through hard work and determination. The difference is their story unfolded on the streets of Los Angeles rather than the streets of New York.

It began when Dan Stathatos, the eldest of three brothers, arrived in America from Greece in 1907. In his early 20s and like so many young men of the era, he longed to go west and soon was on a train bound for Southern California. Having little money, he stayed with friends in Los Angeles while looking for work. Although many friends who came from his island, Cephalonia, had settled in the Redondo Beach area where they were commercial flower growers, Dan turned to selling flowers. He began by selling violets and other fresh flowers on the street corners of downtown Los Angeles until he could save enough money to open his first little flower shop on Broadway between Fourth and Fifth Streets. The year was 1910 and on the strength of his boundless energy and outgoing personality, Broadway Florist began to flourish.

Broadway Florist proudly displays its floral flag around 1915, as Dan Stathatos (senior) supports the flag's left and Peter its right. The gentleman at left is unknown.

Retail Luminaries, continued

dent of the Associated Florists of Southern California and in the early 2000s led the organization of the two "LA Fleur" events at the Los Angeles Flower Market.

Involved in the industry at many levels including education, merchandising, product development, commentating and demonstrating for floral organizations and companies, Jim Lynch was honored for his contributions to the industry by California State Floral Association (2000 Designer of the Year), American Institute of Floral Designers, the Bernice White Service Achievement Award, FTD's J.R. Noocan Designer of the Year in 2000, and several awards from the Associated Florists of Southern California.

Top: Dan (Senior) Stathatos in the original Broadway Florist shop on Broadway in downtown Los Angeles, circa 1912. Stathatos collection. Above: Peter Stathatos, a brother to Dan, poses with the Broadway Florist delivery truck, date unknown.

"Everybody liked him," recalls his eldest son, Dan Jr. "Eventually he was able to employ full-time floral designers and he became the florist to the stars of that time," said his younger son, Jerry. "Harold Lloyd, Fatty Arbuckle, Bebe Daniels, Tom Mix, Mary Pickford and Douglas Fairbanks were among his regular customers."

Eventually he acquired four other stores – three of them located in the city's major hotels: the Biltmore Hotel, the Crystal Florist in the Angelus Hotel at Fourth and Spring Streets, the Ambassador Hotel, and Alexandria Florist on Spring Street.

In 1920 Dan married Diamondo Margaritou, who was also from Greece. The wedding party included his brother Cosmos Stathatos, who had established a floral business in the Larchmont area. By the time their son Dan Jr. was born, the Stathatos family had settled in mid-town Los Angeles and achieved such prominence in the local Greek-American community that a Greek Orthodox archbishop traveled by train from Chicago to officiate at the christening festivities held in the ballroom of the Biltmore Hotel.

In 1925, Dan sold all five shops to a customer, Katherine Clifford, an actress who thought it would be fun to be in the flower business. "We were told that she would arrive at the flower market in a chauffeured car," says Jerry. The following year Dan returned to Greece for a visit and to assist members of his family in launching their own local businesses. He had already brought his two brothers to Los Angeles to work at Broadway Florist. Sadly, his brother Savas died in the flu epidemic in 1918.

Katherine Clifford's entrepreneurial fling failed during the Great Depression and Dan, Sr. found himself back in Los Angeles and in the flower business after purchasing his original shop in bankruptcy proceedings. Because she hadn't been able to pay her bills, he not only paid off all of Clifford's debts but also the growers who thought they would never see their money again. "For years afterward, if one of those growers had flowers that were in short supply, he would make sure my dad received what he needed."

Shortly thereafter, Dan purchased the Alexandria Florist in bankruptcy court and merged the two stores into one. It was his dream that one day his two sons would take over the business that he had worked so hard to build. Every Saturday morning the boys would ride the Red Car from Redondo Beach to downtown Los Angeles. It was a devastating shock when their dad suffered a fatal heart attack at age 58 in 1941. Dan Jr. was seventeen, and Jerry was fourteen. Fortunately, there was a dedicated staff that ran the business while Dan Jr. served in the Army, and Jerry finished school.

Dan Sr. had done his job well. The two young men had watched their father create a successful enterprise with multiple stores. Slowly they begin to expand Broadway Florist, adding new locations and expanding into floral supplies and home decorating merchandise. In addition to purchasing from all the major local

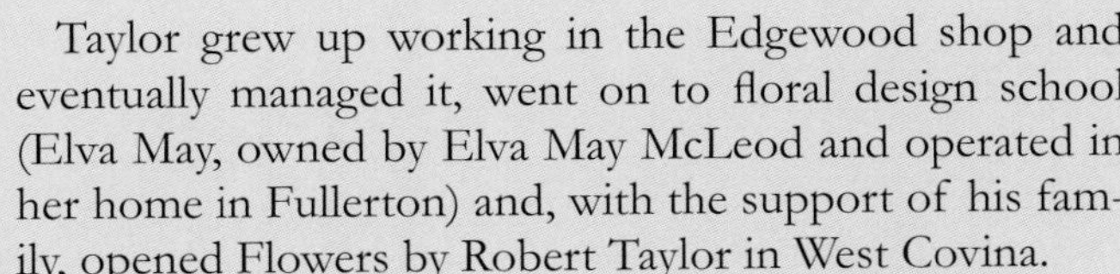

wholesalers and growers at the Los Angeles Flower Market, they also dealt with a leading San Francisco supplier who shipped fresh flowers daily to Los Angeles' Union Station. Their clientele expanded to include Greater Los Angeles, with additional stores in San Marino and Beverly Hills.

"For a number of years, we were always on the top ten list among the thousands of Florists Telegraph Delivery (FTD) members," Jerry recalls. "During the 1950s we created a major annual promotion for Bullock's Department Stores that put us right back in the violet-vending business. Bullock's ordered violets – thousands of them – to give to customers who visited their stores on the anniversary of the day Bullock's first store opened in downtown Los Angeles in 1907."

In 1957 the brothers bought a San Marino flower shop from Erna Thurnher, who had learned her craft in Munich, Germany. She continued to manage the store for them until she retired in 1967. During her long career she decorated several annual Governors' Balls on Oscar Night. Thurnher's classes in professional floral design and her open houses are legendary.

The Broadway Florist chain is now history. The stores were sold in 1985. However, the family continues to operate its popular STATS Floral Supply and Fishbeck's Patio Furniture Store in Pasadena along with locations in San Juan Capistrano, Redondo Beach and Seal Beach. Although Dan Jr. and Jerry are still at the stores nearly every day, the business is now overseen by the third generation: Dan Jr.'s sons Steve, Damon and Philip; and Jerry's son, John Stathatos.

Robert Taylor: A Lifetime Love of Florists and Flowers

On his walk home from grade school one day, Robert (Bob) Taylor followed his heart into a local flower shop and discovered a lifetime love.

Robert Taylor

The year was 1953 and the shop was Edgewood Florist in West Covina, owned by Pat and Howard Spiegel (both are now deceased). Bob Taylor was about eleven years old and fascinated with the colors and textures, the shapes and lines of floral designs in the small shop. It was a wonderful place to hang out and before long, Pat Spiegel had him sweeping cuttings and helping with shop chores.

Taylor grew up working in the Edgewood shop and eventually managed it, went on to floral design school (Elva May, owned by Elva May McLeod and operated in her home in Fullerton) and, with the support of his family, opened Flowers by Robert Taylor in West Covina.

Over the next few years, Bob Taylor became very active in the regional floral industry, serving as president of both the San Gabriel Valley Florists Association and the Inland Florists Association. For a couple years he was the district representative for FTD's District 10A, investigating and getting acquainted with florists from Santa Maria to San Diego and east to Las Vegas.

In the late 1980s, Bob Taylor and florist Ray Tucker bought Flowers by Chris (formerly Mario Del Fante's shop), also located in West Covina, and renamed it Wescove Floral. Ray ran the Westcove shop and Bob managed his own shop until he and Ray sold Westcove about five years later.

For some 25 years, Bob Taylor wrote for *The Bloomin' News*. He began as reporter for the San Gabriel Valley Florists Association, then he reported for the Inland Florists Association. Finally, along came the "Here, There and Everywhere" column in which he chatted casually about the news from the many florists with whom he was in touch frequently through his FTD duties, floral association ties and industry affairs.

"I love florists and loved writing about them," he recalls with pride. "I was so lucky. I knew them all. And we were like family."

Bob Taylor sold his shop in the early 1990s to Bob Bryant, its current owner. Since then, he's kept his childhood dream alive by working part-time for several shops, including his current engagement at Flowers by Kirk in Van Nuys.

Ray Tucker: The Power of the Flower Inspires Him

Like many of our local floral designers, Ray Tucker's entire life has been about flowers. But Ray's exposure to the floral business has extended to teaching and touring and telling thousands of people about flowers.

Ray is the personable guy who leads the walking tours of the Los Angeles Flower District two or three times each year under the sponsorship of Descanso Gardens and Mount San Antonio College. He has also been an instructor of floral design and a full-time florist and designer.

Always enthusiastic when conversing about flowers, Ray Tucker's career began as a data clerk in a Los Angeles bank and as a free lance artist. A casual drop-in visit to the shop of his friend Robert Taylor AIFD in West Covina sparked his interest in floral design. He became excited about designing with cut flowers.

"It was similar to art, my first love," Ray later recalled. He'd earned a bachelors degree in Art at California State University, Northridge, with an emphasis in design and education. He was primed and ready for the beauty of fresh flowers in the arena of design.

"The power of the flower," he says, led him to successive opportunities: working in Taylor's shop, then starting his own shop, then working with Alan Mazal in Glendora, and starting in 1984, teaching floral design at Mt. San Antonio College. As an artist, floral design was "a natural" and he excelled at it.

With his college emphasis on education, he could move easily into an instructional position in his new career. In the early 1980s, Ray began teaching design for the Southern California Floral Association at the Flower Market, where he served on the advisory committee with John Rossi and executive secretary Bob White.

In 1988, Ray started his own school – the Los Angeles Floral Career Center – which he operated at the Los Angeles Flower Market until 2001 when Forest Lawn Mortuary hired him as its floral supervisor. Since leaving Forest Lawn, he's directed his attention to educating others about floral design. He's still teaching at Mt. San Antonio College and in the Regional Occupational Program at Alhambra High School.

This artist-turned-floral designer has served on the boards of FTD, Teleflora and state and regional organizations and commentated at shows and competitions including Flower Market design shows. He has sung in operatic productions in Los Angeles and Orange counties, with greats like Placido Domingo ("I put a spear to Domingo's neck," he says with a chuckle). He's appeared on television, worked with the Tournament of Roses Parade and taught design in Thailand – all made possible because of his love of flowers and design and the great satisfaction he gets from seeing his students succeed.

AIFD Offers Two Professional Design Designations

In 2007, the American Institute of Floral Designers announced it would soon offer a Certified Floral Designer designation to assist both the floral industry and the public in recognizing designers who are proficient in the fundamentals of floral design. The CFD evaluation system compares to the AIFD designation which association members receive for their excellence in floral design and their commitment to the advancement of the art of floral design. Candidates for both designations must participate in design evaluation sessions, take written exams and attend educational sessions. Continuing education is required of those who qualify for the CFD and AIFD designations.

Above: Ray Tucker, 2007
Right: Ray Tucker, center, with early 1990s students from Japan, who came to his classes through the Kintetsu International Tour Company. They posed on the roof of the Los Angeles Flower Market.

The Yack Family: 75 Flower Shops in Nearly 100 Years

As a teenager, Victor Yack remembers peddling fresh cut flowers to patrons in bars and with his uncles and cousins, driving to area towns (Covina, Orange, Covina, Santa Ana, to name a few) to sell flowers to shoppers.

"My uncle would drive the truck, and my cousin and I would be fixing the flowers in the back of the truck, and then we'd hit a little town and put all the bouquets in a basket. And we'd each take a side of the street and go right down the street and try to sell the flowers to all the people. We'd go in and out of the shops."

Like many of the early immigrants who made a living by peddling, the Yack family carved out a niche for themselves in the flower business. Obediah Hasson, Victor's grandfather, was a Turkish immigrant from the Island of Rhodes who, upon arriving in California, sold vegetables and in 1916 added flowers. He found an outlet for his merchandise by transitioning into the wholesale business at the Los Angeles Flower Market of the American Florists' Exchange around 1918, just as the market was beginning to organize itself. Hasson became interested in the future of the Los Angeles Flower Market and worked closely with other wholesalers and growers to establish it.

Obediah Hasson and his wife raised four sons and a daughter in the flower business. Their daughter Mary married Ralph Yack, who quickly entered the business, first by helping Mary's father and then by opening his own flower stand at Adams and Vermont in 1925.

In the early 1930s, Ralph moved his flower business across the street (to make way for the Ralph's grocery supermarket) and expanded it into a retail shop. Ralph Yack bought his cut flowers from wholesalers at the Los Angeles and Southern California flower markets and, with the wealthy residents of West Adams Street as clients, his business thrived.

Eventually, all of Obediah's children owned flower shops. Victor Yack recalled in a 2007 interview that his very large family – including uncles, cousins, second cousins and spouses – accounted for some 75 flower shops from Los Angeles to San Diego.

When one of them got a good deal on a cut flower purchase, he'd share it with the others. They all went to Market in the early mornings, but they were there to take advantage of the bargains at the end of the Market's business day as well. One of Victor's "fondest memories of the Flower Market was meeting my father, uncles and cousins and buying flowers; and then we all used to go out and eat breakfast at the Japanese restaurant."

At the age of ten, Victor started working in his father's shop at Adams and Vermont. That meant tagging along to the Flower Market in the coldest, darkest wee morning hours, and staying late for bargain flowers. For a child, the days were long but the experience proved invaluable.

Victor's brother Allen opened a shop in Arcadia after his father's "Ralph's Flowers" in Pasadena burned to the ground during the 1992 riots. Their father, Ralph, had died several years earlier, but the shop retained his name, and the shop Allen opened in Arcadia carried the Ralph's name as well.

Left: Victor Yack at his flower stand, in front of his retail shop at Fifth and Mission in Pomona, California, May 1960.

Above: Victor Yack, left, is the Sweepstakes winner in this 1962 Las Floristas Headdress Ball. Marilyn (Mrs. Baron) Hilton is pictured in the middle, with Victor's wife Melba on the right. The theme was "When the Swallows Come Back to Capistrano."

Victor Yack owned five flower shops (including Victor's in Covina), representing a business that evolved much like his father's did in downtown Los Angeles. From a little stand on a corner in Pomona, he expanded to a retail shop, then one-by-one, opened four others. Victor nurtured a dream that customers would take his floral design skills seriously, and he entered floral design competitions and made a name for himself as a designer. In 1966, he became a charter member of the American Institute of Floral Designers.

Victor's entries in the annual Las Floristas Headdress Ball at the Beverly Hilton earned him eight prizes, including two Sweepstakes awards. On several occasions, Marilyn Hilton, wife of Baron Hilton, the son of the founder of the Hilton hotel chain, modeled his headdresses. Students from floriculture classes joined Victor's employees, who donated their time, in assembling the headdresses before the big event.

All good things transition to other forms, and eventually, Victor Yack decided it was time to slow down and enjoy life. The problem was that when he wanted to sell his five flower shops, he couldn't find anyone who was willing to get out of bed at two o'clock every morning, work all day and manage shops in different towns and not rest until nine or ten o'clock in the evening. Finally in 1989, he sold a shop called Victor's Florist in Pomona, California to his general manager, the Irvine Florist shop in Irvine, California to his son Ralph and the other three to outsiders.

In the late 1980s, as Victor Yack was beginning to feel a little bored with retirement, son Ralph was starting a floral business of his own and convinced his father to join him. Victor began working half days for Ralph's company, Floral Express in Carlsbad, California, importing flowers from South America.

Ralph had followed in his father's footsteps since he was young, working in the flower shops, buying the Irvine Florists shop (which he quadrupled in sales) and finally entering the floral shipping business. In 2004, Ralph founded a company called FloralShip, which he then sold in October 2007 in order to devote his time to the non profit Kids Flower Foundation and to expand on his role as a flower importer in California and Florida.

The Yack family tradition spans nearly 100 years and their influence upon the floral community goes on and on.

Bill Visser: Growing Visser's Florist & Greenhouses, Inc.

"Bill Visser was a giant and a great businessman" was how florist Victor Levy described the founder of Visser's Florist & Greenhouses, Inc. in Anaheim, California.

At the age of 25, Bill Visser immigrated to the United States from Amsterdam, an award-winning floral designer who had perfected his craft in Holland. For a while, Visser worked in Cedric Nelson's Los Angeles floral shop, where he started at ground level and worked his way up. The entrepreneurial bug had bit him hard, however, and he often took the Red Car from Los Angeles to other cities to look for land and opportunity. As Levy recalls, "one morning as he (Visser) was enjoying his coffee and newspaper, he read that Walt Disney was going to build a park in Anaheim. He took the Red Car to Anaheim, and the rest is history."

In 1956, Bill Visser bought a small flower shop on West Lincoln Avenue in Anaheim from Mary Macres, who had owned it since 1922. Visser named it "Vissers-Macres." Five years later, he moved across the street and began buying up houses in order to grow the business. Now half a century later, Vissers Florist is an Orange County landmark encompassing 12,000 square feet equally divided between shop and greenhouse.

Bill Visser

"We pretty much hit every market and every feeling," said Lynda Visser-Nath about the consumer market for their landmark Anaheim company. Lynda and her sister Lori grew up among the flowers in their father's shop, which they bought from him in 1986, fulfilling his dream.

The Visser daughters carried on the tradition started by Bill Visser, who died in 2001, for almost two decades. In late 2004, they sold to Ted and Cathy Robinson of Placentia, California, and their sons Ted Robinson, Jr and Dennis Robinson.

Erna Thurnher: Sophisticated Floral Designer

"She brought class to the design profession," recalls Stella Berry about Erna Thurnher. This talented floral designer and shop owner loved arranging flowers and planning events for her Los Angeles area customers, many of whom were wealthy and of renown.

A quiet-spoken young Erna Haag, born in Hohenems, Austria in 1902, trained in Buchner Nursery and Flower Shop in Munich, Germany in 1920, where Armin Thurnher, who was a seven-year prisoner of war in Siberia following World War I, apprenticed in the nursery business. The couple married in 1922 and then, responding to Armin's job offer from William Hertrich at the Huntington Botanical Gardens in San Marino, California, they immigrated to the United States in 1923. Armin worked with Hertrich and Henry E. Huntington to develop the Huntington Botanical Gardens and was later selected to build San Marino's Lacy Park. He became a park superintendent and director of landscape planning for San Marino.

In 1939, Erna Thurnher went to work for Lucky Florist on Lake Avenue in Pasadena, where she became manager and in 1942, she purchased the Flower Box on Fair Oaks Boulevard in South Pasadena. In 1947, she opened Erna's Flowers on Huntington Drive in San Marino while still owning and operating the Flower Box, which she later sold to an employee. She sold Erna's Flowers in 1957 to the Stathatos family of San Marino, and the shop became The Broadway Florist/Flowers by Erna. Erna continued to manage the San Marino shop for many years; and she assisted the Stathatos family in their Pasadena and San Juan Capistrano "Stats" stores during Christmas seasons until she retired at age 89.

The years that Erna Thurnher enjoyed her floral design career were filled with hard work and happy events. In her written memories, she reflected, "I think by now it is clear that I enjoyed every minute of what I did in my career. Most enjoyable was the opportunity for creative self expression, and most rewarding was the opportunity for personal growth." The trust that people placed in Erna to plan and decorate dinner parties for 500 people, and organize and design large themed parties, often telling her to be creative, for "there is no limit," touched her and challenged her. She hired teams of free lance artists, concocted one-of-a-kind props (like tall trees constructed of balloons; dancing bears; or live seals in the swimming pool) and called upon area florists and the Los Angeles Flower Market for unusual greens (like tea leaves) and flowers.

During her career, Erna Thurnher designed for The Academy Awards' Governors' Ball dinners, conducted a 40-day flower arranging cruise event for Matson Lines, served on the FTD board of directors, demonstrated at an FTD convention and, with Armin, judged and lectured at flower shows nationwide. At the Los Angeles Flower Market, she presented several professional design classes, and her open house events, held first at Erna's Flowers and then moved to the larger space afforded at the Episcopal Church's parish house, quickly became legend for their elegance and a wonderful tea punch from an old-world family recipe she wouldn't share.

Erna and Armin were a perfect team with her floral arranging and creativity and his nursery profession and flower garden, and they involved the whole family in the flower business. "Bertram tells of accompanying his father late at night out in the fields with flashlights looking for beetles in the chrysanthemums," Erna recalled in 1997. Armin's mums "would win prizes at the flower shows," Erna said, "and they were very popular in the shop and at the wholesale market. On market days, Armin would cut the flowers in the early morning, about 4 a.m., and would bring them to the shop for bundling, which was very difficult as some of the flowers were so large, with heads like cabbages. I would then take them to Market. People would be waiting for me to arrive."

The couple's sons William, Oskar and Bertram grew up in San Marino helping with their mother's flower deliveries to meet hectic seasonal demands. (William died in March 1945 as a U.S. infantryman in Germany.) Oskar now resides in Northern California and Bertram in Orange County, California.

In 1997, Erna Thurnher wrote that on their last trip to Austria, she and her beloved Armin drove to Munich hoping to visit Buchner Nursery, where Armin apprenticed, and "Blumebinderei" (a "flower business"), where she took her early training in 1920. "We looked up and down Augustinastrasse, but it was not there. It had been destroyed in the Second World War. Gone was the wonderful rotunda of leaded glass. It was sad not to find it."

Erna permanently retired in 1967, although she continued to help with special events in the San Juan Capistrano shop. She passed away in 1997 in Laguna Hills, California.

Erna Thurnher as a young woman (left) and in her later years.

Bob Berry Florist, AIFD: "Living Large" in the World of High-Style Flowers

The flower business captured Bob Berry's attention at an early age – he was just ten years old when he started shopping on Wall Street in 1935.

His mother ran a flower shop from the front porch of the family's home in Altadena. She took him with her to the Flower Market early in the morning so she could drop him off at school on her way home. Nobody noticed a boy slipping under the chain meant to keep retailers outside until 6 a.m., the official start of sales to local florists. Prior to 6 a.m., only the shipping companies picking up their orders at the wholesale counters were supposed to be on the Market's floor.

Bob's role was to go to his mother's wholesalers and place her orders. "When the bell rang and the chain was lifted, they had her orders all ready to go because they knew I had to be taken away to school," he explains.

Berry's Flowers got its start during the Depression. Helen Berry needed income so she decided to grow flowers on a friend's vacant lot next door. She and her two sons, Bob and Bud, sold them to people on their way to Mountain View Cemetery just two blocks from the Berry home.

Bob and his brother Bud selling bouquets in front of Berry's Flowers at their home in Altadena, California, 1934.

Bob remembers when someone asked his mother if she could make a casket piece for a funeral. She said "yes", put on her best dress and went to a stranger's funeral so she could see what a casket piece looked like. "She was never one to hesitate on anything that had to do with business," Bob recalls.

Bob took her examples of initiative and customer service with him when he decided to take over the business in 1946, fresh from four years in the U.S. Navy. His mother had built a small shop onto the front of her house but the war years made it difficult to keep going and she was ready to give up the business. Bob says that at the age of 21: "I didn't have a college education or a trade so I thought for the time being, I'll do the flower business."

He has never looked back. Within a few years he opened a walk-in shop in Altadena and did funeral flowers for seven local mortuaries. But he itched to break out of the funeral niche; he already had a taste of event decorating at the Santa Anita Race Track.

Berry Flowers display in April 1953, used in the Southern California Edison company's *Today's Business* magazine in April 1953.

A good friend, John ("Mac") McCormick, who owned Darling's Flowers urged him to move into the downtown area, which was experiencing a building boom. Plus, there was an opportunity for Bob to take over the floral business of Mac's best customer, the venerable California Club, because Mac planned to retire. Bob decided to make the leap.

He kept his Altadena shop open, and worked the California Club business out of a satellite place he called Los Angeles Florist, Inc. at Bill Hatakanaka's wholesale business in the Orchid Exchange Building on Wall Street. He went back and forth between the two places for several years, until in 1969 space in the building at 709 Wall Street owned by Guiseppe (Joe Sr.) Franciosi became available. Bob closed his original store and moved into the first floor space there. He remembers that the Norman Seed Company was upstairs.

First-class stylist for events and venues

Calling Bob Berry a "flower arranger" is like saying the Taj Mahal is a honeymoon cottage or that Magic Johnson played basketball. The label fits but doesn't tell the whole story. Bob's specialty is "large, unusual and elaborate" – floral displays that defy gravity, impress the onlooker and stun the senses. He learned how to craft massive themed displays of flowers, greenery and props from designers such as Cedric Nelson and

San Francisco's Eddie Geoppner and in turn, passed his knowledge along to floral stylists who worked for him.

Bob credits Rudy Ostengaard, head of public relations for United California Bank and one of Mac McCormick's best friends, for offering to mentor him in matters of marketing and presentation. Bob recalls Rudy told him: "If you follow what I say, I'll show you how to get your foot in the door of every major corporation in downtown Los Angeles." The two met once a month for five years. One of the techniques Bob learned from Rudy involved simple but useful etiquette tips and event planning ideas that were mailed regularly to secretaries and administrative assistants. "It was a very professional approach; no hard sell," Bob explains.

Above: Bob Berry, representing the Southern California Floral Association at the FTD convention in Minneapolis, 1963.

As his name became known and his reputation for quality work and a cooperative attitude spread over the next three decades, Bob regularly provided floral arrangements for every bank with a headquarters office in Los Angeles, special events including Opening Night at the Dorothy Chandler Pavilion of the Los Angeles Music Center, events at the Los Angeles Country Club, the Huntington Library in Pasadena and every major private club, including the Jonathan Club and the California Club.

He is especially proud of his work with the prestigious Men's Garden Club of Los Angeles; he decorated their monthly luncheons at the California Club for more than 40 years and has many fond memories of the friends he made there. When Bob closed Los Angeles Florist, Inc. in 1989, he became eligible for Club membership himself. His sponsor was Frank Kuwahara of the Southern California Flower Growers, Inc., who had been a member since shortly after the war. Bob was given a lifetime honorary membership in 2005.

Every month's speaker presentation at the Men's Garden Club had a theme, with floral decorations to match. One memorable set of table centerpieces featured a club member's extensive collection of exotic birds. Bob had arranged tropical flowers, including unusual white and pale yellow birds of paradise, around the tops and bottoms of large gold cages on a massive 30-foot theme table. As one of his freelance designers was transferring a macaw from its cage to a centerpiece cage, it bit the man on the thumb and hung on as the designer cursed and shook his hand vigorously.

Bob laughs as he recalls the bird finally let go and escaped down the "once quiet corridors of the California Club" with its 83-year-old owner in mad pursuit, wielding a large net and commanding at the top of his voice: "Close the windows, close the doors." The errant bird was caught, the designer's finger bandaged, lunch was served on time and the meeting was a great success.

Famous people and industry stars

For more than 50 years, Bob Berry did the flowers for many significant venues and events on Los Angeles' social calendar. His arrangements decorated tables at dinners, luncheons and receptions honoring four American presidents (Gerald Ford, Jimmy Carter, Richard Nixon and Ronald Reagan) and the Emperor of Japan in venues ranging from the Music Center to the Huntington Library, and the Biltmore Hotel to the Century Plaza Hotel in Century City.

He employed a steady crew of sixteen people in downtown Los Angeles to handle logistics and erect displays. One of them was – and still is – his wife of 44 years, Stella, an artist in her own right and his acknowledged "right hand." Bob describes another of the luncheons they did for the Men's Garden Club that had a rural farming theme. Stella painted a colorful backdrop featuring thatched-roof houses to set the stage for a display of prize-winning vegetables donated by the Ventura County Fair. The vegetables were piled in baskets, wheelbarrows and on a cart with two large ceramic donkeys.

Bob figures he trained close to 300 people in floral design over the years – they were employees or attended one of the many design symposiums or schools in which he participated. The designers include René van Rems AIFD, Silverio Casabar AIFD, Osamu Honjo AIFD, Paul Miyahara and Wanda Brady AIFD. He says they all know how to arrange flowers while perched atop a ten-foot ladder.

In 1963, Bob was selected to represent the West Coast on a design panel of florists from the four corners of the U.S. at the national FTD convention. He served numerous times on planning committees for the annual Flower Show when the public was invited to Wall Street. In 1981, he was president of the Southern California Floral Association.

The American Institute of Floral Designers had its genesis in a group of five Southern California-based high-end stylists, including Bob Berry, who thought that floral designers needed a professional organization of their own. The group began meeting around 1963 to discuss an accreditation testing program that allows applicants who have met certain design standards to use the "Accredited in Floral Design" (AIFD) designation with their name.

Off to the races

The Southern California venue with which Bob has had the longest association is Santa Anita Race Track in Arcadia. In racing seasons throughout the 1970s and most of the '80s, Bob employed a separate crew of fifteen designers to decorate five rooms of the facility's elegant Turf Club, working three evenings a week from 6 p.m. until after midnight. Bob recalls it wasn't difficult to find helpers because working on such large and extravagant displays was something they didn't get to do in their "day jobs" – many of them either had their own shops or worked elsewhere.

Bob began working with Santa Anita in 1959. The track's president asked Mary Mikuriya, who had a flower shop in Pasadena's Huntington Hotel, to bid on the contract. It was such a large job, Mary asked Bob to partner with her. Because of their initial inexperience, the track contacted Podesta Baldocchi of San Francisco, the largest flower shop in the U.S. at the time, and asked manager Eddie Geoppner to fly down with a crew to do the major stake events such as Handicaps, Strub Stakes and the Santa Anita Derby.

After one season, Mary and Bob were on their own, although Mr. Goeppner flew down several times to see their creative décor and was so impressed, he offered Bob the chance to work with the Podesta & Baldocchi team on some of San Francisco's most spectacular floral displays. Thus began another mentoring relationship that greatly influenced Bob Berry's floral career.

Above: The Berry crew at work in Santa Anita Park's Turf Club in the Chandelier Room, a job they performed every Monday, Wednesday and Friday evening during the racing season. Circa 1970.

After Mary Mikuriya passed away in 1974, Bob continued working on Santa Anita's floral displays with his wife, Stella. In 2008, their Santa Anita contract was in its forty-ninth year.

Such a long tenure has not been without problems and near-disasters. Bob has had his share, including live flamingos in nine-foot cages that shouldn't have been fed until after the event was over. Bob had to remove the birds from the cages, clean up the unsightly mess and erect large arrangements of anthuriums in their place – all with just moments to spare before the members-only Turf Club opened.

Rhododendrons figured in another Santa Anita display that turned out differently than originally envisioned. Bob had ordered 30 forced-bloom rhododendron shrubs from a grower in the San Francisco area who called just a few weeks before the date they were needed to tell Bob he didn't have enough room in his greenhouses to force both Bob's shrubs and a larger order for Macy's in New York City. Bob approached several local greenhouse growers and wholesalers in Los Angeles to take in his rhododendrons, but no one had enough room for 30 four-foot-diameter plants because Valentine's Day was looming – except for Paul Ecke Jr. in Encinitas: "Sure, bring them on down here."

But a warm spell hit and Paul called Bob: "You better get down here right away because your rhododendron blooms are popping." Bob moved them out of the Ecke greenhouse and placed them in the shade of a large oak tree for a few days, thinking "I'm in big trouble."

When it was time to take them to the track he rented a truck, loaded up and set off for Santa Anita. But the truck had poor suspension and when Bob opened the back door on arrival, he saw that many of the blooms had been jarred loose and the floor was littered with petals. He salvaged some of the shrubs but had to make a quick trip to the Market to pick up ferns and other substitutions. When the event was over, Bob donated the bare bushes to Descanso Gardens; their gardeners knew how to salvage them and the rhododendrons seen there today are from that Santa Anita near-calamity.

"Airlift Saves Track Image" reported *The Los Angeles Times* on March 21, 1969, when weeks of storms wiped out California's flower fields and Bob had to bring in 300 dozen multicolored tulips from Holland. They were, the article reported, "arranged in massive, towering decorations, interspersed with ivy and peach blossoms" by Bob and his crew to be enjoyed by "the thousands of racing fans who expect to see awesome displays" – and did – at the Santa Anita Handicap that year.

Bob often used masses of tulips during the springtime racing season; he remembers currying favor with Tom Kloulekas, a Greek who grew tulips in the South Bay, by buying his breakfast every time he saw him: "I got all the tulips I ever wanted from him."

Bribery wasn't the motive for Bill Yokoyama, a grower on the Japanese side of Wall Street who seemed to go out of his way to accommodate Bob's requests, even when flowers were scarce. "I thought 'Bill just likes Bob' and that's why he always had flowers for us," recalls Stella Berry. Four decades later, Bill told Bob that he remembered meeting him at the internment camp in Gila Bend during the war when Bob drove over on leave from the Navy and spent three days with two Japanese-American friends he had grown up with. "I decided that I would make sure anybody who thought enough of his friends to come see them at that place would get anything they wanted that I grew," Bill said.

Bob Berry's son Ron measures the height of a track prop in Santa Anita's Turf Club, the Brazilian Room, circa 1970.

Flowers seen 'round the world

The equestrian events at the 1984 Summer Olympic Games in Los Angeles were held at Santa Anita. Bob's floral arrangements adorned either side of the jumping gates on the track, and the indoor displays were as elaborate as always.

At 11 p.m. the night before the dressage competition was to take place, track officials came to Bob and said they had underestimated the importance of dressage to the worldwide television audience. There would be fifteen diamond-shaped areas delineating the event's course, each one fifteen feet long. They would like to have the diamonds covered completely with red flowers and with a seven-foot-high arrangement in the center of each. Could Bob do it and have everything in place by the time the competition was to start at 9 a.m. the next morning? A price was agreed to and Bob said: "You're on."

Down on Wall Street, he had the keys to the Greenleaf Wholesale building across the street, with access to flowers and refrigeration space. He offered each of his employees $200 cash if they would stay and work. "Every one of them said they would stay, and we made 300 arrangements overnight, delivered them and had them in place before the event started." Bob remembers that as a proud moment and a highlight of his career. "I had a good bunch of employees, and loved them all."

Bob also did floral decorations for the major 1984 Olympic sponsors at the Los Angeles Coliseum in Exposition Park, for the Los Angeles Music Center, the Huntington Library and Botanical Gardens, and for Rose Parade floats, another widely-televised annual event. For six years beginning in 1990, Bob and Stella helped decorate the float representing the island nation of Indonesia for the Festival Artists float-building company, through their daughter Felicia and son Dan. They also worked on floats for China Airlines.

Bob and Stella Berry by their camellia arrangement at Huntington Library and Botanical Gardens, San Marino, for the International Camellia Convention in February 2001.

Flower Market memories

Bob has seen many changes on Wall Street over his 70-plus years of industry connections. He remembers when cars parked at an angle on the street in front of both Markets and that the drainage was so poor, heavy rains would flood the streets. "The Japanese, with their smaller feet, could easily step inside the five-gallon gladiola cans and use them as boots to wade through the water when it rose about a foot deep." Ethnic divisions were more prominent in the 1930s and '40s than today: "The Japanese side was almost entirely Japanese, while the American side was like the United Nations: Italians, Greeks, Scandinavians, Germans – all the nationalities."

Security guards have always been part of the Flower District scene. Bob remembers that when Chris Colombo brought his lilacs into the American market, the long counter would be piled high with mounds of lilac and a guard was needed to make sure people didn't help themselves to lilac without paying for it. "He was the only local grower who brought lilac to the Market."

Like many floral retailers, Bob opposed allowing the public into the Flower Market until he realized that not enough florists were coming to the Market to sustain it: "I came to see that the Market had to be opened up to the public to ensure its survival."

His insistence on using the freshest flowers is why Bob Berry personally visits the Flower Market to select product: "A first-class florist must buy top-of-the-line merchandise," Bob asserts. "My clientele would know if the flowers weren't first-class."

In 2008, at the age of 83 and still working floral magic for select clients, Bob Berry has "elder statesman" status on both sides of Wall Street. Many long-time members of Los Angeles' floral community – the designers, wholesalers, event planners, design students, commission merchants and others who have worked with him over the years – have been the beneficiary of his talents and counsel.

The Alhanati Family: Florist to Yesterday's Stars Still "On Call"

Stepping into Parisian Florist is a bit like taking a stroll down Hollywood's Memory Lane. It's a busy shop in a colorful building in the Art Moderne style on the corner of Sunset Boulevard and Gardner Street. The door opens with a jingle and the pleasant scent of fresh flowers greets a visitor. In the back room Louis Alhanati is working on a floral arrangement, just as he has since he bought the shop in 1960. Working alongside him are employees who have been at the shop for many years. One of them is Louis' daughter Susan; Susan's own daughter Ryann also joined the staff recently.

Magazine clips, most of which date back many years, decorate the wall across from the cash register. They provide a hint of the clientele that have come and gone over the years for the flower shop in the middle of a Hollywood residential neighborhood.

"Ozzie and Harriet [Nelson] used to walk in here all the time; they lived up the street and came in just to chat," says Louis. "Raymond Burr also lived in the neighborhood; he grew orchids. Clifton Webb often made a pit stop here on his way home."

To Louis, these people were friends: "Robert Mitchum, a very nice man, and Natalie Wood. Desi Arnaz. We were Lucy's florist – she used to call and order flowers all the time. And it was always fun when Jackie Gleason called from Florida. Telly Savalas … he'd say to us: 'Who loves yozu, baby?' on the phone."

Louis' son Bob, who grew up in the family business, also remembers those days: "Paul Lynde was an outgoing, flamboyant character. Nelson Riddle was a kind, caring man who became a family friend. He joined us for birthday celebrations, and even rushed to the hospital when my mom became ill. We loved Nelson, he was a great guy!"

Louis Alhanati, left, Ben Kimura, and Louis' wife Helen at a 1980s open house at the Flower Market. Photo by Harry Sakai.

The Hollywood celebrity with whom Alhanati is most often linked is one he never met: Marilyn Monroe. When she died in 1962, Parisian Florist was tapped to provide the floral casket blanket and the family's floral tribute for her services. The arrangements were made by her half-sister and former baseball star Joe DiMaggio who had been married to Marilyn briefly in 1954.

Then DiMaggio placed a standing order for an ongoing floral tribute to be delivered to her marble crypt in the Westwood Village Memorial Park Cemetery with these instructions: "Six fresh long-stemmed red roses, three times a week … forever."

The deliveries became part of the Alhanati family's lives, as well as a Hollywood legend. In 1972 Louis told a reporter for the *Los Angeles Times**: "We've been delivering roses to Marilyn for ten years, and we've never missed a day. I remember when we started doing it; people came from all over the world… they would go with the delivery boys and photograph them putting the flowers on her grave."

In 1982 word came from DiMaggio's office that "forever" had ended and the contract was terminated. Still, admirers continue to order flowers from Parisian Florist to be taken to her crypt, and groups of fans still drop by to have their pictures taken with Louis on her birthday and the anniversary of her death. "We just sent over a big floral heart because today is her birthday," Louis said on June 1, 2007.

In the 1920s and '30s, Los Angeles' Sephardic Jewish community lived together for the most part around Forty-second Street in the South Central area. Many of them worked in the floral industry. Bob Alhanati, who wasn't born until 1957, remembers the family stories: "My grandparents and the Mayesh grandparents were neighbors. Mr. Mayesh played the lute or the mandolin, and my grandfather made the wine. Then everyone got together to drink wine and dance."

Bob's grandparents, Joe and Rachel Alhanati, had a flower stand at Sixth and Main streets. Louis, who was born in 1927, sold carnation boutonnieres on the streets nearby on holidays. He remembers riding on his dad's wooden pushcart at the Los Angeles Flower Market, and he also remembers that his father's badge number was nine. Other early Market recollections include the days when apartment buildings sat next to the two wholesale markets on Wall Street. "Some of the growers set up shop on their steps, outside the markets. There was no refrigeration so whatever a grower brought in, he had to sell that day."

Refrigeration became a different issue for Louis later on. One of his first jobs was at Consolidated Shippers: "It was too cold for me, working in a refrigerator, but they were the only ones at that time who could package flowers for shipment in a refrigerated room."

He went back to retail, working first for Biltmore Florist ("at that time, it was the largest flower shop west of the Mississippi") and then for the Stathatos family at the Broadway Florist shop downtown. In 1960 he and his older brother Max purchased the Parisian Florist shop which had been in business at the same location since 1924. They were the shop's third owners.

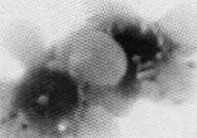

One of Louis Alhanati's favorite things was to go to local farms and buy flowers there. "You could go in any direction – Artesia, Torrance – and in anywhere from a half hour to an hour you'd find a flower field. It was one beautiful sight to see the flowers growing. One farmer I remember had narcissus in the ground and he asked me to take whatever I wanted. He was selling it for 50 cents a hundred. I couldn't get that much; it was too much work for 50 cents."

Louis recalls that during World War II local flower growers were also required to grow produce. "In order to buy their flowers, you had to buy their produce, too. So we always got some good, fresh produce."

And, like all the local retailers who came to the Market in the war years, Louis remembers the pain of waiting around for trucks to deliver flowers that were in short supply. Sometimes they didn't show up until the afternoon: "We used to have to stand in line waiting for a truck to arrive just to get a certain flower, usually roses."

When the Southern California Floral Association produced its promotional film "The Gladiolus Story" in the 1950s, Louis was tapped to play the groom in the wedding scene. He recalls being terrified that the holes in the bottom of his shoes would show when he kneeled for the scene. Louis also made the corsages, wedding bouquets and many of the gladiola displays in the film. "We all did it for free, for the business. Glads in those days were locally grown and they were gorgeous, because the growers let them open up in the field. Not like today."

Louis also misses the spectacle when the industry invited the public to the Hollywood Park Flower Show: "Everyone got involved. The growers would bring in their best product, and there would be competitions in wedding scenes, backyard plant displays, whatever a florist decided to do. I would be out there at midnight arranging flowers. I'll never forget the year we had a bunch of pompon chrysanthemums in the off-season. I was amazed: How in the world did they do that? Well, now we've got them all year 'round."

Louis Alhanati and son Bob at the Flower Market in 1998.

Bob Alhanati worked in his father's shop every weekend as a youngster, and joined the business when he was 21. In September 2007 he purchased the San Fernando Mission Cemetery Florist from Tommy Tomlinson, whose parents started the shop more than 40 years ago.

Bob explains happily: "It used to be on the cemetery's grounds, but now we're right across the street from the entrance. It's a high-volume shop on the bouquet end, plus we have Teleflora and also a gift shop. It's very exciting."

***"Three times a week...forever," Roberta Ostroff, Los Angeles Times, August 6, 1972**

Jacob Maarse Florists: A Signature Look in European Design

"Flower power" came to Pasadena in the late 1960s, as it did to many communities, but in the hands of Holland-born Jacob Maarse it was traditional style with the old-world elegance he was used to.

Jacob's family grew flowers in Aalsmeer, home to the world's largest indoor wholesale flower market, located about eight miles southwest of Amsterdam. After completing floral training and horticultural school in his native country, he visited an uncle in San Francisco when he was in his twenties and decided to stay. He came to the Southland when he was offered a job as manager for Preble's, a high-end produce market that also had a large floral department in the Old Pasadena neighborhood.

In 1966, when Jacob decided to open a full-service shop of his own, he sought out Dutch, German and Swedish floral designers to work for him. He felt that the European trend in floral design – a distinctive "look" to arrangements, the containers that hold them and the materials used to create them – was poised for popularity in America. "He used to say that design in Europe was a little more esoteric than what would work here, so he made a few changes in interpretation to appeal to American tastes," recalls Jacob's son Hank, who now runs the business.

The building housing the original shop was claimed about six years later by expansion of the Pasadena Convention Center, and when the opportunity to purchase what had been a 23,000-square-foot Cadillac showroom nearby arose, Jacob snapped it up. He envisioned a retail home décor shop in which flowers had a place alongside antique furniture, candles, ceramics and other high-end furnishings for home and garden.

Today the shop is the largest in Southern California and has more than 40 employees. It's on every list of "things to see" on a walking tour of Pasadena's vibrant Green Street neighborhood, and is the "go-to" florist for many families and companies in the west San Gabriel Valley. Celebrities, high-profile society events and Pasadena's Tournament of Roses are regular clients.

The Sephardic Clan of Flower People

In the earliest part of the twentieth century, with no refrigeration in their shops, florists were forced to go to the flower market almost every day for fresh flowers, cut just a day or two before in a Southern California field. That coming together several times a week meant that the Los Angeles Flower Market was a hotbed for socializing and camaraderie, where immigrants made connections that helped them establish their businesses.

This was especially true for the immigrants with Sephardic roots (Jewish people of Turkish lineage from the island of Rhodes) who had identified the floral industry as a good way to support their families. "There were a lot of Sephardics in the business," said Victor Yack in a 2007 conversation. His grandfather started in the flower business when he added flowers to his Los Angeles produce market in 1916. Victor's father, uncles, cousins and many in-laws all owned flower shops; he estimates that at one time his family had close to 75 flower businesses from Los Angeles to San Diego. He owned five flower shops himself before retiring in 1989.

The Sephardic Jews were astute businessmen who took risks that gave pause to many others, and embraced a customer awareness that would put many to shame today; they kept their shops open seven days a week and worked late hours. In a way, they were in the real estate business, not the flower business. They made their seed money in the flower business, then put it into real estate. As urban development forced them out, they moved, started over or sold their property and profited.

Early Sephardic immigrants landed at the Union Depot in Los Angeles and settled in the immediate area, near the produce and flower markets. They often left their families in Rhodes when migrating to the United States, wanting to make sure they would be able to support them before they brought them over, too.

According to another floral industry notable, Victor Levy, many Sephardic flower peddlers got started in an empty lot with just an umbrella or in a ramshackle building. As they prospered, they all lived in what is today the South Central neighborhood of Los Angeles. Other well-known family names of Sephardic extraction in the industry are Cohen, Cordova, Mayesh, Alhanati, Hasson, Moskatel, Capilouto and Fisk.

Sephardic flower families shared everything from business acumen to a good buy at the Flower Market.

Jacob is semi-retired and Hank, like his father did before him, still personally selects all the product, even that which is flown in from around the world. Hank visits the Los Angeles Flower Market twice weekly, looking for new and unusual varieties and insisting on freshness: "I've worked with the same growers since I started so when they say the flowers were picked yesterday, I know it's true."

Rose Queens and homegrown roses

Hank joined his father's business in the late 1980s, after he earned a business degree from the University of Southern California and spent a year working sales for one of the major wholesalers, a family friend, at the Aalsmeer Flower Market. He recalls they shipped a lot of flowers to the Middle East at that time, and appreciates the opportunity he had to get a look at how the auction-clock system of buying flowers works: "It was interesting; they take the flower business pretty seriously over there."

In 2008, Jacob still comes into the shop occasionally, as does his wife Clara; they worked together to build the business and its reputation for exquisite arrangements for more than 40 years, and have a warm relationship with many long-time employees.

Hank Maarse, left, and his father, Jacob, in 2001.

Jacob, Clara and Hank Maarse have provided flower arrangements for numerous Academy Awards events, Hollywood premieres, local charity fund-raisers and the Pasadena Showcase House in support of the arts, a special interest for Jacob and Clara. As the preferred floral vendor for the Tournament of Roses since 1996 – and at least a couple of decades "unofficially" before that – their arrangements have decorated events such as the Directors Ball and Rose Bowl Game kick-off luncheon. They have crafted the bouquets carried by many Rose Queens and attendants in publicity photos, at the Coronation Ball and on their parade-day float.

During U.S. President Richard Nixon's tenure, Jacob Maarse was the florist of choice for the Western White House in San Clemente; his floral arrangements greeted Soviet Premier Leonid Brezhnev during his historic visit there in 1973.

In another unusual and old-fashioned floristry twist, Jacob Maarse grows aromatic roses in his home garden in Sierra Madre, to be used in shop arrangements. He planted a couple of hundred bushes around 1992; today his three-acre garden has almost 3,000 bushes, from which 500 to 1,000 flowers are cut daily during the rose season, roughly from April to December, and brought to the shop.

Wordpix

Book List

Barton, Jack, *A Brief History of El Monte*, El Monte, CA (1988)

Brewer, William H., *Up and Down California in 1860-1864: The Journal of William H. Brewer*, Berkeley-Los Angeles – London: University of California Press (2003)

Camp, C.W. ("Bob"), *La Mirada: From Rancho to City*, Fullerton, CA: Sultana Press1970)

Dudley, Frances, *A Centennial History of the American Florist*, Topeka, KS: Florists' Review Enterprises, Inc. (1997)

Dutter, Vera E., *Poinsettia King*, Ecke family and company history (circa 1975)

Floral Product Marketing in Greater Los Angeles, California, United States Department of Agriculture (1997)

Hirahara, Naomi, *A Scent of Flowers*, Southern California Flower Growers, Inc., Pasadena, CA: Midori Press (2004)

Hutchison, Claude B., editor, *California Agriculture*, Berkeley and Los Angeles: University of California Press (1946)

Kawaguchi, Gary, *Living with Flowers: The California Flower Market History*, San Francisco, CA: California Flower Market, Inc. (1993)

Kowalewski, Michael, *Gold Rush: A Literary Exploration,* Berkeley, CA: Heyday Books, in conjunction with the California Council for the Humanities (1997)

McWilliams, Carey, *Southern California: An Island on the Land*, Salt Lake City, UT: Peregrine Smith Books, Gibbs-Smith Publisher (1973-1988)

Melvin, Robert, *Profiles in Flowers: The Story of San Diego County Floriculture*, Encinitas, CA: Paul Ecke Ranch Press (1989)

Northrup, William M. and Newton W. Thompson, editors; Ethel W. Bishop, associate editor and compiler, *History of Alhambra*, Alhambra, CA: A.H. Cawston Managing Editor and Publisher (1936)

O'Flaherty, Joseph S., *Those Powerful Years: The South Coast and Los Angeles 1887-1917,* Hicksville, NY: Exposition Press (1978)

Padilla, Victoria, *Southern California Gardens: An Illustrated History,* Berkeley and Los Angeles: University of California Press (1961)

Reeves, Pamela, *Ellis Island: Gateway to the American Dream,* New York, NY: Dorset Press, a Division of Marboro Books Corporation (1991)

Starr, Kevin, *California: A History*, New York: The Modern Library (2005)

Whitman, Louise Bodger, *The House of Bodger,* Glendale, CA: Louise Bodger Whitman (1981)

Workman, Boyle, *The City That Grew,* Los Angeles, CA: The Southland Publishing Co. (1935)

Yocum, Norma L., *The Life and Times of Norma Yocum*, Chicago, IL: Adams Press (1996)

About the Authors

Peggi Ridgway, an award-winning author of business books and many non-fiction articles, manages a small web and publications design firm in Orange County, California, where she has served the small business community for 20 years. Her interest in the Los Angeles Flower Market began when she became the editor of its *Bloomin' News* newsletter in 1999, a position she holds today. She was delighted to be involved in the research, writing, design and production of the first recorded history of the American Florists' Exchange. She is a frequent visitor to the Flower Market.

Jan Works is a veteran business and marketing communications writer, corporate journalist and publisher whose clients have included major firms and publications. She and her husband self published four books on sport skydiving and an internationally distributed newsletter. She devoted countless hours, miles and phone and Internet time in the research phase of this book, personally interviewing dozens of individuals and the families of early day leaders in the Los Angeles Flower Market.

Index to Photos

Index to Photos

Index

Index

Index

Index

Index

Index

Index

Index

Index

Index

Ordering More Copies of This Book

Sending Flowers to America can be purchased at retail $64.95 plus $6 shipping.
California purchasers add 8.25% tax.

Direct –

Publisher
American Florists' Exchange, Ltd.
754 Wall Street
Los Angeles, CA 90014
(213) 622-1966

Agent
Wordpix Solutions
P.O. Box 218
Buena Park, CA 90621-0218
(800) 200-1101

Los Angeles area booksellers

On-line —

- FlowerMarketHistory.com
- Amazon.com
- Other online retailers

Book Trade –

Bulk orders are available for resale with standard trade arrangements. Please contact the publisher or agent (above) for more information.